Personal Development for Life and Work

9e

Harold R. Wallace

Professor of Occupational & Educational Studies, Emeritus
Colorado State University
Ft. Collins, Colorado

L. Ann Masters

Administrator, Office of the Commissioner of Education
Nebraska Department of Education
Lincoln, Nebraska

THOMSON

SOUTH-WESTERN

Australia · Canada · Mexico · Singapore · Spain · United Kingdom · United States

Personal Development for Life and Work, 9th Edition

Harold R. Wallace and L. Ann Masters

VP/Editorial Director:
Jack W. Calhoun

VP/Editor-in-Chief:
Karen Schmohe

Acquisitions Editor:
Jane Phelan

Project Manager:
Dr. Inell Bolls

Consulting Editor:
Sharon Massen

Marketing Manager:
Valerie Lauer

Production Editor:
Cami Cacciatore

Manufacturing Coordinator:
Kevin Kluck

Production House:
GGS Book Services

Printer:
Edwards Brothers
Ann Arbor, Michigan

Art Director:
Tippy McIntosh

Internal Designer:
Kim Torbeck, Imbue Design

Cover Designer:
Kim Torbeck, Imbue Design

Cover Images:
© PhotoDisc

Photo Researcher:
Darren Wright

For more information about our products, contact us at:

Thomson Higher Education
5191 Natorp Boulevard
Mason, Ohio 45040
USA

Asia (including India)
Thomson Learning
5 Shenton Way
#01-01 UIC Building
Singapore 068808

Australia/New Zealand
Thomson Learning Australia
102 Dodds Street
Southbank, Victoria 3006
Australia

Canada
Thomson Nelson
1120 Birchmount Road
Toronto, Ontario
M1K 5G4
Canada

Latin America
Thomson Learning
Seneca, 53
Colonia Polanco
11560 Mexico
D.F. Mexico

UK/Europe/Middle East/Africa
Thomson Learning
High Holborn House
50/51 Bedford Row
London WC1R 4LR
United Kingdom

Spain (including Portugal)
Thomson Paraninfo
Calle Magallanes, 25
28015 Madrid, Spain

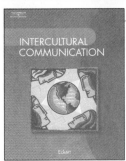
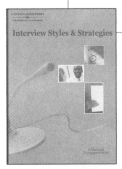

Learning Features

Chapter Opener previews the contents of the chapter and focuses the learner on the topics.

Think About It is a short scenario that previews the concepts, problems, and issues presented in each chapter.

Chapter Focus provides a brief list of expected learning outcomes and achievement expectations.

Getting Along with Your Supervisor

chapter

think about it: Cassandra and Alfred are coworkers at Awards Unlimited, a company that designs, produces, and sells recognition items. Cassandra is the manager in charge of design and production. Alfred is responsible for the salesroom and catalog orders. Larry Hilligas, the owner, is away from the company a good deal. Larry feels that the company is in good hands with his two managers. He spends his days recruiting customers and searching for new markets.

Cassandra enjoys her work very much. She likes the freedom given to her by the owner. She selects the design equipment and raw materials. As long as she can justify her decisions to Larry, no questions are asked. Alfred does not like working at Awards Unlimited. He works long hours, and he feels that Larry gives him too much responsibility. Alfred frequently says, "I don't get paid enough for the type of decisions I have to make! Larry should hang around here once in awhile and find out how tough this business really is!" Larry is very complimentary about the work of his managers.

How can two people working for the same person feel so differently about their employment?

PHOTO © DIGITAL VISION

chapter focus

After completing this chapter, you should be able to:

1. Describe the basic leadership styles.
2. Understand the importance of relating to your supervisor.
3. Demonstrate how to take a problem, share an idea, ask for a raise, or accept a compliment from your supervisor.
4. Demonstrate how to seek, accept, and handle deserved and undeserved criticism.
5. Understand the expectations of your supervisor.

Chapter Highlights

8.1 Know Your Supervisor
8.2 Communicating with Your Supervisor
8.3 Special Communications with Your Supervisor
8.4 What Should You Expect of Your Supervisor?
8.5 What Your Supervisor Expects of You

Chapter Highlights Each main topic in the chapter begins a new section.

8.1 Know Your Supervisor

employees to carry them out without a great deal of direction or close supervision. The laissez-faire leader exercises a "hands-off" policy in dealing with employees. He or she provides information, ideas, guidance, and supplies when asked. This type of supervisor sets goals, then allows the individual or work team to determine how to reach those goals. Depending on the specific job or the level of the employee, the individual or the work team may be expected to decide on policies, tasks, procedures, roles of work group members, and even appraisals.

This leadership style works well in businesses requiring creativity from employees. These businesses need to allow employees to work in a free and open environment. Advertising companies, research organizations, architectural firms, and fashion design firms are examples of businesses in which laissez-faire leadership is often found. Review the characteristics of laissez-faire shown in Figure 8-2.

Characteristics of Laissez-Faire Leadership Style

1. Permits employees to make independent decisions.
2. Encourages initiative and creativity.
3. Allows employees to work independently.
4. Avoids providing specific directions.
5. Provides only general guidance on how to do a job.

FIGURE 8-2 *Characteristics of Laissez-Faire Leaders.*

Laissez-faire leadership is not demonstrated in the "On the Job" example. Jackson was expecting to use his design ability, creativity, and initiative in this position. Obviously being creative was not an option when working in a sales position for Marta.

on the job

Jackson has a talent in the area of interior decorating. He is attending classes and preparing for a career in this field. He is offered a part-time job as a salesperson in a furniture store. He is thrilled because he thinks he will have a chance to work with customers and do some interior decorating work. The position will be beneficial to the customers and provide job satisfaction for Jackson. After a few days on the job, Marta, his supervisor, tells him to stop spending his time sketching and looking for special fabrics and furniture pieces for customers. She tells him that his job is to sell what is on the floor and not waste time doing anything other than selling merchandise.

What suggestion(s) would you have for Jackson? What do you think Marta's perspective is? What lesson should Jackson learn from this experience?

If you are a creative, self-confident, self-directed, assertive person, and you have the ability to set and achieve your own goals, seek a position where you will work for a laissez-faire leader. You can ask questions during the job interview to see if your potential supervisor is a laissez-faire leader. See the "Smart Tip" on page 212 for suggestions. Tailor your questions based on the job that you are seeking. Keep in mind that even in the laissez-faire atmosphere you will want to check with your supervisor periodically to make sure that you are meeting expectations. Also remember that it is often necessary to earn the freedom of working in a laissez-faire environment by showing that you have initiative and drive that will enable you to reach the goals of the organization.

The Democratic Leader
The **democratic leader** will encourage you to participate in the management process.

On the Job presents a workplace scenario and questions to consider. Opportunities are provided for learners to apply chapter concepts to workplace situations.

Smart Tip ▼ ▼ ▼

Ask the following types of questions if you fit the personality profile of someone who wants to work in a laissez-faire environment.
* How much direction will I be given on the projects I work on?
* Will I be able to set goals for myself in this position?
* Will I be given the opportunity to be creative in designing products (or services) for customers?
* Will I need to seek approval before I produce a design?
* Will I have flexibility in the days and hours that I work?
* Will I be able to select the materials and supplies I use in my work?

▲ ▲ ▲ ▲ ▲ ▲ ▲ ▲

This type of leader will seek your ideas, thoughts, and solutions. The democratic leader recognizes that everyone has good ideas, and he or she seeks the input of all workers. The democratic supervisor exercises only a moderate degree of control over employees. He or she has confidence in the employees. Employees have confidence in their employer. This type of supervision is also called *participatory leadership*.

The democratic supervisor may suggest specific policies, procedures, tasks, and/or roles for the workers, but this style of leadership allows the group to participate in the decisions. Under democratic leadership, committees and meetings are part of the work environment. These activities encourage you to share your thoughts and ideas, participate in the decision-making process, and express your opinions.

"Democratic supervision gives every employee the opportunity to be a part of management."
—Anonymous

212

If you believe your thoughts are worthy of consideration and you like the idea of contributing to the success of an organization, you will enjoy working with a democratic supervisor. The democratic supervisor will not allow you to work in isolation. He or she will insist that you become involved and offer ideas, help solve problems, and be an important part of the work team. Workers in this environment are expected to be especially cooperative, empathetic, and participatory.

If you believe your only commitment to an organization is to do a specific job and you prefer not being responsible for decision making, a democratic supervisor is not the type you should seek in the job selection process. The role of the democratic supervisor is clear in this example.

Anna Magid is an entrepreneur who likes to work with her fifteen employees in a democratic style. Each week they have sales meetings, production meetings, and marketing meetings in which ideas are shared and discussed, and decisions for the future are made. Anna seeks ideas about pricing, advertising, merchandising, and production.

Smart Tip suggests helpful hints, strategies, and reminders for key workplace concepts.

LEADERSHIP STYLE SELECTION
Unfortunately, when looking for a job, you will seldom have the opportunity to determine ahead of time the leadership style used or to pick a supervisor with the style you prefer. However, remember to ask questions in the interview that will give you at least a hint as to what the leadership style will be. You will need to adjust your work style to the leadership style in your workplace. Each style has advantages and disadvantages. You should recognize that a supervisor might, at times, use a mixture of styles in order to accomplish a goal of the organization. However, there will always be a primary, underlying style.

When you become angry, frustrated, or displeased with your supervisor (and you will), ask yourself: "Is it the supervisor who angers me, or is it his or her leadership style?" Focusing on the supervisor's style keeps you from being unhappy with the leader personally. If you find there is one leadership style under which you work best, work toward a position where the supervisor suits you and your skills, needs, and work habits. The supervisor's style will probably not change. It is your job to adapt to the style of the supervisor or to find a new workplace.

SELF CHECK

The following phrases describe characteristics of laissez-faire, democratic, and autocratic leadership styles. Identify which is being described by labeling it A, LF, or D. As you read, think about whether or not some of these phrases might apply to more than one style.

_____ 1. Frequent committee meetings are held.

_____ 2. Decisions are made by the work group.

_____ 3. Decisions are made by the supervisor.

_____ 4. Workers are encouraged to be creative.

_____ 5. The supervisor may not be on the work site.

_____ 6. Original work is encouraged.

_____ 7. Everyone's work is valued.

_____ 8. The supervisor gives praise and criticism.

_____ 9. Workers are empathetic, cooperative, and participatory.

_____ 10. Authority is not delegated.

_____ 11. Specific instructions are avoided.

_____ 12. The supervisor prefers to involve employees in the decision-making process.

214

Self Check provides activities for learner self-assessment and exploration.

Technology at Work suggests technology issues and resources to consider and points to helpful Web sites for additional information.

Technology at Work

The Internet presents opportunities both for self-improvement and for creating greater problems. The temptation to "wear a mask" or otherwise hide is even more tempting when using e-mail to communicate. The likelihood that people will see us is less, so we feel that it doesn't matter that we are not being honest. However, we become what we do repeatedly, and repeatedly misrepresenting ourselves makes it more difficult to break this destructive habit.

On the other hand, e-mail can offer us a safe place to try out "removing the mask" for the first time. People can't see how nervous we are, and they will think that the good qualities and honesty that we show are simply natural.

In addition, there are many Web sites on the Internet that offer guidance, assistance, and suggestions on how to improve self-esteem. In your favorite Internet search engine, select the category of social sciences, and do a search using the key word "self-esteem." Reflect on the information you find to see if it applies to you.

SELF CHECK

The following quiz is designed to help you discover your own positive personality qualities. Answer each question by placing a check in either the "Yes" or "No" column.

YES	NO	
____	____	a. Do you sometimes break your promises?
____	____	b. Do you resist giving help to others if it is inconvenient?
____	____	c. Are you frequently witty in a sarcastic way?
____	____	d. Do you have a tendency to gain attention by "topping" the remark made by the previous speaker in a conversation?
____	____	e. Are you usually ill at ease with strangers?

(continued on page 6)

chec**K**point

1. When you really like yourself, you are said to have
   a. personality.   b. self-esteem.   c. morality.   d. performance ability.
2. Using masks to create false impressions
   a. seldom works in the long run.   b. always works in the short run.
   c. can only result in ridicule.   d. is unethical.
3. When you have an experience that you would not expect to happen to a person such as yourself, your inner self is _____.
4. Before you can move ahead with developing self-esteem, you must
   _____
   _____
   _____
   _____

5. There are times when it is okay to hide your true feelings.
   True ____ False ____

5

Checkpoint questions challenge the learner to recall and think critically about key concepts.

applications

1. We all have mental pictures of ourselves. Sometimes they are accurate and realistic, and sometimes they are not. On the grid below, place a check in the first column if the statement represents **what you think you are like**. In the second column check statements that represent **what you think others think of you**. In the third column check statements representing **what you hope will someday be true for you.**

	I THINK I AM	OTHERS THINK I AM	I WANT TO BE
A. HOW I FEEL ABOUT MYSELF			
Inferior to most of my peers	____	____	____
Superior to most of my associates	____	____	____
Equal to most of my associates	____	____	____
Self-confident	____	____	____
Lacking self-confidence	____	____	____
Proud of my achievements	____	____	____
Embarrassed about my achievements	____	____	____
Pleased with my appearance	____	____	____
Disappointed in my appearance	____	____	____
B. HOW I FEEL TOWARD OTHERS			
Tolerant	____	____	____
Intolerant	____	____	____
Friendly	____	____	____
Unfriendly	____	____	____
Like being with strangers	____	____	____
Dislike being with strangers	____	____	____
Like most people	____	____	____
Dislike most people	____	____	____

Applications at the end of each section are designed to help the learner more clearly understand and apply main concepts while providing opportunities for creative problem solving.

and reports when sharing information. Be sure that written documents contain no keying errors or misinformation and that they look professional. For some supervisors, if it isn't in writing, it doesn't exist.

Some supervisors prefer to receive information orally. They like to listen, reflect, and then react. If your supervisor prefers oral communication, use it. Organize your thoughts and what you are going to say prior to providing the information. It is okay to take notes with you and refer to those notes.

on the job

Jeremiah is an office worker in an insurance company. He keeps a very messy desk. Heather's workstation is about six feet from Jeremiah's. The way Jeremiah keeps his desk is very irritating to Heather. She frequently makes remarks about his "mess" to coworkers. She gives him looks of disgust at every opportunity. She finally gets so annoyed that she bursts into the supervisor's office and blurts out, "You have got to do something about Jeremiah. I just can't stand looking at that messy desk." The supervisor is a little stunned by this outburst and replies, "Jeremiah is a good worker. I have more important things to worry about than someone's housekeeping habits."

Was Heather's problem worthy of supervisory attention? What problems may Heather have created for herself with this outburst?

focus on ethics

Olivia and Roger work in a clothing store. Olivia has noticed that Roger puts clothing in his size that he likes in the back of the storeroom. Several times customers have been unable to find items in their size, and Roger has told them that the merchandise is not available. Olivia knows full well that the items are available but have been hidden in the storage area by Roger. During the final sale days, the items Roger has been saving magically appear on the sale racks. He gets the employee discount plus the customer discount. He considers this a perk of working in a retail store.

Should Olivia challenge Roger about his practice? Should she simply remove the clothes from the storage area? Should she speak with the supervisor? Should she remain silent?

Also find out if your supervisor likes to hear from you once an hour, once a day, once a week, or only as needed. This, of course, will depend on the type of work you are doing and the amount ... have in doing it. Whatever ... prefers, *do it.*

If your work site is eq... tronic messaging, use it as ... supervisor. This is a good, ... to communicate.

It is wise to keep a wri... communication with your ... provide him or her with wri... keep a copy. If you use ora... keep some notes about wha... when. This will protect you ... misinterpreted or lost.

On the other side of th... link, you must be a good li... stand what your supervisor ... you, you must be a careful ...

Focus on Ethics presents a scenario and questions that require learners to think critically about an ethical dilemma or difficult situation.

Interpretation: Dan's technical writing skills are weak and need work, but he has good ideas and writes well from a creative standpoint.

These are examples of how you might collect and interpret evidence of praise or criticism from informal feedback. Also, there are occasions when a friend, an employer, a teacher, or anyone in a position to observe your behavior can give you evaluative feedback. You should welcome these opportunities to learn about how others perceive you. Try not to be hurt, offended, or resentful. Even when criticism is given in anger, you should try to learn from it; do not allow the anger to detract from the value of the feedback.

Always try to be open, alert, and sensitive to the feedback that is available, both positive and negative. After evaluating the feedback, you may want to make changes within yourself. ' You should be aware, however, that there are things we can change about ourselves and things we

cannot. Concentrate your energy on what is possible—what is realistic.

A Friend can Help

One good source of feedback is your close friends and associates. Also, counselors, teachers, and possibly employment supervisors or coworkers can help. They can provide you with valuable information about what they see in your behavior. But more importantly, you may feel a sense of trust and safety in talking with them about yourself.

In an environment of trust, you can feel safe to reveal your real self. However, only in an environment of mutual trust can honest, two-way communication occur. The masks have to come off. Be willing to share honestly. Without that openness on your part, your friend may not be willing to be open and candid about negative feedback.

As you share information, think about what you are saying and what you are hearing. Reflect upon it and turn it over in your mind. This process can generate insight and understanding that would not happen without the help of someone to listen, think, and talk things over with.

> *"I have not failed. I've just found 10,000 ways that won't work."*
>
> —THOMAS A. EDISON

Quotes are included to add interest and to reinforce learning.

checkpoint

1. Maintaining a positive self-image while facing reality
   a. is a source of psychological stress.   b. causes others to suspect your motives.
   c. can let failure pave the way for success.   d. creates false impressions.
2. As one grows in self-understanding, there is less discomfort about revealing one's _____ to a caring friend.
3. Feedback is information that you can use to
   _____
   _____

4. When you come to understand and accept yourself, you have paved the way for
   _____
   _____
   _____

12

8 Points to Remember

chapter

Review the following points to determine what you remember from the chapter.

- It is important to know your supervisor and understand his or her leadership style. The basic leadership styles are autocratic, democratic, and laissez-faire.

- You must be able to relate to your supervisor and understand his or her preferred style of communication. If your supervisor likes to communicate orally, you should make every effort to communicate this way. If your supervisor prefers written information, you should write. Keep in mind that supervisors do not like surprises. Keep the lines of communication open and keep your supervisor informed.

- Special attention should be given in your efforts to take a problem to your supervisor, to share an idea, to request a raise, or to accept a compliment. All of these special communication challenges require preparation and thought on your part. You should establish a suitable setting, explain the problem in your own words, present facts that support the problem, ask for understanding, present several alternative solutions, state your recommended solution, and thank your supervisor for listening to your presentation. When sharing a new idea: plan thoroughly for the presentation of your idea, avoid presenting it on the spur of the moment, support the idea

with notes you have researched, be prepared to leave a brief outline of the idea, and close with a positive statement. Be prepared and anticipate that you may get a negative response. Follow the seven-step plan when asking for a raise. Before you ask for a raise, be sure you anticipate questions and have answers related to your performance. "Thank you" is a good response to a compliment.

- Your rights as an employee include: receiving criticism, having a safe work environment, and receiving personal recognition. It is important to remember that criticism is a tool of self-improvement. Seek criticism from your supervisor in order to improve your performance. Supervisors enjoy working with employees who can accept suggestions and criticism. If a situation does arise

Points to Remember provide a recap of the key points from the chapter.

---

key terms

Place the letter of the item in the definition column that matches the key word.

Key Word		Definition
___1. Supervisor	a.	Likes workers to show creativity
___2. Leadership style	b.	Lets someone do something on their own
___3. Laissez-faire leader	c.	Worker does tasks carefully and completely
___4. Democratic leader	d.	Encourages participation in the workplace
___5. Autocratic leader	e.	One who is in charge of one or more workers
___6. Delegate authority	f.	Does not entrust activities to others
___7. Criticism	g.	A form of self-improvement
___8. Diligent worker	h.	Demonstration of loyalty and commitment
___9. Allegiance	i.	Method used by the leader to get the work done

242

Key Terms provide an opportunity for learners to test their recall of new terms and ideas.

---

case studies for critical thinking

Case 1.1

TEARS ON THE JOB

Tanessa is an administrative assistant to the purchasing manager in an electronics firm. Her supervisor, Mr. Rodrigues, was a kind, fatherly man, and Tanessa has worked happily and well. Two weeks ago, however, Mr. Rodrigues was transferred and Tanessa was assigned to work with his replacement, Mr. Kim. The new man is brilliant and efficient, but he is somewhat short on patience. He speaks crisply and concisely to everyone. In Tanessa's anxiety to please, she finds herself making many errors. This fact in itself distresses Tanessa, but when Mr. Kim criticizes her work rather sharply, Tanessa bursts into tears. Mr. Kim takes her tears in stride, but he becomes extremely irritated with Tanessa's continued apologies for her previous errors. Finally, he arranges for Tanessa to be transferred to another office.

1. Would you say that Tanessa has a problem with her self-esteem? What evidence do you see to support this conclusion?

2. Is Tanessa expecting too much of herself? Should she see herself as a "perfectionist" and embark on a self-improvement program, or should she accept herself as a person who occasionally makes mistakes, but learns from them?

3. Assume that Tanessa goes to Mr. Rodrigues for friendly advice. After listening to Tanessa's story, what guidance and advice might he offer?

18

Case Studies for Critical Thinking are thought-provoking exercises in decision making and analysis.

preface

This book is designed to offer the learner a relevant, systematic program for developing self-understanding, promoting personal growth, and preparing for successful employment through a readable and understandable text.

Success in the world of work requires not only the ability to perform according to the requirements of the position, but also the ability to adjust and get along as a member of a working team. A person's personality affects his or her performance on the job. Stress, conflict, and miscommunication in the workplace can often cause difficulties unless positive personality characteristics influence a worker to make personal adjustments and establish comfortable relationships with supervisors and coworkers. Negative personality traits can hamper or prevent individual adjustments and alienate others. The text and learning activities can help the new employee recognize the important role personal qualities play in the work environment and develop the attitudes, interpersonal skills, and values that are in demand by employers.

Personality traits affect productivity as well. The most relevant and effective technical training for the job is useless if the employee is not a good worker. To become a good worker, the employee must have a commitment to personal growth and apply that commitment to developing effective work habits, self-management skills, communication skills, and the ability to think analytically and creatively.

This book helps learners assess their strengths and weaknesses with respect to personality and productivity. It offers direction in using that information to design a specific, focused self-improvement program—to pave the way for learners to attain realistic goals and objectives in preparation for successful employment.

RESEARCH FOR THE TEXT

The chapters have been extensively researched with special emphasis given to updating research studies. The chapters on work adjustment and interpersonal relationships are consistent with recent research and theory in sociology and psychology. This research helped to ensure that the ideas presented are valid and realistic in the typical workplace. A review of literature about employer expectations and causes of failure on the job provided direction for the chapters on developing work habits and thinking and self-management skills. The chapter on getting a job has been revised to reflect current research in application processes and interviewing techniques.

WHAT IS NEW IN THE TEXT

In addition to the chapters being updated, the end-of-section and end-of-chapter materials have been revised to include additional Applications, Activities and Projects, and Case Studies for Critical Thinking. The Summary has been replaced with bulleted Points to Remember correlated to the Chapter Focus objectives. These changes will help students review and assimilate the chapter information. The features so well received by students and teachers in prior editions have been retained, such as Think About It, On the Job, Technology at Work, Checkpoint, Self-Check, Smart Tip, and Focus on Ethics. The Key Terms have been retained but enhanced to include not only definition activities but also short matching activities. A Supplemental Enrichment Resources list has been added to the end of the student text as well as Endnotes to supplement readings.

THE CRITICAL PERSONAL QUALITIES AND SKILLS

- **Success Identity.** Chapters 1–3 are concerned with self-esteem and commitment to personal growth. These chapters set the stage for self-understanding and self-improvement. Specific activities and suggestions help the individual develop positive attitudes and visualize his or her needs for personal development in preparation for successful employment.
- **Communication.** Communication is listed by many employers as the number one human relations skill needed on the job. Chapters 4–6 are devoted to the improvement of communication and conflict resolution skills. Emphasis is placed on the skills needed for good listening as well as conversational and speaking skills.
- **Interpersonal Relationships.** Chapters 7–9 deal with work adjustment and the interpersonal relationships that occur on the job. This section is designed to help the learner face the challenges of fitting in and becoming a member of a working team. Ideas and strategies for developing good relationships with coworkers, supervisors, and customers are presented. Sections are devoted to team and work group activities and customer communication.
- **Productivity.** Chapters 10–12 concentrate on helping learners become good workers. They include information on self-motivation to get the job done—to develop effective and efficient work habits and self-management skills. They also include information on managing stress and, most importantly, developing and using the ability to think.

- **Social Conscience.** Chapters 13 and 14 address problems of potential conflict, misunderstanding, and unfair treatment in the workplace. The objective of these chapters is to help the learner develop a good social conscience and to let it guide his or her behavior as a worker and as a citizen. Chapter 13 deals with issues and problems of personal ethics, loyalty, and standards of personal conduct. Chapter 14 is concerned with discrimination and diversity in the world of work. These chapters have been updated to include laws and acts that affect the workplace and its employees.
- **Career Development.** Chapters 15 and 16 prepare the learner to face the challenges of transition from school to work. This unit includes managing the tasks of finding, selecting, and keeping a job, realistically and aggressively. Chapter 16 prepares the learner for the long road of career development. It provides a framework for building a successful, satisfying career in the world of work. The job process has been revised to include current documents needed in applying for and interviewing for a job.

SUPPLEMENTAL RESOURCES

This edition of *Personal Development for Life and Work* includes the following materials and tools to enrich the learning experience for the student and to give the teacher more effective instructional resources.

- Included in the text, to provide easier access for the student, is a current list of relevant *Supplemental Enrichment Resources*. This reading material is likely available in schools, most public libraries, local bookstores, or on the Internet.
- The updated eManual (Instructor's Manual) on the Instructor's Resource CD-ROM provides expanded general

guidelines for instruction and specific teaching suggestions pertaining to each chapter. Also included are suggested answers to features in the text, key term activities, applications, activities and projects, and case problems. The Supplemental Enrichment Resources are also provided in the eManual.

- An Electronic Test Bank (**Exam***View*®Pro) contains hundreds of questions for comprehensive review and assessment. The software allows for easy generation of tests and editing of individual questions.
- The Instructor's Resource CD-ROM also contains chapter achievement tests with answers, PowerPoint slides, and review materials. In addition, guides to the use of the supplemental video are provided.

ABOUT THE AUTHORS

Harold R. Wallace is Professor Emeritus of Occupational & Educational Studies, Colorado State University. He has held positions as professor in business education and marketing at Utah State, Michigan State, SUNY New York, and the University of Minnesota, where he was Division Head in Business Studies. Dr. Wallace served as advisor and mentor for many teachers and administrators in education and business and also taught summer school courses in marketing, business, and vocational education. A successful author and popular speaker, he has developed and conducted training seminars, and published journal articles and books in the areas of human relations, marketing, management, creative problem solving, school dropout prevention, research methods, program evaluation, and standardized test development.

L. Ann Masters is Administrator, Office of the Commissioner of Education, Nebraska Department of Education, Lincoln, Nebraska. Her extensive teaching experience includes nearly 30 years in business and career education. She has taught a wide variety of communications, human relations, and business courses at both the secondary and postsecondary levels. Her administrative experience includes positions in the Nebraska Department of Education and Member of the National Board of Directors of Future Business Leaders of America. She has published texts in business communication, business English, and human relations and is a frequent conference participant and speaker for state and national career and technical education and business education associations.

ACKNOWLEDGMENTS

The authors wish to thank all of the instructors who have given valuable direction and feedback in the development of this new edition, with special thanks to the following reviewers:

Pat Donahue
Associate Professor
Monroe Community College
Rochester, New York

Doris Youngman
Insurance Coordinator
Florida Sports and Orthopaedic Medicine
Palm Harbor, Florida

MESSAGE TO THE LEARNER

We believe this book will capture your interest and be easy to understand. But we challenge you to do more than just read it. If you apply what you learn, this experience can change your life.

There are three important keys for your success in the workplace. First is the technical knowledge and skills to do the job. Second is the ability and motivation to work effectively. Third is a personality that will allow you to fit in as a member of a working team. This book is based on real-world demands with respect to the second and third keys to success. It is a self-improvement guide.

Self-improvement may not be easy, but it is worth the effort. If you make a personal commitment to become the best that you can be and if you are willing to be conscientious in your study and application of what this book has to offer, our desire and best wishes for your success in the world of work will be realized.

Harold R. Wallace

L. Ann Masters

table of contents

Time Line Assign.
- Personality

Day One
Ch. 1 + 2

Personality Test

Ch. 1 + 2
Baltus

Pg. 127
other book
Ch. 6 - Baltus

Ch. 8 - Baltus

Add → LifeSpan Dev.

chapter 5

Getting Your Message Across 103

Oral Presentation

Ch. 8 Baltus

chapter 6

Communicating to Resolve Conflict 139

Ch. 9 Baltus

chapter 7

chapter 8

Ch. 5 + 10 Baltus

Include Wellness Ch. 11 Baltus

Ch. 7 Baltus

Ch. 13 Baltus

Ch. 12 Baltus

chapter 15

chapter 16

Self-Esteem

think about it: Celia printed a copy of her résumé, turned off the computer, and slumped in her chair. Eva, a friend who shared an apartment with Celia, entered the room. "Something bothering you?" Eva asked. "I'm really nervous about this job interview," Celia replied. "I would love to work in the jewelry department, and I hope Mr. Nelson offers me the position. But I made such a mess of my last interview, I'm afraid I just can't make a good impression. And, if I get by in the interview and get the job, I'm afraid I'll be a total failure as a salesperson. The people who work in that department are so physically attractive and so personable, I just won't be able to fit in."

Is Celia viewing her job qualifications, appearance, and personality realistically? How might Eva respond to encourage and support Celia?

This chapter sets the stage for a program of self-improvement. The goal is to help you become the best that you can be—to reach your potential as a competent, productive worker. When that goal is achieved you will have a clear, realistic image of yourself, and you will like what you see. In addition, your family, friends, and coworkers will respect and appreciate you as a person.

To reach this goal you must:

1. Understand yourself.
2. Develop your **self-esteem**. This means that your attitude about yourself must be positive and constructive. Self-esteem means that you feel good about yourself.
3. Embark on a program of self-improvement. Suggestions for this begin in this chapter and continue in Chapters 2 and 3.

© COMSTOCK IMAGES

chapter focus

After completing this chapter, you should be able to:

1. Explain the meaning of self-esteem.

2. Explain the impact of conflict between real-life experiences and a person's self-image.

3. Learn to believe in yourself and maintain a positive self-image.

4. Avoid using masks and role-playing to hide from reality.

5. Confront the reality of mistakes or failure and, at the same time, maintain self-esteem.

6. Be sensitive to feedback and use it to understand yourself.

7. Use a trusted friend or counselor to help with self-understanding.

The image you have of yourself has many dimensions. It can include your feelings about, among other things:

- Physical appearance
- Aptitude for mathematics
- Athletic skills
- Romantic appeal
- Ethics and morals
- Mechanical ability
- Sense of humor
- Artistic talent

Appreciate the good in your personality.

> "Public opinion is a weak tyrant compared with our own private opinion. What a person thinks of himself [or herself] is that which determines his [or her] fate."
>
> —HENRY DAVID THOREAU

DEVELOP SELF-ESTEEM

When you *dislike* yourself, you have low self-esteem. However, having imperfections in your personality should not cause you to lose self-respect. Everyone has faults and imperfections. Just as you can respect and like your friends who may not be perfect in every way, you should also be able to like yourself—just as you are.

As Norman Vincent Peale wrote in *The Power of Positive Thinking*, "Believe in yourself. Have faith in your abilities. Without a humble and reasonable confidence in your own powers you cannot be successful or happy."

Self-esteem is not conceit or self-absorption. (In fact, self-esteem can make you more humble, since recognizing your own worth can make you more aware of the worth of others.)

Also, liking yourself doesn't mean that you will like everything you do. Self-esteem is an appreciation of your special gifts and your value as a human being, and a desire to both be your best and achieve your potential. Focus on the good, and try to improve what is weak. People with the most self-esteem are the most likely to be working to improve themselves. They understand that liking themselves is not about competing with others, but about caring for themselves and pursuing what is good for them.

Accepting responsibility for your actions is another key aspect of self-esteem. If you try to blame someone else for your actions, or if you feel sorry for yourself, or label yourself as a failure, it is unlikely you will ever experience a strong sense of self-esteem. If you do something wrong, apologize and try to make it right (people admire the strength of a person who can do this). Try to learn from the situation, and try to do better next time. But don't give up on yourself.

Sometimes things happen to you that are beyond your control. At those times, you are only responsible for your reaction. Accept the experience as real, face it, and tell yourself, "I'm still worth caring about."

There is an important distinction between being a good person who has weaknesses and areas that need improvement, and

© BRAND X PICTURES

being a faulty person. When you can appreciate the good in your personality, even with a clear view of your faults and inadequacies, and can genuinely *like* yourself, you are ready to move ahead in planning and working to develop a personality that represents the best that you can be—with even higher self-esteem.

FACE AND ACCEPT REALITY

People often avoid facing and accepting reality in order to maintain a false, unrealistic self-image. They may hide from reality, ignoring experiences that are inconsistent with their self-image. Or they may refuse to accept actions or events as being real. Closing your eyes (or the eyes of your inner self) to reality can prevent you from understanding and accepting the *real* you.

Trouble begins when something happens that is in conflict with an aspect of your self-image that you feel is important. Your inner self is offended. Your self-esteem is threatened. This behavior is something that you would not expect of a person such as yourself. As a result, a kind of tension (anxiety, distress, or conflict) grows inside you. In your disappointment you may feel deep resentment. If the conflict is extremely offensive to your self-esteem, you may blame yourself for allowing it to happen.

When something happens in conflict with your self-image, it is natural to try to ignore it. Here is why. If you can pretend that the event did not actually happen or convince yourself that it was not as it seemed to be, your self-image can be protected temporarily. You convince yourself that the *real* you had nothing to do with the event. However, this creates a serious problem. Using this strategy causes a buildup of psychological stress. The more you use this kind of pretense, the greater will be the stress you will have to endure.

Figure 1-1 shows how some experiences are not allowed to be part of a person's self-image. When the area of the illustration representing experiences denied to awareness is large, the person has an unrealistic self-image and a high level of psychological stress. When it is small, with the self-image including most or all of the experience, stress is low.

Instead of being in denial about events or behavior that you do not want to recognize, preserve your self-esteem by facing up to the fact that something has happened in conflict with your self-image (you understand and accept it as real). Do not allow your self-respect to waver.

You must learn to recognize and accept your experiences as real. Then your self-image will not be in conflict with your life experiences. You will know and like your inner self. Your tension and conflict with reality will disappear. At the same time, the barriers to building your self-esteem will also disappear.

"Friendship with one's self is all important, because without it one cannot be friends with anyone else in the world."

—ELEANOR ROOSEVELT

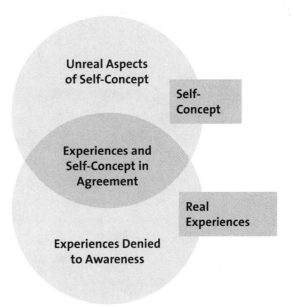

FIGURE 1-1 *Experiences and the self-concept.*

MASKS OFF

Everyone occasionally puts up a false front to **mask** (to cover or hide) his or her true feelings. Or they may put on an

on the job

Alex slumped behind his desk and stared into space. "I suppose it's because I'm so stupid when math is involved," he mumbled. Pages of statistics for his report were scattered on the table and chair where he had been working. "I can't let anyone see how confused and miserable I am when we get together to go over the report." Then Maria walked in and said, "Hey, Alex, how are you doing on the statistics project?" There was a pause. "Are you upset or something?" "No," Alex said as he pressed his hand to his forehead. "I just have a headache. The stats are almost done. But I don't feel like going to that boring review session. Why don't we take an early lunch?"

Is Alex wearing a mask for Maria?

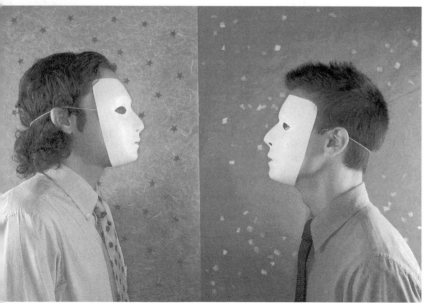

Wearing an emotional mask can cover up one's true feelings.

© THINKSTOCK

act—playing a role to create a false impression. Their purpose may be to inflate themselves in the eyes of others. Or there may be times when a person might wear a mask of being less than he or she really is to avoid the appearance of being smart or stuck-up, or to avoid conflict, or even to escape work or demanding situations.

Sometimes wearing a mask is the right thing to do, considering the circumstances. It would be unrealistic to suggest that one should always share everything one thinks or feels. If people could not mask their true feelings occasionally, the world would be less civilized. For example, if a person has a headache but is required to serve customers, wearing a smile (masking the physical discomfort) is better than complaining.

However, feeling that you always have to wear a mask or play a role can be a tiresome burden. You are not likely to relax and feel good about yourself if you constantly have to keep up false pretenses— trying to present yourself to the world as if you are somehow better than you really are.

To help you visualize and understand how transparent masks can be, think about people in your life who try unsuccessfully to appear ambitious, intelligent, popular, open-minded, courageous, or well-informed about something when they are not.

Although masks may be effective in fooling some people, in the long run they are ineffective. Eventually, people see behind the mask, no matter how carefully the mask is kept up.

As you grow in self-understanding and self-esteem, you will feel better about revealing your true personality to others. You will feel less need to cover up—to present a false image of yourself. You will be willing to take off some of the masks you may have been using to hide your real self or create false impressions.

Technology at Work

The Internet presents opportunities both for self-improvement and for creating greater problems. The temptation to "wear a mask" or otherwise hide is even more tempting when using e-mail to communicate. The likelihood that people will see us is less, so we feel that it doesn't matter that we are not being honest. However, we become what we do repeatedly, and repeatedly misrepresenting ourselves makes it more difficult to break this destructive habit.

On the other hand, e-mail can offer us a safe place to try out "removing the mask" for the first time. People can't see how nervous we are, and they will think that the good qualities and honesty that we show are simply natural.

In addition, there are many Web sites on the Internet that offer guidance, assistance, and suggestions on how to improve self-esteem. In your favorite Internet search engine, select the category of social sciences, and do a search using the key word "self-esteem." Reflect on the information you find to see if it applies to you.

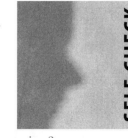

SELF CHECK

The following quiz is designed to help you discover your own positive personality qualities. Answer each question by placing a check in either the "Yes" or "No" column.

YES   NO

____   ____   a. Do you sometimes break your promises?

____   ____   b. Do you resist giving help to others if it is inconvenient?

____   ____   c. Are you frequently witty in a sarcastic way?

____   ____   d. Do you have a tendency to gain attention by "topping" the remark made by the previous speaker in a conversation?

____   ____   e. Are you usually ill at ease with strangers?

(continued on page 6)

check**point**

1. When you really like yourself, you are said to have
   a. personality.   b. self-esteem.   c. morality.   d. performance ability.
2. Using masks to create false impressions
   a. seldom works in the long run.   b. always works in the short run.
   c. can only result in ridicule.   d. is unethical.
3. When you have an experience that you would not expect to happen to a person such as yourself, your inner self is _____.
4. Before you can move ahead with developing self-esteem, you must

   _____

   _____

   _____

   _____

5. There are times when it is okay to hide your true feelings.
   True ____ False ____

SELF CHECK

___ ___ f. Do you have a tendency to be bossy?

___ ___ g. Are you critical of others when you feel they are at fault?

___ ___ h. Do you sometimes make fun of other people?

___ ___ i. Do you frequently laugh at the mistakes of others?

___ ___ j. Do you correct the mistakes of others (in grammar or pronunciation, for example)?

___ ___ k. Do you find it difficult to smile?

___ ___ l. Are you unable to praise and compliment other people easily?

___ ___ m. Do you frequently try to reform other people?

___ ___ n. Are you unable to keep your personal troubles to yourself?

___ ___ o. Are you suspicious of other people's motives?

___ ___ p. Do you frequently borrow the belongings of others?

___ ___ q. Do you enjoy gossip?

___ ___ r. Are you unable to keep out of other people's business most of the time?

___ ___ s. Do you talk a lot about yourself?

___ ___ t. Do you ever use belittling words when referring to those who differ from you in religion, race, or politics?

Evaluating your positive personal qualities: If you are well liked by most of your acquaintances, you probably answered "no" to most of the questions. Take an inventory of needs for improvement in your personality by carefully reviewing your "yes" responses. Do not wait for January 1; make a list of resolutions for positive changes you intend to work on.

Smart Tip ▼ ▼ ▼

Here are some ideas that you might consider as you begin working to build your self-esteem.

• **Celebrate your strengths and accomplishments.**

• **Change the way you talk to yourself; use encouragement, not put-downs.**

• **Accept responsibility for your actions; make wrongs right.**

• **Be sure that you are not setting your standards unrealistically high—or too low.**

• **Remember that beating yourself up for your weaknesses is self-defeating. Instead of running yourself down, set goals for strengthening those areas.**

• **Forgive yourself for your mistakes.**

• **Strike a balance between focusing on improving yourself and focusing on the needs of others.**

• **Keep in mind that being kind to others will help you feel better about yourself.**

• **Don't be defensive when you hear criticism. Look for any truth on which you can act, and ignore any malice.**

• **Never give up on yourself.**

applications

1. People often avoid facing up to reality and accepting that something has happened to them. Discuss some techniques that you could use to avoid having a self-image conflict.

_____

_____

_____

2a. Under what circumstances do you play a role? Do you always project the same image to everyone around you?

_____

_____

_____

_____

_____

_____

_____

_____

_____

2b. Do you find it difficult and stressful to play a role or maintain an unrealistic image—to wear a mask? Why?

_____

_____

_____

_____

_____

_____

2c. Are you willing and able to take off any of your masks? When and under what circumstances?

_____

_____

_____

_____

_____

_____

_____

3. Discuss in a small group how you can tell when someone else is wearing a "mask." What types of masks have you seen on people you know? How do you react to someone else wearing a mask? Are masks easily identified in others? What harm can be created when masks are used? What advantages do masks provide? Record your observations or feelings about the key points of the discussion.

_____

_____

_____

_____

_____

_____

_____

4. In a new job, you will often find that your work takes longer and sometimes fails to meet the quality standards of work done by experienced coworkers. How does this kind of experience feel? How does it influence your self-image?

_____

_____

_____

_____

_____

_____

on the job

Kim was employed as a hair stylist in a salon that went out of business. In her search for a new job she was offered a position with Beautiful Hands. The job included nail sculpture, manicures, tip overlays, and similar jobs requiring good eye-hand coordination. Kim accepted the job and went to work with enthusiasm. She assumed that her successful experience in hair styling was proof of her ability to work successfully at nail sculpting. However, she had problems during her training period. She found that she could not keep up with the other trainees. Also, her trainer gave Kim lower ratings on her work. Often she was required to do the work over again. This caused some customers to ask for another technician when they came in a second time. Kim felt crushed. She had expected to succeed in her new job, but she found herself in a struggle to maintain her composure when confronted with what appeared to be failure.

What should Kim do to maintain a positive, realistic self-image?

FAILURE CAN PAVE THE WAY TO SUCCESS

At first, Kim made excuses for her inability to learn her new job. She told her supervisor that she was not feeling well and could not concentrate. She said that explained why the other trainees were faster and did better work.

Another excuse Kim made to herself was that she was not trying hard enough, so she worked as fast as she could. But that seemed to result in more criticism of her work—more failure.

Finally, Kim found herself at a crossroads. If she continued to make excuses and deny the reality of her failure as a nail technician, she would only create more anxiety and distress for her inner self. If would be very difficult and stressful for her to ignore or hide the reality of her experiences in the training program and, at the same time, maintain her self-esteem.

However, when Kim accepted her experience as real—as a natural thing to have happen in her life—the result would be different.

Kim made the best choice. She confronted the reality of her failure and allowed her inner self to gain insight about this conflict between what she valued and the evidence presented by this experience. She thought, "I tried my best to do the job well and to keep up the pace my supervisor

© RUBBERBALL PRODUCTIONS

Don't let failure ruin your self-image.

expected. But I was unsuccessful. This experience tells me that my natural ability in the skills required for success in nail technician work is less than I had thought. However, that's all right. I can cope with and accept this failure because there is so much in my life that is rewarding and successful. I do not have to be the best at everything. I am good at hair styling. I have artistic ability and good styling skills, and it is realistic for me to see myself as a great hair stylist. I need to find a job where I can use my talents."

Now Kim's experiences and her self-image were in harmony. The stress of maintaining an unrealistic self-image was eliminated.

BE SENSITIVE TO FEEDBACK

If you try to hide from reality, you will find ways to ignore the feedback that comes from negative experiences. However, these experiences provide information, or **feedback**, that you can use to evaluate yourself—to judge how you are doing. For instance, if you want to think of yourself as an excellent student but fear that you are not, you might refuse to look at your report card. Or finding a low grade, you might accuse the teacher of being unfair or incompetent. However, if you are to grow and improve, you need to interpret and use feedback that reflects how you are doing in your life and work.

Be on the Alert for Praise and Criticism

If you are listening and observing, you will pick up all kinds of feedback. If you take the initiative to ask, you will learn even more. Here are some examples:

Feedback: "Paul, the stockroom is still in a mess."
Interpretation: Paul tends to delay and avoid unpleasant tasks.

focus on ethics

Think about a time when you received praise. Also, think about a time when you received criticism. How did you interpret this information? Do you take criticism in the same way that you take praise?

What does your own reaction to praise and criticism tell you about how you should treat others?

Some people use criticism, and even put-downs, to hurt people. They think that this will make them feel more important, and might make others think more highly of them.

How might putting down others undermine a person's own self-esteem? How might it damage the ways others think about the person?

Feedback: "I visited with Mrs. Lucero in the office the other day. She said to tell you that her loan application was approved."
Interpretation: One more satisfied customer. I must be doing my job well.

Feedback: "The supervisor says that we need more training in projecting a positive image over the telephone."
Interpretation: The person who handles the calls projects a negative image over the telephone.

Feedback: Dan reviews the copy he has written for a newspaper advertisement. The copy editor has circled several punctuation and syntax errors, and has written in the margin, "Good selling point!"

Interpretation: Dan's technical writing skills are weak and need work, but he has good ideas and writes well from a creative standpoint.

These are examples of how you might collect and interpret evidence of praise or criticism from informal feedback. Also, there are occasions when a friend, an employer, a teacher, or anyone in a position to observe your behavior can give you evaluative feedback. You should welcome these opportunities to learn about how others perceive you. Try not to be hurt, offended, or resentful. Even when criticism is given in anger, you should try to learn from it; do not allow the anger to detract from the value of the feedback.

Always try to be open, alert, and sensitive to the feedback that is available, both positive and negative. After evaluating the feedback, you may want to make changes within yourself. [1] You should be aware, however, that there are things we can change about ourselves and things we cannot. Concentrate your energy on what is possible—what is realistic.

A Friend can Help

One good source of feedback is your close friends and associates. Also, counselors, teachers, and possibly employment supervisors or coworkers can help. They can provide you with valuable information about what they see in your behavior. But more importantly, you may feel a sense of trust and safety in talking with them about yourself.

In an environment of trust, you can feel safe to reveal your real self. However, only in an environment of mutual trust can honest, two-way communication occur. The masks have to come off. Be willing to share honestly. Without that openness on your part, your friend may not be willing to be open and candid about negative feedback.

As you share information, think about what you are saying and what you are hearing. Reflect upon it and turn it over in your mind. This process can generate insight and understanding that would not happen without the help of someone to listen, think, and talk things over with.

> *"I have not failed. I've just found 10,000 ways that won't work."*
>
> —THOMAS A. EDISON

checkpoint

1. **Maintaining a positive self-image while facing reality**
   a. **is a source of psychological stress.**   b. **causes others to suspect your motives.**
   c. **can let failure pave the way for success.**   d. **creates false impressions.**

2. **As one grows in self-understanding, there is less discomfort about revealing one's _____ to a caring friend.**

3. **Feedback is information that you can use to**

   _____

   _____

4. **When you come to understand and accept yourself, you have paved the way for**

   _____

   _____

   _____

applications

1. We all have mental pictures of ourselves. Sometimes they are accurate and realistic, and sometimes they are not. On the grid below, place a check in the first column if the statement represents **what you think you are like**. In the second column check statements that represent **what you think others think of you**. In the third column check statements representing **what you hope will someday be true for you**.

	I THINK I AM	OTHERS THINK I AM	I WANT TO BE
A. HOW I FEEL ABOUT MYSELF			
Inferior to most of my peers	____	____	____
Superior to most of my associates	____	____	____
Equal to most of my associates	____	____	____
Self-confident	____	____	____
Lacking self-confidence	____	____	____
Proud of my achievements	____	____	____
Embarrassed about my achievements	____	____	____
Pleased with my appearance	____	____	____
Disappointed in my appearance	____	____	____
B. HOW I FEEL TOWARD OTHERS			
Tolerant	____	____	____
Intolerant	____	____	____
Friendly	____	____	____
Unfriendly	____	____	____
Like being with strangers	____	____	____
Dislike being with strangers	____	____	____
Like most people	____	____	____
Dislike most people	____	____	____

2. Sometimes feedback may be provided that is hurtful or something that you think is unfair. This type of criticism can help you learn more about yourself so you can improve in these areas if the criticism is true. Think of a situation in which you received evaluative feedback. You may use any of the items you checked in Application 1. How should you respond to and feel about how others perceive you? Write a brief summary of what you should do to make criticism a positive motivation for you.

_____

_____

_____

_____

_____

_____

_____

_____

_____

_____

_____

_____

_____

_____

_____

1

chapter

Points to Remember

Review the following points to determine what you remember from the chapter.

- Self-esteem is an appreciation of your special gifts and your value as a human being, and a desire to both be your best and achieve your potential. When you really like yourself—when you have a high level of self-respect—you have self-esteem.

- Your self-esteem is threatened when your life experiences are in conflict with your self-image. A natural reaction is to try to ignore the inconsistent experience or to avoid responsibility for it. Accept your experiences as real; then your self-image will not be in conflict with your life experiences.

- You can preserve your self-esteem by facing up to the fact that something has happened that is in conflict with your self-image instead of being in denial about something you don't want to recognize.

- Masks and role-playing can be effective in fooling some people, but in the long run you will be able to relax and feel better about yourself if you avoid using false pretenses.

- Failure and mistakes can be stepping-stones to positive outcomes in your life if you confront them and learn from them. Your self-esteem is deflated when you try to hide from reality and maintained when you face up to it and try to do better.

- Being sensitive to the many sources of feedback (information that you can use to evaluate yourself) can help you set the stage for self-improvement. If you are to benefit from your life experiences, you need to interpret and use feedback that reflects how you are doing in your life and work.

- Simply talking things over with a friend, a counselor, a colleague, or someone with whom you can share your feelings and reflect upon your experiences can generate insight and understanding.

In an environment of trust, you can feel safe to reveal your real self. Reflect upon what you are saying and what you are hearing. This process can help you gain insight and understanding.

How did you do? Did you remember the main points you studied in the chapter?

key terms

Define each term in the space provided.

Self-esteem

Mask

Feedback

activities and projects

1. In a conversation with a trusted friend or counselor—someone who can understand and accept you as you are—talk about the following topics, and write your responses to the following:

What you would like to change or improve about yourself

_____

_____

_____

The events in your life that conflict with your ideal self-image

_____

_____

_____

_____

Your special abilities or talents

_____

_____

_____

_____

Abilities and talents you feel you lack

_____

_____

_____

_____

Your hopes and dreams

_____

_____

_____

_____

2. Think about how you feel about yourself. Do you have a healthy, positive self-image? Review your life experiences over the past few months, then read each of the following items and rate how often it reflects how you have felt about yourself.

1—rarely	2—sometimes	3—often	4—frequently	5—usually

a. _____ I don't like going to work.

b. _____ I am easily bored.

c. _____ I cannot communicate without a strain.

d. _____ I don't perform my job up to par.

e. _____ I get into conflicts with others.

f. _____ I think my friends think of me as a failure.

g. _____ I am late or fail to show up for appointments too often.

h. _____ I am not conscientious about my grooming and appearance.

i. _____ I have unattractive physical characteristics.

j. _____ I can't concentrate on anything for very long.

k. _____ I work hard but accomplish little.

l. _____ I am forgetful.

m. _____ I don't like the people I work for.

n. _____ I lack energy and enthusiasm.

Scoring:

14–20 You're doing well.
21–30 You're okay if you continue building your self-esteem.
31–40 You need to do some serious self-esteem building.
41 and higher—You appear to suffer from chronic low self-esteem. You need to get to work and get help.

case studies for critical thinking

TEARS ON THE JOB

Tanessa is an administrative assistant to the purchasing manager in an electronics firm. Her supervisor, Mr. Rodrigues, was a kind, fatherly man, and Tanessa has worked happily and well. Two weeks ago, however, Mr. Rodrigues was transferred and Tanessa was assigned to work with his replacement, Mr. Kim. The new man is brilliant and efficient, but he is somewhat short on patience. He speaks crisply and concisely to everyone. In Tanessa's anxiety to please, she finds herself making many errors. This fact in itself distresses Tanessa, but when Mr. Kim criticizes her work rather sharply, Tanessa bursts into tears. Mr. Kim takes her tears in stride, but he becomes extremely irritated with Tanessa's continued apologies for her previous errors. Finally, he arranges for Tanessa to be transferred to another office.

1. Would you say that Tanessa has a problem with her self-esteem? What evidence do you see to support this conclusion?

2. Is Tanessa expecting too much of herself? Should she see herself as a "perfectionist" and embark on a self-improvement program, or should she accept herself as a person who occasionally makes mistakes, but learns from them?

3. Assume that Tanessa goes to Mr. Rodrigues for friendly advice. After listening to Tanessa's story, what guidance and advice might he offer?

Case 1.2

CAREER CHANGE?

Carlos was ending his day at the bakery, a family business that he would someday own. After high school he completed a two-year training program—the best in the country; he knew the bakery business very well. He did his job well and felt satisfaction in his achievement.

However, the day seemed long. The routine seemed unchallenging and a bit boring. Now in his mid-twenties, Carlos felt as though he had reached the end of the road in his career. The prospect of another twenty or thirty years in the bakery business (thousands more days like today) was depressing.

1. If Carlos considers a career change, what are some factors that might influence his decision?

2. Assuming Carlos asked you to help him decide what to do (and assuming you are a close friend), what information would you want to obtain, and what information would you want Carlos to consider in the process of reaching a decision?

3. What are the advantages and disadvantages for Carlos if he decides not to make a change?

Advantages

Disadvantages

2 Self-Improvement

chapter

© BRAND X PICTURES

think about it: George answered the doorbell and was surprised to see Leon, a friend from the health club. They had played basketball together and were casual friends. After they exchanged greetings, Leon asked to use the telephone. "My car stalled a couple of blocks from here, and I need to call a tow truck," he explained. "Well, okay," George responded after a short pause. "I hate to have anyone see my place in this condition." Leon looked around, smiled, and quipped, "No problem; it reminds me of your locker back at the gym—but it doesn't smell quite so bad!"

This experience caused George to stop and think about his living conditions. After reflecting on the appearance of his home, his workplace, and the image he was presenting to those around him, he was inspired to make a dramatic change. He resolved to clean up his apartment and his locker at the health club. He thought about how he managed his work environment and realized there was need for improvement there, as well. He decided to develop a reputation for being neat, clean, and orderly.

What are some suggestions you might offer to help George develop neat, clean, and orderly habits?

chapter focus

After completing this chapter, you should be able to:

1. Visualize improvements in your personality that will allow you to reach your full potential.

2. Identify well-defined long-term goals and specific short-term objectives for self-improvement.

Chapter Highlights

2.1 Plan to Improve

2.2 Actively Working to Improve Yourself

3. Develop plans for achieving your self-improvement goals and objectives.

4. Monitor your progress toward goal attainment.

5. Cultivate mentoring relationships with coworkers and supervisors who will support you as you plan and work toward self-improvement.

6. Find and use a professional counselor or therapist, or a trusted friend to help with the process of self-understanding and improvement.

7. Use behavior modification to provide incentives for self-improvement.

8. Use aptitude and interest testing for self-evaluation, setting goals, and making plans for self-improvement.

9. Take specific actions to get your self-improvement program underway.

If you are to take charge of yourself and become successful in your life and work, you must start with a clear, realistic image of yourself. You must also begin to build a clear image of the personality you want to develop. Once you have a good idea of what needs to be accomplished, you are ready to begin making plans—plans for the self-improvement that is needed as you develop your success identity.

Figure 2-1 shows how the process builds toward your self-improvement goals.

Here are the steps in the process of planning for self-improvement:

1. Develop a realistic vision of your future self—an image of the personality that you want and need to attain as you prepare for success in your career and in life. That vision will give you something to plan for and work toward.

2. Analyze the personality that you envision and bring specific goals into focus. Then identify specific, measurable objectives for each goal.

3. Plan the accomplishment of the objectives. The vision of your future self in terms of self-improvement goals and objectives describes what you want to happen. The action plans describe how you will make it happen.

4. Develop your success identity. Your action plans will point the way. As you implement your action plans, remember this: Self-improvement is not a goal to attain. It is a process that continues as you grow into the best person that you can be.

Vision of your
future self

↓

Specific goals

↓

Measurable objectives
for each goal

↓

Action plans for
each objective

FIGURE 2-1 *Planning for self-improvement.*

on the job

Identify someone whom you admire in your workplace—a successful coworker or supervisor. Arrange for an interview and ask for "keys to success" that you might use in your self-improvement action plan. You might invite this person to lunch and, if possible, spend some time observing him or her at work. Here are some ideas for questions or discussion topics:

- What are some experiences that helped prepare you for success in this position?
- What are some of the things you did to improve yourself?
- Tell me about some of the people who influenced you most as role models.
- Are you doing anything now to prepare yourself to be more effective or successful in the future?

Share your information about "keys to success" and discuss what you learned with other class members, coworkers, or friends.

How might you use what you learned to help create your own self-improvement program?

VISUALIZE YOUR BEST SELF

Developing a clear image of your potential begins as you face the reality of your experiences, take off the masks that may be used to create false impressions, and seriously consider the praise and criticism from those who know you well. As you reflect on the masks you found yourself using, think about what you were trying to accomplish with the pretense or role-playing. As you reflect on the praise and criticism, think about the changes in your personality that might eliminate the criticism and bring even more praise. It will help to take notes. As ideas for self-improvement occur to you, jot them down.

Another good way to visualize your potential is by using a technique that psychotherapists call **imaging**. This is a deliberate effort to imagine your renewed and improved personality. Find a quiet, pleasant place where you can relax. Take your time; do not try to hurry. Close your eyes and search your mind for images of yourself doing what gives you satisfaction. If there are sources of distress in your life (anxiety, depression, anger), try to imagine what might relieve the distress.

"Once you say you're going to settle for second, that's what happens to you in life."

—JOHN F. KENNEDY

"Concentrate on finding your goal, then concentrate on reaching it."

—MICHAEL FRIEDSAM

Imagine your improved personality.

© GETTY IMAGES/PHOTODISC

If you follow these suggestions, you should be able to produce a list of notes about the various personal qualities and characteristics you would like to develop. Review and organize these ideas into a profile of your improved personality.

A term for the process of growing to reach your greatest potential is **self-actualization**. This does not culminate in a final achievement of your potential. You should not assume that you will ever be able to sit back and rest in your self-improvement efforts. Rather, you must expect to reassess and redefine your success identity as you move ahead in your career and life. You will need to keep working to maintain your self-esteem. Your success identity will evolve and be renewed as you grow to become the best that you can be.

LONG-TERM GOALS

As you analyze your future personality profile, you will probably see that it can be logically broken down into several categories of self-improvement focusing on:

• career
• social status and relationships
• education and training
• communication skills
• physical well-being
• earning and saving

These elements of your personality profile are the basis for your **long-term goals** (goals for the future) for change. Goals that are too broad or too vague or are built on "psychobabble" ("I want to get my head together" or "I want to be a fully actualized human being") are neither helpful for planning nor are they easily achieved. You must be specific enough in stating your goals to allow for evaluation of your progress and to know when you have achieved your goals.

Following are some examples of long-term goals that are too vague, and more specific statements that may be used for planning:

VAGUE: a good education
SPECIFIC: earn an associate degree in retailing

VAGUE: leadership ability
SPECIFIC: be promoted to supervisor

VAGUE: control my temper
SPECIFIC: avoid shouting matches

VAGUE: self-confidence
SPECIFIC: maintain eye contact in conversations with supervisors

VAGUE: good eating habits
SPECIFIC: avoid "junk food" snacks

VAGUE: develop my musical talent
SPECIFIC: take guitar lessons

SHORT-TERM OBJECTIVES

With a profile of specific goals in view, you are ready to develop the **short-term objectives** that will be the stepping-stones to the achievement of your goals. As you do this, it is important to make the objectives observable or measurable in some way. You must have a clear vision of how you will know that you are making progress. This usually involves including a time frame for your goals and objectives. But be reasonable—no one changes overnight. To get started, for each specific long-term goal, you need to ask yourself:

"What Evidence will Indicate Progress or Achievement of this Goal?"

The answers to this question will be the measurable or observable objectives that will describe the short-term, specific mileposts that indicate progress along the way as you work toward accomplishing your goals. Here are some examples:

GOAL: Be promoted to office manager within four years.

OBJECTIVES:
- Learn basic principles of office management.

- Receive "excellent" or "superior" ratings on performance reviews in my present position.
- Gain experience as receptionist, and work in bookkeeping and inventory control.

GOAL: Improve self-confidence and assertiveness.

OBJECTIVES:
- Have the courage to ask my employer for a new job assignment.
- Learn more about assertiveness and apply it in my life and work.
- Maintain calm, cool, and candid behavior when challenging manipulative friends and coworkers.

GOAL: To be computer literate.

OBJECTIVES:
- Become proficient in keyboarding.
- Learn to use a word-processing program.
- Manage my personal finances using online banking.

"Goals are dreams with deadlines."

—DIANA SHARF HUNT

© GETTY IMAGES/PHOTODISC

Stretch yourself to reach your objectives.

23

SELF CHECK

As you begin to formulate goals and objectives, carefully consider what you know about yourself. Think about your talents, your aptitudes, your skills, your hopes and dreams, your past successes and failures, the kind of person you are, and the kind of person you want to be. You can use this checklist of general categories to help you think of specific areas that you might want to improve.

_____ Do I need to learn or improve technical skills?

_____ Do I need to learn or improve communication skills?

_____ Do I need to break any habits?

_____ Do I understand and use wise money management strategies?

_____ Do I have study habits or skills I need to improve?

_____ Do I have shortcomings or areas of personal weakness that I need to change?

_____ Do I take good care of my physical health?

_____ Does my appearance reflect an image that will help me reach my goals?

_____ Do I have talents or aptitudes I have not pursued?

_____ Do I use my time wisely?

_____ Am I reliable?

_____ Do I have a positive attitude?

_____ Do I treat others with respect?

_____ Is there something I really want to learn?

"If you would hit the mark you must aim a little above it; every arrow that flies feels the attraction of earth."

—HENRY WADSWORTH LONGFELLOW

ACTION PLANS

After you have produced a list of specific objectives for one of the long-term goals, you are ready to develop plans of action (**strategies** and **tactics**) that will ensure the achievement of your objectives.

For each objective, write down what action you plan to take that will bring you closer to the achievement of the objective.

Ask Yourself, "What can I do to Make this Happen?"

Here are some examples of specific actions that might lead to the accomplishment of short-term objectives and, eventually, long-term goals:

- Use a budget to control spending.
- Read a book on assertiveness.
- Practice job interviews with a coworker.
- Join a support group.
- Buy a personal computer to use at home.
- Obtain permission to "shadow" a co-worker to learn about another job.

Review the notes you made during your examination of your potential and analysis of praise and criticism. As you work on identifying your objectives and action plans, combine your ideas of what you need to improve now with your goals for your career and life.

Determining what you would like to do with the rest of your life involves your personality, beliefs, dreams, ambitions, and imagination. Your success identity will depend to some extent on how determined you are to reach your goals. Too often people fail to achieve their goals simply because they get discouraged and give up. Of course, even more people fail because they never set goals in the first place.

Staying focused on your goals helps if you hold yourself accountable for your action plans. One way to do this is by keeping your goals in a journal or diary. Another is by sharing them, when appropriate, with others.

Think of your goals, objectives, and plans as promises—contracts with yourself. If you share what you are doing with your family, friends, coworkers, and employment supervisors, you will have greater

chec**k**point

1. **What problems can you cause for yourself by stating your goals in vague, unrealistic terms?**

   _____

   _____

   _____

   _____

2. **Evaluate "becoming a better driver" as a goal or objective.**

   _____

   _____

   _____

   _____

3. **How might an unconditionally caring friend help you to develop appropriate self-improvement goals, objectives, and action plans?**

   _____

   _____

   _____

   _____

4. **What might you do to visualize where you are at present on the road to becoming the best that you can be?**

   _____

   _____

   _____

   _____

on ethics

Some people don't want to do the work involved in making real changes and improvements, but they still want people to think they have improved themselves. In business, this often takes the form of making false statements on résumés or job applications. This is a dangerous practice, because most companies have policies of instant dismissal if they find out an employee lied. Also, it would be difficult to respect yourself if you know you gave false information—plus there's the fear of getting caught.

What consequences, both short-term and long-term, might be the result of being untruthful on a résumé or job application? What opportunities might be missed or lost?

determination to follow your self-improvement program.

Your motivation to improve will also be sustained by your vision of the benefits of success in your career and by your appreciation of your progress. Remember that you can achieve a realistic goal if it is something you sincerely want, if you carefully plan a way to reach it, and if you have the perseverance to stick with the plan.

"The world stands aside to let anyone pass who knows where he [or she] is going."

—David Starr Jordan

applications

1. Write a short profile of yourself. Include information from your education, work experience, background, and the results of any tests you've taken. Consider other life experiences, such as hobbies, participation in school activities, interest in science, literature, or working with children—whatever might suggest specific talents or abilities that may prepare you for success in life and at work. Discuss how this information can help you set your long-term goals.

_____

_____

_____

2. On a large piece of poster paper, prepare a collage using magazine clippings to represent successful achievement of your personal goals and objectives. A portion of the collage could be devoted to each of your major goals. In a group discussion, share your goals and objectives by asking classmates to interpret the clippings and guess their meaning. Draft your collage here. Then record their responses.

_____

_____

_____

3. Identify someone who has achieved success in a career that seems to fit with the image you have of yourself five years from now. Arrange an interview with that person, and discuss what has gone into developing his or her career. During your discussion, get answers for the following questions:

a. What events or what circumstances paved the way for his or her career decisions?

_____

_____

_____

3b. What personality characteristics, aptitudes, and interests does this person have that correspond to the demands of the career?

_____

_____

_____

_____

_____

3c. What suggestions can he or she offer to someone who might want to follow the same career path?

_____

_____

_____

_____

_____

4. Write a short-term objective regarding an event (perhaps an assignment or a competition) that you have to complete in the next month. Then, write the milestones that you will use to determine how well you are progressing toward the objective.

_____

_____

_____

_____

_____

Actively Working to Improve Yourself

There are many strategies, techniques, or methods you may want to use as you actively work to improve yourself. Several will be described in this section. You may already be using some of these strategies without realizing it, and there may be others that you will want to try.

MENTORING AND COACHING

When you begin a new job, you can expect your employer to be concerned about your training. In most cases there is a period of adjustment to the new work situation. There may be a lot to learn about what the job consists of and how it is to be done. There are procedures, policies, rules, and expectations understood by those who have been on the job for a while. All this becomes the focus of training and adjustment for the new person.

Usually, someone will be assigned to assist the new person with on-the-job training. Also, without a specific assignment to do so, coworkers may voluntarily help with the orientation and training. You can expect support as you learn to fit in, get along, and become productive in a new work situation. The person who takes a personal interest in helping someone with training and development on the job is called a **mentor**.

You could consider a coworker or supervisor who is responsible for your on-the-job training as a resource person, helping you achieve your plans for self-improvement. However, for this person to assume the role of mentor and assist you with your personal self-improvement program, he or she should take a personal interest in helping you reach your potential at work and in life. You may need to put forth an effort to cultivate a friendship with someone, or possibly with several people, who will want to fulfill the role of mentor and coach as you work on your self-improvement program.

COUNSELING

A psychologist describes how the self-improvement process worked for a client named Barbara: "She had come through her divorce successfully, had moved to a new apartment, and was thinking of changing her job. After several sessions we were sorting out the kind of future she wanted. It was the first time in her life, Barbara told me, that she felt truly responsible for her future. The experience was a bit frightening. 'It seems someone else has always made my decisions,' she explained. 'I guess I just came to rely on others for direction in my life.' My job as her counselor is to help Barbara grow. I don't tell her where or how. As we became seriously engaged in the self-improvement process, Barbara was doing the hard work—setting goals for herself and planning her future. 'It's scary,' she admitted, 'but I am taking charge of my life and it feels pretty good.'"

> *"It's what you learn after you know it all that counts."*
>
> —JOHN WOODEN

A mentor can coach you in self-improvement.

© DIGITAL VISION

A professional counselor or therapist can help with the process of developing an understanding and appreciation of who you are and where you are in your personal and career development. Sometimes it helps just to talk to someone about yourself. A mental health professional, school or college counselor, an Employee Assistance Program counselor, or even a relative or personal friend with whom you feel comfortable talking can help you sort out your concerns and help you focus your self-assessment and plans for self-improvement. Often just the process of talking with someone allows you to explore your feelings about yourself. Talking with a counselor can help you appreciate the many positive aspects of your personality, your educational and employment experiences, and your natural abilities.

BEHAVIOR MODIFICATION

An approach to self-improvement that has been successful for many people is to use **behavior modification**. The theory behind behavior modification suggests that people act in ways that bring some kind of reward. If you want to change your behavior, you must have some payoff or benefit as motivation. Psychologists refer to the reward as **reinforcement** of the desirable behavior.

If you develop your own system of rewards, you may be able to use behavior modification to help you carry out your action plans for self-improvement. You might begin by considering what you enjoy. Take a piece of paper and list ten to twenty things that you might use to reward yourself. Do you like to spend time relaxing with a good book or television program? Do you look forward to going out to dinner? Do you enjoy skiing, racquetball, golf, tennis, or hiking? Are you thinking about buying something that you want but do not absolutely need?

© DIGITAL VISION

A compliment from a coworker can be encouraging reinforcement.

Whatever you list as rewards for behavior modification, you should be realistic. If achievement is a step-by-step process, plan additional small rewards at each step along the way. Of course, these rewards must be possible in your present circumstances. You cannot say that you would like to buy a new sports car if you can only afford a used car.

With your potential rewards list at hand, review your self-improvement action plans. Try to match specific objectives or activities with appropriate rewards. Prepare a contract in which you promise yourself that you are going to change in some way. You may decide to use more effective study skills. You may decide to control your bad temper.

Put your ideas for a contract in writing. One way to do this is to keep a card file with each promise to yourself written on a card. It should include a date on which the contract takes effect, what you intend to do ("I promise to..."), and what benefit you expect to achieve. Include something pleasant and rewarding to look forward to when you achieve the objectives in your self-improvement plan. If possible, a realistic date for fulfillment of the contract should be included.

"I am always ready to learn although I do not always like being taught."

—WINSTON CHURCHILL

APTITUDE AND INTEREST TESTING

Your local Job Service Office or career counseling center can provide testing services and help with interpretation and assessment of your strengths and weaknesses. Vocational interest and aptitude tests can help you better understand your potential for success in various career fields. These tests can also help in determining what you need to learn to prepare for success in an appropriate career. Some of the tests measure characteristics that relate to the demands of various work situations. For instance:

- Do you like detail?
- Are you naturally an orderly person?
- Do you like to solve problems?
- Would you do well working with mechanical things?
- Do you enjoy teamwork and cooperative relationships?
- Do you enjoy the challenge of variety and change in your work?
- Do you have an aptitude for selling?
- Do you have an aptitude for work involving mathematics?

Answers to these types of questions will help you focus on your interests, aptitudes, and preferences and can give you clues about what to do as you strive for self-improvement. Also, the information obtained from standardized scholastic aptitude and achievement tests (used by most educational institutions) can provide detailed information about where you are in your preparation for success in your chosen career. Usually, an employment or school counselor will help you with interpretation of your tests and with plans for future career preparation.

"We don't need more strength or more ability or greater opportunity. What we need is to use what we have."

—BASIL S. WALSH

Technology at Work

The Internet is a wonderful place to find information that can help you move ahead in your self-improvement program. Online resources include self-help programs, guidance, and chat rooms for a wide range of areas, from learning the computer or studying writing to dealing with anger, depression, debt, or bad habits. In addition, there are listings of self-help groups available in your area, from Toastmasters (for gaining skill as a public speaker) to 12-step programs (to help in recovery for a wide range of life issues).

Entering the words "self-help" in your favorite search engine should retrieve a good list of options, from business classes to smoking cessation groups to personality tests. Also, a site like About.com, where human guides help in the search, can help you find what you need.

Other search words could include the specific area in which you wish to improve (public speaking, writing, technology, health, continuing education) or issue you need to address (anger, depression, fear of failure or success). The words "anonymous" or "recovery" can help you find support groups, either online or in person.

TRY-OUT EXPERIENCES

A very good way to evaluate your potential for success in an occupation is by trying out actual experiences. For the musician, the athlete, the cook, the taxi driver, the health care worker, or the salesperson, experience provides clear and obvious signs of success and failure. If you have the opportunity in a work environment to test the validity of your new image of yourself as a potential auto mechanic, for example, successful performance is bound to have a positive impact on your self-esteem by strengthening and reinforcing it.

Another kind of **try-out experience** that can help you find and confirm your natural abilities and preparation for a career is to enroll in a course related to the field you want to explore. You can find these courses through adult education programs, community college or high school classes, apprentice training programs, and instruction sponsored by employers in business and industry. If you do not want to enroll in the class formally, you can talk to the instructor and students. You may be allowed to sit in on a few sessions and look at the course outline or text materials. However, you should be aware that what happens in class represents only part of what actually happens at work. This is especially true in classes that serve as preparation for advanced study. For example, an introductory marketing course does not cover what the work is like for an advertising copywriter or a merchandising manager. Keep in mind also that distance education courses, many available online, present other opportunities for you to explore new paths.

Another possibility for testing your interest and ability and building your self-confidence before you fully commit yourself to a career is an internship program. In these programs, classroom and laboratory training is coordinated with on-the-job training in the work environment. It is important that you realize that these skills and strategies are not simply useful for getting started in a career. They can also help you advance in your career or help you to change careers later as you discover new things. Just keep learning and improving.

Smart Tip ▼ ▼ ▼

Here are some things to keep in mind as you plan your self-improvement program:

- **Start now. Don't put it off until you're "ready," because it won't happen.**

- **Start small. Don't try to do everything at once. Focus on the things that are your highest priorities, then add other goals or changes as time goes by. Use your success in these to motivate yourself for the next change.**

- **Involve friends. They can help keep you on course, listen and offer feedback, and help you celebrate your successes.**

- **Don't give up. If you slip up, just get back on your program. Don't think of a slip as defeat; just think of it as a warning sign.**

- **Stay focused on your goals. There are lots of things that will come along and tempt you to go off course, but if you keep your goals in mind, you're more likely to reach them.**

- **Enjoy your improvements. Recognize how far you've come; celebrate a goal reached.**

- **Let every success trigger new goals. There will always be something new to learn, something higher to attain. Keep moving forward.**

▲ ▲ ▲ ▲ ▲ ▲ ▲ ▲ ▲

SELF-IMPROVEMENT ACTION PLANS

Remember, there are no "easy solutions," or "overnight successes." Change takes time. The good news is that, given the time, changes can be made. We are not "stuck" with what we have.

According to Prochaska, Norcross, and Diclemente, the research psychologists who authored the book *Changing for Good: A Revolutionary Six-Stage Program for Overcoming Bad Habits and Moving Your Life Positively Forward,* self-changers are "as successful in their efforts to change as those individuals who choose to enter therapy or join a professionally run program."[1]

So anyone can change who really wants to. It's good to have someone to talk to, but it doesn't have to be an expensive professional.

check✓point

1. **Explain why rewards for success or accomplishment are better ways to provide reinforcement than punishment for failure.**

   _____

   _____

2. **List four examples of try-out experiences that might be of interest to you.**

   _____

   _____

3. **List five personal attributes that can be assessed or measured using aptitude tests.**

   _____

   _____

4. **Name three people with whom you are acquainted who might be willing and able to act as a mentor for you.**

   _____

   _____

5. **Which of the following would *not* be appropriate for you to ask of a mentor: help with behavior modification, job coaching, efficiency tips, personal loan, guidance for career development. Discuss your choice, then talk about how having a mentor might benefit you.**

   _____

   _____

6. **What are some of the benefits of part-time and short-term employment?**

   _____

   _____

applications

1. Explain the concept of behavior modification to your mentor or a good friend. Have this person help you choose suitable rewards for reinforcement of your progress or appropriate behavior. List the rewards below.

2. Go to a library or school counseling center and gather information about vocational interest and aptitude tests. You may also search the Internet for specific types of tests. List below the names of the tests and what they measure.

3. Write or discuss how tests (academic, personality, aptitudes, interests) could help you with your self-improvement program. Why might you want to discuss test results with someone (counselor, teacher, mentor, friend) before using the information to plan your long-term goals?

_____

_____

_____

_____

_____

_____

_____

4. Discuss how a tryout experience may be of benefit to you as you seek to evaluate your potential for success in a particular occupation.

_____

_____

_____

_____

_____

_____

_____

_____

2 Points to Remember

chapter

Review the following points to determine what you remember from the chapter.

- To develop a vision of your best self, you will look realistically at your life experiences and the feedback you obtain through praise and criticism, and imagine your renewed, improved personality. Planning for self-improvement involves the following steps: (1) Develop a realistic vision of your future self; (2) Analyze the personality that you envision and bring specific goals into focus. Then identify specific, measurable objectives for each goal; (3) Plan the accomplishment of the objectives; (4) Develop your success identity.

- Focus on specific categories for self-improvement as the basis for producing specific long-term goals. Focus on your career, relationships, education, training, communication skills, physical well-being, and earning and saving. Use long-term goals to produce short-term objectives that serve as stepping-stones to achievement. Include a time frame for your short-term goals, and make sure the goals are measurable.

- After goals and objectives are in place, a plan of action is needed that will ensure the achievement of your objectives. Design and write down a plan of action you will take that will bring you closer to the achievement of each objective and, eventually, the long-term goals.

- Check on your progress by paying attention to your successes and failures in the attainment of each specific objective. Stay focused on your goals and hold yourself accountable for your action plans.

- To cultivate a mentoring relationship with coworkers or supervisors who will take a personal interest in helping you achieve your plans for self-improvement, you may need to put forth an effort to cultivate a friendship with someone, or possibly several people.

- Seek counseling or just talk with someone about your self-improvement goals, objectives, and plans to help keep you focused. Often just the process of talking with someone allows you to explore your feelings about yourself.

- The theory behind behavior modification suggests that people act in ways that will bring some kind of reward. Develop your own system of behavior modification and use the rewards to reinforce your self-improvement efforts. Make and keep contractual promises to yourself.

- Use aptitude and interest tests to provide clues about what to do as you strive for self-improvement. These tests can also help in determining what you need to learn to prepare for success in an appropriate career.

- Engage in try-out experiences to find and confirm your natural abilities, talents, and interests as you explore different careers in a work environment. Take courses related to the field you want to explore. A very good way to evaluate your potential for success in an occupation is to try out actual experiences. Successful performance is bound to have a positive impact on your self-esteem by strengthening and reinforcing it.

How did you do? Did you remember the main points you studied in the chapter?

key terms

Define each term in the space provided.

Imaging

Self-actualization

Long-term goals

Short-term objectives

Strategies or tactics

Mentor

Behavior modification

Reinforcement

Try-out experiences

activities and projects

1. Interview an experienced worker in a job you think you would like to have. Ask this person to tell you something about the personal qualities needed for the job, especially those that can increase the potential for success, and something about the standards of performance in that workplace. Take notes during the interview and use the information to prepare a list in the left-hand column below indicating the aptitudes, interests, and talents or abilities that a person experiencing success in this job might have. In the corresponding space on the right, evaluate your present qualifications and future potential with respect to each item on the list.

Indicate how qualified you are at present and how qualified you might become if you reach your potential. Use the following: 1 = poorly qualified; 2 = somewhat qualified; 3 = highly qualified.

Personal qualities needed: **Present qualifications:**   **Potential:**

_____   _____   _____

_____   _____   _____

_____   _____   _____

_____   _____   _____

_____   _____   _____

_____   _____   _____

_____   _____   _____

_____   _____   _____

2. Wilma wants to start a program of self-improvement and has asked for your input. Consider the following information about Wilma:

• Her favorite classes in high school were public speaking and English.
• She disliked algebra, science, and history.
• Her favorite activities are dancing, debate, and volleyball.
• She likes her part-time job as a salesperson in a jewelry store.
• She has not balanced her checkbook in the past year.
• Her two older sisters have jokingly called her a "slob."

- She can easily count ten people she considers to be close friends. She says she dislikes no one.
- She has a "B" average in college.

a. What are Wilma's strong points?

_____

_____

_____

b. What are Wilma's weak points?

_____

_____

_____

c. What might be appropriate self-improvement goals for Wilma?

_____

_____

_____

d. Write at least two objectives that Wilma would need to accomplish to achieve a goal of "being a good money manager."

_____

_____

_____

e. Write several strategies or action plans for one of the objectives listed in d. above.

_____

_____

_____

3. List as many resources as you can think of that could assist you in one or more stages of your self-improvement program—from first attempts at assessment through celebrating success. Consider people, books, services, Web sites, organizations—anything or anyone that might help you. When you run out of ideas, join with a partner who is also working on this, and brainstorm together for other resource ideas—not only specific resources, but where to search for more ideas.

case studies for critical thinking

CROSSROADS

Paulo Mendosa has just graduated from high school. He has two job opportunities for the summer. One is a general office job in a large manufacturing company. The other, which pays more, is driving a delivery truck for a nursery and garden store. Paulo likes to drive and enjoys the out of doors. In high school he enjoyed his business and computer courses, and received compliments from his teacher and other students for designing and managing a Web site for the school's athletic department. He also did well in math and accounting courses. Paulo's tentative plan is to go to a nearby community college in the fall to study computer science.

1. Assume that Paulo is in need of and ready to work on a self-improvement plan. Outline a strategy and specific activities that might help him choose a career path and visualize his potential.

_____

_____

_____

2. Paulo sees you as his trusted friend and respects your good judgment. He finds himself torn between the two job opportunities and has become less certain about his plan to study computer science. What advice would you give?

_____

_____

_____

TRY-OUT EXPERIENCES AS A TEMPORARY WORKER

Shari's high school program included several courses in business education. These experiences gave her some understanding of the business world and the variety of job possibilities open to her. For a few months, she worked as a receptionist but found the job to be somewhat frustrating. There were many interruptions, so she could not concentrate on the task at hand. Also, Shari felt pressured because she had to deal with the complaints of dissatisfied clients where she worked. She shared her feelings with a coworker, Sylvia, who had temporarily taken over for someone who was absent from work because of illness. Sylvia explained that she was employed by a firm that provided temporary short-term workers in secretarial, accounting, data processing, and administrative fields. She told Shari about the many different job experiences she had enjoyed over the past several months. She said that the manager was always looking for good workers, and Shari began to consider the possibility of a job change.

1. What are the possible advantages or opportunities for Shari if she obtains temporary positions? What are some risks and disadvantages?

_____

_____

_____

_____

_____

_____

_____

2. How might Shari use her employment to provide try-out experiences in the world of work?

_____

_____

_____

_____

_____

_____

_____

Case 2.3

A NEW DIRECTION

Ben has been working as a meat cutter for seven years. He earns a good salary and likes his work, his coworkers, and his employer. He got the job just before his marriage to Beverly, and now they have three children. The youngest is two years old and stays with Beverly's mother during the day. Beverly recently resumed working as a bank teller. She and Ben had a serious discussion about their future. They concluded that Beverly is content in her banking career, but Ben wants more than meat cutting in his future.

1. Describe what Ben might do to assess his potential to prepare for a new career in business management.

2. Discuss what Beverly might do to support and encourage Ben.

Developing Positive Attitudes

think about it: Phil was assigned to sit between two people on a crowded flight to Anchorage. As a flight attendant walked by, he caught her attention and said, "Could I have a pillow, please?"

"Pillows are all gone. Here's a blanket," she snapped as she tossed it on Phil's lap and walked away.

Trying to make the best of his situation, Phil struck up a conversation with the person next to the window. "Are you enjoying the view?" he asked. "I hadn't noticed," the woman responded. "I guess I was distracted by that flight attendant's behavior." The woman looked up and rolled her eyes. "I've been watching her, and it irritates me to see how she's acting. I think she could have found a pillow for you. And her tone of voice! She was so snippy when you asked for a pillow. Did you notice her body language—hands on her hips, slamming things around in the galley, stomping off and hiding in the cockpit when passengers need her. What a grouch! I work for another airline, and I know we would never tolerate that kind of attitude problem in a flight attendant."

What might happen in the future if the flight attendant does not improve her attitude?

© GETTY IMAGES/PHOTODISC

chapter focus

After completing this chapter, you should be able to:

1. Define attitudes and explain how they develop.

2. Explain how attitudes are visible and how one person's attitudes can influence others.

3. Avoid negative influences and benefit from positive attitudes of others.

4. Take positive steps to improve your attitudes.

5. Develop such attributes as individual responsibility, sociability, and integrity.

Chapter Highlights

3.1 How Attitudes Develop

3.2 Attitudes Are Catching

3.3 Improve Your Attitudes

How Attitudes Develop

Psychologists and educators tell us that human beings are learning constantly. The three general types of learning that take place are knowledge, skills, and attitudes. It would be easy to identify the first two types, but have you given much thought to the third type of learning: attitude?

ATTITUDES DEFINED

A simple definition of an **attitude** is how a person feels about something. If attitudes are a type of learning, then an important part of your personality—the many different feelings you have—is learned. You may or may not be attracted to different people. You may or may not enjoy doing certain things. At a more intense level, you may fear or dislike someone or something.

In another sense, your attitude is the general feeling you communicate to others. You will hear someone say, "He has a bad attitude" or "Her attitude about the project was very positive."

"Nothing can stop the man with the right mental attitude from achieving his goal; nothing on earth can help the man with the wrong mental attitude."

—W. W. ZIEGE

ATTITUDES AND IMAGE

You are constantly sending signals that others pick up. It is almost as if those around you can "tune in" to your attitudes. Your attitudes can cause people to be drawn to you and have positive feelings (or attitudes) toward you. On the other hand, your attitudes can signal others to avoid you. Your attitudes can cause others to see you as attractive or repulsive in varying degrees. Therefore, the image your friends, coworkers, and even casual associates have of you is what you project by your attitudes.

LEARNING ATTITUDES

Each kind of learning requires a different method or strategy, and what works for one

Technology at Work

Because employers understand that much of what an individual does is based on his or her attitudes, a great deal of effort is put into finding out the attitudes of job applicants. An individual's attitudes, values, and lifestyle all go into determining how focused and dedicated the worker will be, how he or she will fit into the workplace team, and how effective the worker will be in developing trusting, cordial relationships with clients and customers. Here is a suggestion that may help you to understand how positive attitudes can have a favorable impact on your career development. In your favorite Internet search engine, select the category of Social Sciences, and do a search using the key word "attitudes."

kind of learning may not work for another. A method that might help you memorize the anatomy of an insect may not work to help you learn to swim. You gain knowledge by studying and by using logical and critical thinking abilities. You develop skills by practice and careful repetition of behavior, with demonstration and coaching to help you improve. However, you do not develop attitudes in the same ways that you develop knowledge or skills.

Educators and psychologists who have studied human learning say that **emotion** is the critical factor in the development of attitudes. Emotions such as fear, joy, anxiety, or compassion seem to shape our feelings about the events in our lives. When emotion accompanies an event time after time, it creates an attitude or feeling that may be very intense and difficult to change.

Here is What Happened:

One of the supervisors came up with the idea of having a "debriefing" after each accident. As soon as an accident happened, all work would stop. The accident victim was required to tell other workers what happened, why, and how it might have been prevented.

There was a dramatic reduction in accidents under that particular supervisor. When these spur-of-the-moment meetings were held in other construction units, the results were the same—a reduction in the frequency of accidents. Where lectures on safety practices in training sessions had failed, the emotionally charged learning that occurred in the debriefing sessions had a powerful effect on the attitudes of the workers.

This example shows that highly emotional experiences can shape attitudes, and those attitudes can effectively influence behavior. These workers had all the knowledge they needed to behave appropriately. What they lacked was the motivation to do what they knew they should. A change in attitudes provided that motivation.

on the job

A firm that was involved in heavy construction found that the frequency of accidental injuries was very high. The training program had stressed safety procedures, and the workers were thoroughly acquainted with what they should do to protect themselves from injury. However, simply knowing the safety rules in this case did not cause the workers to behave in a safe manner. The supervisors concluded that while the workers knew what was expected, they simply were not doing it. Some were found to be welding without safety glasses. Equipment was being serviced without being turned off (as safety codes required). Power tools were being operated without shields, and workers were not wearing gloves when they should have been.

The workers knew the rules, but they had not developed the proper attitudes toward them. What was needed was a learning experience that would create a change in how the workers felt about the rules.

Considering the fact that attitudes change and learning new attitudes can best be accomplished in a situation where emotions are high, what might the supervisors do to create positive attitudes and motivation for the workers to follow the safety rules and be safety conscious?

check*point*

1. Three general types of learning are _____, _____, and _____.

2. What works as effective instruction for one kind of learning is likely to work as well for another. True____ False____

3. An attitude is something you
   a. visualize. b. do. c. know. d. feel.

4. Attitudes are learned
   a. in emotional situations. b. with careful step-by-step instruction.
   c. by memorization. d. by coaching and practice.

5. We are likely to be unaffected by the attitudes of those around us.
   True____ False____

6. It is easy for others to "tune in" to your attitudes. True____ False____

7. Your attitudes can cause others to see you as arrogant. True____ False____

8. People are not likely to make positive or negative judgments about someone because of his or her attitudes. True____ False____

applications

Reflect on your past experiences in school or at work. Prepare written responses and share your ideas in a group discussion of the following:

1. Describe a situation when you demonstrated a negative attitude. How was your attitude reflected in your behavior?

2. Describe an occasion when you demonstrated a positive attitude.

3. Identify a teacher or an employment supervisor who demonstrated an obviously negative attitude. What behavior gave you clues about this person's attitude?

4. Identify someone who you felt demonstrated "the power of positive thinking" that led to a motivational effect on others. Briefly describe the person's attitudes and the behavior that seemed to influence others.

5. Think about an emotionally charged event in your life that influenced your attitude about something. What was the event and what was the attitude change?

6. Discuss a learning situation in which you needed to use a different method or strategy from those you had been using. Why did this type of learning situation require a different strategy or method?

7. Why do experts say that emotion is the critical factor in the development of attitudes?

Attitudes are Catching

One person's attitude can have a powerful influence on the attitudes of others who may be around him or her. This is especially evident when people are involved in a team effort. You have probably experienced the feeling you get when someone causes a positive change in the attitudes of a group. Also, you may have experienced the negative effect produced when someone allows his or her negative attitude to infect others.

on the job

It was a busy Friday afternoon in the tire shop. Arnold, Kimberly, and Mark had been installing snow tires for hours. Because of the early snowstorm, customers' cars were lined up in the parking lot. There was not much conversation. Ray, the shop supervisor, opened the door to the shop area and said, "Hey, we're behind schedule and it's only an hour until we close shop. Can we handle the six cars lined up out there?" No one said a word.

After listening to the clanking of tire irons and the muffled sound of the air compressor for a few seconds, Ray shouted, "Hey, is anyone alive in this disaster area?" Kimberly quickly shouted back, "I am, chief! And I think Mark is showing signs of life. We can handle it!" "Great! After work the sodas are on me," Ray said as he closed the door. Mark looked up, wiped his forehead, and smiled at Kimberly. "Sure, I'm alive—and thirsty." Finally, Arnold said, "What a bunch of eager beavers!" Then he smiled and quickened his pace. By closing time the three were tired but pleased.

What do you see in this situation that shows the influence of one person's attitude on others?

YOUR FEELINGS SHOW

Attitudes are hard to hide. Of course, they are not directly visible. No one can see your inner feelings. But those feelings have such a profound effect on your behavior that it is almost impossible to hide them. Your behavior gives those around you a clear view of your attitudes.

Of course, you would not want to hide a positive attitude. It shines through to create a favorable impression. However, we tend to have negative feelings toward a person when we sense or suspect negative attitudes.

YOUR ATTITUDES INFLUENCE OTHERS

Usually when a group attitude changes, it is because one or possibly several individuals take the initiative to spark the change. Because attitudes are catching, when the leaders of the group let their attitudes show, the effect on the group can be almost electric. You see this when the positive energy of a member of an athletic team ignites a winning spirit in his or her teammates. Everyone seems to respond and performance improves.

This principle was operating when, after being lost in a blizzard, one mountain climber literally saved the lives of her companions because her positive attitude inspired the others to make the effort required for their survival. This principle also applies in the world of work. A positive team spirit and high morale contribute to effective job performance.

A group of people having similar positive feelings and emotions are said to have "high morale" or "team spirit." Even in the face of adversity, a group working together for a common goal can have high morale.

Of course, success in reaching the goals helps keep morale high. As you might expect, when a working team experiences failure, the effect can be depressing on the emotions of everyone. However, even failure doesn't have to affect your attitude. You can still focus on goals, the team, and improving your efforts. This focus will help you get over the negative emotions, rather than letting them harden into negative attitudes. And staying positive improves your chances of being successful the next time.

© DIGITAL VISION

Positive attitudes create team spirit.

on ethics

Be aware that a good attitude is not the same as denial or inaction. Sometimes, there are events or circumstances that are not good, and something needs to be done. A negative attitude is more likely to make it impossible for you to improve the situation, while a positive attitude can empower you to make necessary changes, to help yourself or others, or to stand up for what is right.

In what ways might a positive attitude help you make a difference if you saw someone being treated unfairly? If you were told you couldn't get promoted? If you learned about illegal activities that were occurring in your neighborhood?

SELF CHECK

The fact that you see and judge people by their attitudes can be illustrated with this exercise.

Think of someone you know whom you admire.

Share your ideas about this person with others and have them tell about people they admire. Now respond to this question about the person you have chosen:

What are his or her outstanding qualities?

Write these qualities on a sheet of paper. As you review your list, consider how many of the items are attitudes that tell something about how the person feels, as compared with other qualities such as physical features, what the person owns, or the person's accomplishments.

Your list is likely to show two things. First, most of what you consider important in describing someone would be classified as an attitude. Second, most of the attitudes are positive (integrity, enthusiasm, sincerity, humor, patience, friendliness, outgoing personality, etc.). Your most admired person's attitudes are visible to you, and it is those attitudes that cause you to admire him or her.

What does this tell you about attitudes, and why it is important for you to make certain that yours are positive?

check*point*

1. **Usually when a group attitude changes, it is because**
   a. individuals are allowed to find motivation from within.
   b. negative behavior modification is used.
   c. someone takes the initiative to spark the change.
   d. the group comes to an agreement.

2. **A group of people having similar feelings or emotions are said to have**

   _____

   _____

   _____

   _____

   _____

   _____

   _____

   _____

   _____

   _____

3. **What are some of the negative consequences for those who have negative attitudes?**

   _____

   _____

   _____

   _____

   _____

   _____

   _____

   _____

   _____

   _____

applications

1. Consider the following quotation by Reginald B. Mansell:

"A pessimist is one who makes difficulties of his opportunities; an optimist is one who makes opportunities of his difficulties."

Do you agree with this statement? If so, why? If not, why not?

_____

_____

_____

_____

_____

2. Give an example from your personal experience when your attitude influenced your behavior and the behavior of others.

_____

_____

_____

3. From your experience give an example of an occasion when someone caused positive change in the attitudes of a group.

_____

_____

_____

4. Give an example of an occasion when someone created a negative influence by allowing his or her negative attitude to infect others.

_____

_____

_____

5. Find a group of people engaged in casual conversation. You might join a group taking a break at your workplace or school. Other possibilities are a group of students in the cafeteria, team members in a locker room, or a family around the dinner table. Listen to the conversation, and observe the body language of individuals. Prepare a list of attitudes that are revealed and the actions or behavior that gave you clues about each one.

ATTITUDES   ACTIONS
Example: Boredom   *Example:* Yawning, eyes wandering

_____

_____

_____

_____

_____

6. How may failure affect a team and its attitude? What should one do if feeling depressed over failure?

_____

_____

_____

_____

_____

It may not be easy, but there is one person you can "get tough with" without fear of reprisal. There is, in fact, one person you can change. That person is you! Changing your own attitudes can be very satisfying. It can also be enlightening.

THREE STEPS TO IMPROVE

Developing positive attitudes and eliminating negative ones is the best kind of reforming you can do. But how should you start? There are no steps for self-improvement that will work for everyone. However, these ideas and suggestions can be helpful if you have the inner strength to put them to the test. Remember, because attitudes are shaped under the stress of emotions, it may take courage for you to try these suggestions. The reward can be a more positive attitude.

Here are three steps in the process of attitude improvement:
1. Identify the attitudes you want to improve.
It may help to write a brief description of the image you have of yourself after you have achieved your attitude-improvement goals. Keep in mind the image of the kind of person you wish to become. Your mental picture must be so clear and so constantly present that it can create a pattern for your behavior.

2. Resolve to develop those attitudes.
They are a reflection of your ideal personality. It should be your goal to cultivate those qualities because they are needed as a model for your self-renewal.

3. Use the image of your ideal personality as a model for your behavior.
By practice and effort, you can make the desirable behavior come naturally, and the improved attitudes will transform your personality.

AVOID THE NEGATIVE

Everyone is negative some of the time. Negative feelings, negative comments, and negative actions are depressors of the spirit. They drag you down instead of lifting you up. You can get up in the morning feeling great, but if you meet four or five friends during the day who tell you of depressing happenings, who complain, or (worst of all) who criticize you or call attention to your mistakes, your happy mood will soon disappear. Fortunately, this works both ways. If you are tired and discouraged, your mood can change when you meet someone who gives you a sincere compliment or greets you with a smile.

"The greater part of our happiness or misery depends on our dispositions and not on our circumstances."

—MARTHA WASHINGTON

Imagine for a moment that you are another person—a person with an attitude problem. You have been having trouble with your supervisor. You feel you have been criticized too much and too often, and you (being human) have tried to get even. Perhaps you were sullen. You may have answered abruptly, or you may have threatened to quit.

Ask yourself what other tactics you might have tried. How would a person with a positive attitude have responded?

For example, you might have said sincerely, "I know I made an error. You were right to tell me about it, and I appreciate it. Is there anything you can suggest or do to help me correct it? I want to improve."

What response might the supervisor in this situation have?

Even though your supervisor may have been stern and demanding, your remarks would probably have created a positive response. Chances are your supervisor might have said, "That's all right. I'm sure you can improve. Here is a suggestion about how to handle it next time."

Even if the response you receive does not match this ideal, why would you still be better off with a positive attitude?

SELF CHECK

> *"A stumbling block to the pessimist is a stepping stone to the optimist."*
>
> — ELEANOR ROOSEVELT

> *"...so many of us undermine our creativity by self-discouragement."*
>
> — ALEX F. OSBORNE

While occasional negative feelings are normal and inevitable, it is important to not let them become ingrained attitudes. Negative attitudes can creep up on us because it is so easy to be negative. It is easy to let a feeling of self-pity steal over you. Every day has its disappointments. The easy way is to let them engulf us. It does take effort to replace negative thoughts with positive ones, but the effort is well spent.

Here are some suggestions that may help you create a positive atmosphere.

Avoid the negative as much as possible as you interact with people.

Smile

You can create a smile, even though it may not at the time feel natural. Simply raise your eyebrows and turn the corners of your mouth up instead of down. Make a real effort to look pleasant and interested in what is going on around you. Under the stimulation of your own interest, those around you may become interesting!

Say Something Pleasant

Think of something positive, good-natured, or complimentary to say to someone else at every opportunity. This will do wonders for those around you. It will also keep you busy thinking of positive things to say and you will not have time to be negative.

Take a Positive Approach

Another way to survive in a negative atmosphere is to view the negative situation as a challenge. Is there a coworker you dislike? Is there a friend who rubs you the wrong way? Whatever it is, try the positive approach. Try to change the situation by being positive. You may become a positive influence, as Kimberly was in the tire shop incident.

Here is a case in point. Let's say you have a friend, Antonio, who gets on your nerves. He talks about himself all the time. He boasts about everything—his car, his job, his school. Ask yourself, "What can I say that is positive?" Suppose he begins to tell you about a test on which he knew all the answers. Why not say, "Antonio, I wish I had your confidence." If you keep out the sarcasm and say it sincerely, this may cause Antonio to stop and think a minute. He may not have too much confidence, and his bragging helps boost his self-confidence. He may say, "To tell you the truth, I've always thought you were the confident one." If something like this should happen, the hostility on both sides will begin to evaporate. Your campaign to become more positive will get you over a big hurdle. When you learn to look at problems with a positive attitude, you can begin to solve them more easily.

COPING WITH OTHER PEOPLE'S NEGATIVE ATTITUDES

You may recall a time in your life when the emotions and attitudes of those around you were negative. You felt yourself getting negative too. Just by being aware of them you can resist and avoid negative influences on your attitudes. For example, when your coworkers get together to complain, gossip, or create dissension at work, you can refuse to participate. You can walk away or simply ignore what you hear and see.

Of all the many factors that influence a person's success, one of the most important is a positive attitude. You can improve your attitude and help others to improve by following the suggestions outlined in this chapter. Your improvement campaign will pay off in greater satisfaction and in greater ability to fit in and get along on the job and in daily life. As your positive attitude develops, the people around you begin to respond accordingly. They think of you as being enthusiastic, willing to learn, cheerful, and easy to get along with. Their favorable image of you causes them to expect positive, productive behavior. As you sense these positive expectations, your motivation to live up to your image is increased. The result is a cycle of reinforcement and improvement, greater appreciation of your positive attitude, and even higher levels of self-esteem.

In addition to the beneficial effect of your positive attitude on your own behavior, you find yourself in a new position of power. The influence of your positive

on the job

Audrey was in good spirits as she began her new job in the produce department of a supermarket. But soon her positive attitude was threatened. At coffee break she joined a group of coworkers. No one smiled or welcomed her. An older man wearing a dirty gray sweatshirt seemed to be leading the conversation. He talked about how "management is greedy and the union representatives are their puppets." He complained that "the only way to get a fair share of overtime work (for time-and-a-half pay) is to be one of the favored few." Then the conversation turned to gossip about an absent member of the meat department crew.

Is hearing this conversation likely to influence Audrey's attitudes about management, the union, and the meat department crew?

Assume that Audrey had unfavorable information about the absent crew member's behavior. Should she join in and participate in the gossip?

© DIGITAL VISION

Your attitudes are showing.

attitude on other people allows you to influence them—to help them improve their self-esteem and develop positive attitudes. Your personal attributes of responsibility, sociability, and integrity will likely be more visible in your behavior.

Smart Tip ▼ ▼ ▼

Doctors have found that there is a very strong connection between our minds and our bodies. Your attitudes can dramatically affect your health, for good or bad. Conversely, your body can help you develop better attitudes. Next time you feel negative, try the following:

- Smile—it doesn't just impress others, it actually improves how you feel.

- Sit up or stand up straight, shoulders back. It's hard to maintain a negative attitude with really positive body language.
- Take a deep breath and let it out slowly. Sometimes stress affects our attitudes, and breathing helps reduce stress.
- Focus on what is good. Think about your goals and dreams, recall a happy incident, or look at pictures of beautiful scenery. Focusing on what is negative increases stress, but thinking positive thoughts and looking at beautiful scenery triggers the relaxation response.
- Take care of yourself; feeling unwell often makes things seem worse.

▲ ▲ ▲ ▲ ▲ ▲ ▲ ▲ ▲ ▲ ▲ ▲ ▲ ▲ ▲ ▲ ▲

chec**K**point

1. The process of self-improvement consists of three steps. They are

   a. _____

   b. _____

   c. _____

2. It requires little effort to replace negative thoughts with positive ones.
   True_____ False_____

3. If you want to improve your attitudes it may help to
   a. smile.   b. say something pleasant.
   c. take a positive approach.   d. all of the above.

4. When your coworkers get together to complain, gossip, or create dissension at work, rather than join in you should

   _____

   _____

   _____

   _____

applications

1. Following are three examples of attitudes that a person might want to improve. For each attitude, describe actions or behaviors that might help bring about the desired changes. You might share your ideas and brainstorm with other students as you complete this assignment.

a. *Present attitude:* I feel disorganized. My workplace, my bedroom, and my garage are a mess.

Future attitude: I feel organized. I will keep my workplace, bedroom, garage, and other living places neat and clean.

To help bring about this change, I will

b. *Present attitude:* I feel impatient. I become anxious and distressed when I have to wait in long lines. When I want something, I want it right now.

Future attitude: I feel that I have patience. I can relax and feel free of distress and anxiety in situations that require patience.

To help bring about this change, I will

c. *Present attitude:* I feel compulsive about sweets. I love ice cream, pastries, and candy. Constantly "grazing" on these foods seems to be an almost uncontrollable habit.

Future attitude: I feel in control of my desire for sweets. I only eat at mealtimes and I rarely find myself buying or eating sweet foods that are not included in healthful meals.

To help bring about this change, I will

2. Identify three attitudes you have resolved to improve following the suggestions in Chapter 3. The three examples in Application 1 illustrate how you should respond here. You should describe each as a reflection of how you feel now and how you expect to feel when you achieve your objectives for improvement. In the third space, list the behaviors you want to exhibit or actions you intend to take as you strive for improvement.

a. *Attitude now:* _____

Future attitude: _____

To help me change, I will _____

_____

_____

b. *Attitude now:* _____

Future attitude: _____

To help me change, I will _____

_____

_____

c. *Attitude now:* _____

Future attitude: _____

To help me change, I will _____

_____

_____

3. Practice creating a smile. Then explain to another person (a classmate, friend, relative, or employer) why a smile is important for maintaining a positive outlook.

_____

_____

_____

_____

3 Points to Remember

chapter

Review the following points to determine what you remember from the chapter.

- Attitudes are a reflection of a person's inner feelings. The image they project to your associates can cause them to be drawn to you, or they can signal others to avoid you. Emotion is the critical factor in attitude development.

- Attitudes are hard to hide. Your behavior gives those around you a clear view of your attitudes. Because attitudes are catching, when the leaders of the group let their attitudes show, the effect on the group can be almost electric. A positive team spirit and high morale contribute to effective job performance.

- When those around you exhibit negative emotions and attitudes, you can resist their influence by ignoring or avoiding what is negative in their behavior. Developing positive attitudes and eliminating negative ones are important in the process of fitting in and getting along in the world of work.

- To develop a more positive attitude, take the following steps: (1) identify the attitudes you want to improve, (2) resolve to develop those attitudes, and (3) use the image of your ideal personality as a model for your behavior. Other ways to improve your attitude is to make an effort to smile and show an interest in what is going on around you. Also, your attitudes can improve when you say something pleasant to compliment or encourage others and when you take a positive approach in a negative situation.

- As your negative attitudes disappear and positive ones are developed, your self-image will improve and the image you project to others will be more positive. This will motivate you to greater productivity and success. Your positive attitude will allow you to influence others. Your personal attributes, such as responsibility, sociability, and integrity, will likely be more visible in your behavior.

How did you do? Did you remember the main points you studied in the chapter?

key terms

Define each term in the space provided.

Attitude

Emotion

activities and projects

1. Sean had worked for a year in a large company that employed twenty people who worked at computers responding to Internet e-mail inquiries and orders for auto parts. During this time some of his friends—coworkers doing the same job as Sean—had been assigned to higher-level jobs and to supervisory positions. Sean felt he was just as competent and productive as those who had been advanced. Every time someone was promoted or assigned to a better job, Sean made sarcastic remarks, complained about not being recognized for his good work, and showed his resentment by sulking for several days. He knew, of course, that he should not show these negative attitudes, but he wanted his supervisor, Ms. Nelson, to know how he felt. He had disliked Ms. Nelson's crisp manner when they first met, and he was sure that she was doing everything she could to keep Sean from moving to a better job. You are a friend of Sean's. You have not wanted to interfere, but now you believe that something must be done.

a. What attitudes and feelings that he has about himself might be contributing to Sean's resentment?

b. Do you think Ms. Nelson harbors negative attitudes about Sean? Why or why not?

c. As a friend, what would you say to Sean? Consider what he might say and do to repair and improve his relationship with Ms. Nelson.

2. The search for a person to set up and operate a computer network for a real estate agency was narrowed to two excellent candidates. The brokers who were making the selection agreed on the following:

• Both people were well trained in computer technology.
• Both had very good references from previous employers.

- Candidate A had a better "track record" with computer network management—exactly what was needed in this job.
- Candidate B appeared to be more enthusiastic and pleasant. She had been a teacher, and her students adored her.

a. Write a short essay or participate in a small group discussion about the potential for success of each candidate.

_____

_____

_____

_____

b. Choose the candidate who you believe should be selected. Explain why you believe this person's area of weakness can be corrected and how it might be done.

_____

_____

_____

_____

3. Study the following conversation. Then, either as a small group or working individually, develop a list of five to ten circumstances or events that might have caused these attitudes to develop.

Four people are carpooling to the office. Here are some comments made in a discussion of why their office is or is not a good place to work.

- The work is boring.
- There's no future in a dead-end job like mine.
- The boss is stupid.
- The benefits are poor.
- The pay is low. We deserve more.

What are some circumstances or events that might have caused these attitudes to develop?

Example: Last year we received only a 1 percent pay raise.

_____

_____

_____

_____

_____

4. Review the information about the carpool conversation in Activity 3 above. Also, review the responses concerning possible circumstances and events that might have led up to this situation. Assume you are a member of this carpool group that has developed such negative attitudes. Prepare an outline of a plan, including some specific actions that might result from turning this negative atmosphere into one that is positive. The outcome will be a pleasant, upbeat ride to work that will get the day started on a positive note.

_____

_____

_____

_____

_____

_____

_____

_____

case studies for critical thinking

ATTITUDE ADJUSTMENT?

Kim worked in his family business in Korea during his teen years. There he learned the value of "suggestion selling." He applied these lessons as a salesperson in a downtown San Francisco department store. Soon after he began his new job selling fine china and silverware, Kim became the top salesperson in his department. The merchandising manager was pleased, but Kim's coworkers were not. Sally and Fred took him aside and expressed their feelings. "Hey, squirt, you're overdoing it. If you don't slack off, the rest of us will look bad," Sally said. Fred continued, "Management doesn't appreciate all this customer attention, and they will only assume you're sucking up to them."

At that moment Kim almost caved in to the emotional pressure. He clenched his fists, looked down, turned away, and said, "I'm only doing what they pay me for." Then he walked away. As the weeks passed, Kim continued selling as before, and his coworkers continued trying to discourage him. They spoke to him only when necessary and never with a smile or pleasant tone of voice. Occasionally Kim found his sales invoices missing or altered. Once, someone put trash in his locker along with a note suggesting that he needed an "attitude adjustment."

1. What are some clues about the attitudes of Sally and Fred, and how do you interpret those clues?

2. What, if anything, do you think Kim did wrong? What did he do right? Give reasons for your answers.

3. Write a continuation of this story—a script giving specific words and actions by the participants—that will lead to the development of improved attitudes for Sally and Fred.

Case 3.2

THE GROUCH

B. J. was in charge of the copy room where college faculty and staff took work to be done. The work included production of tests, teaching materials, brochures, text materials, and instructional aids. Following are some bits and pieces of B. J.'s conversations in a one-hour period. "No, I'm not having a good day." "You forgot to sign for the transparency masters. You can't just take what you want without recording it, you know." "Who messed up the cover of this brochure?" "No, I can't afford to go to lunch at the student center. I'll just eat my peanut butter sandwich by myself." "Tell Professor Nelson not to send students in here. He should know the rule about student use of the copy machine." "How does she expect me to read these instructions? You would think someone with a Ph.D. could write so a person could read it."

1. Can you recognize some specific attitudes demonstrated by B. J.'s conversation? For each of her comments, list an attitude that is apparent from it.

2. What attitude changes would you recommend for B. J.? Explain.

Case 3.3

BODY LANGUAGE

"Who does she think she is, Queen of the Universe?" Carl tossed the sweater he had just tried on back on the display table. His friend Bill smiled and said, "Don't let the attitude of that salesperson keep you from buying that sweater. You look good in it." Carl stuffed his hands into his pockets and looked at the floor. Then he slowly began to move toward the door of the sporting goods store. "I don't need the sweater," he said. "When she said that a short guy with a full figure shouldn't wear horizontal stripes and looked down her nose at me that way, I got her message." "Oh, really?" Bill said. "What *was* her message?" Carl looked at the floor and said, "That tall, good-looking women think short, chunky guys are dirt."

1. What are some examples of behavior that might have caused Carl to interpret the salesperson's attitude as he did?

_____

_____

_____

2. What suggestions do you have to help Carl cope with the influence of the salesperson's negative comment?

_____

_____

_____

3. Do you think Carl's attitude could have affected his interpretation of the salesperson's remark? Do you think low self-esteem might be an issue?

_____

_____

_____

4. How might the salesperson's attitude affect sales?

_____

_____

_____

5. Should the salesperson's supervisor be made aware of the comment? Why or why not?

_____

_____

_____

Case 3.4

WORKING OVERTIME

Francisco was tired and depressed and ready to call it a day. However, work was still piled up on his desk and then he saw his department manager making his way toward him.

As his department manager stopped, he spoke quickly to Francisco: "We have a rush job that just came in and it must be shipped by eight tonight. Unfortunately, Larry slipped out before I could ask him to process the shipment. Could you get it done for me? I really am in a bind right now and need to get this order out to the customer."

1. Keeping in mind that Francisco is tired already, what do you think he should say to the department manager?

2. If you were the department manager, what could you do about this order instead of asking Francisco for his help?

Communication Channels

think about it:	"Good morning, Tadd. Happy Monday to you."
	"Thanks, Megan. How was your weekend?"

"It was great. I spent some time with the radiology staff. I got caught up on the latest hospital gossip. Did you know that Dr. Benjamin is going to be sued for malpractice? Some of the radiology staff might be named in the lawsuit. I hope those of us in the accounting department don't get involved. Part of the suit involves overcharging patients."

"That's news to me, Megan. Thanks for the scoop. I'll talk with you at lunch."

"Hi, Tadd. How's it going?"

"Fine, Luis. Have you heard that Dr. Benjamin is about to have his license to practice revoked for malpractice? Megan spent the weekend with staff from radiology. They are all scared stiff that they are going to be involved in a lawsuit involving the hospital related to the Benjamin revocation. I'll bet Megan knows more than she shared with me. I've heard that the radiologists don't do a thorough job of reviewing x-rays. Everybody knows that Benjamin has been overcharging patients and doing unnecessary surgeries for years. Our records are going to be scrutinized in this whole mess." "Thanks for the information, Tadd. I want to give Sharon a heads-up on what is happening."

What problems have surfaced in this scenario?

© THINKSTOCK

chapter focus

After completing this chapter, you should be able to:

1. Describe what takes place in the communication process to convey thoughts, feelings, and ideas.

2. Identify the barriers to communication.

3. Demonstrate the use of open communication to persuade and develop a positive attitude.

4. Demonstrate passive, aggressive, and assertive communication styles.

5. List the components of good listening.

Communication

Communication is the act of transmitting information and meaning from one individual or group to another.[1] Communication comes in many forms in the workplace. It may arrive in written form: You can expect to receive letters, memos, electronic messages, bulletins, newsletters, bulletin board messages, periodicals, or maybe even a note scratched on the back of an envelope. Oral communication may be even more common, whether it's face-to-face, by voice mail, through an intercom, or in telephone conversations. Information is often communicated orally by coworkers, customers, supervisors, suppliers, or government regulators. While speaking and writing are both **verbal** (that is, they use words), you will also receive **nonverbal** (that is, no words are used) messages. Body language is probably the most common way of sending or receiving nonverbal messages. Even the clothing of others can communicate a message to you. If a friend shows up at your door in tennis clothes, you know at a glance that he or she probably wants you to play tennis.

The "rumor mill," or "the office **grapevine**," are informal terms used to describe the circulating of information. Although often inaccurate, it is a source of information in the workplace. You can see gossip in action in the opening situation. Sources may not be reliable, and information is often altered or inflated in the retelling.

In spite of all the experiences we have in communicating, we still do not seem to be very effective at it. Why not?

> *"Young people do not perceive at once that the giver of wounds is the enemy and the quoted tattle merely the arrow."*
>
> —F. Scott Fitzgerald

COMMUNICATION TAKES TWO

Communication is a two-way process. The **sender** is the originator of a thought, information, or idea to be transmitted to another. The **receiver** is the individual to whom the thought or idea is transmitted. The thought or idea is called the **message**. The message may take many forms. The request *Please turn on your computer,* whether written or spoken, is an example of a verbal message. Nonverbal messages are sent without words, such as when you wink an eye or glance at the clock to indicate your awareness of another or concern about time. Beware! Remember the adage . . . Actions speak louder than words. If your words convey one message and your nonverbal message gives another, the nonverbal message will be the stronger.

What nonverbal messages are sent by these actions?
1. Raising a brow
2. Pointing a finger
3. Winking
4. Crossing the arms across the chest
5. Tapping a foot
6. Placing hands on hips
7. Nodding the head

Communication cannot take place until the message moves from the sender to the receiver and the receiver understands the message intended. In other words, for communication to be successful, both the sender and the receiver must share the same meaning of what is being communicated.

In order to know if the receiver has received your message, you watch or listen for a response. This response is called **feedback**. Feedback is what tells the sender whether or not the message is understood. Feedback, like the message, may be written or spoken, verbal or nonverbal. For example, if you tell a coworker a joke and his or her reaction is laughter, you can assume the receiver "got the joke." Feedback may also be solicited, that is, if you need to make certain that the message was received, you can ask questions of a listener or request the recipient of a memo to respond. Figure 4-1 diagrams this full communication process.

Remembering the ways in which messages are received and processed can help you communicate. The mode (the medium or route) in which the message is transmitted is known as the **channel**.

Among the channels available to us, the most important to keep in mind are our senses. Each of our senses is the channel for a different type of message. The sense of hearing receives and delivers to the brain sound messages, from a kind word to the sound of a slamming door. With the sense of sight, the eyes are the channel for receiving visual messages: the written word, images, actions, nonverbal communication, and so forth. If the sense of touch is used, the channel is the skin. Touch can send powerful messages, but a caution to you: be careful about how and with whom you use it.

You may choose to use more than one channel to get your message across. If you are apologizing to a friend by saying, "I apologize for my thoughtlessness," you might strengthen your message by using the sense of touch—touching the friend's shoulder or hand.

Poor communication is said to be one of the biggest problems in the workplace and in human relationships. Sometimes, it is because the complete two-way communication process does not take place. Often, senders and receivers do not share the same understanding of the message, and communication just doesn't happen. There are many barriers to the communication process. The barriers can block communication, and

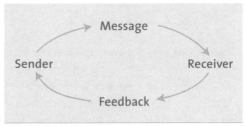

FIGURE 4-1 *Diagram of communication model.*

blocked communication can lead to confusion, mistrust, and misunderstanding. We will discuss some of these barriers in Section 4.2.

"That which we are capable of feeling we are capable of sending."

—CERVANTES

on the job

Norma and Stuart were talking quietly at their workstation. The conversation related to a new reporting format from the accounting department. Mitzi, an employee in the accounting department, concluded they were looking at forms she had created. Stuart said to Mitzi, "Hey! Come on over. We want to talk with you." Mitzi smiled and shuddered to think what they were talking about. Norma and Stuart were talking about how easy it was to read reports placed in the new format. Mitzi assumed they were being critical of her work and doubted her abilities. She had heard them mention her name several times, but she couldn't hear most of what was being said. Mitzi decided to ignore their request to come over and enter the conversation and continued on with her work. Stuart and Norma wanted to compliment Mitzi on the new format. Mitzi missed an opportunity to communicate with coworkers and receive positive feedback about her work. Stuart and Norma are now confused about why Mitzi didn't want to talk with them. Mitzi remains suspicious of Norma and Stuart and manages to avoid them for the remainder of the workday.

What may be the results of this ineffective communication? How might the exchange have been improved?

Smart Tip ▼ ▼ ▼

One good way to determine how you communicate, and which areas you might need to work on, is to videotape a few different conversations with friends or classmates. As you review the videotape, look for some of the following things:

- Are you speaking clearly so that others can understand your message?
- Can you tell if the receiver understands the message you are sending?
- What signals did you receive that indicate understanding?
- What nonverbal messages are you sending?
- Do your nonverbal signals support or detract from your spoken message?
- Do you offer feedback when the other person is speaking?
- Do you respond appropriately to feedback?
- Are you sending and receiving messages using more than one channel?
- What channels are you using?
- What do you notice in your conversation that works?
- What do you notice that could improve your communication?

▲ ▲ ▲ ▲ ▲ ▲ ▲ ▲ ▲ ▲ ▲ ▲ ▲ ▲ ▲ ▲ ▲

checkpoint

1. Who are the principal persons in the communication model?

   _____

   _____

2. What is the thought or idea transmitted from one person to another called?

   _____

   _____

3. What is the response of the receiver of information called?

   _____

   _____

4. What is the media or mode (route) that a message takes called?

   _____

   _____

5. What does feedback tell you? How may feedback be provided?

   _____

   _____

6. What are some nonverbal messages that you typically send each day?

   _____

   _____

applications

1. What nonverbal messages have you observed in others, in addition to those mentioned in the lesson? Have all the messages been conscious, that is, have you observed people sending nonverbal messages without intending to do so?

2. Think of a situation that you have been in that involved an unintended miscommunication. Was the misunderstanding ever cleared up? Describe the situation, and discuss how it could have been avoided.

3. Draw the communication model, using the following situation: to illustrate the parts of the model. Edward told Sierra that her voice mail message was unclear. Sierra told Edward that she was sorry and repeated the message for him.

4. Explain the role of feedback in the communication process. Describe at least two types of possible feedback.

Communication Barriers

The first step to removing barriers to communication is to identify them. The following section will assist you in recognizing and avoiding the barriers as you work to improve your communication skills.

CHOICE OF WORDS

Word choice is the most common of the communication barriers. Often, the problem begins when people don't understand the words you are using, whether it's because of differences in work or personal experiences, age, education level, or because listeners are from a different culture.

The problem continues when a word has more than one possible interpretation or meaning. Words have different meanings for different people. Take the word *spicy*, for example. For one person, this may mean salt and pepper, while for another it could mean blisteringly hot or zesty. However, a noun like *clock* probably has the same meaning for everyone. But other words, such as *mean, cheap,* and *awesome*, are vague and could be interpreted in a variety of ways. Use precise words to get your message across, as well as words that are not likely to be misinterpreted. Think about the person you are communicating with as you select your words.

If you are in doubt about how someone is interpreting your words, ask! Feedback is your best tool when trying to determine if people understand your message. Do not use a word that confuses or misleads the listener. The key to communication is either using words your audience will understand or else making certain they understand the words you need to use.

As you work with people from diverse backgrounds and experiences, be aware that misunderstandings are more likely, since differences in background and knowledge may give different connotations to your words. You might offend a coworker, customer, or supervisor through ignorance by using a word that sends the wrong message. Remember that your listener may interpret words with multiple meanings. An example of this situation was when a company executive from Germany, Hans, spoke with a group in an American plant. The conversation was about building a partnership to improve production. Several times the German speaker used the word "signatory." The word wasn't familiar to the Americans and after several misunderstandings, finally someone spoke up and said, "Hans, what do you mean by the word "signatory"? Hans replied, "Partner." Everyone had a good laugh and the conversation continued. The Americans had their vocabularies expanded. Hans and the Americans now understood that signatory can be a synonym for partner.

When you use a term that is offensive or confusing, you can unknowingly build a communication barrier. You probably can't anticipate every word that might offend someone, so it is important to always be open, polite, and request feedback. People should know that you're not the type of person who would say something unkind, and therefore they will be more likely to offer feedback that would let you know what your words mean to them.

Ask others who are from backgrounds different from yours to let you know if you say something that is inappropriate, offensive, derogatory, or unkind. Also, offer to do the same for them. Listen to others with the thought in mind that what they are saying may not be what you are hearing. Always remember that your role as the receiver is part of the communication process, so offer feedback and make sure you know the real message.

SELECTIVE COMMUNICATION

Are you guilty of allowing selective communication to be a barrier in your communication with others? **Selective communication** means hearing or reading only what you want to hear or read. It is a common human characteristic to skip over the uncomfortable, the unpleasant, or the difficult to comprehend. This often happens when you hear or read something that is in conflict with your personal thoughts, convictions, or viewpoints. Or you may be selective when you receive information that you do not want to hear or that you feel is difficult to understand—or even that is simply being presented at an inconvenient time or not to your liking. Selective communication is not an option in the workplace. You need to pay careful attention to everything that is said.

Jargon

All workplaces have a specific language that is related to the work environment. The language is often referred to as jargon. **Jargon** is the technical terminology or characteristic words and ideas that belong to a specific type of work or field of knowledge. Jargon can be unintelligible to someone new to a setting. Jargon may be unfamiliar terms, or may be acronyms or shortened words. For example, your coworker might say to you, "Bring me a copy of the RFP." RFP is an example of an acronym. But even if it was explained that this stood for "request for proposal," you still might not understand "RFP" without further explanation.

Jargon may also be terms that sound familiar but that are defined differently in different fields. For example, the word *mouse* means something entirely different if you're working at the computer than it does if you're in the pest removal business. The language of each workplace is different and can be a barrier until you learn the jargon of

on the job

Hal's supervisor at AERO provides him with some instructions each morning. Today, he tells Hal to move the pallets in the storage room to Level B and place them in Area A. While Hal is on Level B, he is to pick up packets for the sales department and take them to Ellen Ramsey. Further, he is to drive over to the Atlantic Hotel at 9:30 a.m. and pick up Alfred Wid, an AERO Board member, and take him to the airport. Then, he is to stop at the post office and sign for the Certified Mail and bring it to Marian Aksamit in the mailroom. He also tells Hal to call the airport freight office to see if a part for maintenance has arrived.

Hal decides that the pallets are okay where they are. He goes to Level B and picks up the packets prepared for the sales department and drops them at the sales receptionist's desk. He can't remember who he is to pick up at the Atlantic, and he doesn't like to fight the traffic around the hotel, so he calls the Atlantic and tells the person answering the phone at the front desk that if anyone is waiting to be picked up by someone from AERO, he or she should take a cab to the airport. He drives over to the post office and signs for the Certified Mail and drops it off in the mailroom. He drives to the airport freight office for the maintenance part and finds that it hasn't yet arrived.

How do you think the supervisor will react to Hal's work for the day?

the environment. As you enter the workplace, keep a list of the jargon that is new to you. It will soon be second nature. Also, explain the jargon of the workplace as you work with new employees or those unfamiliar with your work environment. If this doesn't happen, jargon will continue to be a barrier.

Jargon tends to be most difficult in government offices, education institutions, engineering facilities, and law offices.

Think about your word choice when you refer to an occupation. Circle the words that might have negative connotations. In the spaces provided, write the appropriate occupation title of the words that you circled.

Shrink _____

Sanitation worker _____

Cop _____

Garbage hauler _____

Ambulance chaser _____

Chef _____

Secretary _____

Bean counter _____

Sexist words should be avoided in your word choice. Think of a word that would not be sexist for each of the following and place it in the blank.

Fireman _____

Congressman _____

Businessman _____

Waitress _____

Stewardess _____

Chairman _____

Foreman _____

"To effectively communicate, we must realize that we are all different in the way we perceive the world and use this understanding as a guide to our communication with others."

—ANTHONY ROBBINS

© GETTY IMAGES/PHOTODISC

Move in closely when necessary to improve communication.

Physical or Distance Barriers

Sometimes communication does not take place because the receiver is simply unable to hear what has been said or he or she only partially hears the message. This barrier is common in the workplace because background noise (equipment, conversations of others, telephones, radios) may interfere with the communication process.

This is usually a relatively easy barrier to overcome. When you are communicating, speak up. Use the volume necessary to be heard in that environment. If you are the receiver, step closer or ask the sender to speak louder. If you are working with equipment or machinery that creates noise, you may want (if possible) to turn it off or down, or step away from it, to better hear what is being transmitted. If you are in a meeting, sit in the front of the room so that you can hear what is being said and see any illustrations that are being used.

chec**K***point*

1. **How can your choice of words affect communication?**

    _____

    _____

    _____

    _____

2. **What is selective communication?**

    _____

    _____

    _____

    _____

3. **What is jargon?**

    _____

    _____

    _____

    _____

4. **List three jargon terms used in a workplace with which you are familiar.**

    _____

    _____

    _____

    _____

5. **Identify some ways that physical or distance barriers can be overcome.**

    _____

    _____

    _____

    _____

applications

1. Imagine that someone is starting a new job. Write several things a new employee might say: First write something that someone might say if he or she was not careful in word choice, and therefore created a bad impression. Then write the same ideas over, but in words that would create a good impression.

_____

_____

_____

_____

_____

_____

_____

_____

2. Go back and reread the "On the Job" story about Hal and his work at AERO on page 73. Make a list of the problems he may have caused through his selective communication.

_____

_____

_____

_____

3. Think about situations where you have witnessed—or experienced yourself—selective communication. What was the message that was missed? What was the result of the selective communication? What suggestions would you make to both the sender and receiver of the message to help prevent selective communication in the future?

_____

_____

_____

_____

_____

_____

_____

4. Think of a time in which a physical barrier has affected communication for you. Describe the barrier and how it affected communication. What did you do to solve the situation?

_____

_____

_____

_____

_____

_____

_____

4.3 Communication Openers

"I am still determined to be cheerful and happy, in whatever situation I may be; for I have also learned from experience that the greater part of our happiness or misery depends upon our dispositions, and not upon our circumstances."

—MARTHA WASHINGTON
(1732–1802)

The sharing and understanding that are essential in good communication will more likely occur if a comfortable climate exists in the workplace. This type of atmosphere can be created with a friendly smile, a good attitude, and an attempt to understand others. If people are comfortable with you and feel that you care, they will be more likely to communicate with you. Thus, two-way communication will flow and improve the workplace problems in communication.

on the job

Rachel was hired as a radiology technician at the Legacy Retirement Center. This was her first job after training, and she was eager to put her skills into practice and succeed. On her first morning of duty, she followed several veteran employees in from the parking lot. She suddenly felt a bit anxious. Her thoughts were: "I'm new. I don't know anyone. Will I understand the procedures? Will the workers and patients accept me? Are my skills good enough?" Rachel paused at the entrance door, took a deep breath, and said to herself, "They'll like me. I can do a good job. I am well trained. I will ask questions when necessary. Now get to work." She entered the room where the supervisor was preparing to brief the staff on new patients. Rachel looked at each of her coworkers, smiled, introduced herself, and said, "I'm ready to get to work. I hope you'll be patient with me when I ask questions and review the procedures." Rachel had no problems in establishing herself as part of the team at Legacy.

Do you think Rachel will be successful at Legacy? Why?

FRIENDLY ATTITUDE

A friendly attitude aids effective communication. If your work brings you into contact with many people, a friendly, cheerful, open attitude is essential. Be warm and kind to all of your coworkers, supervisors, and customers. At first you may have to work at it. Take every opportunity to say "thank you" with a smile. Offer help to others whenever appropriate. Look for something positive in everyone you meet. Each new acquaintance will bring a new dimension to your life.

USING POSITIVE PERSUASION

In the workplace, there are times you will want to persuade others. **Persuasion** is attempting to get others to adopt or agree with an idea of yours. Persuasion will be a channel opener for you. You should sharpen up some techniques you now use and perhaps become familiar with some new ones. If you have new ideas, share them at the appropriate time and make sure that your suggestions are valid. You will not be persuasive on the first day. The concept of "I'm going to fix this place" can be dangerous. Go slowly.

Questioning Technique

When you use questions to persuade others, use nonchallenging and positive thoughts with the person you are trying to persuade.

Lora says, "Mike, did you know that 2,500 people right here in our community do not have a warm bed to sleep in every night? Isn't that disturbing?"

Mike replies, "That is upsetting. I haven't heard that statistic. What is being done about it?"

Lora says, "Would you be interested in being the company representative for the fund drive to expand the bed capacity for the homeless in our community?"

In this example, Lora most likely persuaded Mike to be a recruit to help the fund drive before he realized he was being asked.

Sharing a Story

The sharing of an anecdote or a story is a great persuasive technique. Almost everyone likes to hear a story. Have you noticed that when listening to a sermon, lecture, or a serious discussion you really perk up when someone uses a phrase such as, "Let me share a story with you?" The story doesn't need to be funny to be persuasive.

Perhaps a similar story could help convince people in your life to join you in an activity—or might encourage them to not give up on someone who might be hesitating. Other stories might be used to get a supervisor to listen to your ideas, a customer to try a new product or service, or a coworker to tackle more challenging assignments.

HELP THE OTHER PERSON FEEL IMPORTANT

A way to help others feel important is by asking for their opinions, seeking their advice, getting their points of view, and making them a part of the group. Seek opportunities to give recognition, to build others up, and make others feel important. Take a look at the story about Manuel.

You will not succeed if you allow other people to feel unimportant. If you brag about how well you are doing, you may make others doubt their own success. If you treat others as if they are inferior to you, you will cause them to doubt their own value. For example, if you begin speaking

with the phrase, "You may not understand this, but . . ." you may cause your listeners to feel incapable of understanding what you are about to say. This is not the way to open up the channels of communication.

REWARD THE POSITIVE; IGNORE THE NEGATIVE

When someone says something positive about you or your work habits, respond warmly. You need to respond this way so the sender of the message will feel free to communicate

"Persuasion is often more effective than force."

—AESOP

"One of the best ways to persuade others is with your ears— by listening to them."

—DEAN RUSK

on the job

Albert was struggling with his senior managers to get them to encourage all of the new staff to be team players. He got their attention when he said, "I want to share with you a story about Manuel. Manuel and I had worked together for several months. Manuel had a good education and some experience in the advertising field but he was quiet, unsure of himself, and not contributing much to the company. I was concerned that he was in danger of losing his job. We were working hard to secure a big advertising contract with the Fellman Corporation. I told Manuel that I was really struggling with writing copy for the Fellman ad campaign and needed all the help I could get. Manuel indicated that he and his family had used Fellman products for many years and liked them. He jotted down his positive comments and dropped them at my desk. Wow, from that point on copywriting came easy for me. Manuel was thrilled when he saw his thoughts in the presentation to the Fellman Corporation. We got the account. Manuel gained confidence. He felt valued. His work took on new meaning."

Do you think Manuel's attempt to share a story will "get to" his staff? Can you think of a similar story for Albert to share that might work as well or better?

with you in the future. Many of us have difficulty in accepting compliments or kind words. Be prepared to respond to individuals who compliment you with a warm response. Practice saying something warm, "giving back" to the person who compliments you. Try saying, "It makes me feel good to hear you say that. I appreciate your kind words," or at the very least, a sincere "Thank you." Accepting compliments takes practice. Avoid phrases such as, "Oh, it was nothing." Show the other person respect, and let him or her know that the compliment is appreciated —especially if you want to hear kind things in the future.

When someone complains about your actions or job performance, let him or her talk. Just listen. As you listen, ignore the part of the conversation that is directed wrongly at you personally. Listening may also give you a clue or two about improving your job performance. Mean, negative statements are best forgotten. Just concentrate on what you can learn from the experience.

Gossip

In your effort to keep channels of communication open, keep in mind that a very powerful channel of information in any organization is gossip. Gossip surfaces when people are curious about a situation and the facts are not available. When this happens, speculation begins and the informal communication network known as the "grapevine" goes into action. Check out the accuracy of gossip you hear before you communicate it to others or apply it to yourself. Often, gossip is based on speculation and guesses. Sometimes, the source of a story intends to spread misinformation. In addition, even accurate information can change when it moves from person to person, because, for example:

1. The receiver may not hear the whole message and will pass along only the parts heard.

2. A word may be added in place of a word that has been forgotten.

3. A poor word choice may confuse the next person who hears the message.

4. Part of the message may have been forgotten before it is passed along.

5. The receiver may misinterpret what was said.

6. Someone along the way may deliberately sabotage the message.

© BRAND X PICTURES

Beware of the evils of gossip.

When you hear a message that is gossip or has the potential of being gossip, listen carefully. Repeat the message to the sender to be sure you have accurately heard the message. Then check with someone who would know the accuracy of the message. Avoid hurting a coworker or supervisor. When someone starts malicious gossip about a coworker, it is often wisest to refuse to listen. If you do hear malicious gossip, do not pass it along. You may even want to turn over the information to someone who can put a stop to it.

on ethics

George heard a rumor that his supervisor, Henry, was going to be fired for personal use of company equipment. Supposedly, Henry was using his e-mail account to communicate with family and friends around the country and visiting Web sites not related to his work. According to the rumor, Henry is going to be fired and will have to pay the company back for the minutes spent sending and receiving messages on company time or risk a lawsuit. The rumor has it that the company plans to make an example of the supervisor so that other employees will get the strong message that company equipment is not for personal use. George was eavesdropping and wasn't sure if he had missed some of the conversation.

What should George do? What would you recommend George not do?

chec**K***point*

1. **How does a friendly attitude in the workplace environment enhance communication?**

   _____

   _____

2. **What two techniques can be used to persuade others?**

   _____

   _____

3. **Why do you think gossip is so popular? Why is it so dangerous?**

   _____

   _____

applications

1. How can you help another person feel important? Based on your experiences, what phrases have you heard or used in the workplace or your personal life to help others feel important? Write out these phrases and share them with others. What are the possible benefits to you personally, and to the workplace in general, of making others feel important?

_____

_____

_____

_____

_____

_____

2. Think about a person you know in the workplace or someone you know personally who appears to be unhappy or down at this point in his or her life. Make a list of things you could do to improve this person's attitude and open up the communication channels to him or her.

_____

_____

_____

_____

_____

_____

3. Use one of the persuasion techniques in this chapter to create a dialogue in which you try to persuade a coworker to exchange lunch hours with you next week. You want to work her lunch hour of 12 to 1 p.m. rather than your usual 11 a.m. to 12 p.m. You want to be free to have lunch with a friend who cannot change his lunch hour. Your supervisor has approved the change with the understanding that your coworker will cooperate with the exchange. Draft a preliminary dialogue you would use to persuade your coworker.

_____

_____

_____

_____

_____

_____

_____

_____

4. List some phrases that you might use in response to the following compliments: "You did a great job in preparing that report!" "You've shown you know what you're doing. I'm glad you're part of the team." "You are a tremendous asset to this agency!" "You dress very professionally!" Your responses should indicate that you appreciate the comments.

_____

_____

_____

_____

_____

_____

_____

Standing up for your rights in the workplace is important. However, when you do this, you need to communicate in an open, effective manner. Consider your personal communication style. Are you a passive, an aggressive, or an assertive communicator?

PASSIVE COMMUNICATION

Passive communication is accepting communication without response. It happens when you simply give in without expressing your feelings or rights. If you communicate and behave in a passive manner, never standing up for yourself, you may be treated as a "doormat" by others. For example, if someone steps in front of you in the grocery checkout line and you do not indicate that you were in line, you are exhibiting passive behavior. The danger of being passive is that, as your rights and feelings are trampled, your anger and frustration can mount. The result may be resentment, depression, and a loss of self-esteem.

Do not, however, mistake good manners for passivity. Sometimes it is simply the kind thing to say, "That's okay." Context is what makes the difference. You always have the option of being generous, but that is not the same as being taken advantage of in a situation.

on the job

Philip and Emily decide to continue their business meeting over dinner. At the restaurant, Emily orders fettuccine Alfredo with chicken. Carl orders his fettuccine Alfredo with shrimp. When the meals are served, Emily finds her dish delicious and exactly what she ordered. Philip, however, finds that his dish doesn't contain shrimp but rather chicken. Philip does not like chicken. Philip mentions to Emily that the cook missed putting the shrimp in his meal. He laboriously picks the chicken out and eats only a few bites. Philip doesn't say anything to the server. He leaves a small tip and they leave the restaurant. Emily is surprised that he didn't request that he receive what he had ordered. She also wishes that he had spoken up and requested what was rightly his. He tells Emily on the way out that he will not return to this restaurant because they don't understand the term "customer service."

Who is hurt in this situation? Why? How might Philip's passivity affect Emily's opinion of him as a business associate?

AGGRESSIVE COMMUNICATION

Aggressive communication is the opposite of passive communication. If you use this style of communication, you communicate your feelings in a strong, vigorous manner without regard to the rights or feelings of others. For example, upon ordering a rare steak and receiving one that is well done, the aggressive communicator might say loudly, "Get this piece of meat off of my plate. I ordered a rare steak, not a piece of shoe leather. For the prices you charge in this place, you should be able to get an order correct." The aggressive communicator is very defensive, faultfinding, and judgmental. This type of behavior definitely communicates your feelings, but steps on the rights and feelings of others in the process. Aggressive communication can even result in physical contact—pushing, nudging, shoving. Aggressive behavior is embarrassing and offensive to others in the area. Aggressive behavior may leave a lasting impression on others but not the kind of impression that is preferable.

ASSERTIVE COMMUNICATION

Assertive communication is a more positive and effective communication style than either the passive or aggressive styles. Assertive communication occurs when you stand up for your rights but do not impinge on the rights of others. Being assertive allows you to express your feelings and ideas in a positive manner. You are important enough to have your rights respected. Everyone is important. It does not matter whether you are a student, an accountant, a flight attendant, a supervisor, an attorney, a housekeeper, or a jockey—all are important. You have the right to express your feelings in your own words, without guilt or remorse, and others have the right to express theirs. As you work to use assertive and clear language, you should identify and express what you are thinking or feeling in the most caring, thoughtful manner possible. Assertive communication is a positive step in effective two-way communication.

Assertive communication is not only what you say, but also how you say it. You recall that earlier in this chapter it was said that nonverbal communication is very strong and often will overshadow the verbal message. In addition to stating your feelings and saying the right words, you will need to remember the following:

1. Establish eye contact with the receiver of your message. Eye contact is important. It indicates that you are serious, you mean business, and you want to command the receiver's attention. Do not stare at the other person. Just comfortably look into the receiver's eyes. Some people have a difficult time looking directly at others; begin working on this skill now. Without this skill you will have difficulty in communicating assertively.

2. Do not use gestures that are threatening or that could be interpreted as aggressive. Never point or shake a finger at someone.

3. Your body position is also important. Stand or sit erect, but not stiff. Position yourself so that your eye level is about the same as the receiver. Stand or sit just a little bit closer than you normally would, but be careful not to get too close. You will know you are too close if the receiver steps or moves back. If you get too close, you are approaching aggressive communication.

4. Speak in a normal tone of voice. Speak loudly enough to be heard, and speak clearly. If you raise your voice, you will appear aggressive. If you speak too softly, it will be difficult for the receiver to take you seriously.

"The basic difference between being assertive and being aggressive is how our words and behavior affect the rights and well being of others."

—SHARON ANTHON BOWER

on the job

Denise and Doug are standing in line waiting to get a ticket to a concert they want to attend. Just as they are nearing the ticket booth, two young men crowd in line in front of them. Denise speaks to them in a calm, firm voice and looks them in the eye. Denise stands closer to them than she would under normal circumstances. She says, "Guys, we've been standing here for some time. You've crowded in front of us. You will need to move to the back of the line and wait your turn." Doug is pleased with Denise's assertive communication skills—as were the people behind her in line. Doug is also pleased as he and Denise are able to get tickets and get into the arena in time to hear the first number. Denise stood up for her rights without being defensive, pushy, critical, or judgmental.

What did Denise avoid by being assertive rather than passive or aggressive?

Passive people are usually unhappy because they cannot state what they think and feel. Aggressive communicators get their ideas, thoughts, and feelings heard, but they usually create more problems for themselves and others because of their aggressive tactics. The ability to be assertive takes thought and practice, but it is the most effective option and well worth the practice time.

checkpoint

1. **What is passive communication? Why is passive communication generally not a good choice?**

   _____

   _____

   _____

2. **What gestures may be considered inappropriate when you want to communicate in an assertive manner?**

   _____

   _____

   _____

3. **What actions are appropriate when you want to communicate in an assertive manner?**

   _____

   _____

   _____

4. **What are the characteristics of aggressive behavior?**

   _____

   _____

   _____

5. **What is the difference between assertive and aggressive communication?**

   _____

   _____

   _____

applications

1. Label the following comments as passive, aggressive, or assertive.

a._____ This report is lousy. Get it out of here. Rewrite it. Now!

b._____ No Sundays off for the remainder of the year. Oh, I guess that's okay.

c._____ Thank you for not smoking. Smoke bothers my eyes.

d._____ Put out that cigarette. Don't you know cigarettes cause cancer? Why do you want to endanger my health?

e._____ I'm returning this set of dishes because of their poor quality. One of the cup handles was broken when I got it home. Don't you look over merchandise before it leaves the store? I want my money refunded or a better quality of dinnerware as a replacement.

2. Rewrite the comments that you labeled as aggressive in Application #1 to make them more assertive. In addition to your comments, describe the nonverbal communication that you would use to communicate your message.

_____

_____

_____

_____

_____

_____

_____

_____

_____

3. How would you assertively tell a coworker that you no longer want her to take or use supplies and personal items from your desk drawers? Your coworker borrows scissors, pens, and office forms. She uses your hand lotion, tissues, and breath mints. Draft a sample dialogue.

_____

_____

_____

_____

_____

_____

_____

4. What does eye contact mean, and why is it important?

_____

_____

_____

_____

_____

_____

_____

_____

Listening: A Vital Part of Communication

Listening is the process by which we make sense out of what we hear. Hearing alone is not listening because hearing only means that you recognize that a message is being sent; you may or may not be translating the information and attempting to bring a common understanding between you and the sender of the message. Have you had the experience of listening to an entire lecture or sermon and, at the end, you realize you remember nothing that has been said? You may have heard it, but you weren't listening.

Listening is an art that needs to be practiced in order to be perfected. If you were to measure the amount of communication that you are involved in each day, you would find that more time is spent in listening than in speaking, reading, or writing. Yet you have probably spent a good share of your educational time learning to speak, read, and write, but not learning to listen.

BARRIERS TO LISTENING

Many roadblocks can stop you from receiving a message. Let's review some of those roadblocks so that you can eliminate them from being barriers to your listening skills.

Noise

Unusual sounds or too many sounds at one time can be barriers to your listening. Focus on what you are listening to. Block out what is not important. Other things can be considered "noise" because they can take your thoughts away from the message. Concentrate to avoid being distracted by the unusual attire of a speaker, the pronunciation of a word, an unusual voice quality or dialect, or the sound of an airplane passing over.

Thinking Ahead

In a conversation, people take turns speaking and listening. Sometimes you may take the time for listening to think about what you will say next. If this happens, you are hearing but not listening. Your reply may not make sense because you did not listen to the words of the speaker. He or she may have moved the conversation to a new topic and you missed it.

Mind Moving Too Fast

People think at a much more rapid rate than they speak. Most speakers talk at a rate of about 120 to 150 words per minute. Most receivers listen and think at a rate exceeding 1000 words a minute.[2] If you are listening at 1000 words a minute, you are ahead of the speaker. Thus, your thoughts can wander while you are listening. You may begin to daydream, think about what you need to do later, or wonder what your friends are doing. When this happens, you miss the points of the speaker because your mind is elsewhere. If you find yourself ahead of the speaker, use this valuable time to review what the speaker has said, but try to keep your mind focused on the speaker.

Lack of Attention

Good listening requires keeping one's thoughts on what is being said. When you do not pay close attention to the speaker and his or her message, you are not listening. Paying attention will prevent you from missing important information. For example, if you are being given directions on the job and you are not paying close attention, you may do something wrong and cause injury or expense to your employer or a coworker.

GOOD LISTENING SKILLS

Listening takes practice. Work on the following good listening techniques:

1. Prepare yourself to listen.
2. Learn to shift from speaker to listener.
3. Listen actively.
4. Avoid emotional responses.

Prepare Yourself to Listen

Your efficiency as a listener will improve if you prepare yourself, both mentally and physically, to listen. Block out miscellaneous thoughts that are running through your mind. Attempt to erase competing thoughts, such as what was said in the carpool, the dentist's bill you need to pay, and your plans for Sunday afternoon. You cannot act on any of these thoughts now, so push them aside and prepare yourself to listen. Do some self-talk: *"I'm going to concentrate on what's being said. I need to listen to this information."*

To prepare physically, sit or stand in a way that is comfortable and will help you listen. Be alert. Look at the speaker as you prepare yourself. A visual bond between speaker and listener is important for effective listening. Put yourself in a place where you can hear the person speaking.

Shift from Speaker to Listener

Keep in mind that one of the barriers to good listening is planning what you are going to say next, rather than listening to the speaker. Spend your time listening and not

1. thinking about what clever thing you are going to say next or
2. planning the next question you want to ask.

The next time you are the listener in a conversation, ask yourself: "Am I preparing a speech, or am I listening?"

"The reason why so few people are agreeable is that each is thinking more about what he [sic] intends to say than about what others are saying, and we never listen when we are eager to speak."

—LaRochefoucauld

"So when you are listening to somebody, completely, attentively, then you are listening not only to the words, but also to the feeling of what is being conveyed, to the whole of it, not part of it."

—Juddu Krishnamurti

Listen Actively

Since a person is capable of receiving words faster than a person can speak them, you can use the "extra time" as "think time." While still listening, begin to process the information you are receiving. Paraphrase and interpret what is being said. This is called **active listening**.

Active listening is hard work, but the rewards are great. An active listener will make better decisions—decisions based on more information, including the opinions and experiences of others. The active listener

1. takes the time to listen,
2. shows the speaker that he or she is interested by looking at the speaker and using body language to indicate that listening is taking place,
3. blocks out noise,
4. jots down the main ideas (when appropriate),
5. listens with an open mind, and
6. provides feedback.

Now look at points 5 and 6 again. When you are in the listening role, keep an open mind. If you have an open mind, you will listen to ideas and opinions with which you may disagree. You are willing to hear the other side and learn. (You may still disagree, but you will learn about the other person and may gain valuable information.) Avoid judging the speaker's message while he or she is speaking. Absorb the information and formulate your opinions later. Disregard looks, actions, and personality. Attempt to understand the speaker's feelings and respect his or her thoughts.

Asking questions or making comments shows the speaker that you are listening. You can also provide the speaker with nonverbal feedback as you listen; use eye contact, a smile, or a nod to let your speaker know you are an active listener. If you frown, yawn, or turn your eyes away, you indicate to the speaker that you are not interested in the message.

Technology at Work

On the Internet, there are many Web sites that offer information on listening skills. You may want to look at the following Web sites to discover new ways to improve this important skill.

http://listen.org

http://www.kidsource.com/kidsource/content2/How_Can_Parents_Model.html

http://www.infoplease.com/homework/listeningskills1.html

http://www.d.umn.edu/student/loon/acad/strat/ss_listening.html

Avoid Emotional Responses

Many times, as you listen, it is difficult to control your emotional responses to the speaker's message. Each of us has a list of words that trigger emotional responses—whether positive or negative. What are some words that cause an emotional reaction in you? Perhaps some of the words on your list are feminist, Republican, Democrat, or racist. Poor listeners spend their time reacting to "red flag" words and frequently miss the message.

SEPARATE FACTS FROM OPINIONS

At times you will need to separate facts from the opinions of those who are speaking to you. This is called **critical listening**. A critical listener determines the accuracy of the message and identifies the main ideas and details being imparted. You will need to evaluate each message by deciding what is fact and what is opinion. This is done with respect for the opinion of the sender of the message.

As a critical listener, you will want to play detective. Your game will include

separating facts from opinions. Separate things that can be proven, which are called **facts**, from opinions. **Opinions** are based on personal beliefs or feelings. They are what people think about what they have seen, heard, learned, or experienced. Opinions may not always be based on fact. This does not, however, mean opinions are not true. If someone says, "My red hair is unattractive," this is an opinion and while it may not be based on a fact, it is still true that the person believes his or her red hair is unattractive.

"The reason we have two ears and only one mouth is that we may listen the more and talk the less."

—UNKNOWN

on the job

Chip wants to tell Audrey about the possibility of a job opening that she is qualified to hold. Chip tells her that the job involves working with accounts payable for the Dryden Corporation. Audrey asks, "What does the Dryden Company produce? How many accounts are held by the company?" Chip tells her.

Chip further explains that the salary will be determined based on her experience and education. Audrey asks, "Do you know what the salary range might be? Is there a fringe benefit package provided by the company?" Chip responds that there is a fringe benefit package but he isn't sure about the salary. Audrey asks, "Does the fringe benefit package include dental insurance? How can I find out the salary range being considered?" Audrey pulls a small notebook from her handbag and jots down some notes.

Audrey attempts to ignore the boom box blaring from the street and moves a little closer to Chip. Chip talks about the hours, the job duties, and the other personnel involved in accounts payable. Audrey replies, "Now, let's make sure I have this correct. The hours are 7:30 a.m. to 4:30 p.m. Tuesday through Saturday. There are eight paid holidays during the year. I would be lead accountant in accounts payable." Chip assures her that her notes are correct.

What active listening skills did Audrey demonstrate in this example?

When in doubt about a fact . . . check it out!

© DIGITAL VISION

Where critical listening is important is not when people are sharing what they feel, but when opinions are expressed as facts—"This is the best candidate" or "This is the perfect product."

Facts and opinions are illustrated below.

FACTS
—The oven is set for 350 degrees.
—The invoice for the refrigerator was for $1,496.59.
—The race car runs at 130 miles per hour.
—The elevator will hold 13 people.
—The dog bit her on the leg.

OPINIONS
—The oven is still hot.
—The refrigerator was expensive.
—The race car is fast.
—The elevator looks full.
—The dog is dangerous.

chec**k**point

1. **Why is thinking ahead a barrier to listening?**

_____

_____

2. **What is active listening?**

_____

_____

3. **What are the characteristics of active listening?**

_____

_____

4. **What is critical listening?**

_____

_____

5. **What is the difference between a fact and an opinion?**

_____

_____

applications

1. Write five (or more) words that could bring an emotional response from you when you are listening. Write or discuss why these are "triggers" for you. Describe what you might be able to do to keep yourself from being sidetracked by these "red flags." Your goal is not to react emotionally when you hear these words.

_____

_____

_____

_____

2. Fill in the blanks with sample facts or opinions that match the given information.

FACTS   OPINIONS

a. It reached 102 degrees today.   a. _____

b. The Eiffel Tower is in Paris.   b. _____

c. _____   c. The Democratic candidate will win the election.

d. _____   d. Indian food is spicy.

e. _____   e. Suzy's hair looks cute.

f. The laptop weighs 5 pounds.   f. _____

3. Identify situations in which it would be especially important for you to be a critical listener. List three situations in the workplace. List three situations in your personal life.

_____

_____

_____

_____

_____

4. Think of a time when you have found a barrier to listening based on your lack of attention. What was the situation at the time? What could you have done to avoid this barrier from interfering with communication?

_____

_____

_____

_____

_____

_____

_____

_____

_____

_____

Points to Remember

4

chapter

Review the following points to determine what you remember from the chapter.

- Communication is a two-way process. The sender of information produces the thought or idea to be transmitted to the receiver. The receiver is the individual to whom the thought or idea is transmitted. Both the sender and the receiver must share the same meaning of what is being communicated if communication is to take place. The route or medium (mode) in which the message is transmitted is known as the channel. The receiver responds to the message with feedback.

- There are several barriers to watch out for as you communicate in the work-place: (1) choice of words, (2) selective communication, (3) use of jargon, and (4) physical or distance barriers.

- Strive to keep the channels of communication open by keeping a friendly attitude, using positive persuasion, helping others feel important, rewarding the positive and ignoring the negative, and being aware of the pitfalls of gossip.

- Passive communication is accepting communication without response. You give in without expressing your feelings or rights. Aggressive communication is the opposite of passive. You communicate your feelings in a strong, vigorous manner without regard to the rights or feelings of others. Assertive communication occurs when you stand up for your rights and feelings without stepping on the rights and feelings of others. In addition to stating your feelings and saying the right words, you will need to: (1) establish good eye contact with the receiver of the message, (2) use gestures that are not threatening or aggressive, (3) position yourself at the eye level of the receiver, and (4) speak in a normal tone of voice.

- Listening is the process by which you make sense out of what you hear. The good listener: (1) prepares to listen, (2) avoids thinking about what he or she is going to say next, (3) listens actively, and (4) avoids emotional responses. The critical listener separates facts from opinions. Barriers to good listening include: (1) noise, (2) thinking ahead, (3) mind moving too fast, (4) lack of attention, and (5) poor attitude.

How did you do? Did you remember the main points you studied in the chapter?

key terms

Place the letter of the item in the definition column that matches the key word.

Key Word	Definition
____1. Communication	a. Hearing or reading only what you want to hear or read.
____2. Sender	b. Separating facts from the opinions of those who are speaking to you
____3. Receiver	c. Paraphrasing and interpreting what is being said
____4. Message	d. Based on personal beliefs or feelings
____5. Feedback	e. Give in without expressing your feelings or rights
____6. Channel	f. The process by which we make sense out of what we hear
____7. Selective communication	g. The technical terminology or characteristic words and ideas that belong to a specific type of work or field of knowledge
____8. Jargon	h. Tells the sender whether or not the message is understood
____9. Persuasion	i. Produces the thought or idea that is to be transmitted to another
___10. Passive communication	j. Individual to whom the thought or idea is transmitted
___11. Aggressive communication	k. Thought or idea
___12. Assertive communication	l. Information that can be proven
___13. Listening	m. Opposite of passive communication
___14. Active listening	n. Act of transmitting information
___15. Critical listening	o. The route that a message takes to get to the receiver
___16. Facts	p. Attempt to get others to adopt or agree with an idea you have
___17. Opinions	q. Communicating without the use of words
___18. Grapevine	r. A positive and effective use of words
___19. Nonverbal communication	s. Informal circulation of a message
___20. Verbal communication	t. Communicating with words

activities and projects

1. Ron and several of his coworkers from a retail clothing store were having a friendly discussion during a lunch break. Ron was very interested in fashion and wanted to compliment Lucy, a new coworker, on her trendy new outfit. "You look great in your new suit," he said. Lucy got up from the table and walked away without saying a word. Even though Ron's comment was innocent, Lucy was offended by the compliment because she had been the victim of sexual harassment in a previous job.

a. What would you recommend Ron do at this point?

b. Should Aggie, Ron's friend, have spoken up at the table and explained the interpretation Lucy had made of the comment?

c. Should Lucy have explained her feelings?

d. What listening skill might Lucy want to practice?

e. How could Ron have avoided this incident?

2. Place an O in the space provided before a statement you would ignore in the workplace. Place an X in the space provided before a statement you would check out before you dismissed the gossip.

_____ Xavier is going to be transferred to the Atlanta office. Maybe he'll fit in better there.

_____ Did you hear that Mae's brother was fired for sexual harassment?

_____ Our paychecks won't be ready on Friday.

_____ Payroll didn't take FICA out of last month's checks.

_____ Did you know the plant manager wears a toupee?

_____ I hear you are going to be fired because you are missing too much work.

_____ I heard the agency cafeteria is infested with roaches.

_____ Hanh has lost a lot of weight. Do you think she is sick?

_____ Rumor has it that all of us are subject to drug tests.

3. Discuss in a small group why you think it is so difficult to learn to listen well. Think about attitudes and experiences, as well as skills and techniques. Take notes on things that you think apply to you, and try to find solutions to improve them.

_____

_____

_____

_____

_____

_____

_____

_____

_____

_____

4. Explain how you would assertively tell a coworker that he takes too many personal calls during work hours. The calls are distracting to you and others because he frequently raises his voice and his language is often inappropriate. The work he doesn't complete is shifted to your workload. If he didn't spend so much time on the telephone, he would have time to complete his share of the work.

_____

_____

_____

_____

_____

_____

5. Think about the situation in item 4. Explain what might happen if you used passive communication in this situation. Passive communication means that you don't say anything to your coworker; you continue to carry some of his workload and continue to be distracted by his personal telephone calls.

_____

_____

_____

_____

_____

_____

case studies for critical thinking

Case 4.1

OPINIONATED MENTOR

Mesha is a new employee in a large city library. She has not had previous experience in a library but she is eager to learn. Charles has worked in the library for about ten years and has agreed to serve as a mentor for Mesha. During her first week on the job, Charles explains the library policies, the checkout procedures, and begins to talk with her about how the books, reference materials, and periodicals are arranged within the library. As he explains the procedures to her, he tells her that Tim Davis, the head librarian, got his job because his wife is related to the city mayor. He has also shared other information about Mr. Davis that is very negative.

Mesha is a critical listener and is struggling to separate Charles' opinions from fact. In truth, she is only interested in learning to do her job well and doesn't want to hear personal information about her employer. She has an opportunity to deliver some materials to Mr. Davis. While she is waiting for him to arrive in his office, she notices some certificates hanging on the walls; he has two degrees in library science and an award for his work as a librarian in another community. She now has a strong clue that Charles is sharing his opinion with her, not the facts. It is obvious that the head librarian is credentialed and recognized for his work. Mesha will be mentored by Charles throughout her probationary period of six months.

1. Should Mesha be passive about this information and not respond to the comments by Charles? Why or why not?

2. Should Mesha be aggressive and tell him to stop talking about their employer and just continue telling her about the workings of the library? If so, why? What might be the fallout of this tactic?

3. What recommendations would you have for Mesha in this situation?

Case 4.2

HOW TO HANDLE A COMPLIMENT

Bonnie and Bev have worked together for a number of years. They spend social time as well as work time together. Bev said to Bonnie, "You are such an asset to our bowling team. Your average keeps us alive." Bonnie replied, "Oh, it is nothing. Are you going to work next Saturday?"

1. List four appropriate responses for Bonnie following Bev's compliment about her contribution to the bowling team.

_____

_____

2. How do you think Bev felt when her comment on Bonnie's bowling skill was ignored?

_____

_____

3. How could Bev help Bonnie learn to accept a compliment?

_____

_____

Case 4.3

AGGRESSIVE COMMUNICATION

Eric is a medical records clerk in a small rural hospital. He takes his job very seriously. He knows that a mistake in a medical record could jeopardize a patient's health, and possibly even the patient's life, and could also damage the reputation of the hospital. Melissa is the night shift emergency room nurse. On the chart of one of her patients, she states that the left toe of an emergency room patient was crushed in a workplace accident. As Eric is putting the records together for the patient, he notes that the doctor and the ambulance driver had noted that the patient's right toe was injured. Eric rushes out of his office, locates Melissa, and begins shaking the medical record at her. He begins to yell at her. "How could you be so negligent? Do you know right from left? Do you realize you put the patient in jeopardy with this type of error? Don't you care about the reputation of this hospital? Where did you get your license to practice nursing?" This outburst takes place within earshot of the family waiting room.

1. What was Eric's style of communication? What characteristics of the style were demonstrated by Eric in this example?

_____

_____

2. Who may have been embarrassed by Eric's choice of communication? What damage may have been done because of where he chose to speak to Melissa?

_____

_____

_____

_____

3. What words and nonverbal communication could have been used by Eric to send his message in an assertive communication style?

_____

_____

_____

_____

4. What could Melissa have said back to Eric after his outburst?

_____

_____

_____

_____

5. What kind of worry is now on the minds of the family in the waiting room?

_____

_____

_____

_____

Getting Your Message Across

think about it: Max and Jess were busy attempting to solve a problem involving a new piece of equipment designed to provide more safety for factory line workers. Nathan, a fairly new employee, was walking through the area and hesitated as he passed them. Nathan had considerable experience in working with this equipment, but he hesitated to offer advice because he did not know Max and Jess very well. Max noticed Nathan and said, "Hello." Nathan responded with a "Hi." Nathan then moved out of the work area. Max said to Jess, "He sure isn't very friendly. I hear he is really sharp, but I can't seem to get more than a word or two from him." Jess replied, "I think he thinks he's too good to talk with other employees. I'll bet he comes on strong with conversation when management is around." Max said, "Yes, I notice that he spends a lot of time in the boss's office."

What habits has Nathan developed that make him appear unfriendly and perhaps aloof? What habits have Max and Jess developed that may make them less than good coworkers?

© DIGITAL VISION

chapter focus

After completing this chapter, you should be able to:

1. Demonstrate the ability to get a message across clearly to others.

2. Participate in a conversation.

3. Explain what to say in a conversation.

4. Explain the purpose of giving a speech before a group.

As you communicate with others, you may be the speaker or the listener. The following rules for workplace communication may apply specifically to the sender. You are a sender when you speak or write.

BE CLEAR

Your message will be received accurately only if you make your statements or requests so clear that they cannot be misunderstood. In an effort to make your message clear, be brief, use variety, and itemize.

Brevity

Typically, your communication will be clearer if you use short words, short sentences, and short paragraphs. Brevity is key to clear workplace communication, because the receiver will both absorb and understand your message more easily and quickly. Be selective with your words; don't add any that aren't necessary. Don't use a six-syllable word if a one- or two-syllable word will do. A six-line paragraph is easier to digest than one containing twelve lines.

However, be sure that in your attempt to be brief, you do not omit some important part of your message.

Variety

Your communication will get attention if you use variety in your speaking and writing. One way to put variety into what you say or write is to avoid using the same words or phrases over and over. Avoid using trite and meaningless phrases like "you know," "in terms of," "like," "okay," and "at this point in time." Also, avoid the tendency to write several sentences in succession that start the same way or are the same length.

Itemization

Clarity is also improved if you itemize steps or lists you wish to communicate. Notice

how difficult it is to understand the following written instructions: *"Please find the files on Case #04-04, the Commissioner vs. Tony Abernathy and pull the affidavit from the Franklin file. This is an old breach of contract case. Make three copies of the affidavit in the file, send one to the law office of Smith, Leonard, and Smith. Send another to Abernathy. And, send one to the Lancaster District Court."*

If these instructions were written or spoken in an itemized form, they would be much easier to follow:

1. *Make three copies of the Franklin affidavit in Case #04-04 file.*
2. *Send a copy to Smith, Leonard, and Smith.*
3. *Send a copy to respondent Abernathy.*
4. *Send a copy to the Lancaster District Court.*

Notice how you automatically eliminate unnecessary words as you itemize instructions. You realize it is redundant to say the name of the case file. You have given the number. It isn't necessary to say that this is an old breach of contract case. You don't have to mention the affidavit twice. Itemization helps with clarity and brevity.

SAY NO IN A POSITIVE WAY

In previous chapters you have learned the importance of being positive. However, there are times when you must say "no." Therefore, in your study of getting the message across, it is important to learn and practice how to say "no" in a positive manner.

Imply the Negative

In some circumstances you can say "no" or send a "no" message by simply implying it. For example, if a coworker asks you to cover her phone over the lunch hour you might answer, "I'm having lunch at a restaurant across town with my sister, and

I'll be gone at the same time your lunch hour is scheduled."

Note that you did not say "No, I will not cover your phone over the lunch hour."

Say What You Can Do

To avoid being negative, you can say what you *can* or *will* do without saying what you cannot or will not do. If a patient requests an appointment at 2:45 p.m. on Friday and you realize that time is not available, rather than saying, "No, this is not possible," say, "We'll have time for you at 3:30 p.m. or 4:30 p.m. on Friday."

Use Sentence Structure

When you must say "no," remove the sting of the word by putting the "no" part of the sentence in a dependent clause of the sentence. For example, rather than saying, "You failed to put the letters you want monogrammed on the sheets you ordered, and we can't get them to you in two days," say, "If you'll let me know what letters you want monogrammed on the sheets you want, we'll get them to you within five working days."

© GETTY IMAGES/PHOTODISC

You may be the speaker or the listener at times in a conversation.

Depersonalize the Negative

Make the "no" part of your sentence relate to a thing rather than a person. If you say, "This wallpaper appears to be warped," the listener will easily accept your statement. But if you say, "Did you store this wallpaper in a damp place?" your statement sounds accusatory, and your listener may resent the remark.

chec**k**point

1. **Why is brevity the key to clear communication?**

   _____

   _____

2. **Why is variety in your speaking and writing good for communication?**

   _____

   _____

3. **What are four ways you can say "no" in a positive way?**

   _____

   _____

applications

1. In the first column, list the words and phrases that you or others use that are trite or overused. In the second column, list phrases that could replace the overused words. If the words or phrases are unnecessary and add nothing to the message, write "eliminate" in the second column.

_____   _____

_____   _____

_____   _____

_____   _____

_____   _____

_____   _____

_____   _____

2. How would you tell a customer that the DVD he desires is out of stock and won't be available until your next shipment arrives on the following Monday?

_____

_____

_____

_____

_____

_____

_____

3. How would you tell your supervisor that you won't cover up an error he made in estimating a painting contract without actually saying "no"?

_____

_____

_____

_____

_____

_____

_____

4. Think of a time when you said "no" in a positive way. How did the receiver react to this type of communication? Would saying a definite "no" have made the receiver think or react differently?

_____

_____

_____

_____

_____

_____

_____

Conversational skills are important in the workplace. Take advantage of conversational opportunities to get to know your supervisors and coworkers better. If this opportunity frightens you, that is normal. Take a deep breath, and start a conversation whenever it is appropriate. The secret of being a good conversationalist is to just *be yourself*. If you try to impress others by attempting to be someone you are not, you will be uneasy and guarded. This will make you and the receiver(s) of the message uncomfortable. Such a statement, however, is certain to raise the question, "How can I improve my conversation?" The following paragraphs give you suggestions; after that, you will need to practice.

on the job

Bart was a foreman in a large food processing plant. When he spoke to his employees, he often talked in a very loud, booming voice because he was accustomed to talking over factory noise. Bart was a very active, aggressive man, and always in a hurry. Chen and Emily were called into Bart's office for an explanation of a new procedure. Bart talked to them in the same very loud voice he used on the floor of the plant. The loudness of his voice made it hard to concentrate on the message. Bart was in a hurry as usual. He talked very fast, didn't pause for questions, and left in a hurry. His parting words were: "Please go back to the line and explain to your coworkers how we are going to implement this procedure." Chen and Emily left his office very confused, frustrated, and not very knowledgeable about the new procedure they were being assigned to implement. They were so intimidated by the voice volume that they didn't hear the message and felt incapable of sharing the information.

Why was Bart's message so hard to understand? What suggestions would you have for Bart? How should Chen and Emily prepare for their next conversation with Bart?

VOICE QUALITIES

Part of your conversational ability will be based on your voice qualities. Your voice qualities are part of your personality. Work on good voice qualities. There is no right way to speak. Listening would be very dull if everyone spoke and sounded alike. There are, however, several characteristics of a good voice that you will want to work on as you develop your skills as a speaker and as a conversationalist. They are as follows:

1. good pitch
2. appropriate volume
3. good inflection
4. enunciation
5. pronunciation

Pitch is the high or low sound of your voice. The length, tension, and thickness of your vocal cords determine pitch. You have no control over the length or thickness of your vocal cords, but you do have control over the tension you exert on them. When your vocal cords are too tense, they produce high squeaky tones. Your listener then realizes you are tense. Relax and take a deep breath; your pitch will be smooth and improved.

Many people perceive that a lower pitch gives the impression of authority and influence. Some of us do not have the vocal cords for a lower pitch. If you try to create a lower pitch, you may experience a crackly sound known as a "fry." Working toward the lower limit of your voice can produce a sound similar to a radio not quite tuned into a station. This is not only an unpleasant sound but it can also damage the vocal cords. Don't try for any dramatic changes in pitch without consulting a speech therapist.

When you are in a conversational setting, you must work to avoid raising your pitch at the end of a statement. If you raise your pitch at the end of a statement, you may sound hesitant and insecure.

Do you understand how to operate this machine? If not, I'd be happy to demonstrate. (Pitch should drop at the end of a sentence to signify the end of a statement.)

Do the best you can with the pitch you were given. Know the times when you are susceptible to a pitch shift due to stress or nervousness. A deep breath will help your pitch.

Volume is the loudness or softness of your voice. Have you ever noticed how exhausting it is to try to hear someone who speaks too softly? Speak up so that others can hear your message. Do not tire others by forcing them to strain to hear you or miss your message because they could not hear what you were saying.

Listening to a very loud voice can also be annoying. Adjust your voice so that others can hear you clearly. You don't want to assume the role of the "workplace megaphone." If you are unsure of your volume, ask the help of others. Say, "Can you hear me?" "Am I speaking loudly enough?" or "Am I speaking too loudly?"

If you consistently hear from others that your voice is excessive in volume, you may want to have your hearing checked.

The inability to monitor or control volume could be an effect of a hearing impairment.

Most people instinctively do a good job with volume control by taking the following into account:

1. *The amount of background noise in the setting.*
2. *The distance between ourselves and our audience.*
3. *The degree to which we want to publicize a message.*

Inflection is the rising and falling of your voice, as shown in Figure 5-1. If you speak with no inflection, you speak in a **monotone**. A monotone is a voice with no expression. It always sounds the same. Use your voice to help express the meaning of your words. Be sure your voice is not always the same. Ask others for help: "Is my voice flat?" "Does my voice always sound the same?" Put the enthusiasm in your voice that you feel inside.

Conversation is improved when your voice shows emotion. Read these sentences and put feeling into them. Work at using inflection in your voice.

Happy birthday!
Amy, did you enjoy your vacation?
The game is over! We won!
Yes, I want to work with you on this new project.

Enunciation is pronouncing each part of each word clearly. The more carefully you enunciate, the more likely you are to be understood. Be careful to speak clearly

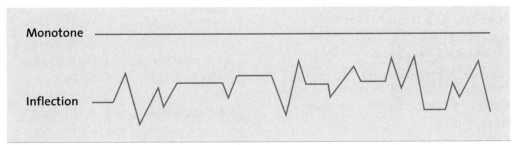

FIGURE 5-1 *Conversation is improved when your voice shows inflection.*

and not run your words together. Avoid the carelessness of running frequently used phrases together, and take special care not to leave out part of a word or syllable. If you do not enunciate, your speech will be sloppy and difficult to understand.

Check to be sure you avoid the jumbling of common words or phrases like:

postta	suppose to
havta	have to
dunno	don't know
uzhly	usually
wuncha	wouldn't you
can'tcha	can't you

Pronunciation is saying a word correctly. Pronunciation requires that you know how words are supposed to be said. If you mispronounce words, you should know you make a bad impression or fail to communicate your meaning. Good pronunciation is a quality of an articulate person. If you are unsure of how to pronounce a word, check a dictionary, or ask.

Smart Tip ▼ ▼ ▼

If you feel you are not being taken seriously when you speak, you may want to work on your pitch. When you speak, you want everyone to listen.

To find your best or most comfortable pitch, say the phrase "uh-huh" without an effort. If it sounds much lower than the pitch you normally use, it is possible you are speaking at a higher level than is necessary. You can also use this technique in a stressful situation. Find your best pitch by saying "uh-huh" out loud or mentally, and then begin your speech on that note.

▲ ▲ ▲ ▲ ▲ ▲ ▲ ▲ ▲

Don't Talk Too Fast

Good conversation is meant to be relaxing, so do not talk too fast. When you speak very rapidly, your receiver will sense a feeling of tenseness. Rapid speech can indicate a sign of stress and make your listener uncomfortable and anxious. Put some pauses into what you have to say. This will slow down your speaking tempo. A technique that may help you is called one-two. Count one-two in your mind at natural pauses. *"I would like to tell you a story (one-two), about my first day on the job (one-two). I started off on a good note (one-two), by arriving on time."* With enough practice of this technique, your speech will slow down and be more understandable and believable. As you slow down the speed of your conversation, you will enunciate more clearly. It will be easier for your listener to understand your message.

Silence is Okay

Do not be afraid of a brief silence in conversation. Constant chatter can be extremely tiring, and an occasional pause or short silence can be refreshing. Silence can provide a moment or two for you and your listener to summarize and think about what has been said. Silence is an improvement over saying "um" or "ah." Some speakers will say "um" or "ah" when they need a break to think. The "ums" and "ahs" can be very distracting to the listener.

Learn to Listen

You read about the importance of being a good listener in Chapter 4. Good listening is also a very important part of being a skilled conversationalist. If you think of your conversational group as a basketball team, for example, it may help you to see the necessity of giving each player a chance to move the ball toward the basket. Pass the conversation, listen to others, listen actively, and show interest with your face and body language. Doing this will make others think you are a gifted conversationalist. You will not need to say much yourself if you make the conversation of others seem important. Do this by nodding your head and making short statements of agreement or interest. A good listener must avoid criticism, too. If you have negative thoughts, "This person doesn't really know what he is talking about," "I wish she would get to the point," "I'm out of here," your face or body language may give you away, defeating what you have been trying to accomplish.

RESPECT THE SPACE OF OTHERS

The distance between you and your listener is called **personal space**. It has an impact on how well you get across your conversational message. Violations of personal space can cause deep discomfort. Have you noticed how people react in a crowded elevator? They stand rigid, do not talk, and stare at the floor indicator above the door or at the floor. This reaction demonstrates a discomfort because in a crowded elevator, people are "in your personal space." This also happens in conversation. If you get too close when talking to someone, your message may be lost and the conversation will soon terminate. (You will know if you are too close when the listener steps back or moves away.)

We usually give little conscious attention to the role of personal space in our communication—until someone is standing too close or too far away for our comfort. The way in which others use space gives strong clues to what they are thinking and how they are communicating with us. There are many variables that influence our use of

space when communicating—status, gender, culture, and context are but a few.

Through our body language and manipulation of objects we unconsciously let others know our space needs. For example, where you place chairs or couches in an office, where you choose to sit in a meeting, or the length of the desk you choose all tell something about our needs. You have a right to have your space respected, as your listener has a right to have his or her space requirements respected.

Status (position or rank) affects the distance that is maintained between speakers and listeners. Studies show that when people of different status levels converse, they tend to stand farther apart than do individuals of equal status. People of higher status may close the distance between themselves and people of lower status, but seldom do people of lower status move to close the distance between themselves and a person of higher status.

Genders (male or female) tend to differ in their space patterns. But the differences in part hinge on whether the communication is with someone of the same or opposite gender. In same-gender situations, men prefer, and usually establish, greater conversational distance than women do. Opposite-gender distancing depends on the intimacy of the relationship.

Culture (customs, beliefs, traits, and social forms of a group) produces a wide range of differences in the way individuals use distance while communicating. What an American would consider acceptable conversational distance would almost certainly be different from what a person from Latin America or the Middle East would find acceptable. The important thing is to recognize that different cultures are accustomed

"Drawing on my fine command of the English language, I said nothing."

—ROBERT BENCHLEY (1889–1945)

"We all need to have a creative outlet—a window, a space—so we don't lose track of ourselves."

—NORMAN FISCHER

Check the speaking skills you possess. I . . .

_____ 1. itemize my thoughts.

_____ 2. use familiar, understandable words.

_____ 3. avoid trite phrases.

_____ 4. put inflection in my voice.

_____ 5. enunciate each word.

_____ 6. listen to the person with whom I am talking.

_____ 7. recognize the space needs of others.

_____ 8. establish eye contact.

_____ 9. give others a chance to speak.

_____ 10. speak loudly enough to be comfortably heard.

In which areas do you need to improve? Think about how you might gain or practice skills in which you are not strong.

to different amounts of personal space. If you work with people who are culturally diverse, ask them about the space needs of their culture, do some research on your own, or observe the distance set when they are talking with others.

The standards for space requirements in the United States are usually quoted as follows:

Formal distance: three to six feet apart.
Comfortable conversational distance: two to three feet apart.
Close friend distance: one and a half feet apart.

Context (the setting) also influences the space that is maintained between individuals. For example, people in line at an automated teller machine usually stand back far enough to give the person using the machine the feeling that his or her transaction is not being observed. But passengers waiting to board a plane or bus ordinarily stand close together to avoid losing their places.

ACHIEVE EYE CONTACT

Eye contact is important if your listeners are to take your message seriously. If you are talking to several people, you will need to establish eye contact with each person. This will make each of them feel included. It may be hard to move your eyes away from someone who seems to be responding to you, but, if you are to get across your message, you must make an effort to do so. If eye contact is difficult for you in small group conversations, just look at the nose of your listeners. This will suffice until you have practiced eye contact enough to become comfortable with it. Also, be aware that more than five seconds of eye contact can be interpreted as a stare, which would make a listener uncomfortable.

Some ethnic groups show respect by dropping their eyes. Recognize this act as a cultural characteristic and don't feel slighted because of the lack of eye contact.

LET OTHERS SPEAK

Keep your comments brief. If you tell a story, keep it short. If you explain the way you think about something, give the highlights only. You need to work at this so you will leave time for others to speak. When you are talking, you are not listening or learning. Give others a chance to speak.

AVOID BEING SHY

If you are a shy person, having a conversation is easier said than done. If you feel comfortable fading into the background, fight it. Your shyness or lack of conversation may make others think you are aloof, cold, uninterested, or unfeeling. People may become uncomfortable in your presence. If you start by showing an interest in what others are saying, it will not be long before you will want to participate in the conversation. Your ideas are valuable, others want to hear them, and they need to be shared.

checkpoint

1. **What does it mean to enunciate?**

   _____

   _____

   _____

2. **What is voice inflection?**

   _____

   _____

   _____

3. **What is personal space?**

   _____

   _____

   _____

   _____

   _____

4. **Why is eye contact with the listener important to the communication process?**

   _____

   _____

   _____

   _____

   _____

   _____

5. **Is voice volume in a conversation important? Why?**

   _____

   _____

   _____

   _____

   _____

applications

1. Sharpen your speaking skills by practicing aloud the following:

a. Say the *t* and *d*.

don't you   did you   told you
won't you   would you   found you

b. Say the long *o*.

Swallow   mellow   fellow   pillow

c. Say the *ing*. Do not omit the sound of the *g*.

making   taking   sewing   going   seeing   helping   doing   thinking

d. Practice saying these frequently mispronounced words. Do not reverse the order of the italicized letters in the following words:

Apron   hundred   proposal   children

Do not add a syllable to these words:

athlete (ath let)   film (film)   drowned (dround)
grown (gron)   burglar (bur gler)

2. Look up each of these frequently mispronounced words in a dictionary. Write the preferred pronunciation, and practice saying the word correctly.

a. apricot _____

b. pecan _____

c. chic _____

d. pianist _____

e. greasy _____

f. roof _____

g. aluminum _____

3. List six questions you could use to establish a dialogue with people you have never met before. Imagine you are at a picnic with a friend. The friend is talking with others in a private conversation. You find yourself around a picnic table with several people you would like to meet.

a. _____

b. _____

c. _____

d. _____

e. _____

f. _____

4. Think of a time when you were talking to someone and he or she stepped back away from you or you saw this situation happen to another person. Why would that happen? What did you or the other person do in response?

_____

_____

_____

_____

_____

_____

_____

Conversation—What do I Say?

So far this chapter has focused on how you should act and what you should do in a conversation. Now you need to concentrate on what to say.

KEEP YOUR STATEMENTS PLEASANT

As you begin thinking about your conversational skill, put yourself in a positive frame of mind. Try to avoid unpleasant topics, criticism of others, sarcasm, and pessimism. In fact, it would be a good idea to avoid these types of conversations entirely. Refrain from derogatory remarks for three reasons: (1) Others do not admire the person who makes such remarks, (2) They destroy the spirit of cooperation that can be built by good conversation, and (3) Others enjoy talking to someone who is upbeat and positive.

GET INVOLVED

Be prepared to talk as you move to a conversational setting. A good starter may be to pay an *honest compliment* to one of the speakers. You might want to use a phrase such as, "How interesting. I had never thought of that." "You have given this topic some thought!" This is complimentary to the person speaking because it shows you are thinking about what has been said. Another way to involve yourself in a conversation might be to ask questions. Speakers are always glad to be asked a question because this gives them a chance to talk to a definite point and lets them know you are listening. If someone has been talking about his or her child, you might ask, "How old is your child?" "Where does he or she go to school?" A question is another sincere form of flattery. It is an easy way to get involved and expand a conversation.

If you are attempting to start or become engaged in a conversation, don't give up after one question. You may need to ask several questions before you become a part of the conversation. Your questions will eventually encourage responses. If your first question does not work, try a few more questions to see if you can determine an interest of the person with whom you want to talk. See an example of expanded questioning in the On the Job scenario.

When you use a question to begin a conversation, be careful to choose one that cannot be answered with a single word. For example, "Do you like your job?" The

on the job

Henry wanted to establish a good working rapport with a new coworker, Mitch. Henry said, "Good morning. How was your weekend?" Mitch replied, "Quiet!" Henry did not give up; he kept going. "Great. Did you hear the final score of the Yankees game?" Mitch said, "I don't follow baseball." Henry responded, "Sorry, I forget that not everyone is a baseball nut." Henry tried again, "Wasn't the weather beautiful this weekend?" Mitch replied, "Yes." Henry asked, "What sports do you enjoy?" Mitch replied, "Oh, my sport is hockey. I grew up in northern Wisconsin where hockey is very popular, and I've never lost that interest." Henry thought, "Aha. I finally asked the right question." He said, "It's a small world. I grew up in Milwaukee and played hockey in high school and college." The conversation was off and running.

Why was it important for Henry not to give up on the conversation? Why do you think some people are more difficult to engage in conversation than others?

answer you will likely get from the question will be "yes" or "no." You might try a question like, "What do you enjoy about your work?" If you get a one-word answer, "nothing," do not give up. Follow up with "Why don't you tell me what kind of job you would like to have?"

Some conversation starter questions should be avoided. These include personal questions, particularly those involving health, religion, politics, and money. If you are in doubt as to whether a question is too personal, put yourself in the other person's place. Would you like someone to ask you if you have gained weight or what you paid for your car or why you had surgery?

People usually like to talk about themselves. You might ask questions like these: Where are you from? Where did you go to high school? What do you do? What are your interests? Getting the other person to talk about himself or herself can be a strong motivator for continuing the conversation. This is especially true if you listen carefully and use follow-up questions to keep the person talking if necessary.

KEEP AN OPEN MIND

A good conversationalist keeps a tolerant attitude. If you preach, if you dictate, if you pass judgments, others will not enjoy listening to you. Keep your mind open to the ideas of others. A conversation is meant to be a free exchange of ideas. Do not try to dominate the conversation or have the final word on every subject. If you do this, you will actually block the conversation and miss the opportunity to hear the ideas of others.

AVOID TOTAL DISAGREEMENT

A good conversationalist avoids putting a sudden halt to the conversation. If you suddenly express an opposite viewpoint to

the one being related, or if you contradict or interrupt the speaker, you are being rude. Even more unpleasant, however, is that you will usually stop the conversation dead. A mild remark is much more effective and may eventually open the door for you to make your point without being offensive. A remark like, "Do you really think so?" is much more tactful than "You are completely

"The real art of conversation is not only to say the right thing at the right place but to leave unsaid the wrong thing at the tempting moment."

—DOROTHY NEVILL

focus on ethics

The manager of your section tells your work group that the section will be closed within the next couple of months and everyone will be relocated to a community about five hundred miles away. Your coworkers are very upset. They are not interested in moving; they own homes, they have children in school, and their spouses have employment in this community. You know this information is not true. The branch manager is your neighbor, and he recently told you that your section would be expanded at the present site. You know from past experience that your section manager operates on rumors. This manager also likes to stir up trouble.

Do you correct the section manager at the time he makes the announcement? Do you share your inside information with your coworkers? Do you tell the branch manager what has been said? If you did decide to mention it, what conversational techniques could you use to help introduce your information without upsetting the manager?

wrong!" Work to eliminate all feelings of competitiveness in conversation. There is no winner or loser; instead, there should be a feeling of friendliness and open exchange among the participants of a talking group.

ENCOURAGE FEEDBACK

If you can show with a nod or smile that you understand the message presented in a conversation, you will be using a good conversational technique. A good speaker also creates a climate in which others feel comfortable giving feedback.

Here are several ways to encourage feedback.

Give Reinforcement

If you have asked for feedback, give reinforcement to the listener who responds to your question. For example, suppose you ask a coworker, Joe, how he likes the new health insurance plan. Joe responds, "I think the new program

"The art of conversation consists as much in listening politely, as in talking agreeably."

—ATWELL

is too expensive for the employee with children." If you say, "Well, you're lucky you have insurance," Joe will probably terminate the conversation. To encourage Joe, you might say, "I understand it is more expensive for employees with families, but what are your thoughts about the benefits for quality medical care needed for your kids?" This comment may help continue the dialogue.

Outline the Kind of Feedback you are Seeking

Try not to ask general or vague questions about feelings, ideas, or behaviors; phrase your questions specifically. If your feedback is vague, it may be interpreted as insincere. Rather than saying to a coworker, "Let me know if there is any way I can help you," try being specific. "Do you want help with putting those numbers in a database program?" "When I pick up my son at day care, would it help if I pick up your daughter and give you an extra couple of hours this evening?"

check✓point

1. **What are two ways to get involved in a conversation?**

   _____

   _____

2. **Why does a statement of total disagreement stop conversation?**

   _____

   _____

3. **How can you encourage feedback from your listener during conversation?**

   _____

   _____

   _____

applications

1. Explain why the following comments should be avoided in conversation. Point out the specifics of the phrases that concern you the most.

a. What kind of surgery are you having?

b. I can't stand being around smoke.

c. How can you say that you don't approve of the president's budget?

d. You should wear brighter colors.

e. You are wrong. I saw the accident.

f. Does your church believe in absolution?

2. Rewrite the sentences in Item 1 so that they would be acceptable in good conversation.

_____

_____

_____

_____

_____

3. Assume you are sitting on a plane next to a nervous flyer. Your seat partner appears to be shy, but you get the feeling she wants to talk. You are interested in a conversation with her. List six questions that you could ask to engage her in conversation and keep the dialogue going.

_____

_____

_____

_____

_____

4. Laura is a new employee at the Matthews Upholstery Factory. She is eager to get to know her coworkers, but Laura is a shy person. Fran and Allison are fabric cutters. Alexis is a frame builder, and Laura is a finish worker. Fran and Allison have been at the factory for many years, and they are good friends. Alexis has been on the job only a few months; however, she has worked in the upholstery business for twenty years. Laura's coworkers are friendly, but Laura does not seem to be able to engage in conversation with them.

a. How could Laura become involved in the conversations?

_____

_____

_____

b. What specific techniques could she use to be a part of the conversations?

_____

_____

_____

_____

c. What will Laura want to avoid in her effort to get acquainted through conversation?

_____

_____

_____

_____

d. What questions would you suggest for Laura to ask her coworkers?

_____

_____

_____

_____

_____

_____

_____

5.4 Speaking Before Groups

In the workplace or in your personal life, you may have the opportunity to speak before a group of coworkers, a committee, or an organization. You may be asked to join a panel, give a report, teach a class, or make a speech. A speech is a more formal, prepared presentation of comments, ideas, and/or information. When giving a speech, the speaker sends a message with a specific purpose. A speech may be given to:

on the job

Bernice was an established member of her neighborhood watch organization. She had worked on several committees, had attended safety conferences, and had helped other neighborhoods form their own watch groups. The local police chief asked Bernice to talk at a community-service organization about the benefits of a neighborhood watch program and to encourage their membership to form watch groups within their neighborhoods. Bernice was terrified. She would have to talk to sixty-five strangers. She couldn't tell the police chief "no"—he had done so much for her community. She thought about ways to get out of speaking: scheduling a vacation; calling the chief a few days before the presentation and telling him she was ill. But she knew that this was important and would be worth doing. She went to the library to research neighborhood watch groups. She didn't find much recent information. With her neighbors, she discussed what the programs had accomplished for them. She talked with her husband and friends about anxiety, and even considered going to her doctor to request some antianxiety medication.

What positive step(s) did Bernice take as she prepared to speak? What suggestions do you have for Bernice as she prepares for this experience?

Inform

An informative speech enhances an audience's knowledge and understanding by explaining what something is, how something works, or how something is done. Your goal in this type of speech is to present information clearly and accurately, while making the learning experience as enjoyable as possible for the audience.

Persuade

The persuasive speech is intended to change listeners' beliefs, attitudes, or behavior, or to encourage them to take action by advocating or gaining acceptance for a point of view. In a persuasive speech, the speaker must present evidence that supports the speech's objectives, and needs to use logic to demonstrate the connection between the evidence and what he or she hopes the listeners will believe or do.

Entertain

This type of speech provides enjoyment and amusement. Speeches that entertain may be humorous in nature and often occur on special occasions. This type of speech is light, original, and appropriate for the situation.

Rarely does a speech serve only one function. A single speech may contain aspects of all three purposes.

Some people have a great deal of anxiety about speaking before others. This anxiety can be eliminated if you prepare for the speaking experience. Your preparation includes selecting the subject, preparing your message, and preparing to deliver the speech.

SELECTING THE SUBJECT

Often the subject you talk about has been determined for you. Many times, however, you get to select the subject based on your own purpose for giving the speech. Whichever is the case, you need to review three rules of selecting the subject to help you tailor your subject to the audience and prepare the speech.

1. Consider the interests and needs of the audience.

Find out as much as possible about your audience so that you can include information that connects with their interests, concerns, expectations, and level of knowledge. This is vital. Direct your comments, examples, and stories to the audience. Be sure your audience can understand what you are talking about. A speech should make each listener feel that you are really talking to him or her. No speech should be given without relating what is being said to the listening audience.

2. Consider what you know about the subject.

As you begin, jot down what you know about the subject. Determine what you want your audience to know. Allow yourself time to research and verify your information or seek new information to present to your audience.

3. Break the topic into manageable points.

You will want to cover your selected topic in the time you have been given. Topics like "weather," "art," or "gardening" are too broad. Break the topic into manageable points. "Hurricane Conditions," "Characteristics of Monet," or "Growing Orchids" would be more reasonable.

PREPARING THE SPEECH

Good preparation begins early. Give yourself time to prepare a quality presentation.

Decide the specific purpose of your speech. Refer to the purposes of a speech

© IMAGE SOURCE

Visuals help the speaker illustrate points being made in the speech.

Smart Tip ▾ ▾ ▾

Key questions for selecting the subject:

- **Does the subject merit the audience's attention?**
- **Can you make the subject understandable to everyone in the audience?**
- **Is the subject of sufficient interest to you that you will be motivated to present it effectively?**
- **Do you have adequate knowledge of the subject?**
- **If you are not familiar with the subject, will you be able to learn enough about it to give an informed speech? Is there time for you to do the adequate research on the topic?**
- **Is the subject appropriate for the situation in which you will present it?**

▲ ▲ ▲ ▲ ▲ ▲ ▲ ▲ ▲

described at the beginning of this section. If you decide what it is you wish to tell the listener and why you wish to tell him or her, the rest of the organizing will be easier.

Use an outline to organize your speech. The speech should have three basic parts:

Introduction

The introduction must be designed to get the attention of the listener. You might want to tell a story, make a startling statement, use an example, ask a question, or share a series of interesting facts. Your introduction should also let your audience know where you are headed. This will assist your listeners in feeling grounded and secure.

Body

The body simply tells the audience what it is that you want them to know. The important thing is to organize your information into logical points so that it is easily understood. As you organize the information you want to present, ask yourself the following questions as you put in the pieces you are considering.

Will the listeners gain from hearing this?
Is this too brief or too detailed for this circumstance?
Will including this take away from my purpose?
Am I including this information for me or the listeners?
Include in the body a balance of facts, examples, and anecdotes.

Conclusion

The conclusion will give you the opportunity to give a brief summary of what you have said. The conclusion is the last chance you will have to get across your message to the audience. What do you want them to remember? You might use a personal example that shows your

audience the value of the information presented. You could tell a story or joke that will reinforce your message. You could use a bold statement that shows the audience what will happen if the information you presented is not used. Try to repeat a portion of your opening so that the listeners will have the feeling that they have heard a complete, well-planned presentation.

Now all you need to do is fill in the blanks of the outline.

Let's see what an outline might look like for a speaker who is going to talk about an employee wellness program for a company.

The best way to write your outline is on index cards. The cards can be easily held in your hand. See the boxed sample outline in Figure 5-2. Do not be concerned about the audience being aware of your cards; the cards signal to them that you are prepared. You will want to write out and memorize your opening and closing remarks. You should choose the wording of the rest of the talk as you are speaking. That way you will not need to keep your eyes glued to your notes, and your audience will feel like you are talking to them. Your index cards are simply a security device to help you keep your comments, statistics, and main points organized. Of course, you will have planned carefully, thinking through what it is you want to present. However, even the most experienced speakers can lose their train of thought—the index cards are a lifesaver in this event.

PRESENTING THE SPEECH

If your speech is well prepared, there is no reason for you to be anxious about the delivery. You have something to share that your audience wants to hear. If they did not want to hear you, they would not be present. Consider the following suggestions:

1. To reduce your anxiety, practice giving your speech before a mirror or before family or friends.

2. Learn to relax your throat. Yawn. Notice how your throat feels. When you yawn, your throat is open. Try to keep this feeling when you are speaking. If you learn to relax, you will benefit in another way. That same sense of relaxation will be conveyed to your audience, helping them to hear your message.

3. If possible, make small talk with your audience prior to your presentation.

4. Drink a small glass of warm water to open your throat before speaking. (Do not drink cold water as it can cause your muscles to constrict.)

5. Avoid consuming dairy products before speaking. They can create mucus, causing the need to clear your throat.

6. When it is your turn to speak, walk quickly and confidently to the front of the room and wait for everyone's attention before you begin. Look at the audience, smile, take a deep breath, and share your thoughts and ideas.

7. As you present your speech, keep in mind that your message is important and everyone will want to be able to hear you. Speak to the people in the back of the room, and your voice will be heard. You will lose your audience in a hurry if they cannot hear you.

8. If, as you are talking, you find yourself stuck for a word or thought, glance down at your notes, think about what you just said, and just wait for the word or thought to come. Silence is acceptable. Silence may be used to emphasize a point as well as provide you with a few seconds to regroup your thoughts. Do not fill in the time with "oh, uh . . . ." Do not apologize to the audience if you get stuck. Just go on with the speech.

9. Be aware of what is happening with your hands. The best thing to do is use your hands naturally to show conviction or honest enthusiasm. Your hands should be relaxed and make influential gestures. Don't go to great lengths to hide them—put them behind your back, put them in your pockets, or hide them below the podium. Also, avoid moving your arms wildly about or repeating the same gesture over and over.

10. Be careful not to allow your body language to interfere. Avoid meaningless and repeated gestures like scratching, fiddling with your clothing, or pulling on your ear. Do not lean against the

---

Employee Health and Wellness Program

I. Introduction—The Bergman Company instituted a health and wellness program and reduced absenteeism by 25 percent in the first year of the program. A health and wellness problem could assist our company.

II. Body
A. Why should we consider a health and wellness program?
B. Do we need a health and wellness program?
C. Who will design the program?
D. What changes to our facility will be necessary?
E. What activities and services will be included in the program?
F. What costs will be absorbed by the employee? the company?

III. Conclusion—We, too, could reduce absenteeism by instituting a health and wellness program. Review points. Tell story of how one woman at Bergman discovered a dangerous cholesterol level while in the program. Her doctor has proclaimed that the program may have saved her life.

FIGURE 5-2 *Speech outline example.*

"Make sure you have finished speaking before your audience has finished listening."

—DOROTHY SARNOFF

lectern or a wall. Stand on both feet, and do not rock from one foot to another.

11. Look at your listeners. Glance at your note cards only as you need to. Pick out four or five people in different parts of the room and speak to them, shifting your eyes from one to another.

12. As you approach the end of the speech, do not drift off or allow your voice to decline in volume. Give your last thoughts with force. Smile. Say "thank you for listening." Sit down. Do not end with a meaningless phrase, such as "I guess that's all I have to say" or "I think that's about it."

Technology at Work

Many Internet sites offer free information on how to improve your speaking skills. If you are new at the business of public speaking, you may want to visit some of these Web sites for additional support and information.

http://www.fripp.com/speaking_
newsletter.html
http://www.presentations.com
http://www.school-for-champions.com/
speaking.htm
http://www.speechtips.com

The last site listed provides special help for the nervous or stressed speaker. Check it out. It may help you.

checkpoint

1. **What is the goal of an informative speech?**

   _____

   _____

   _____

2. **What is the goal of a persuasive speech?**

   _____

   _____

   _____

3. **What are the three basic parts of a speech?**

   _____

   _____

   _____

   _____

4. What should be discussed in the body of your speech?

_____

_____

_____

_____

_____

_____

5. What should a speaker do after he or she reaches the lectern or speaker's station?

_____

_____

_____

_____

_____

6. Why are note cards important to a speaker?

_____

_____

_____

_____

_____

7. What should a speaker do with his or her hands while speaking?

_____

_____

_____

_____

_____

_____

_____

applications

1. Write an opening paragraph for a speech to persuade an audience to support a "plant a tree" program for your community.

_____

_____

_____

_____

_____

_____

_____

2. Write the closing paragraph for a speech to persuade an audience to support a "plant a tree" program for your community.

_____

_____

_____

_____

_____

_____

_____

3. Imagine that you have been asked to make a presentation about how to select a laptop computer for business and personal use. Prepare an outline for your presentation.

_____

_____

_____

_____

_____

_____

_____

_____

_____

_____

_____

4. The following topics are too broad for acceptable speech topics. Give an example of a topic from each broad area that would be an acceptable speech topic.

a. Art _____

b. Education _____

c. Meat _____

d. Computers _____

e. Housing industry _____

f. Music _____

5 Points to Remember

chapter

Review the following points to determine what you remember from the chapter.

- In order to share your knowledge and get across your message, you need to be clear. In an effort to make your message clear, you should be brief, have variety, use itemization when needed, and be positive, even when you have to say no. Good conversation requires that you (1) be positive, (2) use good voice qualities, (3) be a good listener, (4) respect the space of others, (5) achieve eye contact, (6) let others speak, and (7) avoid being shy.

- The secret of being a good conversationalist is to just be yourself. Conversational skills involve the development of your voice qualities. Several characteristics of a good voice that you will want to work on as you develop your skills as a speaker and as a conversationalist include (1) good pitch, (2) appropriate volume, (3) good inflection, (4) enunciation, and (5) pronunciation.

- How do we get involved in a conversation? A good starter may be to pay an honest compliment, such as "How interesting. I had never thought of that." Ask questions. A question is an easy way to get involved and expand a conversation. Be careful to choose one that cannot be answered with a single word. Avoid personal questions involving health, religion, politics, and money.

- You may have the opportunity to speak in front of a group. A speech is a more formal, prepared presentation of comments, ideas, and/or information. An outline should be one of the first things you develop as you research material for your speech. The purpose of a speech may be to (1) inform, (2) persuade, or (3) entertain. When giving a speech, the speaker sends a message with a specific purpose.

How did you do? Did you remember the main points you studied in the chapter?

key terms

Place the letter of the item in the definition column that matches the key word.

Key Word		Definition
___1. Pitch	a.	Pronouncing each part of a word
___2. Volume	b.	The high or low sound of your voice
___3. Inflection	c.	Voice with no change in expression
___4. Monotone	d.	Loudness or softness of the voice
___5. Enunciation	e.	Distance between you and your listener
___6. Personal space	f.	Rising and falling of your voice
___7. Pronunciation	g.	Saying a word correctly

activities and projects

1. Rewrite the following paragraph using some of the techniques studied in Chapter 5. When you finish, the document should be easier to understand. Eliminate information that is not important to Sherrill.

Sherrill, I want you to plan for a meeting of the Mental Health Board. They are scheduled to meet on Thursday, April 5, and the agenda will probably take about two hours. Be sure to have coffee, tea, and water available. Prepare folders for each of them and include an agenda, the new brochure on Project 12, the auditor's report, and anything else that Murt thinks should be included. Be sure you have decaf coffee for Board member Jurgens. He is a pain. Use the black folders with the company seal. Make sure we have enough. Put together the agenda, get the agenda items from Murt. They like to meet in a well-lighted room with extra comfy chairs. Why don't you call the Mega Hotel or the Libra Hotel or just get someplace to meet? Be sure the place you find for us to meet has equipment to show a PowerPoint presentation. I don't like PowerPoint slides because everybody just stares at the slides and drifts off and thinks about something else. Get the Board member names from Murt. Use their home addresses when you send them the information about the meeting. I don't want any staff at the meeting—just the Board. Get this done by Thursday.

2. Prepare an outline for an informative speech you are to present to a civic group in your community. The group is interested in hearing about the new plans for a Vietnam War Memorial in honor of the men and women who served there.

_____

_____

_____

_____

_____

_____

_____

_____

_____

_____

3. Name three speakers whom you find to be especially effective. What contributes to their effectiveness?

_____

_____

_____

_____

_____

_____

_____

4. You are preparing to speak on drug testing in the workplace for a company in your community. You don't know much about the company or their testing policies, and are uncertain of your audience's views. What should you know about your audience? How would you go about getting the information?

_____

_____

_____

_____

_____

_____

_____

5. Your peers often tease you about talking with your hands. You have even been known to knock things off of a table because of how you use your hands. You have a speech before a service organization next month. How are you going to avoid the overuse of gestures?

_____

_____

_____

_____

_____

_____

_____

_____

6. Nancy is scheduled to address her coworkers next week on company policy regarding acceptable use of company equipment—phones, Internet, cars, copy equipment, fax machines, and supplies. The policy is important as violation of the policy can result in the dismissal of an employee and there have been several known violations in the past month. The employees indicated they weren't aware of the acceptable use policy, thus, the reason for the speech. The following information is to be presented. Organize an outline for Nancy to use.

Violation of these policies may result in dismissal.

Too many personal phone calls are being taken and placed when workers should be on the job.

Paper, pens, pencils, ink cartridges, copy toner, and all other supplies are for company use only.

Games found on the Internet are not to be played on company equipment. No exceptions.

Essential personal telephone calls may be accepted or placed but should be kept short.

Do not check your home e-mail from your office equipment. This could spawn viruses or worms, and cause us local area network problems.

Calls to babysitters, dentists, doctors, and other essential personal communication may be necessary at times other than breaks. If so, they should be brief.

No personal products or services may be ordered online from your work computer.

No long distance calls should be placed from your work phone.

No computer software is to be loaded onto company equipment. If a program is needed, call our technology section and arrange for it to be purchased and loaded.

Too many people are checking with stockbrokers.

If a pornographic site pops up on your computer, delete it immediately and report the incident to our Webmaster.

Copy and fax machines are for business use only.

case studies for critical thinking

FEAR OF SPEAKING

Chen Li has worked for Smith and Fields Industry for several years. An opportunity came up for Chen to be promoted to a division director. Chen felt qualified for the position and was excited about the opportunity. His one concern was that he would be expected to give monthly oral reports to the upper management team. The thought of speaking to a group of 20 to 25 people terrified Chen.

1. Would you encourage Chen to turn down the promotion if he doesn't feel comfortable with accepting all of the duties of the position?

2. Who could Chen talk with regarding his concerns about speaking to groups?

3. What suggestions and support would you give Chen if he came to you for help?

Case 5.2

TOUGH CALL

Louie works in a small company that publishes newsletters for companies too small to hire staff to write, edit, proof, and send newsletters to their customers. One of the customers, Christensen, Inc., is owned by Donald Christensen. Christensen insists on writing the copy for the newsletter and does not like to have his work edited. Louie is assigned the Christensen account and is really struggling with the copy submitted. Christensen uses trite, overused phrases. He writes sentences that ramble, and nearly every paragraph begins with the word *I*.

1. Based on the human relations skills you have read about earlier in this text and the information you have just read about the importance of getting your message across, what advice would you give Louie?

2. What communicating techniques would you specifically recommend to Donald Christensen?

3. Would you print the newsletter as you think it should be? Or would you just print it the way Christensen wrote it? Explain your reasoning.

Case 5.3

CULTURAL AWARENESS

Toya Blackhawk is an American Indian. Toya has just moved into your apartment building. You noticed her on the day she moved into the building; you didn't make an effort to meet her at that time because she appeared to be busy with the movers and the family member who had come to help. Today you see her in the department adjacent to your workplace. You recognize her, and go over to introduce yourself. Toya looks at the floor during the introduction and barely acknowledges your presence. You let her know that you work in the adjacent workplace and you live in her apartment building. You suggest that she might want to ride to work with you as you have a company assigned parking space. Toya doesn't really give you an answer. You return to your office. You see her after work in the elevator. She doesn't acknowledge you. She just looks at the floor. As you exit the elevator, you ask her if she could use a lift home. She says yes; however, she barely says a word all the way home. You want to get acquainted.

1. How do you proceed to get to know Toya?

2. Does the fact that Toya is an American Indian play a role in her shyness? How can you learn more about the American Indian culture?

3. What topics might you bring up to encourage conversation?

Case 5.4

CUSTOMER SERVICE NEEDS

You have just been placed in charge of the customer service representatives for your company. You note that several of the representatives do not speak well on the telephone as they talk to customers. Some of them say *um* and *huh* several times and you have noted that a few of them slam down the telephone receiver when ending a call.

1. What training would you suggest to the training department?

2. Do you think the customer service representatives realize they need help in their speaking skills? How would you propose the training to the representatives?

Communicating to Resolve Conflict

think about it:	Melodee works in the sales department of a kitchen cabinet shop. She has learned the business from the bottom up. She began working there

just out of high school and has been employed for about seven years and has learned a great deal about the business. She keeps up on the latest in kitchen design by reading design periodicals, attending exhibits and product shows, and asking many questions of the carpenters and other cabinet workers. The designers and carpenters are pleased with her ability to help the customers. She did the primary design work on the kitchen in a very expensive show home which has brought in many new customers.

Mark, the shop owner, is very pleased with Melodee's work and doesn't want to overwork her. Thus he decides to hire an additional salesperson. The new salesperson, Michaela, has a degree in interior design and is very eager to get started. Melodee is cordial to her and is happy to help her get started in the business. Jeff, one of the carpenters, takes Michaela out to see the show home to help familiarize her with their work. Michaela is very critical of the design work in the show home kitchen. She tells Jeff the kitchen isn't functional and that the lack of color and texture in the kitchen makes it very dull. Michaela says, "The design work on this job must have been that of an amateur." Jeff doesn't know how to handle Michaela's comments. He is very loyal to Melodee but doesn't want to get in the middle of a potential conflict.

What would you do if you were Jeff? Why would Michaela, a new employee, make negative comments about the project? What potential problems do you see in the shop?

© GETTY IMAGES/PHOTODISC

chapter focus

After completing this chapter, you should be able to:

1. Define conflict.

2. Identify the types of conflict and their causes.

3. Identify ways to avoid conflict in your personal and professional life.

4. Explain the phases of conflict.

5. Identify positive and negative ways of dealing with conflict.

6. Recognize a problem; devise and implement a plan of action to solve it.

Conflict is something you often experience at a very young age. As a child you may have had conflicts or squabbles with a sibling or friend. You have read about conflicts in courtrooms; you see conflict on the nightly news; you have read about conflicts between countries; and you have probably experienced or heard about labor-management conflicts. Conflict is a communication concern as it can stop the flow of communication.

There are many definitions of conflict, with the precise meaning depending on context. In this chapter, where the context is the workplace, the term **conflict** refers to a difference of opinions caused by opposing attitudes, behaviors, ideas, needs, wants, or goals. The word *conflict* is usually associated with negative thoughts, unpleasant situations, or unpleasant memories.

Workplace conflicts can erupt abruptly and cause delays in productivity as well as other losses in work goals.

© GETTY IMAGES/PHOTODISC

Everyone has his or her own likes and dislikes, ideas, habits, flaws, needs, and personality. Often, these personal differences can lead to conflict. While it is certain that there will be conflict in your life, the good news is that there are many ways to cope with conflict, avoid conflict, and sometimes change a conflict to a positive experience. Conflict forces choice, and making a choice can help you test the merits of the specific attitudes, behaviors, needs, or goals that are in conflict.

TYPES OF CONFLICT

You will be better able to deal with conflict if you understand the types of conflict, recognize the basic causes, and consider the possible resolution to the conflict.

Simple Conflict

Simple conflicts are usually over a fact, such as these: What was the net profit for the company last year? What is the longest landing strip in the United States? Where is the Nile River? What day did you call me about the Everett contract?

A conflict over facts can easily be resolved by consulting a source of information that is considered "expert" on the part of those involved in the conflict. Simple conflicts are seldom serious as the resolution is simple. When you find yourself in conflict over a fact, end the conflict by checking a source immediately. If you are right, do not gloat. If you are wrong, simply say, "Well, you were right. That's a fact I won't forget." Do not allow a simple conflict to harm a personal or professional relationship or the flow of communication.

Ego Conflict

Ego is your feeling of self-worth. Conflicts involving egos are probably the most damaging to relationships. This is because, in an **ego conflict**, the individuals view "winning" or "losing" the conflict as a measure of their expertise and personal worth.

Ego conflict escalates when one or both parties introduce personal or judgmental statements. When conflict is tied to your personal worth, the conflict becomes an ego conflict. Once your ego becomes involved in conflict, your ability to behave in a rational manner is jeopardized. Ego conflict is difficult to resolve without bringing in emotions. You must be careful to separate the content of a conflict from your potential ego involvement.

False Conflict

There are situations when you think a conflict exists, but in reality it does not. This type of conflict is called a **false conflict**. For example, suppose you are a supervisor and one of your staff has not appeared for work on Monday morning. You are concerned and angry because you were counting on this person to help you with a special project. A few minutes later you see the person walk into her office with a stack of papers. The employee says, "I came to work a few minutes early this morning so I could use the quality copy machine on the fourth floor. I thought that would give us a head start on the day." This situation was an example of a false conflict.

The first thing to do when you feel a conflict coming into place is to determine whether the conflict is real. Do not jump to conclusions. The energy devoted to getting upset over a false conflict is wasted. In the example above, what do you think might have happened if the supervisor spoke first?

Values and Beliefs Conflict

Values and beliefs conflicts arise when people differ in their thoughts about life in general (or an aspect of life), and these differences are brought into focus on a

on the job

Julio and Nicole were discussing the Pulitzer-prize winners in the field of music in the 1980s. Julio said that John Harbison won the award in 1987. Nicole insisted that Harbison won the honor in 1983 for his work, "The Flight Into Egypt." The discussion became heated when Julio mentioned that he was a music major in college and had studied the prize winners in a music appreciation class. He said he knew what he was talking about. Nicole replied, "Are you saying that I don't know what I am talking about because I don't have a college degree?" Julio said, "I do have an advantage over you." The conversation escalated to name-calling and severely damaged the relationship between Julio and Nicole. Communication came to an end in their personal and professional relationship.

Was there a point in this discussion where it could have been reduced to a simple conflict? How can communication be restored between Julio and Nicole?

particular issue. You have determined what is important to you.

The values or beliefs you have about certain aspects of life may not be the same as those of others. For example, maybe you feel that society should take care of people who are in need in the form of a welfare system. A coworker believes that everyone is responsible to take care of himself or herself. If you and your coworker are to get along, you should probably talk about topics that do not include welfare, unemployment compensation, or other entitlement programs. Do not risk unnecessary conflict with someone who has different values or beliefs from yours.

Can values and beliefs conflicts be resolved? Perhaps over a long period of time they can. Our values may change some

"Difficulties are meant to rouse, not discourage. The human spirit is to grow strong by conflict."

—WILLIAM ELLERY CHANNING

on the job

Betty and Audrey work in the same government office. They report to the same supervisor. They are not only coworkers but also good friends outside of the office. Audrey notices that Betty has been in and out of the supervisor's office several times during the morning. At lunchtime, Audrey hears through the grapevine that Betty will be representing the office at a meeting in Chicago next month. Audrey is upset and furious. She has decided that Betty has been spending extra time with the supervisor, Mary Alice, persuading Mary Alice to send her to Chicago. Audrey had hoped to attend the Chicago meeting. Audrey was thinking, "Betty hasn't said a word to me about going. She will probably get promoted over me because of her national meeting connections. I hope she is satisfied . . . and I thought we were friends." Audrey ignores Betty the remainder of the day. Audrey leaves work early and doesn't say good-bye to Betty. Betty is confused. The next day Betty ignores Audrey because she is confused by her behavior. A conflict between coworkers and friends has begun. Mary Alice calls Audrey into her office shortly before lunch and asks if she would be willing to attend the upcoming meeting in Chicago. Audrey is elated. She says, "I heard that you were sending Betty." Mary Alice responds, "I'm sending you both. Sorry I was so busy yesterday that I didn't get to talk with you about the trip. Are you willing to attend?"

What was the perceived conflict? Who jumped to conclusions? What actions on Audrey's part would have solved a day of conflict and confusion? How should Audrey approach Betty and explain her behavior for the past day?

"If you want to make peace with your enemy, you have to work with your enemy. Then he [sic] becomes your partner."

—NELSON MANDELA

from one period of life to another, but they do not change quickly. It is not bad for people with differences in values to discuss those thoughts, provided that each person recognizes that he or she is not likely to change the other person. It is often said, "You can change no one but yourself." Recognize that you are not likely to change the values or beliefs of others. Perhaps you can agree to disagree. Learn to respect the values and beliefs of others.

HOW TO AVOID CONFLICTS

There are several ways to avoid conflicts in your personal and professional life. The following practices may help you steer clear of conflict.

1. Discuss problems before they elevate to a conflict. Whenever you see a conflict on the horizon, begin to discuss and search for solutions before the problem elevates to the status of a conflict.

2. Whenever you find it necessary to express anger, use "I-messages." You use the word "I" rather than "you."

   "You make me so angry when you take supplies without asking."

   A statement like the above sends a blaming message and puts the other person on the defensive. When you say "I," not "you," the conversation is about your feelings, not the other person's perceived errors or failures.

   "I feel angry when you borrow my supplies without asking, because I don't realize when we are low on needed items."

   The above statement gives a reason for your feelings that helps the other person understand your point of view and provides an opportunity for you to ask for what you want and need, which gives the other person a chance to do the right thing. "I" messages can help avoid conflict.

3. Stop and think before you act or react. Thomas Jefferson suggested that one should count to ten when angry, and count to one hundred when very angry before you speak. This is great advice. Try to think ahead and predict the consequences of your words or actions. Slow down and ask yourself questions such as: Is my comment going to result in a conflict? Will my words result in hurting someone else? Will my words put me in a risky situation?

4. Find ways to compose and relax yourself when you're feeling angry or frustrated about a possible conflict. Give yourself some time to work through your own feelings. Try some of these simple techniques: take a walk; listen to peaceful music; read a book or some poetry; do some deep breathing exercises (take a deep breath in through your nose and hold it while you count to five, breathe out slowly through your mouth); or get into a relaxed position and clear your mind by thinking of an enjoyable experience. After these activities, you should be relaxed enough to move forward in a positive manner.

Decide whether the following are (S) simple conflict, (E) ego conflict, (VB) values and beliefs conflict, or (F) false conflict.

_____1. Rachel wants to live with Robert, but Robert wants the two of them to get married.

_____2. Adienne insists that Arbor Day is in April. Liz says it is in June.

_____3. John believes that since he is a college professor of accounting, Jacob should not dispute his knowledge of taxes.

_____4. Lung called his wife to say that he is bringing his boss home for dinner. His wife replied, "No, you're not! The house is a mess."

_____5. Phyllis says, "Herb, pick up your clothes! I'm not your maid!" Herb replies, "I thought we agreed that it's your job to take care of the house; I take care of the car and the yard."

_____6. Malcolm believes in the hereafter. Marcia does not.

_____7. "Based on my experience with computers, I know that you are wrong."

_____8. "Where are you going?" asks the wife. "Out," says the husband. She thinks he is going out to sneak a cigarette, but he is actually going out to get her birthday gift.

_____9. Juan says that Yellowstone Park is in Wyoming. Ramon insists it is in Colorado.

___10. Henry says, "You were hired as my assistant." Joel replies, "I have a college degree and I didn't earn it just to make coffee for you."

check*point*

1. **What is the definition of conflict?**

   _____

   _____

   _____

   _____

2. **What are the four types of conflict?**

   _____

   _____

   _____

   _____

3. **What are four ways of avoiding conflict?**

   _____

   _____

   _____

   _____

4. **What is the best way to resolve simple conflict?**

   _____

   _____

   _____

   _____

5. **What is ego?**

   _____

   _____

   _____

   _____

6. **Why is false conflict so dangerous?**

   _____

   _____

   _____

   _____

applications

1. Describe an ego conflict or a values or beliefs conflict in which you or someone you know has been involved. What were the circumstances? How did you feel? Was the conflict ever solved? How?

_____

_____

_____

_____

_____

_____

2. List three conflicts of which you are aware from your personal or work life, or that you read about in the news. Describe each conflict and determine if it is simple, false, values and beliefs, or ego conflict. (There may be some combinations.)

_____

_____

_____

_____

_____

_____

_____

3. List three resources that you could check to solve a simple conflict over who pitched the winning game of the World Series in 2001.

_____

_____

_____

_____

4. Identify whether the following conflicts are examples of simple conflict, ego conflict, values and beliefs conflict, or a false conflict.

_____ Emma says that the quote, "Silence is a true friend who never betrays" was penned by Shakespeare. Niki says, "You're wrong. The quote comes from Confucius."

_____ Hanh says, "Why don't you answer that phone?" Her coworker, JoAnne, says, "Why don't you? If you've got time to tell others what to do, you have time to answer the phone."

_____ Jean regards herself as an artist, and when Judy challenges her knowledge of Monet, a conflict follows.

_____ Sue is a vegetarian. James, her coworker, laughs at her and tells her that she is going to be sick because her body needs protein from meat. Sue disagrees and is angry.

5. List ways that you can relax when you are restless or confused because a conflict may be pending.

_____

_____

_____

_____

_____

_____

Simple, ego, false, and values and beliefs conflicts can occur in the workplace. Conflicts among coworkers are very destructive because they can destroy the morale of the people involved, divert energy from the important tasks that need to be performed, reduce the cooperative spirit of the work team, increase stress, and harm positive communication. It is important to understand the phases of conflict, so that conflict can be prevented or, once started, can be successfully resolved. Regardless of the cause or kind, conflicts in the workplace typically pass through the following four phases.

PHASE I—TAKING SIDES

A conflict in the workplace may begin with two individuals; however, it does not take long for others to learn about the situation. The first step of a conflict is taking sides.

It seems to be a natural phenomenon for others to take the side of one of the individuals involved in the conflict. Taking sides is harmful, as it can split the workforce, the family, or a friendship. Taking sides may also destroy teamwork, destroy productivity, and cause a great deal of tension and stress.

PHASE II—KEEPING SCORE

The second phase of conflict is keeping score. The teams that have now developed often keep track of what the other team "does to them." (See Figure 6-1) During this phase, each side tries to prove the other side is unreasonable.

The "score keeping" may not even be related to the original conflict. If you know of an office or a family that has a long record of keeping score, chances are they do not even remember the original source of the conflict.

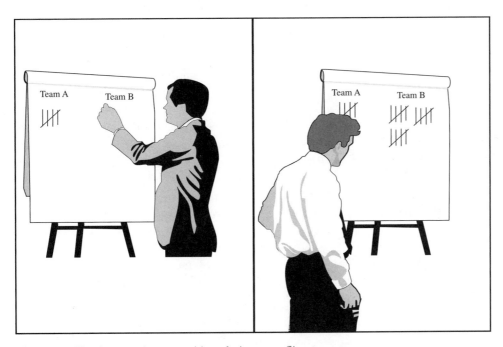

FIGURE 6-1 *Keeping score is not a positive solution to conflict.*

PHASE III—SHOWDOWN

The most dangerous and volatile phase is the showdown. The people involved in the original conflict, or the teams that have developed, will decide that they "have had it" or they "just can't take it anymore." They then decide to confront the other person or team. This confrontation can be a constructive activity involving talking over the situation and coming to a compromise or an agreement.

However, not all showdowns are constructive. A showdown can be a destructive experience if the people threaten each other physically or verbally, or use some other negative techniques for handling conflict. This destructive type of showdown should *always* be avoided.

PHASE IV—ADJUSTMENT

After the showdown, one or both sides may decide to make some changes in their behavior. The adjustments that people make determine how well the conflict is settled. For example, if only one side makes the adjustments, the conflict may start all over again. The adjustment can also be made so that the conflict is settled in a constructive manner. Opening up and discussing issues will usually lead to a satisfactory adjustment that is agreeable to both sides. A positive result from a conflict can be that it helps build a spirit of teamwork among people as they share the conflict, celebrate its settlement, and learn more about each other in the process. The adjustment process is a good time to build open and positive communication in the workplace.

This example illustrates positive showdown and adjustment phases.

Ted and Ben have been in conflict for several weeks over the fact that Ted refused to help Ben with a special work-related project on a Saturday morning. Ted belongs to a church that worships on Saturday. Ted considers Saturday a day for worship, rest, and family. Ben was aware of Ted's religious practices, but he could not understand why Ted would not make an exception and work on a Saturday morning to complete the project they needed to present on Monday. The tension between Ted and Ben was building, and it was affecting their ability to work together. Finally Ted said, "Ben, we've got to talk about the animosity that is building between us." Ben replied, "Yes, I agree." They talked through their lunch hour about the incident that had caused the conflict. The value conflict was settled after Ben explained that he felt you could worship any day and Ted explained how important Saturday was to him, his church, and his family. Ted promised to respect Ben's traditions. Ben vowed to respect Ted's feelings. Both Ted and Ben decided that

on the job

Jerry and Sandra had worked together for several months. They had a good working relationship. Sandra shared with Jerry that she was having very severe headaches. Jerry told her that he was a firm believer in the use of herbs and natural cures for headaches. He offered to go on his lunch hour to the health food store and pick up a helpful powder. Sandra laughed and said, "Get real. The use of herbs and that other junk is a joke." Jerry was offended by her remark and walked away from her. He told others in the work area about their conflict and soon the workers were talking about the conflict. Sandra was also telling others and laughing about Jerry's belief in alternative medicine. Jerry and Sandra were both uncomfortable about the conflict that had occurred and their relationship became strained.

How should Jerry and Sandra proceed? What is their phase of conflict? What recommendations would you suggest for resolving this conflict? What impact will this conflict have on the workplace?

working late one or two weeknights would get the work done without creating conflicts for either of them. The constructive conversation was a positive showdown and a successful adjustment.

What other solutions might have been possible to the above scenario?

Technology
at Work

The complete understanding of conflict and conflict adjustment requires additional study. If this is a special area of interest for you, you may want to seek additional information on the following Web sites.

http://www.geocities.com/Athens/8945
http://www.conflictresolver.com
http://www.conflict-resolution.net

© DIGITAL VISION

Workers who avoid conflict as they interact will experience a more pleasant relationship on the job.

check✓point

1. **What are the typical phases of conflict?**

   _____

   _____

   _____

2. **Why is taking sides in a conflict in the workplace a negative step?**

   _____

   _____

   _____

3. **Is the "score keeping" in Phase II always related to the original conflict?**

   _____

   _____

   _____

applications

1. Indicate whether the following statements about conflict are true or false. Place a "T" to indicate a statement is true. Write "F" to indicate that a statement is false. Check your answers by referring to the previous section in the chapter.

a. _____ The showdown phase of conflict means that the sides have resorted to physical violence.

b. _____ The last phase of handling conflict is adjustment.

c. _____ All showdowns are constructive.

d. _____ Confrontation can be a constructive activity.

e. _____ Conflict usually strengthens the team building process.

2. Which of the four phases of conflict is the most volatile? Describe why this phase has the potential to be explosive, and what might be done to prevent the explosion.

_____

_____

_____

_____

_____

_____

3. In your own words, react to this statement: Conflict is only destructive to a relationship if the parties involved engage in personal attacks and are unwilling to negotiate.

_____

_____

_____

_____

_____

_____

4. Why do people usually take sides in a conflict?

_____

_____

_____

_____

_____

_____

_____

The adjustment phase of conflict needs further exploration. Phase IV might lead you to believe that positive or acceptable adjustment always follows a showdown. Unfortunately, this is not true.

NEGATIVE CONFLICT ADJUSTMENT

There are three negative ways to handle conflict; they are withdrawal, delay, and aggression. As you read the scenarios within the text of this section, think about why these are not constructive methods of dealing with conflict.

Withdrawal

A common way of handling conflict is to avoid it or withdraw from it. You choose to remove yourself physically or psychologically from the situation.

This is typically done by avoiding the person, refusing to think or talk about the conflict, changing the subject when the conflict is brought up, or maybe even doing something as drastic as quitting a job. Withdrawal can be very frustrating to those involved in the conflict in the workplace.

You may find it very difficult to focus on your work when you spend most of your time thinking about avoiding a situation or an encounter. The conflict needs to be faced, and a suitable solution or adjustment needs to be determined. Read the following example, which further illustrates what it means to withdraw from conflict.

Martha told Carol that she was disappointed with her because she refused to be the department representative for the United Way charity drive. Carol respects her superior, Martha, but Carol

"The greatest conflicts are not between two people but between one person and himself." [sic]

—GARTH BROOKS

has served as the department representative for several years and feels that it is someone else's turn to do this job. Martha, however, told Carol it was necessary for everyone to support this community effort and continued on about civic responsibility, etc. Carol now avoids Martha. If Carol sees Martha coming toward her, she gets involved in a phone conversation or moves to another area of the department. If Carol arrives at the restroom at the same time as Martha, she uses the restroom on another floor. Carol has started parking across the street so that she does not see Martha in the parking lot before or after work. Carol has rearranged her schedule over a conflict that needs to be discussed and resolved.

Delay

Another way to handle conflict is to delay resolution. You may settle a small part of the conflict, but not handle the critical issues. The excuse you use is that you are "cooling off" the situation temporarily. This method is not entirely negative. Sometimes postponing a discussion over a conflict gives a new perspective and allows people to calm down, think, and reach a rational compromise, adjustment, or solution.

The following situation demonstrates what delaying a solution means.

Randall and Goro work in the pressroom of a major newspaper and know the importance of getting the paper out to the delivery people. On Thursday evening, Goro is especially eager to leave the pressroom to see his son play football. A breakdown in the equipment occurs about 3:30 p.m. and will take a couple of hours to repair. Everyone will have to work late to get the papers out for delivery on time. Goro says, "I'm tired and have worked my share of the overtime. I'm going to leave at 5." Randall replies, "We need you. You have to stick it out and help." Some unkind remarks fly back and forth between Randall and Goro. The supervisor, Mac, steps in and offers to help Randall, and Goro leaves at 5. The conflict was temporarily settled but the initial conflict is still in need of attention.

Aggression

The poorest way to handle a conflict is through aggression. Through aggression, you attempt to force another to accept your ideas. **Aggression** is an emotional response to conflict. Verbal aggression can be emotionally damaging to those involved in the conflict, as well as those in the area where the conflict takes place. Physical aggression is the absolute worst way to handle a conflict. It can cause injury and will not bring about a suitable adjustment to the conflict, and, if extreme, can result in job loss and/or legal action.

POSITIVE CONFLICT RESOLUTION

The negative conflict adjustments described above will not lead to resolving conflict. The trick to handling conflict is to put the emotional energy generated by the conflict toward a constructive solution. If you are involved in a conflict, or if you are attempting to mediate a solution, you must first establish the correct frame of mind.

Conflicts can be resolved only when both parties
1. agree to cooperate,
2. believe the problem has a solution,
3. recognize that a difference of opinion is not a personal attack,
4. respect the opinions of all involved, and
5. make an effort to be patient.

Once these attitudes are in place, a step-by-step resolution to the conflict can be attempted.

The basic problem-solving technique is often referred to as the scientific

© GETTY IMAGES/PHOTODISC

Verbal aggression can be emotionally damaging to those involved in the conflict as well as to those in the vicinity of the conflict.

on the job

Tim and Nathan work in a chemical plant. Proper care of the chemicals is a constant safety issue. Tim asks Nathan if he has secured some of the chemicals as they are about to leave for the day. Nathan responds, "I can't remember. Why don't you check them for me? I want to call my girlfriend." Tim responds, "It's your job! Why don't you check them yourself?" Nathan jumps up and says, "Get off my back!" Nathan shoves Tim. Tim takes a swing at Nathan. This act of aggression causes the chemicals not to be checked and creates a conflict that will need to be resolved between Tim and Nathan if they are to continue to work together.

What are the consequences of this conflict? Do you have some suggestions for Tim and Nathan on how this conflict might be resolved?

method, because it has been used successfully in solving scientific problems. The **problem-solving technique** leads to the solution of a conflict by answering five key questions.

Let's go through each of the steps listed in Figure 6-2.

What is the Conflict?

This sounds like a simple question, but as you try to put into words exactly what the conflict is, you will realize that this might take some work. It has been said that a conflict well stated is half solved. As you put the pieces of the conflict together, you may begin to find some solutions. You may know something is wrong—you are in conflict with another person—but you cannot quite describe what the conflict is. As you attempt to state the conflict, take care (1) to be nonjudgmental; (2) to be objective; and (3) to consider the feelings of all involved. Just state the conflict in specific terms.

The following example will help lead you through the appropriate steps of problem solving.

Charles and Amelia are engaged in a discussion. Amelia says, "Let's buy a new house." Charles agrees, "Yes, I think the market is right." Amelia replies, "I've always wanted a ranch-style house. Let's call the real estate agent and request that a search be conducted for a ranch-style house." Charles responds in a loud, harsh voice, "What do you mean a ranch-style house? You know I want a town house where someone else does the yard work and snow removal."

> "It is through cooperation, rather than conflict, that your greatest successes will be derived."
>
> —RALPH CHARELL

What is the conflict? Charles and Amelia do not agree on the type of house they want to buy.

You will notice in this statement that **no** attempt at a solution is made. There is no right or wrong in the statement of the problem.

What are the Facts?

The answer to "What are the facts?" is important to write down. Take note: You are writing down facts, not opinions or value judgments. The facts listed must relate specifically to the problem. Drop any "oughts" or "shoulds." There are several facts in the Charles and Amelia scenario.

1. They agree it is time to buy a house.
2. Amelia wants a ranch-style house.
3. Charles wants a town house.
4. Charles and Amelia need to discuss what they want in a house.

What is the Overall Objective?

This answer can be difficult, but it does have to be considered. Perhaps you have never really thought about the main objective involved in a conflict. Again, it helps to write down exactly what the overall objective is going to be. Charles and Amelia's objective is not difficult to see. The overall objective is to find a home that is pleasing to both of them.

What are Some Possible Solutions?

To answer this question, write down as many solutions to the conflict as you can think of. One method of clearing the way for a good solution is to write down the extreme solutions first. Charles and Amelia's extremes might be as ridiculous as buying two houses or getting a divorce so each one can live in the house he or she likes best. After the ridiculous and extreme solutions are written, it is time to devote your attention to some realistic and solid possibilities.

Five-Step Problem Solving

1. What is the conflict?
2. What are the facts?
3. What is the overall objective?
4. What are some possible solutions?
5. What is the best solution?

FIGURE 6-2 *Five-step problem solving.*

The possibilities might include:

1. Look for a ranch-style house in a town house subdivision.
2. Look at houses that are located in a neighborhood where there is an association that cares for the lawn and garden areas.
3. Design their own house with features they both like.
4. Stay in their present house.

What is the Best Solution?

The last question is answered by choosing the best solution of the possibilities that have been listed, and also by considering all of the facts listed in response to question two. The best solution must improve the situation as it stands and must help, not hinder, you in reaching your overall objective. What would you say is the best solution for Charles and Amelia? It could be 1, 2, 3, 4, or a combination of a couple of the solutions.

With the five-step problem-solving technique, you are equipped to solve the conflicts that come up in your line of work. It can also serve you well in your personal life. One reason for the success of the five-step method is the mental attitude you must adopt if you are to follow the first three steps. You cannot answer the first three questions (What is the conflict? What are the facts? and What is the overall objective?) until you become detached emotionally from the situation. When you can shelve your emotions temporarily and put your mature self in charge, you may find

that the correct solution to a conflict appears to you even before you get to step four. The secret of quality problem solving is to use mental judgment rather than the emotional pitfalls of "getting even" or "showing who is in charge."

focus on ethics

Most of the employees of an upscale retail store appear to get along well, but two seem to be having problems. One evening, as another employee, Helen, is leaving the store, these two are caught up in a physical struggle in an area where customers might observe them. Helen is concerned, but leaves without saying anything. The next morning, she confronts one of the two coworkers about what she witnessed. He tells her to mind her own business. Helen is worried about his behavior and attitude. The other coworker comes to work with a very bruised eye and says he walked into a door. Helen is anxious about what she should do.

Should Helen speak further with the involved coworkers? Should she talk with her supervisor? Why or why not?

Smart Tip ▾ ▾ ▾

Remember these points as you think about conflict.

- **Conflict is destructive when the resolution of the conflict ends with a winner and a loser.**
- **Conflict motivates behaviors, and when it forces us to do things that we don't want to do, it can be destructive.**

- **Conflict can keep us from doing our work or feeling good about ourselves and others.**
- **Conflict can be destructive in proportion to the importance of the goals to the individual.**
- **Conflict can be destructive if the individuals involved act aggressively, or if they accuse each other of causing the problem.**

▲ ▲ ▲ ▲ ▲ ▲ ▲ ▲ ▲ ▲ ▲ ▲ ▲ ▲ ▲ ▲ ▲

check✓point

1. **What are the five attitudes that must be in place if a conflict resolution is to be attempted?**

   _____

   _____

   _____

   _____

   _____

2. **What are the five steps of problem solving?**

   _____

   _____

   _____

   _____

   _____

3. **What must you take care to do as you attempt to state the conflict?**

   _____

   _____

   _____

   _____

   _____

applications

1. Imagine that you are walking down the main street of your community. You see Abby, one of your coworkers, coming the other way. You and Abby have not been getting along. Abby feels that you try to do her job. You feel that you have to do Abby's job to keep the department running. You think Abby is unmotivated and lacks the skills necessary to do her work. As Abby approaches, you cross the street to avoid meeting her. Close your eyes and envision the above scene. Answer the following questions:

a. What kind of reaction to conflict did you use in the above situation?

_____

_____

_____

b. Are you pleased with the reaction? Why or why not?

_____

_____

_____

c. How did you feel about your reaction? What emotions did you experience?

_____

_____

_____

_____

d. Did your action take a step toward solving the problem between you and Abby? Why or why not? If you had a second chance, would you have crossed the street? If you *don't* cross the street and meet Abby, what might you say to Abby?

_____

_____

_____

_____

2. Find an article that describes a conflict between two or more persons. It could be a labor dispute, a conflict between neighbors, a disagreement among city or state officials, a conflict between countries, or any other conflict that you can find.

Clip the article and attach it to a worksheet on which you list the following questions. Use your own ideas about what is the most beneficial solution. Base your solution on facts and good judgment. Try to keep your emotions out of your decision.

a. What is the conflict?

_____

_____

_____

_____

b. What are the facts?

_____

_____

_____

_____

c. What would be the desirable outcome?

_____

_____

_____

_____

d. What are some possible solutions to the conflict?

_____

_____

_____

_____

e. Could this conflict have been avoided? How? Why?

_____

_____

_____

_____

3. What is aggression and why is it the poorest way to try to solve a problem?

_____

_____

_____

_____

6 Points to Remember

Review the following points to determine what you remember from the chapter.

- Conflict, in the workplace, refers to a difference of opinions caused by opposing attitudes, behaviors, ideas, needs, wants, or goals. Conflict may occur when there is a simple disagreement over a fact; when your ego, values, and beliefs are questioned; or when a situation arises that you only perceive as a conflict.

- There are four specific types of conflict: (1) simple conflict (over a fact); (2) ego conflict (tied to your personal worth); (3) false conflict (when you think a conflict exists, and it really does not); and (4) values and beliefs conflict (when people have different thoughts about life in general).

- Avoid conflict whenever possible. Here are four easy steps that will help you: (1) discuss problems before they elevate to a conflict; (2) use "I messages" to express anger; (3) stop and think before you act or react; and (4) find ways to compose and relax yourself when feeling angry or frustrated about a possible conflict.

- Conflicts in the workplace typically go through four phases: (1) taking sides (people take one side or the other of the conflict and agree with that person); (2) keeping score (keeping track of what each side does to the other); (3) showdown (people decide to confront the other side because they have had it); and (4) adjustment (both sides may make changes to settle the conflict).

- Approaches to conflict can be negative or positive. Three negative ways to handle conflict involve withdrawal (avoid it), delay (postpone it), and aggression (attempt to force another to accept your ideas). The positive approach of following the problem-solving technique also referred to as the scientific method can lead to the solution of a conflict.

- The five steps of the problem-solving technique, which leads to the settling of a conflict, require answers to five questions: (1) What is the conflict? (2) What are the facts? (3) What is the overall objective? (4) What are some possible solutions? and (5) What is the best solution? This is the best way to solve a problem and implement a plan of action for a resolution.

How did you do? Did you remember the main points you studied in the chapter?

key terms

Place the letter of the item in the definition column that matches the key word.

Key Word	Definition
___1. Conflict	a. The solution of a conflict by answering five key questions
___2. Simple conflict	b. Refers to a difference of opinions caused by opposing attitudes, behaviors, ideas, needs, wants, or goals
___3. Ego	c. Emotional response to a conflict
___4. Ego conflict	d. You think a conflict exists, but in reality it does not
___5. False conflict	e. Your feeling of self-worth
___6. Values and beliefs conflict	f. Conflict over a fact
___7. Aggression	g. The individuals view "winning" or losing" the conflict as a measure of their expertise and personal worth
___8. Problem-solving technique	h. Arise when people differ in their thoughts about life in general, and these differences are brought into focus on a particular issue

activities and projects

1. Read this discussion. (You may want to role-play it with a friend to get the full impact of the situation.) Martin is the supervisor.

Darren: The air I'm forced to breathe in this place is disgusting. I have a sinus headache.

Martin: What do the environmental conditions have to do with your headache?

Darren: This building wasn't designed to have the windows sealed and temporary walls blocking air flow. I think I'll stop and see my doctor on the way home. Maybe I should also stop and see a lawyer. I wonder if it's legal to require people to work in an environment that is impure and unclean.

Martin: You complain too much. You probably have a sinus infection, and that's causing the head problems.

Darren: If that's the cause, I must have a chronic sinus condition.

Martin: Don't show that kind of an attitude with me.

Darren: I'm not showing attitude. I just want you to do something about the air in this place so that I can breathe.

Martin: (walking off) Please get some work done.

a. What is the conflict?

_____

_____

_____

_____

b. What are the known facts?

_____

_____

_____

_____

c. What stage is this conflict in? How can you tell?

_____

_____

_____

_____

d. What additional conflicts may result after this discussion?

_____

_____

_____

_____

e. What are some possible solutions?

_____

_____

_____

_____

f. What is the best solution? (Based on the facts.)

_____

_____

_____

_____

2. Finish the script started in Item 1 on a separate sheet of paper. The script should develop an agreeable adjustment resulting from good problem solving. Use the space below to draft a few ideas.

_____

_____

_____

_____

_____

_____

_____

_____

_____

_____

_____

3. Find a problem in your environment. (Your community may be looking at water issues, land restrictions, smoking bans, cell phone bans or speed zones, as examples.) Look at the sides of the controversy and determine which stage of the conflict the problem is in currently. Develop a plan for the resolution of the conflict.

case studies for critical thinking

PAT AND LYNNE AT ODDS

Lynne and Pat have worked together for several years. They have a very good personal relationship outside the workplace. They are often assigned to work on projects as a team. This week has been particularly stressful—several deadlines are approaching, two members of the support staff are out on medical leave, their work area is in chaos because it is being renovated, and Pat's daughter has been experiencing serious problems at school.

Pat and Lynne both receive a short memo from their supervisor, Mr. Andrew, that says: "Pat and Lynne, research this competitor's product and send me a product comparison report by noon on Monday. A product sheet on the competitor's item is attached." Pat is away from the office trying to get things smoothed over at her daughter's school. So Lynne drops her other projects and does some Web site research and makes a few calls in order to get started on Mr. Andrew's request. Pat stops in Lynne's office upon her return and brings the memo from Mr. Andrew with her. Pat immediately spots the competitor's Web site on Lynne's computer screen. And she says in a louder than normal voice, "What are you doing? My name was first on the note from Mr. Andrew, and therefore, I am the lead person on this assignment. Why did you start without direction from me? Are you trying to jump one ahead of me and get extra points with Andrew?" Lynne is a bit taken aback by Pat's comments and tone of voice. Lynne sharply replies, "Well, you were out and somebody needed to get started on this. This is Friday and he wants it on Monday." Pat says, "Well, you just don't worry about it. I'll get this done and ready for him on Monday. I won't need your help." She walks out of the office in a huff.

1. What type of conflict(s) have developed in this scenario?

_____

_____

_____

2. Should Lynne have started on the project without consulting Pat?

_____

_____

_____

3. Were Pat's opening remarks to Lynne appropriate? Why or why not?

_____

_____

_____

4. How might this conflict have been avoided?

_____

_____

_____

5. What type of work atmosphere will most likely be present in this office on Monday?

_____

_____

_____

6. How can this conflict be resolved?

_____

_____

_____

7. What will happen if the conflict isn't resolved?

_____

_____

_____

Case 6.2

TWO TALENTS

Tara is an assistant in the art department of a major publishing company. Dean is an assistant in the editing department. Both employees are well known for quality work and are highly praised by their supervisors. Dean takes some copy to Tara and asks her to fit the copy into the caption of an illustration she has designed. Tara says, "You expect me to destroy the message of this illustration with a trite caption like the one you've written?" Dean retorts, "The caption supplements the meaning of the illustration. By the way, it isn't a trite line. Not everyone sees what you see in an illustration." Dean is quite upset by Tara's attitude. Tara is annoyed with Dean's comments. They must continue to work together, but after this confrontation, adjustments will need to be made.

1. What type of conflict is this?

_____

_____

_____

2. What is the conflict?

_____

_____

_____

3. Is this the type of conflict that may lead quickly to the phase of taking sides? Why?

_____

_____

_____

4. Why would the negative technique of withdrawal not be an option in this situation?

_____

_____

_____

5. What are the facts?

_____

_____

_____

6. What is the major overall objective?

_____

_____

_____

7. What are some possible solutions?

_____

_____

_____

8. What do you think is the best solution?

_____

_____

_____

Case 6.3

NOT ALWAYS FUNNY

Frank Lloyd has worked at Hy-Volume Electric for many years. Over time, Frank has been crowned the prankster of the company. Frank jokes with everyone, from the plant manager on down the ladder. Most people enjoy his humor and find his antics day brighteners. Kim Le has been with Hy-Volume for only a few months and, of course, has met Frank. Frank tells Kim Le a joke that includes racial slurs. She is proud of her cultural heritage and feels that no joke is funny that puts down a group of people. Kim Le said, "Frank, in the future I'd prefer that you stay away from me and keep your jokes to yourself. Please leave me alone." Frank is hurt by her remark because it is important to him to be liked by everyone. He doesn't understand what he did to offend her. He attempts to apologize but Kim Le walks away. The next morning Frank and Kim Le are assigned to work together on a project.

1. What is the conflict? What type of conflict is it?

_____

_____

_____

2. Is there more than one conflict in this case?

_____

_____

_____

3. What impact might the conflict have on the workplace?

_____

_____

_____

4. Was Kim Le within her rights to say what she did to Frank? Why or why not?

_____

_____

_____

5. How can Kim Le begin to adjust to the new work situation?

_____

_____

_____

6. How can Frank begin to adjust to the new work situation?

_____

_____

_____

7. What is the best solution to this problem?

_____

_____

_____

Working with Others

think about it: Oki was graduated with honors from a health occupations program in a well-respected community college. Her excellent grades and clinical experiences helped her get a good job in a large metropolitan hospital. During her first weeks on the job, Oki received compliments from her supervisor on her clinical skills and her attention to detail. One of the staff physicians told her that she had a great future in the medical field. At the end of her new employee probationary period, her supervisor called her in for an evaluation conference and informed her she was going to remain on probation. Her supervisor told her that her coworkers found her unpleasant and difficult to work with. According to the floor nurses, she had been rude and unpleasant with patients and other medical professionals. The probationary period was extended for six months with no pay increase. Oki was devastated. She thought her work was going very well. Oki snapped at the supervisor and firmly stated, "I do quality work. I am not here to be cheerful!" Oki stormed out of the office, slammed the door, and muttered something about being unfairly judged.

What would you say to Oki if she were your friend and she shared the content of the conversation with the supervisor? Should Oki have a further discussion with her supervisor? What should she say to her supervisor? What would you suggest that Oki do to improve her chances of getting off probation and earning a salary increase?

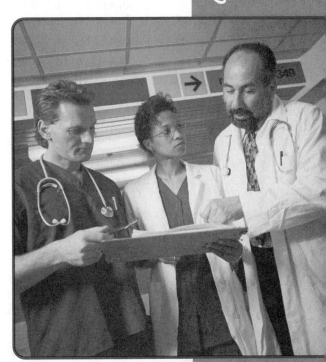

© GETTY IMAGES/PHOTODISC

chapter focus

After completing this chapter, you should be able to:

1. Describe the qualities and traits to strive for to be a success in the workplace.

2. Identify negative qualities and traits to be avoided in the workplace.

3. Eliminate personal habits that may detract from your effectiveness in the workplace.

4. Describe the personality traits conducive to working with others and contribute to group efforts with ideas, suggestions, and effort.

5. Describe the importance of being a team player and being able to participate as a member of a team.

6. Recognize the traits of the non-team player, and describe the techniques to enable you to get along with difficult coworkers.

Value-Added Qualities

Think about the last person you know who was dismissed from employment. What was the reason? Chances are the person was unable to fit in and get along with others. Surveys in many industries indicate that the most common reasons for failure on the job involve difficulties in working with others. You may spend several years working hard and studying to become technically competent for a position, and you may have special talents that enhance your abilities, but if you cannot get along with others, job success may escape you.

There are specific personal traits and qualities that are valued in the workplace. Think of these as **value-added qualities** because they *add value* to the skills and assets you already possess, such as your technical skills, knowledge, expertise, and work experience.

You do not have to be the most popular, interesting, entertaining, and charming person to be successful on the job. You simply need some positive characteristics that others expect and appreciate. These characteristics will not only help you get along with your coworkers, but they will also increase your chances for promotion. Your employer will expect you to get along with your coworkers so as not to reduce the productivity of your work area. Employers cannot afford to keep employees who interfere with the company's ability to get the job done. Consider these value-added qualities—cheerfulness, sense of humor, tactfulness, empathy/sympathy, and willingness to participate. These value-added characteristics will make you a better team player.

CHEERFULNESS

Cheerfulness is contagious. If one employee is cheerful, the mood will be "caught" by others. You can test this theory: Get into an elevator with several people and say something relevant but positive, such as, "Isn't this weather wonderful!" Say this with a smile on your face, and look directly at several of the elevator occupants. Did you get some smiles? Did you get some agreement? Did you get someone else to make a cheerful remark?

A cheerful atmosphere is a productive one. This is why employers try to hire and retain cheerful people. These people are often promoted because of their special personal traits. Note the negative experience of Oki at the beginning of the chapter.

The single trait of cheerfulness will make your coworkers want to work with you and enjoy working with you. Think about the people you enjoy being around; chances are they are cheerful. A cheerful worker makes things less difficult, dispels

Value-added qualities add meaning to your experiences as an employee and to your life in general.

PHOTO: © DIGITAL VISION

gloom, makes others happy, and looks at the brighter side of life. A cheerful worker energizes others.

Remind yourself each day to be cheerful. Cheerfulness will keep you in a positive frame of mind, and you will be happier with yourself and more pleasant to others. Try it. It is "catching." Cheerfulness is a quality you can *add* to make yourself a more valuable employee.

SENSE OF HUMOR

Most people appreciate a good sense of humor. Yes, there is a place for humor in the workplace as well as in your daily life. Humor is considered necessary by many for mental, emotional, spiritual, and physical well-being. How is your sense of humor? Is this a value-added characteristic you will take to the workplace? Do you appreciate humor? Do you appreciate the humor of others? Can you laugh at yourself?

A sense of humor is something you can cultivate if you feel it is a quality you lack. Typically, there are two reasons why people exhibit little or no sense of humor. First, they may not appreciate humor most of the time. What appears to be funny to others is not funny to them. Second, they may not react when something appears to be funny to everyone else. When others are laughing, this type of person barely cracks a smile. Such a person may actually enjoy a funny joke or situation but does not show this enjoyment. If you think either or both of these situations describe you, work on them. If you do not see humor where others do, you will need to sharpen your sense of humor. This does not mean that you should begin laughing loudly every time someone else does. Don't act like you "get it" when you do not. Pretending will just make you feel and appear foolish.

Try these suggestions to develop your sense of humor:

1. Make every effort to look for humorous elements in difficulties or errors. For example, if you find yourself pushing on a door marked "pull," think about how funny that could be in a television sitcom or home video program. If you embarrass yourself by being tongue-tied or getting your words scrambled, make every effort to laugh about your stumbling. Admit you are human and laugh at yourself. Laughter is an assurance of our humanness and can help you to create bonds and friendship. Your laughter will make others more empathetic, and gives you a chance to back up and try again. Realize that everyone sometimes says something that comes out differently than planned. If you do something "silly," take advantage of the opportunity to laugh at yourself. It is one of life's great pleasures.

2. Ask a friend to explain a joke when you "don't get it." There is nothing wrong with admitting you missed the punch line or failed to see the humor. For example, you may read a "Dilbert" cartoon and miss the point because you do not have enough political knowledge or office savvy to understand it.

3. Make a habit of watching comedies on television and seeing funny movies and plays. Discuss funny parts with others. This will help you become more sensitive to humor.

If you do not laugh when everyone else does, work at reacting to humor. Simply allow yourself to be more expressive. At first, it may make you feel uncomfortable to laugh aloud when you normally only smile or giggle. (People who are shy are less likely to laugh out loud.) Keep in mind that laughing aloud is a good emotional release. With a little practice, you should be able to relax and bring your reactions up to a level that shows others you really do have a sense of humor.

As you work on your sense of humor, remember that jokes that are crude, poke fun at others, or put others down as individuals or groups are not in good taste anywhere—especially in the workplace.

Think about this famous quote from Sir Max Beerbohm. (Sir Beerbohm, an English essayist and caricaturist, was well-known for his charm and wit.)

"Strange when you come to think of it, that of all the countless folk who have lived before our time on this planet, not one is known in history or in legend as having died of laughter."

TACTFULNESS

Tact is the ability to do or say the right thing when dealing with people or difficult situations. It is diplomacy, the skill to maintain good relations with others without offending them. Tact has been defined as the ability to change a porcupine into a possum, the ability to hammer home a point without hitting the other person on the head, or the ability to make your guests feel at home when you wish they were.

Tact involves understanding the other person's needs and wishes. You can make life much easier for yourself and those around you by using tact as a value-added quality. You may be a tactful person by nature, or you may need to practice being more tactful. Wanting and intending to be tactful is not good enough. It takes good judgment, thought, and careful wording of your remarks.

Some suggestions to consider when you are working to improve your tactfulness:

1. Avoid the number of confrontational words you use. Confrontational words are those that imply you are pointing at the other person and thereby confronting him or her. This is not tactful because the result is your listener will become defensive and challenged. Confrontational words might include: *think, and, you, opinion,* and *but.* Check this conversation to see the result of confrontational words.
   Sally: I do not vote because my vote doesn't count.
   Janet: How can you think that way? You don't feel your opinion counts! What is the matter with you!
   Sally: Get off my back!
   Watch your e-mail language, too! E-mail language must also be tactful. Boldface type, underlining, all capitals, italicized type, and red ink can be interpreted as confrontational language.
2. Never respond immediately when a response requires tact. Pause, and determine the best way to design your response to the other person. This moment of silence may also be helpful to the other person.

EMPATHY AND SYMPATHY

Another quality closely associated with tact is empathy. **Empathy** is the ability to participate in another person's feelings or ideas, to understand and feel another person's emotions—"to walk in another's shoes." For example, if you have a friend who has suffered the loss of a parent, you can understand his or her feelings of sadness if you have experienced the same loss. If you are sensitive to the feelings of others, you will try to make them feel at ease. The ability to make others feel at ease is important in getting along with others.

Each of us has problems of one kind or another that may influence the way we act in the workplace. The display of emotions or feelings by others may annoy or disturb you, but you must realize that there are reasons for their actions. Try to be understanding.

There is a distinction between *empathy* and *sympathy*. Both terms have to do with how you respond to another person's emotions. Many people use the terms interchangeably, but the difference is real and important. **Sympathy** involves identifying with, and even taking on, another person's emotions. Their feelings become your feelings. A sympathetic response is, "I'm furious about the new policy, too." An empathetic response is, "I can understand how that policy makes you angry."

There are times when you will share another's feelings. However, responding to coworkers with sympathy can put you on an emotional roller coaster and leave you exhausted at the end of the day. It is appropriate to be emotionally aware and sensitive to the needs of others without becoming too emotionally involved. When you stay in control, you respond with empathy. This allows you to be ready, willing, and able to assist your coworker. Empathy permits you to be professional and caring at the same time. Save sympathy for close friends and family.

As with sympathy, feeling sorry for or pitying is not empathy. When you pity another, you look down on him or her. You may think "How terrible" or "What a sad situation that person is in" or even "What a dreadful deal. Thank goodness I'm not in that situation." Pity sets you apart; empathy has the capacity to bring you together.

Here is an example of empathy in practice.

Emily knew that Arthur, her supervisor, was having a difficult time with his youngest son. He had been arrested for several misdemeanors, he was often truant from school, and had been experimenting with illegal

on the job

Myra, Clarise, and Juanita are coworkers in a factory where being on time is important. Clarise and Juanita are anxious because Myra is late. They are production line workers and depend on Myra to get the line started. They like to start on time because they are paid by the completed piece. Myra finally arrives about thirty minutes late. She was involved in a traffic accident. Clarise says, "Nice you could finally join us, Myra. You know we can't start the line without you. You're taking money from my paycheck and food from my children's mouths. What happened? Did you have a late date last night?"

Juanita is embarrassed by Clarise's remarks. She says, "Hi, Myra. Glad you are here. You look upset. Is everything okay?"

Who was more tactful? How is Clarise going to feel when she finds out why Myra was late? What may have clued Juanita into the fact that there was a good reason for Myra's lateness? What should Clarise say or do next?

drugs. Emily had had similar problems with her stepchildren.

At one point, Arthur raised his voice at Emily for a very minor error in a monthly report, which could easily have been corrected. Emily recognized that Arthur was really shouting because of frustration about his personal life, which enabled Emily to understand Arthur's outburst. Later, Emily asked Arthur to have lunch with her and gave him the opportunity to talk. Arthur appreciated Emily's perceptiveness and empathy.

Treat others as you would like to be treated. Take time to be kind to those with problems or troubles. Be sensitive to others' moods without intruding on their privacy. You may think that there is no room in the workplace for empathy, but this is

"You can't understand another person until you walk a few miles in [his or her] moccasins."

—NATIVE AMERICAN PROVERB

Participation with coworkers will pay benefits both in and out of the workplace.

PHOTO: © PHOTODISC GREEN

For example, companies may sponsor park cleanup days, transportation of senior citizens to the polls, or walk-a-thons for charitable organizations. As your schedule allows, participate in as many of these activities as you can. You will make friends and work for the public good. Working side-by-side with coworkers in community improvement activities will enhance your ability to fit in and get along. When you are called upon to contribute to charitable organizations, donate your time cheerfully. Your employer will recognize your willingness to help others.

not true. There is always time for an expression of empathy.

WILLINGNESS TO PARTICIPATE

As you grow in your ability to get along with your coworkers, you may want to spend some time with them away from the job. Many employers have programs for just this purpose—softball teams, company picnics, or bowling and golf leagues.

In some companies, employees can volunteer to participate in civic activities.

Technology
at Work

Do some additional study on cheerfulness by checking out this Web site.
http://humanityquest.com/topic/Index.asp?theme/=cheerfulness

Have fun learning more about being a team player at
http://www.fabjob.com/tips171.html

Further sharpen your sense of humor by visiting
http://www.theallineed.com/ad-self-help-2/self-help-043.htm

chec**k**point

1. **Describe why good technical skills supported by value-added characteristics are necessary for job success.**

_____

_____

_____

2. Explain why the characteristic of cheerfulness is considered contagious.

    _____

    _____

    _____

3. List two suggestions for further developing your sense of humor.

    _____

    _____

    _____

4. What is tact?

    _____

    _____

    _____

5. What communication formatting should be avoided in e-mail when you want your message to be tactful?

    _____

    _____

    _____

6. Explain the difference between empathy and sympathy.

    _____

    _____

    _____

7. Explain the difference between empathy and pity.

    _____

    _____

    _____

    _____

    _____

applications

1. What qualities or characteristics do you look for when you choose friends? List these qualities. Are they similar to the value-added qualities listed in this section?

2. Read the comic section of a Sunday newspaper. Share the humor of two of your favorite cartoons or comic strips with a friend, family member, or coworker. This will help you get in the habit of sharing humor. Comment on their reactions.

3. What are some potential business advantages to participating in events or projects sponsored by the company you work for? What are some of the potential personal advantages? Are there any disadvantages?

4. Think about the following situations, and describe how you might address them tactfully.

a. Ask a coworker about a close relative who has been ill.

b. Tell a customer that your store policy does not allow sale merchandise to be returned.

_____

_____

_____

c. Tell your supervisor that you have found a better paying position and you plan to take it.

_____

_____

_____

d. Make visitors feel at ease as they are kept waiting.

_____

_____

_____

e. Ask for a raise in pay.

_____

_____

_____

f. Ask the name of someone with whom you are talking, but whose name you can't remember.

_____

_____

5. Discuss a situation in which you needed to express sympathy for a situation.

_____

_____

_____

Negative Traits to Avoid

Some key positive value-added qualities have been discussed in the first part of this chapter. Now let's take a look at some of the negative traits you will want to *avoid* in order to achieve success on the job. These include resentment, irritating habits, envy and jealousy, and self-pity.

RESENTMENT

Nothing consumes a person more quickly than the harboring of resentment. **Resentment** is a feeling of displeasure over something you believe (correctly or incorrectly) to be a wrong, insult, slight, or injury. Resentment, expressed openly, comes out as grumbling and complaining. Eventually, the grumbler finds himself or herself alone and excluded by coworkers. Those who complain and grumble because they resent others, the workplace, or a specific situation are not pleasant people to be around. Eliminating this trait may require extra effort. You already know that cheerfulness is contagious; unfortunately, complaining is also contagious. If you constantly complain, you may be creating a very unhealthy work environment. Perhaps you resent a coworker who was promoted, or someone who didn't speak when you passed. Dwelling on these feelings will not help. When you find yourself continually complaining and whining, do something about it! The best cure for this type of behavior is to take some positive action. Do something you enjoy. Do a part of your job that you find interesting, take a walk during your break or lunch period, go for a ride, or do anything that is fun for you. Combining action with enjoyment will overcome resentment and put the original cause for resentment in a better perspective as shown in Figure 7-1.

Action + Enjoyment − Resentment = Proper Perspective

FIGURE 7-1   *Winning formula.*

Another way to break the whining habit is to surround yourself with cheerful and positive people. This can cure the "grumbling" disease.

IRRITATING HABITS

Like it or not, you may have an irritating habit or two that you need to eliminate in order to fit in and get along. You may not always recognize your own unwelcome, annoying habits. Check the following list to see if you have any habits that could be offensive to others. Also think about other habits you could add to the list.

Irritating Habits

- Continually clearing your throat
- Popping or snapping gum
- Fiddling with your hair
- Sniffing repeatedly
- Playing with your jewelry
- Constantly adjusting your clothing
- Whispering when others are talking
- Jiggling change or keys in your pocket
- Tapping your fingers or a pen or pencil
- Picking your nose
- Continually interrupting in a conversation
- And . . . many others

When you discover you have irritating or objectionable habits, work to eliminate them. If you think you are quite perfect and have no irritating habits, check with a good friend and his or her response may surprise you. Don't be upset. To release an undesirable habit, be aware that you practice it. Desire to get rid of it; then stop it.

ENVY AND JEALOUSY

The closely related feelings of envy and jealousy are two of life's most destructive emotions. If you want to fit in and get along, these traits need to be controlled. Whenever you feel these emotions, think about the old adage: "Every time you turn green with envy, you're ripe for trouble." **Envy** is desiring something someone else has. **Jealousy** is feeling a rivalry toward one who you believe has an advantage over you.

In our highly competitive world, these feelings often occur. You may never eliminate these emotions completely, but you can continually work to accept the advantages enjoyed by others and express happiness over the accomplishments of coworkers. The key is to be glad for others and hope for the same or similar rewards for yourself, but not at the expense of others. If you can become the kind of person who is pleased when you hear words of praise for someone else, you will have taken a giant step toward your own emotional health. If this step is not taken, you can become consumed with envy and jealousy that could destroy any happiness or pleasure you might experience with others.

You may find yourself having to share honors that you feel rightfully belong to you alone. You must realize that your superior or coworkers may be praised for your work, ideas, contributions, or plans. Developing an unselfish attitude is not easy. Try to eliminate feelings of envy and jealousy by helping another person accomplish a goal and then praising that person. This is the way to begin. You can receive great pleasure from the success of someone you have helped. Enjoy the success of others as well as your own.

SELF-PITY

If you wish to fit in and get along, dump your feelings of self-pity. **Self-pity** is feeling sorry for yourself and your situation

on the job

Mario and Denise share a small office. Mario was continually irritated because every time a customer called with an unusual or seemingly unreasonable request, Denise would slam the phone down at the end of the conversation and make disparaging remarks about the customer. Mario figured that all requests by customers should be treated as legitimate. Mario finally lost his cool and said, "Denise, I wish you would quit slamming the phone down at the end of conversations. I find that very annoying!" Denise looked at Mario and said, "I wish you would stop popping your gum. I find that very annoying!" A silence came over the room and the coworkers went back to work. They didn't communicate the remainder of the day unless it was absolutely necessary.

What is illustrated by this example? What would you suggest Mario and Denise do the next morning when they arrive at work?

PHOTO: © PHOTODISC RED

We all have irritating habits. What are yours?

without looking at the good things in your life. If you talk continually about your problems, and dwell on them, others will get tired of hearing about them. Rehearsing your problems will drag you down, too. If you have the "poor little me" syndrome, get rid of it. "Pity parties" can result when this trait takes over. The bad thing about a pity party is that no one else wants to attend. Every now and then you will naturally feel sorry for yourself. Recognize your self-pity, and put a time limit on how long you are going to let these feelings last. Then turn your thoughts to the things in your life that are working well for you, and focus on your successes.

How much of the following monologue would you like to hear on a regular basis?

"I'm so tired. I work here all day and then go home and meet the challenges of house and yard work. Then I get up and start all over again. My neighbor stays home all day and has time to shop, play cards, and golf. I'll never have that kind of luxury. I wish I made more money so that I could buy some new clothes. I'm tired of wearing the same old things day after day. My old car is about to give out. It has developed a clanking noise, and I'm sure it is going to cost me big bucks. My kids constantly need school supplies. Don't we pay taxes so that schools can provide what kids need? Everything costs so much to repair these days. I don't feel very well today. I feel a bit nauseated. Yesterday my head ached all day."

This kind of self-pity talk can be exhausting to those around you, and to you.

focus on ethics

Carol had attended several conferences with Jeff. Carol appreciated the financial support and time the company provided for her conference participation. She also found the meetings very helpful to her work. Jeff always took his golf clubs and casual clothes to the conferences. Carol would fly to the meetings with Jeff, and the next time she would see him would be when they met at the airport for the return trip. Jeff did not attend the meetings. He used his time and company money for pleasure. At staff meetings upon their return, Carol always shared with others the ideas and thoughts she had heard at the conference. Jeff would just second whatever Carol had to say. Carol resents Jeff's behavior.

In this case, do you think Carol's resentment is justified? What can she do to keep the resentment from hurting her? How might she resolve the situation? If the situation cannot be resolved, what could Carol do to reduce or eliminate her resentment?

If others seem to be avoiding you, think about what you have said in the past few days. Does your conversation sound like the previous paragraph? Self-pity can be a bad habit. Break it.

chec**k***point*

1. Write the formula that will lead you to the proper perspective.

   _____

   _____

   _____

2. List three habits that some people possess that might be irritating to you or others. Suggest ways to eliminate them.

   _____

   _____

   _____

3. What is resentment? How can you eliminate it?

   _____

   _____

   _____

4. What is envy? How can it be controlled?

   _____

   _____

   _____

5. What is the difference between envy and jealousy?

   _____

   _____

   _____

6. What is self-pity? Why is it damaging to relationships?

   _____

   _____

   _____

applications

1. Have you ever had a "pity party"? How long did it last? What brought about the self-pitying mood? How could you have avoided these feelings of self-pity? How long did you allow this mood to last?

2. Write a paragraph on why envy and jealousy are often called the destructive emotions. You may want to refer to your own life experiences or the experiences of others.

3. As a result of reading this section, have you set any new goals for yourself? If so, list them and describe how you plan to reach them. Who might be able to help you set and reach these new goals? If you have not set any new goals, identify the reasons.

4. What does this quote mean to you? "Love looks through a telescope; envy, through a microscope." —Joseph Billings (1818–1885)

In addition to improving the value-added traits that help you and eliminating the negative traits that can hurt you, it is important that you learn how to work effectively with others. On the job, getting the work done is a team effort. You will enjoy your work more if you have a good relationship with your coworkers, and the productivity of the work team will be improved. Your supervisor, of course, is also an important member of this working team.

To better understand how important it is to get along with coworkers—to be a team player—imagine that you are a member of the bucket brigade engaged in putting out a fire. Long lines of people pass the buckets of water from a stream at one end to the fire at the other. Each person in the brigade is an important element in putting the fire out, and a break in the line would create problems. So it is in the workplace. Everyone has an important role in getting the job done.

KEYS TO GETTING ALONG WITH OTHERS

Wouldn't it be terrific if you could decide with whom you would work each day? However, while companies do try to hire people with the value-added qualities that will help them fit in, they cannot hire people based on shared interests, personalities, and backgrounds. Rather, they hire people who have the specific skills and knowledge needed to get a job done. Therefore, establishing a harmonious working team is not always an easy task. Those with whom you work may perceive things very differently from the way you do. They may have values, habits, traits, and beliefs that are different from or in conflict with yours.

Your behavior as a worker affects, directly or indirectly, everyone else in the workplace. Everything you do matters: the way you perform your job, the way you speak, the way you feel, and even the way you look. All of these things influence, in one way or another, the general effectiveness of your work group. It is necessary that you carry out your job tasks properly and work to develop desirable traits that will help produce "team spirit." Coworkers are counting on you—just as you are counting on them. There are some personality traits or characteristics that are vital to helping you work well with your coworkers.

Cooperation

One key to working with others is to be cooperative. **Cooperation** is the ability to work well with others, keeping in mind that you are all working toward a common goal. Imagine that you're on a tug-of-war team. You have no chance of winning unless you are all pulling, and all pulling in the same direction. Cooperation involves pulling your own weight, plus pitching in and helping whenever necessary. It may require going out of your way to help others, or helping when you have a few free moments. Cooperation is like a savings account. As with a savings account, cooperation may demand that you give up short-term conveniences for the sake of future rewards. In the workplace, cooperation may mean:

- a simple act of sharing your materials or equipment with a coworker
- stopping by someone's office on your way to the mail room to see if he or she has anything to send
- helping to cover the territory of another salesperson
- putting things away for a coworker who gets called to a meeting
- holding back when you want to disagree
- being a good sport when you have lost a sale

- showing tolerance in listening to the ideas of others when you feel that your own ideas are superior
- helping someone move a file cabinet, box, desk, or another large object.

Cooperation is not just necessary between coworkers. Sometimes you need to cooperate with the company as a whole. In all careers, you will be expected to cooperate often and in varied circumstances. For example, you may be asked to:

- work overtime willingly
- offer services even when you are not obligated to do so
- help with work that is not specifically related to your job
- surrender your own ideas if someone else's are better for the welfare of the work team or company
- inform others of devices or ideas that may make their work easier
- pass ideas or results of your experiences to others
- listen to others when they try to help you as a result of their experience.

"No matter what accomplishments you make, somebody helped you."

—ALTHEA GIBSON

"Power consists in one's capacity to link his [or her] will with the purpose of others, to lead by reason and a gift of cooperation."

—WOODROW WILSON

Politeness

Being polite is valuable in any context, but is expected in business. **Politeness** is exhibiting courtesy and consideration to others. Positive body language and pleasant words are very powerful in developing a good work environment. Expressions of politeness are signals to others that you care about them and appreciate them. They make you appear kind and good-mannered. And, more importantly, they indicate to others that you think they are important. An example of how politeness helps can be seen in the following situation.

Bob's morning was not off to a good start. His uniform was missing a button, his boots were scuffed, and the breakfast food box was empty. He got caught in the rain between home and the bus stop without an umbrella. As he entered the work area, his coworker, Bella, greeted him with a big smile, a cup of coffee, and a cheerful "good morning." Bob couldn't help responding to this warm greeting in the same manner, and he began to feel his day turning around for the better.

Politeness contributes to a pleasant, cooperative, productive working environment. *Hello, good-bye, sorry, excuse me, please, thank you,* and *you're welcome* are good words—practice using them. But as important as polite words are, they need to be accompanied by polite actions: hold the door for someone whose hands are full; don't cut in line—be polite.

Patience

Learn and practice the fine art of patience. It is often said that **patience** is the capacity to bear pains or trials calmly and *without complaint.* The emphasis on this statement should be on the words "without complaint." You may be able to remain calm; however, if you complain about a situation, you are not being patient. Not everyone "catches on" to tasks and routines at the same rate. Try to remain calm as you help a coworker with a new process, even when you must explain the process more than once. Be patient when coworkers ask questions that you believe are unnecessary. A less-than-patient attitude may lead to conflict and a negative work environment. Lack of patience has the capacity to produce fear, anxiety, discouragement, and ultimately failure. Patience can create confidence, certainty, and a realistic outlook—the ingredients for success.

When your patience is running thin, take a deep breath and do some self-talk: "Take it easy." "Don't lose your patience." "I can do this." "Let's try it one more time."

As you prepare for the workplace, keep in mind the old Dutch proverb: "A handful of patience is worth more than a bushel of brains."

Enthusiasm

Enthusiasm is a very contagious emotion. If you are enthusiastic, it seems to spread to others. **Enthusiasm** means to inject energy into your work. People who are enthusiastic are inspired to do their work. They enjoy what they are doing, and it shows. If you are enthusiastic and eager about your work, this will often cause others to get work done more quickly and easily. The positive effect of enthusiasm is illustrated in this example.

Emma said, "This is an impossible task. How can we separate all of these charts and graphs and make any sense of them? I just don't want to do this. It's impossible." But Murray said enthusiastically, "I think if we work together, we can make some sense of this information in short order. Let's get to it, get it done, and have fun while we are putting this together." "You think so?" Emma replied. "Well, if you're willing to tackle it, I'm with you. Maybe we can do it."

Murray's enthusiasm and spirit of cooperation has already begun to inspire Emma, and the task will be completed.

If you do not look forward to going to your workplace and cannot express genuine enthusiasm about your job, it is probably time to look for other employment opportunities. You will be doing yourself and others a great favor.

Dependability

Another key to getting along with coworkers is to be **dependable**. Teamwork is based on the ability of one worker to depend and count on another. Think of mountain-climbing teams. The life of one climber may depend upon the actions of another.

on the job

Sheila was explaining the company's benefits package to Paul, a new employee. The package was somewhat complex because it included information about health and life insurance, the retirement plan, and profit sharing. Because this was Paul's first job, he was not familiar with the terms used to describe benefit programs. After Sheila had completed her explanation, she asked for questions. Paul had many questions that Sheila felt she had already answered. Although Sheila answered Paul's questions, her body language let Paul know she didn't like the questions. Paul said, "If you didn't want to answer my questions, why did you ask if I had any?" Sheila replied, "If you had been paying attention, you wouldn't have needed to ask any questions."

Who lost patience in this case? What will likely be the result of this situation? What would you suggest to Sheila the next time she prepares to talk with a new employee?

Their teamwork is built upon dependability. While the life of a coworker may not be in your hands, your coworkers depend on you.

A dependable coworker will be punctual, committed to deadlines, helpful, patient, and positive.

Loyalty

Loyalty is believing in your place of employment and being committed to it. Can you find loyalty in the following example?

Dennis works for a large discount store in his community. He tells his neighbors and friends that many of the products sold at the store are seconds or rejects from other larger stores. He takes every opportunity to "bad mouth" the store's service and tells others that the store takes advantage of

"Have patience. All things are difficult before they become easy."

Are you dependable? In the space provided, write yes or no.

_____ 1. Can your coworkers count on you to be punctual?

_____ 2. Do you have a good attendance record?

_____ 3. Do you complete tasks on time?

_____ 4. Can coworkers depend on you to assist them if they get overloaded with work?

_____ 5. Are you enthusiastic about your job?

_____ 6. Can you be patient as you help another learn a new task?

_____ 7. Can you be patient without complaining?

its workers. He has gone so far as to say that the working conditions in the store do not meet the Occupational Safety and Health Administration (OSHA) standards.

Obviously, Dennis is not a loyal employee. He does not respect the discount store where he is employed. Dennis believes that the store pays for his time and effort to work in the plant. He does not think he is paid for loyalty to the company. If you have questions about the quality of products, services, or working conditions of your employer, discuss your concerns with your employer, not your friends and neighbors.

Loyalty goes beyond respect for your employer. Loyalty is key to getting along with your work team. Your work team counts on you for support and commitment, just as your employer does. This means supporting your coworkers by helping them. Ignore or correct gossip about coworkers. Support their efforts whenever appropriate. Would you remain friends with a person who frequently tells others about your faults and secrets? You probably would not.

"An ounce of loyalty is worth a pound of cleverness."

—ELBERT HUBBARD

You want and expect your friends to be loyal. The same expectations hold true for coworkers.

Loyalty and faithfulness to your workplace are important to your success on the job. If, due to serious disagreement with or objections about the products or policies of your company, you are not able to be loyal to your coworkers and cannot promote the place where you work, you may be in the wrong job.

Building the Self-Esteem of Others

Another key to working with coworkers is to do whatever you can to bolster the self-esteem of others. Positive remarks, simple gestures, or the demonstration of an interest in others can do a lot to enhance how others feel. Think about how you feel when someone pays you an honest compliment. Wouldn't you like to share that feeling with others? Positive people provide a great work environment. Review the following list of ideas for building the self-esteem of others.

• Nod in agreement when you concur with others.
• Use people's names when talking to them.
• Pay deserved compliments and pass on compliments from third parties.
• Inquire about others' interests.
• Support coworkers when they are stressed.
• Ask others for help and write down their ideas.
• Ask for the opinions of others.

An effort to be cooperative, polite, patient, enthusiastic, dependable, loyal, and supportive of others will help you succeed as you work to build a team. As you develop these characteristics, you will set an example for others. It is not fair to expect others to demonstrate these traits unless you are willing to exhibit them also.

Smart Tip ▼ ▼ ▼

As you work at building the self-esteem of others, keep in mind that everyone has

- **his or her own opinions, values, and beliefs.**
- **his or her own way of learning and thinking in special ways.**
- **a personality that is different from everyone else's.**
- **special interests, secret desires, and unique gifts.**
- **some strong feelings and fears.**
- **problems that he or she may not share often.**

▲ ▲ ▲ ▲ ▲ ▲ ▲ ▲ ▲

YOUR POSITION ON THE TEAM

Think of yourself as playing a certain position on your organization's team. No single employee, no matter how good he or she may be, can make a company successful. As an employee, make it your business to be a team player. Do not focus on what great work you can do. Focus on what great work your organization can do because you are on the team.

For example, your job may be keeping records. If it is, make sure that the records are accurate and thoroughly checked. If you are a shipping clerk, see that each order is filled out perfectly; see that there is no slipup on your part of the team effort. If you write the first draft of a report, check the information that goes into the report. Do your very best to see that the report is written as well as you can do it.

Remember that, like the player in a football game who throws a forward pass, you pass your part of the report to the person who will write or dictate the final draft. That person will make the touchdown, but you will be the team member who made it possible for someone else to catch the ball and carry it over the line. Also, like being a member of that football team, working to improve your own skills helps the whole team, while making you a more valuable player.

You can see why, as a worker, you must understand why people behave as they do. Computers may supply facts and figures, but people still make the business enterprise go—or break down. Being a good team player every day is a tough job. Do your best every day. Others are counting on you.

BEING A GOOD TEAM PLAYER

As with any team, there are behaviors you want to avoid, as well as the positive ones you want to develop. As you think of yourself as a team player, keep in mind these

on the job

Evelyn was a new administrative assistant in an insurance company. After several weeks on the job, she was feeling very comfortable with her work and the relationships she was developing with coworkers. Jeanette was especially helpful to her during those first rough days. During Evelyn's fourth week, Jeanette explained to her that she needed to be away from the office for a few minutes to take care of a personal matter. She asked Evelyn to skip her break and cover her phone while she was out. Evelyn was happy to help out. However, Jeanette began to ask Evelyn to watch her phone more often. Soon, it seemed that, whenever Evelyn had an opportunity for a break, Jeanette needed help or had some errand to run, leaving Evelyn to handle both jobs.

What is Jeanette doing? How do you think Evelyn should handle this?

"don'ts." They are pitfalls that you should carefully avoid.

Don't take advantage of others.

It will be necessary at times to ask a coworker to assist you in some way or to take care of some of your assigned responsibilities. However, you should never take advantage of others or shirk your own work.

It is obvious that Jeanette was taking advantage of a new employee. This type of arrangement is not conducive to teamwork. When someone does assist you with your work, be sure to thank him or her, and return the favor whenever possible. It is not necessary for you to allow someone to take advantage of you. However, it is equally important that you do not take advantage of others.

Don't speak before you think.

You should feel comfortable about expressing your ideas when you think they are appropriate. However, it is important in most business situations to think about what you are going to say and to use good judgment in deciding when you should speak up and when it is better to keep silent. There may be some situations when you should comment, or even protest, but you should always listen to the ideas of your coworkers, supervisors, or customers. Many times, others will have a different perspective or will have noticed details that you may have overlooked. If a decision is made and your ideas are overruled or rejected, you must accept the decision of the majority in a cheerful manner.

In a good working environment, effective communication is vital. Knowing when to speak, when not to speak, what to say, and what not to say is an important skill to develop, especially when working for advancement. Remember that sometimes silence is golden. And always put your mind in gear before engaging your tongue.

Don't make hasty judgments about others.

Trying to understand the possible reasons for others' behavior will keep you from making unfair or hasty judgments about coworkers. If, for example, Maureen's desk is next to yours, and she challenges everything you say, it may be tempting to stop speaking to her altogether. But this will not solve your problem, and it will not help build team spirit. Attempt to figure out why Maureen feels the need to contradict and challenge your comments and decisions. She may feel inferior to you. She may feel extremely insecure in her position. She may have no idea how to seek help for real or imagined inadequacies. You can help by providing her reassurance now and then. Your help may stop the challenges she tosses at you. (Of course, if you are kind and show consideration, you may get closer as time goes by, and she may tell you the reasons, and even ask for your help.)

Your coworkers are struggling along in life just as you are. Sometimes unattractive personality traits cover up a reality that is the exact opposite. The clown may be unhappy; the braggart may be insecure; the person who laughs too much may be nervous; the aggressive person may not feel secure; the person who seems to be avoiding you may be shy. In addition, there are often stresses or problems in people's lives that affect their moods or ability to cope at work. Give others a chance before passing judgment.

Smart Tip ▾ ▾ ▾

Consider the following guidelines for speaking up in the workplace.

- A beginning worker should be slow to suggest changes in procedures. Before you make suggestions, study the reasons for the present processes. You might learn that your changes would not be practical. Suggesting changes just to prove you are alert and aware of current practices can be detrimental to you.

- Before you speak, think about with whom or to whom you are addressing your remarks. If it is a more experienced employee or a supervisor, you need to be aware of whether your remarks might be seen as challenging his or her authority.

- When you do speak up, come directly to the point. If explanations are essential, organize them in a logical fashion. State your case, and answer the questions that result from your comments. It may be that your employer will welcome your suggestions.

- Think about how you are going to phrase what you want to say. Should you be informal (more appropriate with coworkers) or formal (better with managers)? Can you make a comment sound more positive?

- If you find that your supervisors have different ideas on the subject, amicably respect and abide by their decisions.

▲ ▲ ▲ ▲ ▲ ▲ ▲ ▲ ▲ ▲ ▲ ▲ ▲ ▲ ▲ ▲

check*point*

1. Good teamwork creates increased work productivity.
   True _____ False _____
2. You should immediately assume that someone who is quiet is a snob.
   True _____ False _____
3. Loyalty is believing in your place of employment and being committed to it.
   True _____ False _____
4. What is cooperation? Why is it so critical in the workplace?

   _____

   _____

   _____

5. What are the three don'ts of being a good team player?

   _____

   _____

   _____

applications

1. List five characteristics you would like the person working most closely to you to have. Compare your list with the lists of others. What traits do your lists have in common? Rate yourself on each characteristic on a scale of 1 to 10, with 10 being the highest rating. List the qualities you have that would make you a good coworker.

_____

_____

_____

_____

_____

2. This chapter stresses the importance of politeness. For a two-week period, keep a log of polite comments or gestures that you make in your work, school, or family life. Each day, try to increase the number of genuine polite gestures or comments that you make. Also, keep a log of polite mannerisms you see others demonstrate. At the end of each week, review both logs. After your review, list what you can do to increase your politeness.

3. Review the situation about Dennis who works at the large discount store. (See page 187.) Answer the following questions about this situation.

a. Why would Dennis make negative remarks about the company and the working conditions in the store?

_____

_____

_____

_____

b. If the supervisor hears that Dennis is making negative remarks about the store, what do you think might happen? Why?

_____

_____

_____

_____

c. If you are a customer at the discount store and hear what Dennis is saying about the products, would you quit buying from that store? If not, would you discuss the remarks with someone? With whom?

_____

_____

_____

_____

d. What could be the long-term impact of Dennis's statements and the future of the discount store in the community?

_____

_____

_____

_____

4. Think of a situation in which you had to exercise patience while working with someone on the job or in a school activity. What happened in the situation? How did you handle it?

_____

_____

_____

_____

Now let's talk about how you can better understand the way members of a work group interact, and how you can even help others to fit in. Most workplaces are made up of groups of people. A group consists of two or more individuals who are aware of one another, interact with one another, and perceive themselves as a group.[1] If you work now, or plan to work someday, you should learn as much as you can about group psychology or, as it is sometimes called, group dynamics. What makes groups tick? How does group behavior differ from individual behavior? Why is the study of group behavior important?

The study of group behavior is important because whatever you do affects the way someone else in your group feels. When your actions make others feel positively toward you and toward the group, you help others do a more effective job. When your actions cause friction and bad feelings in the group, you hold others back from doing their best work.

Thus, your actions will diminish the effectiveness of your group. You then need to work on yourself. Be the type of person who brings out the best in people in the group, not one who contributes to the problems that may exist when people work closely together.

HELPING THE PROBLEM COWORKER

Even if you personally do not create problems in your group, you can aggravate problems if you don't know how to react to difficult coworkers. You can do much to help others. You've already learned about empathy, patience, and politeness, which can be valuable in these situations. To help someone who is new to feel less awkward,

Technology at Work

The Internet can be a good place to research information about topics such as *group dynamics, group sociology, work groups,* or *team building.* Select a topic and enter the search words in your browser. Share the information you find with your classmates as directed by your instructor.

you may want to share with him or her a problem you had when you first joined the group, or you may try commenting favorably on something someone else did to make work go more smoothly.

To change or guide the behavior of members of your work group who are having difficulties, you may need to use a technique such as **shaping**. The theory behind shaping is to help a group member work better within the group by reinforcing positive behavior. With shaping, you pay no attention to irritating things the group member does, but you give rewards or praise for the things said and done that are helpful and correct. See Figure 7-2 and note the shaping formula.

Most of the difficulties people have when they become part of a group are caused by lack of confidence. Praise is a good confidence builder. Don't worry about being in a position to offer "real" rewards; give the "rewards" that you can give, such as acceptance, a smile, a kind word. These work and can be given sincerely, even when praise is not really appropriate.

When you decide to help guide coworkers toward changes or improvements,

Shaping = Rewarding
        + Praise
        − Acknowledging Irritating Things

Shaping = **More Confident Person**

FIGURE 7-2   *Shaping formula.*

you may need to proceed indirectly. People do not like to be forced to do things, even if it is for their own good. You should never be unkind. And you should never try to change a worker to please yourself, only to help the work group operate more smoothly.

Of course, as with all techniques designed to encourage better performance among others, shaping works best when you take the lead and set a good example. Like enthusiasm and cheerfulness, a good example can be contagious.

For example, when you are more truthful in dealing with your coworkers, that truthfulness becomes a habit. In an organization where everyone is truthful and considerate of others' feelings, bad relationships that can hurt a group's effectiveness are minimized. Work no longer seems like work in such an organization. It becomes a pleasant experience.

IDENTIFYING SPECIAL COWORKERS

Most working groups have several types of characters. Those characters may be recognizable at once, or they may be hiding behind a mask. This is one reason why you should take your time in joining one of the many informal groups you will encounter in the workplace.

The following paragraphs describe some of the typical characters, and give suggestions on how you may want to interact with them.

on the job

Tonya wears clothing that is inappropriate for the office environment. She often wears dresses made of satin or velvet; her rhinestone jewelry would be more appropriate for evening wear, and her high heels are too high for comfort or safety. Tonya has become the talk of the office. People walk past her office each day just to see what she is wearing. Tonya's skills are excellent, but she is causing a disturbance in the work group. She doesn't appear to understand what is happening, why people avoid her, or why others stare at her. You like her and want her to fit into the dynamics of your work group.

What sort of shaping activities could you engage in to help Tonya?

Complainers. Most work groups have one or more complainers. The complainer can be a very dangerous member of the working team because complaining, like so many other traits, can be contagious. It is important to give the complainer positive and cheerful statements whenever possible. Whatever you do, do not let the complainer influence your thinking so that you become a complainer, too. Consider the following strategies for dealing with the complainers you know. (Don't use these strategies, however, if the complaints relate to real, serious, or potentially illegal activities, such as harassment. These strategies are to be used with complainers who simply pick apart every little thing, and who can always find the bad side of anything.)

1. Attempt to minimize the other person's troubles.
You might say, "Now is half an hour of overtime really that bad?" or "Don't take everything so hard. Let's take a look at your

complaint together." This technique may not be effective with complainers who may feel that you are not willing to listen.

2. Repeat the complaint but in different words.

Suppose the complaining coworker says to you, "I'd like to take the day off. I'm tired of working on this stupid project. Byron has been on my case all day." You might respond by saying, "I can tell Byron has made you unhappy and that this day is not going well for you." This technique is an attempt to put the person's feelings into words. By doing this, you are not saying that you agree with the feelings or that you condone the outburst, but you do let the complainer know that you understand the feelings behind the complaint.

Counselors use this technique, commonly called a **nondirective approach**, to reflect back what the person has said. This approach eliminates your natural tendency to give advice, to agree with, to preach, to take sides, or to defend the complainer. The nondirective approach also has positive benefits for the complainer. It draws out negative feelings and provides an opportunity for the complainer to pause, take stock of the situation, and think it through.

Angry people. Anger is an unpleasant but common behavior in the workplace. If you talk with someone who is angry, use the nondirective approach. Take responsibility for your actions when a coworker yells or expresses anger at you. For example, in response to, "Why did you leave that file drawer open for me to trip over? How can you be so careless?" answer calmly, "I did leave the file drawer open. I'm sorry I was careless." Admitting your own faults is almost guaranteed to defuse some of the anger of your coworker.

"It is a waste of energy to be angry with a man [sic] who behaves badly, just as it is to be angry with a car that won't go."

—BERTRAND RUSSELL

You must keep all traces of sarcasm from your voice as you give your calm reply. Any other response or increase in the tone of your voice may escalate the anger. Bad feelings and conflict between people do not just happen. There is usually a cause. Without knowing it, you may be part of the cause. If you can take the giant step of admitting your part in causing the trouble, you will help the other person take the equally hard step of admitting to a share of the blame.

It is key in dealing with anger not to aggravate the problem. Keep your cool, keep your voice calm, and use the nondirective approach.

The grouch. Generally every group has a grouch. The grouch is not mad, angry, or unhappy with you. Usually the causes for the grouch's behavior and feelings are unrelated to the workplace. Physical problems, family conflicts, or financial troubles may cause the grouch's behavior. Also, recognize that some people have little or no reason for their grouchy moods and seem never to have an interest in changing their behavior. If you are pleasant and caring and refuse to take the grouch's complaining personally, you may help such a person become less of a grouch.

The tattletale. You can recognize a tattletale by the stories he or she tells about other employees. Do not tell your own stories about other employees, no matter what the provocation. Gossip is unwise at any time, but gossip with a tattletale can be disastrous.

The tattletale feels the need to talk about the bad habits or deeds of others, possibly to make himself or herself feel more important. When the tattletale starts telling you about another person, be polite but firm. You might say, "I don't want you to share that information with me" or "Why are you telling me this?" Or say you have work to do and don't have time to talk. The tattletale will leave you alone if he or she does not find you to be a receptive audience.

The boss non-boss. This person criticizes everything you do (and everything others do, too). The non-boss has suggestions, commands, and recommendations for everyone in the workplace. These bossy coworkers are primarily dissatisfied with themselves. Calling attention to the faults of others is just a way of trying to feel satisfied with themselves. Pay little or no attention to the suggestions or demands of the bossy person who is your coworker. Do your work to the best of your ability. You are responsible only to complete your tasks to the satisfaction of your assigned supervisor (boss).

The favorite. The employee labeled "the favorite" is the one who seems to have the "inside track" with the supervisor. Avoid labeling a coworker as a favorite. Your coworker may have good rapport with the supervisor because he or she is a quality worker. Recognize the good qualities of the coworker and emulate them. Avoid the name calling. If you find yourself to be "the favorite," it is important not to capitalize on such favoritism. Continue to treat your supervisor with respect and a formality that indicates an appropriate employer/employee relationship.

The arguer. You may have coworkers who actually enjoy an argument. When you meet the arguer, arm yourself with two ingredients—relaxation and patience. If someone makes a controversial statement or attempts to get you to argue, relax. Take a deep breath. Consciously let your muscles go limp. Then patiently wait and listen until you have heard the whole story. Many arguments are merely the result of not letting the other person finish. Decide to say nothing until your "opponent" has finished talking. By that time, particularly if you are relaxed, you will find yourself much less likely to say something rash, something that might hurt the other person's feelings, something that you will regret later, or something that will raise the situation to a level of conflict. Perhaps you can help "the arguer" realize that arguing is not conducive to a good work environment.

Jerome says, "I don't understand why you won't support our efforts to get management to change our summer work hours from 7 a.m. to 4 p.m. rather than the usual 8 to 5. What's wrong with you? Don't you want to support your coworkers? Are you trying to become the favored employee? What are you doing, bucking for a promotion?" Abby is tempted to defend herself after several of his comments. However, she takes a deep breath and tells herself to relax and let Jerome finish. Then she replies as calmly as possible. "I understand that you would like to change the work hours this summer. The time adjustment you are recommending would not work for me, as my childcare arrangements are not available at 7 a.m. I hope you will understand and respect my point of view."

After Abby expressed her thoughts, she went back to her workstation. She did not cause the argument to escalate by raising her voice or by becoming defensive. She simply stated her position and feeling. It may be difficult for Abby to overlook Jerome's harsh words, but based on the way she handled the situation, she may even get an apology from him.

chec**K**point

1. Ignoring the tattletale is one way to change his or her behavior.
   True _____ False _____

2. Reflecting back on what someone else has said is called the nondirective approach.
   True _____ False _____

3. The nondirective approach should not be used in dealing with an angry person.
   True _____ False _____

4. You should realize that "the grouch" is angry at you.
   True _____ False _____

5. Why is it important to think about group behavior?

   _____

   _____

   _____

   _____

   _____

   _____

   _____

   _____

   _____

applications

1. You have read that the way to avoid an argument is to relax and wait for the whole story before you respond. The next time you are tempted to argue with someone, say nothing until he or she is through speaking. Just be patient and listen. Write down the results of your experience. Did you accomplish anything? How did the other person react? Do you feel that this is a helpful solution for you?

_____

_____

_____

_____

_____

_____

2. Since it is likely that you will spend most of your life working and/or living with groups of people, it is important that you understand how groups work together. Do some research on group dynamics, either consulting books at the library or doing research on the Internet. Share with the class either a list of recommended sources or an item of information about group dynamics that you discover.

_____

_____

_____

_____

_____

3. Draw or paste below a cartoon that depicts "the grouch," "the complainer," "the arguer," or "the bossy non-boss." What does the cartoon say about working with these "characters"?

----

 4. Identify a special coworker with whom you have worked with who was a complainer, a grouch, or exhibited any one or more of the behaviors discussed in the chapter. You do not need to provide the real name of the person, but discuss the situation and how you handled it; could you have done a better job after reading this chapter?

Points to Remember

7

chapter

Review the following points to determine what you remember from the chapter.

- The development of the value-added qualities, cheerfulness, sense of humor, tactfulness, empathy and sympathy, and the willingness to participate are essential if you are going to succeed in the workplace. Each day analyze how you did with the value-added qualities.

- As your goal is to fit in and get along, avoid the negative traits of allowing feelings of resentment (feeling of indignant displeasure over something that you believe to be a wrong, slight, insult, or injury), envy (desiring something someone else has), jealousy (feeling of rivalry toward someone who you believe has an advantage), or indulging in self-pity (feeling sorry for yourself) to be a part of your personality. These traits can only lead to feelings that will not make your work more pleasant.

- Work at eliminating any irritating habits such as fiddling with your hair, playing with your jewelry, popping or snapping gum, or jingling change in your pockets.

Other habits such as clearing your throat constantly, sniffing, or tapping something are also irritating.

- Each day in the workplace, you will want to show a cooperative spirit and exercise politeness in dealing with others; you will also want to demonstrate patience, enthusiasm, dependability, loyalty, and help build the self-esteem of others.

- You will recognize that to be happy in your job, you will need to be a team player. If you are a team player, you will not take advantage of others, speak before you think, let your emotions get ahead of you, or make hasty judgments or decisions about others.

- Problem coworkers usually exhibit behavior by complaining, being angry, being a tattletale, arguing, or playing the favorite in a work situation. You will recognize and deal with problem coworkers and non-team players using such techniques as shaping and the nondirective approach.

How did you do? Did you remember the main points you studied in the chapter?

key terms

Place the letter of the item in the definition column that matches the key word.

Key Word | Definition

_____1. Value-added qualities

a. Feeling of displeasure over something you believe is wrong.

_____2. Tact

b. Personal traits valued in the workplace

_____3. Empathy

c. Inject energy into your work

_____4. Sympathy

d. Believing in your place of employment

_____5. Resentment

e. Guide or change workplace behavior

_____6. Envy

f. Ability to do or say the right thing when dealing with people or difficult situations

_____7. Jealousy

g. Identifying with another's emotions

_____8. Self-pity

h. Ability to participate in another's feelings

_____9. Cooperation

i. Desiring something someone else has

_____10. Politeness

j. Feeling sorry for yourself

_____11. Enthusiasm

k. Feeling a rivalry over someone you feel has an advantage over you

_____12. Loyalty

l. Exhibiting courtesy and consideration to others

_____13. Shaping

m. Capacity to bear pain calmly and without complaint

_____14. Nondirective approach

n. Reflect back on what a person has said

_____15. Patience

o. Ability of one worker to count on another

_____16. Dependable

p. Ability to work well with others

activities and projects

1. Think about this sentence: "Don't just envy another's good fortune; duplicate the work that helped earn it." In the column on the left, list some of the people or situations you might envy. In the column on the right, list how you might earn or achieve what you envy. This activity will help you turn the destructive emotion of envy into positive ideas and action and may help you reach your goals. This is an activity that you will not be asked to share with your instructor or classmates.

I envy

a. _____

b. _____

c. _____

d. _____

e. _____

I will earn or achieve by

a. _____

b. _____

c. _____

d. _____

e. _____

2. This chapter emphasizes that making quick, incorrect judgments about people can be dangerous and may lead to conflict. What judgments have you made about others that turned out not to be true? Did your judgments lead to conflict? How did you discover that your judgments were not accurate?

_____

_____

_____

_____

_____

3. Getting along with others is an ongoing process. Try the following steps, which may win you new friends as well as help you fit in wherever you go.

a. All day Monday, smile at those you meet at school or work. Praise at least one person you greet.

b. On Tuesday, relay a kind or encouraging word to every close associate with whom you talk during the day.

c. On Wednesday, seek out someone who needs a friend or who needs a helping hand, and help that person out.

d. On Thursday, talk to someone with whom you do not often talk. Discuss only that person's interests, not your own.

e. On Friday, write a friendly letter or e-mail to someone.

Of course, you could do any or all of these things each day, but set a goal of doing at least these things. At the end of the week, evaluate your experiences. Do you feel more friendly with someone? Did things go more smoothly at work or school? Did someone surprise you with his or her response to your interest or kindness?

_____

_____

_____

_____

4. Discuss the meaning of dependability and how it may and usually does affect production in a company. How does dependability relate to you in your job or even in your class work? Is being dependable a quality you would want in a coworker?

_____

_____

_____

_____

case studies for critical thinking

GREGORY THE GROUCH

Your coworker, Gregory, begins the morning by telling you that you should not have parking lot privileges as you have been with the company only a short time. A few minutes later Gregory growls that you spend too much time away from your desk. At midmorning Gregory comes by and says that he thinks the room temperature is set too high and he is going to complain to management. He asks you in the early afternoon who you are trying to impress by keeping your suit coat on all day. You note that you are not the only victim of Gregory's comments. He makes similar remarks to others.

1. Is Gregory angry or unhappy with you?

2. How can you help Gregory to be a comfortable member of the work team?

3. What can you say in response to Gregory's comments to you?

4. Is Gregory dangerous to the success of the work team?

5. Can you accept Gregory the way he is?

_____

_____

_____

NEW ELECTRONIC PROCESS

Kate is a new employee in a large government agency. One of her tasks is to put together the agenda and support materials for the agency's governing board. The Board materials are sent to Kate from all areas of the agency. She rekeys the materials, puts them in a suitable outline, and sends them to the Board members, the media, and other people as required by law. Kate finds this process cumbersome and time consuming. She soon develops a plan to do the entire process electronically, thus eliminating mounds of paperwork and postage expenses. The other employees and her supervisors did not accept the idea as they felt the old process had worked well for many years and didn't see the necessity to change. Kate and her ideas were ignored. Kate was frustrated by the rejection of a streamlined process and quit.

1. Did Kate (who needed the job) do the right thing?

_____

_____

_____

2. Was the new method of putting the Board materials together a good idea? Why or why not?

_____

_____

_____

3. How could Kate have gained acceptance of the new idea?

_____

_____

_____

4. What steps could Kate have taken to be accepted again as a part of the agency team?

_____

_____

_____

Case 7.3

CONTAGIOUS ATTITUDE

Edward has been a productive worker in an advertising agency for seven years. He has enjoyed his work and his coworkers. Keiko, his newest coworker, seems to have many problems. She is a single parent of two children with health problems. She is responsible for an elderly mother, and she feels her salary is not adequate. Each day she finds fault with the weather, the government, the plant, her coworkers, and life in general.

Edward listens empathetically to Keiko during break periods and hears her negative mutterings and comments while they are on the job. He begins to notice that her attitude is affecting his. He thinks of the negative aspects of life and starts to feel a general dissatisfaction with the workplace. Edward recognizes the change and decides he must do something about it.

1. What would you suggest that Edward do?

_____

_____

_____

2. Based on what you know about Keiko, do you believe that her feelings about life are justified?

_____

_____

_____

3. How could Keiko help herself enjoy life more?

_____

_____

_____

4. Should Edward help Keiko attack her attitude? Or, just work on his own?

_____

_____

_____

5. Should Keiko's attitude be of concern to management?

_____

_____

_____

Getting Along with Your Supervisor

PHOTO: © DIGITAL VISION

think about it: Cassandra and Alfred are coworkers at Awards Unlimited, a company that designs, produces, and sells recognition items. Cassandra is the manager in charge of design and production. Alfred is responsible for the salesroom and catalog orders. Larry Hilligas, the owner, is away from the company a good deal. Larry feels that the company is in good hands with his two managers. He spends his days recruiting customers and searching for new markets.

Cassandra enjoys her work very much. She likes the freedom given to her by the owner. She selects the design equipment and raw materials. As long as she can justify her decisions to Larry, no questions are asked. Alfred does not like working at Awards Unlimited. He works long hours, and he feels that Larry gives him too much responsibility. Alfred frequently says, "I don't get paid enough for the type of decisions I have to make! Larry should hang around here once in awhile and find out how tough this business really is!" Larry is very complimentary about the work of his managers.

How can two people working for the same person feel so differently about their employment?

chapter focus

After completing this chapter, you should be able to:

1. Describe the basic leadership styles.

2. Understand the importance of relating to your supervisor.

3. Demonstrate how to take a problem, share an idea, ask for a raise, or accept a compliment from your supervisor.

4. Demonstrate how to seek, accept, and handle deserved and undeserved criticism.

5. Understand the expectations of your supervisor.

Chapter Highlights

8.1 Know Your Supervisor

8.2 Communicating with Your Supervisor

8.3 Special Communications with Your Supervisor

8.4 What Should You Expect of Your Supervisor?

8.5 What Your Supervisor Expects of You

Know Your Supervisor

Your future in the work world may hinge on your ability to establish a good working relationship with your supervisor. Your supervisor will most likely determine whether you are retained, promoted, or terminated. A good working relationship with your supervisor does not mean "apple-polishing" (conniving or manipulating to assure that you are in good standing with him or her). A good relationship between you and your supervisor means making a conscious effort to manage your relationship so that it achieves the best possible results for you, your supervisor, and the organization that pays both your salaries. Your relationship with the supervisor should be one of mutual respect.

A Supervisor is a Real Person

A **supervisor**, for discussion purposes in this chapter, is a person who is in charge of one or more workers. Supervisors are human beings. They have the same type of feelings as you. Supervisors, like everyone else, have strengths and weaknesses, good and bad days, hopes and fears, personality quirks, and irritating habits. They are skilled at some things and not others. They may be football fans, archers, pet lovers, readers, golfers, songwriters, gourmet cooks, or distance runners. The thing that sets supervisors apart from other workers is that they are assigned the task of leading a group of people toward the development of a quality product, the sale of merchandise, or service to customers.

Keep this information in mind as you seek to understand, respect, and respond to your supervisor. He or she is a *real* person with special responsibilities. Get to know this real person, his or her likes and dislikes, hobbies, personality, and other information that may help you understand more about this human being. You will want to get to know these things, not so that you can be friends or buddies, but so you can better understand his or her expectations, needs, and leadership style.

Leadership Styles

The method the supervisor uses to get the work done is called a leadership **style**.[1] This style is how he or she manages people to help accomplish the goals and objectives of the organization. One of your first tasks in a new position will be to become acquainted, not only with your supervisor as a person, but also with his or her style of leadership.

There are three basic leadership styles: laissez-faire, democratic or participatory, and autocratic as shown in Figure 8-1. Each has its own set of characteristics. Be aware, as you study the styles, that a supervisor may have developed a combination of styles, or may vary his or her style depending on the situation.

Three Basic Leadership Styles

1. Laissez- faire
2. Democratic, or participatory
3. Autocratic

Figure 8-1 *Leadership styles.*

The Laissez-Faire Leader

Laissez-faire is a French phrase meaning "to allow to do; to let someone do something on their own." The **laissez-faire leader** is portrayed in the business situation that opens this chapter. Mr. Hilligas gives his managers responsibilities and expects the employees to carry them out without a great deal of direction or close supervision. The laissez-faire leader exercises a "hands-off" policy in dealing with employees. He or she provides information, ideas, guidance, and supplies when asked. This type of supervisor sets goals, then allows the individual or work team to determine how to reach those goals. Depending on the specific job or the level of the employee, the individual or the work team may be expected to decide on policies, tasks, procedures, roles of work group members, and even appraisals.

This leadership style works well in businesses requiring creativity from employees. These businesses need to allow employees to work in a free and open environment. Advertising companies, research organizations, architectural firms, and fashion design firms are examples of businesses in which laissez-faire leadership is often found. Review the characteristics of laissez-faire shown in Figure 8-2.

Characteristics of Laissez-Faire Leadership Style

1. Permits employees to make independent decisions.
2. Encourages initiative and creativity.
3. Allows employees to work independently.
4. Avoids providing specific directions.
5. Provides only general guidance on how to do a job.

FIGURE 8-2 *Characteristics of Laissez-Faire Leaders.*

Laissez-faire leadership is not demonstrated in the "On the Job" example. Jackson was expecting to use his design ability, creativity, and initiative in this position. Obviously being creative was not an option when working in a sales position for Marta.

on the job

Jackson has a talent in the area of interior decorating. He is attending classes and preparing for a career in this field. He is offered a part-time job as a salesperson in a furniture store. He is thrilled because he thinks he will have a chance to work with customers and do some interior decorating work. The position will be beneficial to the customers and provide job satisfaction for Jackson. After a few days on the job, Marta, his supervisor, tells him to stop spending his time sketching and looking for special fabrics and furniture pieces for customers. She tells him that his job is to sell what is on the floor and not waste time doing anything other than selling merchandise.

What suggestion(s) would you have for Jackson? What do you think Marta's perspective is? What lesson should Jackson learn from this experience?

If you are a creative, self-confident, self-directed, assertive person, and you have the ability to set and achieve your own goals, seek a position where you will work for a laissez-faire leader. You can ask questions during the job interview to see if your potential supervisor is a laissez-faire leader. See the "Smart Tip" on page 212 for suggestions. Tailor your questions based on the job that you are seeking. Keep in mind that even in the laissez-faire atmosphere you will want to check with your supervisor periodically to make sure that you are meeting expectations. Also remember that it is often necessary to earn the freedom of working in a laissez-faire environment by showing that you have initiative and drive that will enable you to reach the goals of the organization.

The Democratic Leader

The **democratic leader** will encourage you to participate in the management process.

Smart Tip ▾ ▾ ▾

Ask the following types of questions if you fit the personality profile of someone who wants to work in a laissez-faire environment.

- **How much direction will I be given on the projects I work on?**
- **Will I be able to set goals for myself in this position?**
- **Will I be given the opportunity to be creative in designing products (or services) for customers?**
- **Will I need to seek approval before I produce a design?**
- **Will I have flexibility in the days and hours that I work?**
- **Will I be able to select the materials and supplies I use in my work?**

▲ ▲ ▲ ▲ ▲ ▲ ▲ ▲ ▲

"Democratic supervision gives every employee the opportunity to be a part of management."

—ANONYMOUS

This type of leader will seek your ideas, thoughts, and solutions. The democratic leader recognizes that everyone has good ideas, and he or she seeks the input of all workers. The democratic supervisor exercises only a moderate degree of control over employees. He or she has confidence in the employees. Employees have confidence in their employer. This type of supervision is also called *participatory leadership*.

The democratic supervisor may suggest specific policies, procedures, tasks, and/or roles for the workers, but this style of leadership allows the group to participate in the decisions. Under democratic leadership, committees and meetings are part of the work environment. These activities encourage you to share your thoughts and ideas, participate in the decision-making process, and express your opinions.

If you believe your thoughts are worthy of consideration and you like the idea of contributing to the success of an organization, you will enjoy working with a democratic supervisor. The democratic supervisor will not allow you to work in isolation. He or she will insist that you become involved and offer ideas, help solve problems, and be an important part of the work team. Workers in this environment are expected to be especially cooperative, empathetic, and participatory.

If you believe your only commitment to an organization is to do a specific job and you prefer not being responsible for decision making, a democratic supervisor is not the type you should seek in the job selection process. The role of the democratic supervisor is clear in this example.

Anna Magid is an entrepreneur who likes to work with her fifteen employees in a democratic style. Each week they have sales meetings, production meetings, and marketing meetings in which ideas are shared and discussed, and decisions for the future are made. Anna seeks ideas about pricing, advertising, merchandising, and production. She recognizes the value of her employees' suggestions as they interact with each other and customers each day. Shawn is a new employee who works in the production area. He attends the production meetings but does not contribute anything, even when his coworkers and Anna prompt him several times. Anna talks with Shawn after one of the meetings and asks why he did not participate. Shawn says, "I get paid to work in production and I do quality work. I am not here to jabber in a meeting that takes me away from my job. You make the big bucks for thinking." Anna plans to assist Shawn in finding another job because she believes Shawn does not like working under her style of supervision.

The Autocratic Leader

The **autocratic leader** is an "in charge" type of person. He or she solely develops policies and procedures, defines and assigns tasks, and, in general, dictates how work is to be done. If you are working for an autocratic supervisor, there will be no question that he or she will be the leader and the employees will be the followers. You will be told what to do, when to do it, and how it will be done. Your goals will be established for you. You will usually not be asked for your opinions or ideas. The autocratic supervisor gives personal praise or criticism of individual contributions.

The autocratic supervisor usually does not **delegate authority**. In other words, he or she does not totally entrust an activity, a decision, or a responsibility to an employee. This type of supervisor retains all authority.

You may prefer working for an autocratic supervisor because you will not be responsible for the difficult tasks of planning and making decisions. On the other hand, you will need to be patient, cooperative, accepting, and reliable in order to function in this leadership setting. It is also very important that you follow directions carefully and always adhere strictly to the rules, regulations, and policies of the organization. An advantage to working for this type of leader is that you always know where your job begins and ends. If you are the type of individual who feels comfortable taking directions and prefers being given specific job instructions, you will enjoy working for a supervisor who exercises an autocratic leadership style.

The following example may give you a better understanding of the autocratic leadership style.

Marcus Lightfoot, the supervisor of 31 quality-control technicians in a circuit breaker manufacturing plant, is an auto-

PHOTO: © DIGITAL VISION

Democratic supervisors enjoy capturing the best thoughts from all members of the group.

cratic leader. Marcus is very proud of the quality product produced by the company. He refers to the technicians as his technicians. He assumes responsibility for the job that each of his technicians completes. He is very specific in his instructions to the employees about the specifications for each circuit breaker sent from the plant. He has strict rules about the number of minutes allowed for lunch and breaks, the order in which the circuit breaker sections are to be checked, the specifics to be checked for each product, and the procedures to be used in approving a completed product.

Rosie Delgado, a quality-control technician, says that she enjoys working for Mr. Lightfoot. She likes knowing what is expected of her and how her work will be evaluated. She likes doing a quality job and does not want to be involved in the decision-making activities of the plant.

LEADERSHIP STYLE SELECTION

Unfortunately, when looking for a job, you will seldom have the opportunity to determine ahead of time the leadership style used or to pick a supervisor with the style you prefer. However, remember to ask questions in the interview that will give you at least a hint as to what the leadership style will be. You will need to adjust your work style to the leadership style in your workplace. Each style has advantages and disadvantages. You should recognize that a supervisor might, at times, use a mixture of styles in order to accomplish a goal of the organization. However, there will always be a primary, underlying style.

When you become angry, frustrated, or displeased with your supervisor (and you will), ask yourself: "Is it the supervisor who angers me, or is it his or her leadership style?" Focusing on the supervisor's style keeps you from being unhappy with the leader personally. If you find there is one leadership style under which you work best, work toward a position where the supervisor suits you and your skills, needs, and work habits. The supervisor's style will probably not change. It is your job to adapt to the style of the supervisor or to find a new workplace.

SELF CHECK

The following phrases describe characteristics of laissez-faire, democratic, and autocratic leadership styles. Identify which is being described by labeling it A, LF, or D. As you read, think about whether or not some of these phrases might apply to more than one style.

_____ 1. Frequent committee meetings are held.

_____ 2. Decisions are made by the work group.

_____ 3. Decisions are made by the supervisor.

_____ 4. Workers are encouraged to be creative.

_____ 5. The supervisor may not be on the work site.

_____ 6. Original work is encouraged.

_____ 7. Everyone's work is valued.

_____ 8. The supervisor gives praise and criticism.

_____ 9. Workers are empathetic, cooperative, and participatory.

_____ 10. Authority is not delegated.

_____ 11. Specific instructions are avoided.

_____ 12. The supervisor prefers to involve employees in the decision-making process.

chec**k**point

1. **What makes a supervisor different from other workers?**

_____

_____

_____

_____

2. **What are the three basic leadership styles?**

_____

_____

_____

_____

3. **The leadership style of all quality supervisors is the same.**
   True _____ False _____

4. **What personal qualities do you need to work well under the supervision of an autocratic leader?**

_____

_____

_____

_____

5. **What personal qualities do you need to work well under the supervision of a laissez-faire leader?**

_____

_____

_____

_____

_____

_____

_____

applications

1. List five types of businesses in which laissez-faire leadership would be beneficial in the workplace. Explain why.

_____

_____

_____

_____

2. Under what leadership style do you think you would prefer to work? Explain your answer.

_____

_____

_____

3. Using what you have learned about leadership styles, how would you proceed in the following situations if you were working for a laissez-faire supervisor, a democratic supervisor, or an autocratic supervisor? Why?

Situation A: You have discovered a new way to speed up a work process.

Laissez-faire _____

_____

_____

Democratic _____

_____

_____

Autocratic _____

_____

_____

Situation B: You would like to inquire about the possibilities of supporting a local charity by asking your coworkers to participate in a walk-a-thon. You want the support of the supervisor.

Laissez-faire _____

_____

_____

Democratic _____

_____

_____

Autocratic _____

_____

_____

4. Review the leadership styles discussed in the chapter. Think about three or four people with whom you interact daily. Write their names below and the style of leadership you think each person is projecting. Is there a common leadership style among the group?

_____

_____

_____

_____

_____

_____

Communicating with Your Supervisor

To establish a good working relationship with your supervisor, you must maintain an open line of communication. With an open line of communication, you will know what is expected, your supervisor will know what is going on, and you will know how to respond to your supervisor's directives. The following tips will help you establish a good rapport with your supervisor.

ALLOW NO SURPRISES

Any time there is a problem, crisis, or new development in your work area, make sure that your supervisor hears about it from you first. Supervisors do not like surprises. They need to be kept aware of what is going on in order to make quality decisions.

Marina works in the shipping department of a large aircraft production company. She receives a call from a major supplier about the possibility of a steel shipment being held up because of a rail strike. Marina decides not to mention this possible delay to her supervisor, Carmela. She does not want Carmela to worry unnecessarily about the shipment. Marina decides that she will check on it later. Carmela hears from another worker about the possible late shipment. She is surprised and alarmed that she has not been kept informed.

Keep your supervisor apprised of all situations and potential situations. Your supervisor cannot be everywhere at one time; therefore, communication from you is essential. Supervisors always appreciate a "heads up."

> "Problems are just challenging opportunities."
>
> —ANONYMOUS

Smart Tip ▼ ▼ ▼

The body language you display when talking with your supervisor should be very positive. Your body language should transfer determination and sincerity.

Here are some tips to help you use body language effectively.

- Whenever possible, position yourself at the eye level of the supervisor. If the supervisor stands, you stand. If the supervisor sits, you sit.
- Avoid looking downward.
- Keep your hands out of your pockets during conversation.
- Sit up straight and don't slump or slouch in your chair.
- Lean forward from the hips slightly.
- Keep your hands and legs quiet.
- Keep eye contact with your supervisor.
- Don't cross your arms over your chest.
- Avoid aggressive gestures.

▲ ▲ ▲ ▲ ▲ ▲ ▲ ▲ ▲

UNDERSTAND YOUR SUPERVISOR'S COMMUNICATION STYLE

People have favorite styles of communicating, so it is important for you to become familiar with how your supervisor prefers to receive information. Some supervisors like information in writing backed with facts, statistical data, and other support documents. If your supervisor prefers this style of communication, use it. Prepare memos and reports when sharing information. Be sure that written documents contain no keying errors or misinformation and that they look professional. For some supervisors, if it isn't in writing, it doesn't exist.

Some supervisors prefer to receive information orally. They like to listen, reflect, and then react. If your supervisor prefers oral communication, use it. Organize your thoughts and what you are going to say prior to providing the information. It is okay to take notes with you and refer to those notes.

on the job

Jeremiah is an office worker in an insurance company. He keeps a very messy desk. Heather's workstation is about six feet from Jeremiah's. The way Jeremiah keeps his desk is very irritating to Heather. She frequently makes remarks about his "mess" to coworkers. She gives him looks of disgust at every opportunity. She finally gets so annoyed that she bursts into the supervisor's office and blurts out, "You have got to do something about Jeremiah. I just can't stand looking at that messy desk." The supervisor is a little stunned by this outburst and replies, "Jeremiah is a good worker. I have more important things to worry about than someone's housekeeping habits."

Was Heather's problem worthy of supervisory attention? What problems may Heather have created for herself with this outburst?

focus on ethics

Olivia and Roger work in a clothing store. Olivia has noticed that Roger puts clothing in his size that he likes in the back of the storeroom. Several times customers have been unable to find items in their size, and Roger has told them that the merchandise is not available. Olivia knows full well that the items are available but have been hidden in the storage area by Roger. During the final sale days, the items Roger has been saving magically appear on the sale racks. He gets the employee discount plus the customer discount. He considers this a perk of working in a retail store.

Should Olivia challenge Roger about his practice? Should she simply remove the clothes from the storage area? Should she speak with the supervisor? Should she remain silent?

Also find out if your supervisor likes to hear from you once an hour, once a day, once a week, or only as necessary. This, of course, will depend on the type of work you are doing and the amount of experience you have in doing it. Whatever your supervisor prefers, *do it.*

If your work site is equipped with electronic messaging, use it as desired by the supervisor. This is a good, immediate way to communicate.

It is wise to keep a written record of all communication with your supervisor. If you provide him or her with written information, keep a copy. If you use oral communication, keep some notes about what was said and when. This will protect you if information is misinterpreted or lost.

On the other side of the communication link, you must be a good listener. To understand what your supervisor expects from you, you must be a careful listener. When you are discussing a topic, listen carefully. Listen not just for what the supervisor is saying, but also for what he or she means and what implications there might be. If you are not getting the supervisor's "drift," state what you *think* has been said and ask for clarification. After the discussion, summarize what you have learned to make sure you understood. Write down key points so they are not forgotten. To reinforce the importance of good listening, you may wish to review Chapters 4 and 5.

chec✔point

1. **What options for communication with your supervisor are usually available?**

   _____

   _____

   _____

   _____

2. **Why is it important to find out the preferred communication style of your supervisor?**

   _____

   _____

   _____

   _____

3. **Why is it important to write down or keep records of your conversations with the supervisor?**

   _____

   _____

   _____

   _____

4. **List three body language tips that are important to remember as you communicate with a supervisor.**

   _____

   _____

   _____

   _____

applications

1. List the body language items that you feel would require work on your part as you think about talking with your supervisor.

2. What notes would you record after the following conversation with your supervisor?

Clarence: I would like to tell you about a safety concern that I have in my work area. Many workers from the engine room go through my work area on the way to the break room and track in grease. The grease creates a very slippery situation. The grease is cleaned up by the night crew; however, by noon the area becomes slippery. I wouldn't want anyone to fall.

Supervisor: Clarence, thank you for bringing this situation to my attention. I didn't realize that the tracking of grease from the engine room was creating a safety hazard. I'll work on a solution soon. Please share with your coworkers the information about the slippery spots in your work area.

3. You need to discuss a production problem with your supervisor but know that she does not like to receive written information about serious problems. She is interested in hearing the problem and the solution. Think of a situation when you used oral communication. How would this situation differ if you had used written communication?

Special Communications with Your Supervisor

There are several situations when an extra effort needs to be made in communicating with your supervisor. There will be times when you need to communicate with your supervisor about a particularly troublesome problem, an idea that you have generated, or a request for a raise. You also need to feel comfortable accepting a compliment. Thinking through these situations beforehand will help you communicate more effectively.

TAKE PROBLEMS TO YOUR SUPERVISOR

Your supervisor wants to be aware of problems. However, you need to exercise some judgment about taking problems to your supervisor that may not be appropriate or worthy of his or her attention. It is important that you approach your supervisor with problems. Generally, these problems should be work related; however, if you are having a significant personal problem that could affect your work, keep your supervisor informed.

The following steps can help you organize your thoughts and information so that you will take a minimal amount of your supervisor's time when presenting a problem.

1. Establish a suitable setting.
You are sharing a problem with your supervisor, not the entire workforce. Step into a private office, canteen area, or quiet hallway. This will help ensure that you have the supervisor's full attention.

2. Explain the problem in your own words.
Use terms that accurately describe your concerns and feelings. Do not try to toss in a $5 word when a 50-cent word will do just as well in conveying your feelings.

3. Present facts that support the problem.
These facts should be carefully gathered prior to the presentation of your problem. Do your homework! Your facts should be specific, documented, and accurate. You will lose credibility by stating generalizations, half truths, and innuendoes. Avoid using phrases such as "I hear that . . . ." "I assume . . . ." or "Rumor has it . . . ." If you do not have the facts in order, you are not ready to talk with your supervisor.

4. Ask for understanding.
Pause and ask your supervisor whether or not he or she understands the problem and if you have explained it clearly enough. (Notice that you have assumed a leadership role in this process.) This step will allow your supervisor the chance to ask questions or clarify points that you have made.

5. Present several alternative solutions.
Be prepared with some suggestions as to how the problem might be solved. If you do not have any solutions in mind, you are not ready to talk with the supervisor. Do your homework! Be prepared with alternative suggestions.

6. State your recommended solution.
Indicate the solution that you think is best and why after you have presented several alternatives. However, do not insist that your recommendation is the one that must be followed. Welcome his or her input. There may be options that you have not considered.

7. Thank your supervisor.
Thank your supervisor for his or her time and attention. If appropriate, request a follow-up to the conversation at a later date.

After you have completed this seven-step process with your supervisor, return to your workstation and resist the temptation to share the conversation with coworkers. They will be curious, but the employee who is skillful in communicating with a supervisor and who can keep those conversations confidential has an edge over coworkers who do not realize the importance of this skill.

SHARE YOUR IDEAS

After you have been with an organization for awhile, you will have some ideas that you would like to promote and share. You should seek a position in an organization where creativity and initiative are welcome. You may hesitate to share your thoughts and ideas with the supervisors because you fear having your idea rejected or "shot down." Dispel those thoughts! You owe it to yourself and the workplace to share your ideas.

There are some appropriate points to consider when you are ready to advance an idea to your superior. (1) Plan thoroughly for the presentation of your idea. It is essential that you research all aspects of your idea and check your idea to be sure that it is congruent with company policy. (2) Avoid presenting your idea on the spur of the moment. Arrange the presentation at a convenient time for your supervisor. (3) Support yourself with notes from research. Let your supervisor know that you have thought about all areas and aspects of the new concept. As you talk about the idea, be concise and hit the key points of your proposal. Do not oversell by using too many superlatives. Place the emphasis on objective, well-thought-out features of your idea. (4) Close with a positive statement. "Please give some thought to this concept and I'm confident you will like the idea and be willing to support it." (5) Be prepared to leave a brief outline of your presentation with the supervisor.

Be prepared for and anticipate a negative response. You may hear: "I won't be

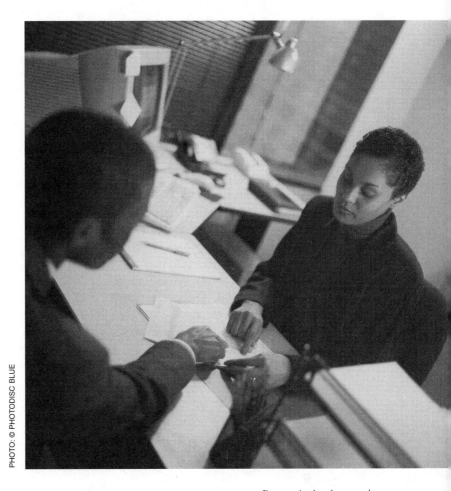

PHOTO: © PHOTODISC BLUE

Be organized and prepared to present a new idea to your supervisor.

able to review this immediately." You might respond: "I know you are a very busy person with a great deal of responsibility, but I think you'll find this idea worth your time." Or, you might hear: "We're so busy right now. We just can't take on another idea." You might respond: "I agree. But, I would still like to get your thoughts on this even if we can't get to it right away."

Leave the setting with a handshake, a friendly smile, and say sincerely, "I look forward to hearing from you. Thanks so much for listening."

"Man's [sic] mind, once stretched by a new idea, never regains its original dimensions."

—OLIVER WENDELL HOLMES

ASK FOR A RAISE

There will come a time in your career when you feel it appropriate to request an increase in your salary. As with other special communication situations with your supervisor, this conversation must be held in a private setting. Also prepare, prepare, and prepare for this conversation.

Step 1: Prepare for the conversation by looking at how you meet and exceed the expectations of your job. It is not necessary to tell your supervisor that you run a wonderful department or that you are a great worker. Let your research show why you meet and exceed expectations.

When I took this job, the company was outsourcing the monthly newsletter at a cost of $5,000 per issue. I reviewed the software already available in the company and now with the help of my assistant, the newsletter is published in-house. The only cost is that of a few hours of our time and the paper. I have trained 14 of our representatives on the use of PowerPoint software and all 14 of them are now using PowerPoint presentations. Our sales are up 11 percent for the quarter and at least in part the increase may be due to the improved communication between our sales staff and the customers.

Step 2: Complete a review of what others doing the same work that you are doing are earning both in the company and in comparable settings. If your review shows that you are below the average, bring this fact to the attention of your supervisor. If your salary falls within the average, explain how you exceed the expectations of the position. If your salary is above the average, consider yourself well paid and wait until another time to request a raise.

Step 3: Make a list of all of your accomplishments since you joined the organization. Present this list in writing or orally,

depending upon the communication preference of your supervisor.

Step 4: Once the above work is complete, you should prepare yourself emotionally to request the raise. If you are convinced that you deserve it, ask for it. The focus must be on your job performance. The fact that you want or need a raise for a personal reason (your child needs braces, you need a better car, or your house needs a new roof) is not justification for a raise to your employer.

Thanks for seeing me today. I have been with the Woodrow Company for the past five years and I've enjoyed my work very much. My duties and responsibilities have steadily increased over time. I have been given the responsibility of the Christensen account, I am now responsible for supervising two people in the accounting department, and I have been asked to represent our branch at the monthly Board of Directors meetings. As I said, I take pleasure in my work at Woodrow and very much appreciate the opportunities that I have been given. As I have accepted many new responsibilities, which are further explained in the summary (hand the summary to the supervisor), I would like to respectfully request that my salary be aligned with my responsibilities.

Step 5: Be prepared with a dollar amount that you think is fair and equitable for the work that you do.

Step 6: Thank your supervisor for his or her time. End with a phrase like:

"May I expect a response from you during the next week?

ACCEPT A COMPLIMENT

This conversation should be an easy one. However, many people find it difficult to accept compliments. You may have been told at different times in your life that it isn't appropriate to be boastful or "full of yourself." Thus you may find yourself uncomfortable when kind words of praise are said to you. If you are complimented by your supervisor, your first words should be "thank you." The "thank you" should be said sincerely and with eye contact. You can take the opportunity to share your positive thoughts with your supervisor. If appropriate, acknowledge the contribution of coworkers who also deserve the compliment or praise. Be specific about the others. For example:

Supervisor: "Lora, I want to thank you for the extra work you did to highlight the good work of the department during the presentation before the Board of Directors."

Lora: "Thank you very much. I am glad you were pleased and felt the presentation went well. Your part of the presentation was outstanding. Denise and Cheryl were of great help to me in putting the PowerPoint presentation together."

As you practice accepting compliments, remember that it is okay to accept a compliment by giving a compliment. Avoid "confessing" your concerns regarding the compliment or explaining why you doubt the compliment. This doesn't make you look modest. It makes you look awkward and embarrassed.

Supervisor: "Max, that is a very smart-looking suit you are wearing."

Max: "This old thing? I bought it on sale when Hardy's went out of business. I have always felt like it looks cheap."

Max shows in this example what *not* to say. Max's comments could be interpreted as saying to his supervisor, "Hey, you don't have good taste if you think this suit looks smart." The correct thing for Max to say is, "Thank you, you look sharp yourself."

check**point**

1. **Should all problems be taken to your supervisor? Why or why not?**

_____

_____

_____

_____

2. **What kind of setting is recommended for discussing a problem with your supervisor? Why is the setting important?**

_____

_____

_____

_____

3. What steps should be followed when taking a problem to your supervisor?

_____

_____

_____

_____

_____

_____

_____

_____

_____

4. Why is it important to do some preparation before you request a raise?

_____

_____

_____

_____

_____

_____

_____

_____

_____

5. Why is it hard for some people to accept a compliment?

_____

_____

_____

_____

_____

_____

_____

_____

_____

applications

1. Step 3 in explaining a problem to your supervisor is: "present facts that support the problem." Choose from the following statements those that would be appropriate in communicating with your supervisor that you need to adjust your work hours (8 a.m. to 4:30 p.m.) to 7:30 a.m. to 4:00 p.m. The company does offer flex hours.

YES   NO

_____ _____   My youngest child gets out of school at 3:45 p.m., and I would like to be home close to the time that she arrives home.

_____ _____   I hear people in accounting can work whatever hours they choose.

_____ _____   Maybe I could get Carey to cover my phone from 4 to 4:30 p.m.

_____ _____   Rumor has it that everyone will be working 7:30 a.m. to 4 p.m. after June. I want to work those hours now.

_____ _____   My spouse works in Cortland (30 minutes away) and cannot adjust his work hours to be at home when our daughter gets home from school.

2. Using the items you have placed a check before in Application 1, write down what you would say to your supervisor if making the above request.

_____

_____

_____

3. Why is it important for you to make a point of not discussing with coworkers any conversation you have with supervisors? What might you say if a coworker says, "Hey, I saw you with the boss in the break room. What was that all about?"

_____

_____

_____

4. Tony Waldron works as a front-end cashier and assistant manager in a discount store. Tony knows the merchandise well, and he wants to be considered for a promotion when one becomes available. Tony's present supervisor, Ruth Brooks, is pleased with Tony's work, his pleasant way with customers, and his knowledge of the products within the store. Ruth plans a vacation and leaves Tony responsible for the store in her absence.

While Ruth is on vacation, Tony observes Ed and Bob stocking the inventory. Ed and Bob appear to have a personality conflict and frequently argue in front of the customers. Ed and Bob are good workers, but they cannot get along. They get in each other's way. Tony thinks that their duties should be reassigned. Ed could stock aisle shelves 1 through 8, and Bob could stock aisle shelves 9 through 17. This would mean they would not work together, and it would prevent arguments in front of customers.

As soon as Ruth returns, Tony asks to visit with her. Tony wants to share what he perceives to be a problem and offer a solution. How should Tony explain the problem and his solution to Ruth? Write down what Tony should say in each of the steps presented in this section on how to take a problem to your supervisor.

a. _____

_____

_____

b. _____

_____

_____

c. _____

_____

_____

d. _____

_____

_____

e. _____

_____

_____

f. _____

_____

_____

g. _____

_____

_____

5. Mallory has several ideas that she feels will put patients more at ease as they enter the out-patient clinic where she works. Mallory has been at the clinic for two years. Her ideas include: providing a less businesslike atmosphere in the reception area, providing coffee and soft drinks for the patients, and having someone on hand at all times to explain the procedure(s) that the patient will have done. What advice would you have for Mallory before she presents her ideas to her supervisor?

_____

_____

_____

_____

_____

_____

What Should You Expect of Your Supervisor?

Relationships between supervisors and employees are better when each helps to meet the other's needs. You have a right to expect to be evaluated and criticized, to work in a safe environment, and to receive personal recognition. You also have the right to expect explanations for decisions, clarification of policies, and fair evaluations of your work. If your expectations are reasonable but not met, you should employ the seven steps of taking a problem to your supervisor (see page 222) and discussing the situation with him or her. Bring your concerns to the attention of your supervisor, not your coworkers.

"A just criticism is a commenda- tion, rather than a detraction."

—Henry Jacob

YOUR RIGHT TO CRITICISM

The right to receive criticism from your employer is a fair expectation. You may be thinking: "What do you mean? Why should I want to seek or expect criticism?" The truth is that you *need* criticism. Criticism should not be viewed as a negative word. **Criticism** is the route to self-improvement and should be regarded as such. Without criticism and suggestions from your supervisor, you will be unaware of how to improve. No matter how skilled you become on the job, improvement is always possible. Improved skills may lead to additional self-confidence, promotions, and income.

Many supervisors may try to avoid providing you with adequate criticism. When constructive criticism is not given, your employer is denying you a right. Many supervisors find offering criticism to be a very difficult and unpleasant task. Think of yourself as a future supervisor. It is doubtful that administering criticism will be one of your favorite duties. Other reasons supervisors avoid giving criticism are as follows:

1. Many supervisors hope that if you work at a job long enough, you will figure out what you are doing wrong and correct the problem.
2. Some supervisors dislike upsetting the "status quo" in any way. If things are going reasonably well, they take the position "Why bother to upset anybody?"
3. Supervisors may fear confrontation in any form and dislike any show of emotion from employees. Some people do not take criticism well and respond in an emotional manner—pouting, crying, or other emotional outbursts.

Thus, some supervisors may not want to risk the consequences of giving criticism. When this happens, you (the employee) are the loser because you will not receive information that will assist you in becoming a more productive employee.

It is important for you to communicate with your supervisor that you appreciate and can accept suggestions and guidance. This can be done by asking your supervisor about your job performance. Speak up during performance evaluations, and ask for suggestions on how to improve. Whenever suggestions are shared about your work, accept them graciously, with a sincere vow to make improvements. Thank the supervisor for his or her interest in your success.

AVOID NEGATIVE REACTIONS TO CRITICISM

Consider your own reactions to criticism from others. If you react positively, you may receive helpful information. If you react negatively to criticism, your employer may not share with you some information that would be useful to your work. Avoid the following common negative reactions when you receive criticism.

Giving excuses. If the criticism you receive is deserved, do not give flimsy excuses and alibis. This is tough, because there is a natural tendency to make excuses. If a friend says, "You're in a sour mood today," the typical human response is, "Well, you would be too, if you had the problems I have." Excuses can carry over to your work life too. "There are errors in this report because my work area is so noisy. I can't concentrate." Responses such as this are not an appropriate way to indicate to your supervisor that you can handle criticism. A better response about errors in a report would be "Thanks for pointing those out. I'll correct them right away."

Verbally attacking. You may have a desire to "verbally attack" in response to criticism. Fight it. "Attackers" focus the spotlight away from themselves and blame someone else for the error(s). A verbal attack may be oral or written, and may be directed at anyone. "Well, if your directions had been clear, I would have gotten it right" or "I did a lousy job on proofing that copy because I had to answer Melodee's phone and couldn't do two things at once."

The attacker does not handle criticism well and may be creating an unnecessary conflict with a coworker or even with the supervisor. A better response in this situation may be "I do need to go over that copy again. Thanks for giving me the opportunity."

Withdrawing. You may react to criticism by withdrawing or feeling guilty and inadequate. Those who react in this manner ask no questions on how to improve but rather give up and take the "What's-the-use" attitude. This type of behavior is inappropriate, unprofessional, and obvious to your supervisor. Again, you will be the loser because the supervisor may not want

to deal with this attitude in the future. And worse, you will not have improved your performance.

If you react to criticism by making excuses, attacking, blaming others, or withdrawing, you are experiencing a lot of emotional pain without much healing. When you fail to use criticism to your advantage, you suffer loss of self-esteem, as well as the opportunity to improve your work. Begin to take a healthier attitude about criticism; recognize it as a tool for self-improvement.

HANDLING CRITICISM

Work hard to accept criticism with professionalism and maturity. Step one in this process is to evaluate the criticism. Is it deserved or undeserved?

Deserved criticism. Handling deserved criticism is not difficult. Use the following steps to handle deserved criticism.

1. Listen very carefully to the suggestions being made. Fight the impulse to be defensive. Keep eye contact with your supervisor.
2. Ask questions, if necessary, to clarify the error that you made or the suggestions being offered.
3. Offer to correct the error(s), if possible.
4. Pledge an effort to try suggestions.
5. Thank the supervisor giving the criticism.

After you have completed these steps, leave the situation with your self-esteem in place and go back to work. Do not share with your coworkers either remarks made about you or your response. The comments made were between you and your supervisor. Your supervisor will recognize that you can accept criticism and will be willing to communicate recommendations to you in the future.

Undeserved criticism. Coping with undeserved criticism requires more self-control and courage. At some point in your

"He [or she] only profits from praise who values criticism."

—HEINRICH HEINZ

on the job

Xiao Li has worked part-time for Dr. Eliza Goodwin for several months. The job is important to her, and she enjoys the work and the extra income. Dr. Goodwin is chairperson of the anthropology department at the state university. Xiao Li seldom sees her because she gets her work assignments from the administrative assistant, Mildred Christensen.

One day, Dr. Goodwin unexpectedly calls Xiao Li into her office and says, "Young woman, sit down!" Shaking her finger at Xiao Li, she says, "You just cost the university $2,000." She tosses a letter at her. It misses Xiao Li's lap, and Xiao Li leans over to pick it up. Because of this treatment, she now has a lump in her throat and tears are brimming in her eyes. Xiao Li tries to say, "I don't understand. What has happened?" Her words are unclear, because of her emotional state. Dr. Goodwin says to her, "This letter you keyed offers a part-time assistantship to a graduate student. You keyed the figure $22,000 rather than $20,000. This guy is a smart one, and he has informed us that he'll accept the offer of $22,000 as stated in our letter." Xiao Li has now recovered somewhat and looks at the letter. She realizes that she did not work on the day the letter was keyed and does not recognize the name of the recipient. Most importantly, the reference initials at the bottom of the page (MC) are not hers. She states, "I didn't key this letter." Dr. Goodwin replies, "Well, how do you know that?" Xiao Li tells her. Dr. Goodwin pauses, looks at her, and says, "Oh, I see. Well, I had better talk to Mildred about this." Xiao Li is upset for the remainder of the day and is concerned about the wrath that is about to come down on Mildred.

Could Xiao Li have handled the unjust criticism better? What might she have done differently?

career, you will be unfairly criticized or blamed for something that is not your fault; it happens to everyone. The following series of steps should be followed carefully to deal with this unfortunate circumstance.

1. Listen carefully to your accuser. Do not interrupt. Do not try to deny. Do not say, "but," "wait a minute," "you're wrong," or "no, that's not what happened." Just keep quiet and listen. Keep eye contact with your accuser.

2. After your accuser is finished, take a deep breath and ask a series of calm questions. Your questions should be polite, reasonable, responsible, and related to what you have just heard. Do not become rude or raise your voice. Stay calm!

3. Through your questions, lead your accuser to the conclusion that you are being unfairly criticized.

4. Accept the apology of the accuser if one is offered. Keep in mind that apologies are difficult for some people and none may be forthcoming.

5. Say "Thank you for your time." (This might be tough, but say it.)

6. Return to your workplace and do not discuss the incident with anyone.

Above all, do not keep a "chip" on your shoulder and do not take on the attitude of "Well, I guess I got that straightened out." This strategy may become clearer to you as you see it played out in the "On the Job" example.

Handling undeserved criticism is tough and takes practice. The rewards, however, are great. It is important to your relationship with a supervisor that you are able to demonstrate an ability to handle either type of criticism. If you approach criticism positively, you will find that it can be as valuable as praise. You are probably aware of your strong points. Criticism allows others to help you improve your weaknesses.

Your goal in responding to deserved or undeserved criticism is to appear open, willing to listen, willing to change, and above all, willing to cooperate.

SAFE WORK ENVIRONMENT

The right to criticism is a big expectation and has taken a lot of space in this chapter. There are other things you have a right to expect. A safe work environment is one of them. When you come to work, you have the right to expect a clean, safe environment. For example, in eating establishments where spills are common, floors should have nonslip surfaces or floor mats, and they should be cleaned regularly.

Businesses of all types must have clearly marked fire exits. Workers who may be exposed to dangerous chemicals should be provided with protective gear. Workers should not be expected to work in areas where mold, high levels of lead, or asbestos are present. Machine workers must be provided with protective gear (as appropriate)—steel-toed shoes, eye goggles, or earplugs may be required.

If you are encountering hazards or unsafe working conditions on the job, point them out to your supervisor. If the dangerous conditions are not corrected, you can seek help from the Occupational Safety and Health Administration (OSHA). OSHA is a federal agency that sets and enforces standards for job safety. You have a right to expect safe working conditions! You also have a right to a workplace that is free from discrimination and harassment of any kind.

PERSONAL RECOGNITION

Another right you have is the possibility of personal recognition. If you are doing your job well, your supervisor should acknowledge your work. This doesn't mean that you should expect daily recognition, frequent pay increases, plaques, or honors. It means that your employer should recognize your contributions to the organization. This is most often accomplished by an occasional "pat on the back" that will likely take the form of a personal comment or a note to you.

Many organizations have special days of recognition for employees, bonus programs, or special recognition programs, such as employee of the month or the year. These activities are publicly rewarding, but may not be available in your workplace.

Regardless of company policies and programs, if you are conscientious and work hard, you do have a right to expect some personal recognition from your supervisor. Everyone who is diligent needs to be told that he or she is doing a good job. In the past (and perhaps still at some companies) the regular paycheck and retaining your job were often considered the only "recognition" needed. However, in today's job market, where change is more common, stress can be higher, and overtime is almost inevitable, companies are beginning to realize that employees need to be recognized when they excel. If you are not appreciated, it is difficult to be loyal, diligent, enthusiastic, and show initiative.

check*point*

1. You have a right to seek criticism from your supervisor.
   True _____ False _____

2. It is preferable to work for a supervisor who offers little or no criticism.
   True _____ False _____

3. If you receive undeserved criticism, it is best not to make waves and just accept it.
   True _____ False _____

4. What three expectations should you have of your supervisor?

   _____

   _____

   _____

   _____

   _____

   _____

   _____

   _____

applications

1. Have you ever received undeserved criticism? What were your feelings? How did you handle the situation? Write out the situation and what you should have said using the steps for handling undeserved criticism given in this section.

_____

_____

_____

_____

2. Have you ever received criticism that was helpful? Explain the criticism and how it helped you.

_____

_____

_____

_____

3. How would you respond to this comment of undeserved criticism by your supervisor? "I am not pleased with the quality of your work. You are making too many mistakes. And, you spend too much time talking on the phone and with coworkers."

_____

_____

_____

_____

What Your Supervisor Expects of You

You have been reading about your rights and what you can expect of a supervisor. Turn the table and spend some time thinking about your supervisor's expectations of you. If you understand those expectations, your chances of getting along with the supervisor will be enhanced.

BE PRESENT AND ON TIME

Know that your supervisor will expect you to be on the job regularly and on time. Your absence can cause work inefficiency, disruptions in the work of others, and a general frustration for those who are called upon to fill in for you. Even being late causes problems at work. Chronic absenteeism and tardiness both show a lack of consideration for others, and communicate to your supervisor that you may not take the job seriously. Being at work and on time shows your supervisor that you are responsible, conscientious, and a good team player.

If you have an emergency, illness, or another unavoidable problem, let your supervisor know as soon as possible. Offer to help out in any way you can to make up for your absence: come in early when you get back to work, or stay late to make up for lost time. Continual absenteeism from the job will not be allowed by your supervisor and will result in your termination. Chronic tardiness can also result in your being dismissed.

SHOW DILIGENCE AND INITIATIVE

A **diligent worker** is one who does his or her work carefully and completely. The diligent worker is industrious, constant, and persistent with each task. Supervisors notice workers who do more than just what is expected. When bonuses, promotions, and pay raises are considered, dividends may be in store for the diligent employee.

Supervisors also value personal initiative. Ambition, drive, energy, and motivation to a task and the workplace demonstrate initiative. When you have finished your assigned tasks, do not just sit and wait for your supervisor to tell you what to do next. Look for something that needs to be done on your own or assist someone else. Work for your best possible performance. Do your best; do not accept second best from yourself. Be aware of your own strengths and make efforts to use them.

ALLEGIANCE

Allegiance is the demonstration of loyalty and commitment to your supervisor. Make an effort to speak well of your supervisor to your coworkers and those outside the organization. Do not "bad mouth" your supervisor, even if it seems to be acceptable behavior in your workplace. It is not acceptable for you. If you find you are dissatisfied with your supervisor and have nothing good to say about him or her, be a professional and say nothing. You read about the importance of loyalty in Chapter 7 as a part of getting along with your coworkers. It is equally important, perhaps more important, as you strive to get along with your supervisor. Allegiance is expected.

ENTHUSIASM

You also read in Chapter 7 about the importance of being enthusiastic around coworkers. Enthusiasm is also important and expected by your supervisor. Many supervisors believe that the best employees are those who like their work and show enthusiasm for it. All jobs have some unpleasant parts. Do not dwell on the tasks you dislike; instead, focus your thoughts on the parts of the job that you enjoy. When someone asks you about your position, tell him or her about the things you enjoy. By focusing on and sharing the positive parts of your job, you will be a more productive and successful employee. Supervisors like to sense enthusiasm within the workplace. It makes their jobs easier.

CHANGE

You are living in a fast-paced age, so your supervisor will expect you to be flexible and adaptable to the ever-changing work-place. A piece of equipment you are work-ing with today may be obsolete tomorrow. You need to be ready to accept this kind of change and be willing to adapt to new chal-lenges and tasks as they come to you.

on the job

Pedro has been working for Boyer's Construction Company for a few weeks. He likes his work. He enjoys being a part of the home-building business. Pedro's primary responsibility is to assist with the framing. Occasionally he has spare time because materials have not yet arrived at the site. Whenever this happens, Pedro volunteers to help others with their tasks or spends time cleaning his work area. Mort Boyer, general manager, notices that Pedro is busy all the time. He makes a mental note to consider him the next time a site-framing supervisor is selected.

Why do you think Mr. Boyer would consider Pedro for promotion? What have Pedro's actions communicated to Mr. Boyer?

Technology at Work

Do a little thinking and researching about the role of a supervisor.

These Web sites present in-formation about successful supervisors and provide a broader perspective of management.

http://ut.essortment.com/
    leadershipstyle_rrnq.htm
http://tx.essortment.com/
    howtoaskraise_rsme.htm

Keep an open mind toward change. Fear of change is natural. The fear comes when you do not understand why the change is taking place. Keep asking questions and seeking answers until you are comfortable with the change. Do not allow yourself to become obsolete by being stubborn and resistant to change. Change will keep you fresh, challenged, and enthusiastic about your work.

If you meet the expectations of your supervisors, you are more likely to meet with success, no matter what career you choose.

"Fear of change is always a brake on progress."

—ANONYMOUS

check✓point

1. **Why is being on time so important in the workplace?**

   _____

   _____

   _____

   _____

2. **What is a diligent worker?**

   _____

   _____

   _____

   _____

3. **Why is enthusiasm important in the workplace?**

   _____

   _____

   _____

   _____

4. **How can you control fear of change?**

   _____

   _____

   _____

   _____

   _____

   _____

   _____

   _____

   _____

applications

1. Attendance on the job is very important in any position. Missing work requires a good reason. Place a check mark by the statements that you believe are acceptable reasons to miss work. Be prepared to defend your choices.

a. _____ You are ill with a cold and cough and have a temperature of 101 degrees.

b. _____ A friend is in town just for the day and you want to show her your community.

c. _____ A close friend dies and you want to attend the funeral.

d. _____ You have a slight headache and decide you need to take a "mental health" day.

e. _____ You have had a fun-filled, long weekend. You feel you are too tired to go to work.

f. _____ Your special friend is leaving for duty in the armed services. You will not see her for one year. You want to spend the day with her.

Comments on any of the above statements: _____

_____

_____

_____

_____

_____

_____

_____

_____

_____

_____

2. Write a paragraph about a change that has occurred in your workplace, home, or school that required you to adapt to the change. What was the change? How well did you accept the change? How did you adjust to the change? How are you handling the change now? What did you learn from your reaction to change and from the process of adapting? What might you do differently in the future?

_____

_____

_____

_____

_____

_____

_____

3. Write a paragraph explaining why tardiness on the job may affect productivity and other workers. What do you think happens when people are frequently tardy?

_____

_____

_____

_____

_____

_____

_____

8 Points to Remember

chapter

Review the following points to determine what you remember from the chapter.

- It is important to know your supervisor and understand his or her leadership style. The basic leadership styles are autocratic, democratic, and laissez-faire.

- You must be able to relate to your supervisor and understand his or her preferred style of communication. If your supervisor likes to communicate orally, you should make every effort to communicate this way. If your supervisor prefers written information, you should write. Keep in mind that supervisors do not like surprises. Keep the lines of communication open and keep your supervisor informed.

- Special attention should be given in your efforts to take a problem to your supervisor, to share an idea, to request a raise, or to accept a compliment. All of these special communication challenges require preparation and thought on your part. You should establish a suitable setting, explain the problem in your own words, present facts that support the problem, ask for understanding, present several alternative solutions, state your recommended solution, and thank your supervisor for listening to your presentation. When sharing a new idea: plan thoroughly for the presentation of your idea, avoid presenting it on the spur of the moment, support the idea with notes you have researched, be prepared to leave a brief outline of the idea, and close with a positive statement. Be prepared and anticipate that you may get a negative response. Follow the seven-step plan when asking for a raise. Before you ask for a raise, be sure you anticipate questions and have answers related to your performance. "Thank you" is a good response to a compliment.

- Your rights as an employee include: receiving criticism, having a safe work environment, and receiving personal recognition. It is important to remember that criticism is a tool of self-improvement. Seek criticism from your supervisor in order to improve your performance. Supervisors enjoy working with employees who can accept suggestions and criticism. If a situation does arise where the criticism is undeserved, there are steps that can be taken to remedy the situation if you remain calm and businesslike.

- Remind yourself frequently of the expectations the employer has of you in addition to doing quality work—being on time, being diligent in your work, demonstrating initiative, showing loyalty and enthusiasm, and adapting to change as needed.

How did you do? Did you remember the main points you studied in the chapter?

key terms

Place the letter of the item in the definition column that matches the key word.

Key Word

_____1. Supervisor

_____2. Leadership style

_____3. Laissez-faire leader

_____4. Democratic leader

_____5. Autocratic leader

_____6. Delegate authority

_____7. Criticism

_____8. Diligent worker

_____9. Allegiance

Definition

a. Likes workers to show creativity

b. Lets someone do something on their own

c. Worker does tasks carefully and completely

d. Encourages participation in the workplace

e. One who is in charge of one or more workers

f. Does not entrust activities to others

g. A form of self-improvement

h. Demonstration of loyalty and commitment

i. Method used by the leader to get the work done

activities and projects

1. Create a list of questions that you could ask a supervisor in an effort to get to know his or her leadership style.

2. Arrange to interview someone who works in a supervisory capacity. Determine his or her leadership style by asking your questions. Submit a written report to your instructor giving your findings.

3. The parts manager in the automotive department is getting an illegal rebate from one of the wholesalers. You have discovered this information from a reliable source. Plus, you have witnessed a financial transaction between the parts manager and the wholesaler. You decide you must take the problem to your supervisor.

   Is the problem worthy of the supervisor's time and attention? Why or why not? What would you say to the supervisor? (Refer to the seven steps for taking a problem to your supervisor in Section 8.3, page 222.)

4. During your performance evaluation, the supervisor says that you are doing a good job and all of your ratings are good. You decide this is not enough feedback. You want to be the best worker you can be. What questions might you ask to get your supervisor to share more with you?

_____

_____

_____

_____

_____

_____

5. You have been a clerk in the Henderson Retail Store for three years. You have made your weekly sales quota every week of those three years. You need money because your rent is being raised. You have heard that another clerk receives a salary that exceeds yours by $3 per hour. You need some dental work done but have been putting it off because you can't afford it. You have helped devise a new inventory program for the cosmetic department that saves at least 20 hours of employee time when inventory is taken. You want a new car. The overall sales in your department have increased by 15 percent over a three-year period. During the last quarter, sales increased by 22.2 percent.

Outline how you would approach your supervisor and ask for a raise. You can select whatever information you wish from the information given.

_____

_____

_____

_____

_____

_____

case studies for critical thinking

ALLEGIANCE

Michael works in a government office responsible for services to senior citizens. His supervisor, Jenny, has worked in government for about 30 years. Jenny is considered competent and has been recognized publicly many times for her service to the clientele of the office. Michael does not like Jenny. He believes she expects too much of employees and coddles the senior citizens coming into the office. Michael tells workers from other offices that it is time for Jenny to retire. He frequently makes unkind comments about her decisions and seems to enjoy doing imitations of her. Michael's comments get back to Jenny and she must decide what to do about Michael.

1. Is Michael's behavior acceptable? Why or why not?

_____

_____

_____

2. What do you think of his behavior? Explain your thoughts.

_____

_____

_____

3. What information would you like to have about Michael and Jenny that might help you give advice to Jenny about what she should do?

_____

_____

_____

4. Should Jenny dismiss Michael? Would you dismiss Michael? Why or why not?

_____

_____

_____

Case 8.2

No Surprises

Kevin has the responsibility of preparing checks for the 44 employees of the Campbell Nursery. The checks are to be ready for employees on the last working day of each month. Kevin is ill for several days, and Teresita covers his duties. When Kevin returns he finds that Teresita has not entered overtime pay and has somehow lost data in the computer. Kevin does not panic because he has several days to get everything straightened out in order to meet the payroll. He calls a computer technician in to try and locate the missing data. The day before checks are to be given out, he realizes that they are going to be delayed. At this point, he informs his supervisor, Mr. Webb. Mr. Webb is furious and demands, "Why didn't you tell me there was a problem?"

1. Who is to blame for the problem?

_____

_____

_____

2. What should Kevin have done upon returning to work and encountering the problem? Explain your answer.

_____

_____

_____

3. Why is Mr. Webb upset? What other workplace problems may result because of this mix-up?

_____

_____

_____

Case 8.3

Leadership Style

Megan has a new job in state government in the area of disability determinations. She is to work with clients who have mental or physical handicaps that entitle them to apply for government assistance. Megan's supervisor, Frank, has only recently been transferred to disability determinations. On her first morning, Frank tells Megan the rules, assigns her cases, and reviews the policy manual in detail. Frank shows her to her desk and tells her that he expects to see her there every work day, all day, except for during her approved 15-minute morning and afternoon breaks and one hour lunch. Megan feels that Frank is a bit brisk but decides he is okay—she knows exactly what to do.

During her second week, Frank calls her to his office and lets her know that he is dissatisfied with her work. He has checked her desk several times and she wasn't present. She has violated policies 2.3 and 5.4 of the manual. He tells her this type of thing will not happen again. The reason Megan has been away from her desk is that she finds several of her clients are more comfortable talking about their disabilities in an area away from others. She checks policies 2.3 and 5.4 and finds that they have to do with putting exact times and dates on forms.

1. What leadership style is Frank displaying? What evidence of this style do you see in the case study?

_____

_____

_____

2. Should Megan try to explain her absence from her desk? Should she seek permission to interview clients elsewhere?

_____

_____

_____

3. Megan doesn't feel that the details in policies 2.3 and 5.4 apply to the situation, and she doesn't understand why they were brought up. Should she challenge Frank about them?

_____

_____

_____

4. Megan is a "people person." She wants her clients to feel comfortable. She doesn't feel that the atmosphere in her area is conducive to comfortable discussions. How do you propose (or do you propose?) that Megan approach Frank with her concerns?

_____

_____

_____

Case 8.4

Attendance/Tardiness

Charley's of Toledo has been a profitable company for many years. Management is very excited about the efficiency and effectiveness of its employees. However, recently attendance has become an issue with employees being absent one or more days per week in most departments. Tardiness has also increased. As president of the company, John Charles is at a loss to understand this problem. He asks his vice president and general manager Henry Watts to investigate and determine the reasons for these issues.

1. Do you think the president has reason to be concerned about these problems?

2. What, if you were Henry, would you do to solve these problems? How should he go about learning what the reasons are?

Relating to Clients and Customers

think about it: Gabrielle has worked for Donley Medical Supply for several months. She feels competent about the information that she gives customers—so confident, in fact, that she no longer refers to product manuals. Albert McManus came to the supply house to purchase a wheelchair for his wife. Gabrielle showed him several floor models and others in their catalog. Albert emphasized that it was necessary for the back to be adjustable because of his wife's condition. Albert liked Model No. 212. Gabrielle did not have this model on the floor, but she could order one. Again, he asked for assurance that the back was adjustable. Albert finally said, "Fine, have one shipped to my home address." When the chair arrived at the McManus home, Albert discovered that the back was not adjustable. Albert was not pleased and called the store to announce that they should pick the chair up, return his check, and that he would shop elsewhere where he could get reliable service and find knowledgeable clerks.

Why did the company lose this customer? How could this have been prevented?

PHOTO: © STOCKBYTE GOLD

chapter focus

After completing this chapter, you should be able to:

1. List the reasons why customers are important.

2. Identify the expectations of customers and how these expectations can be met.

3. Communicate that you are working to serve the customer.

4. Communicate the attitude that the customer is right.

Chapter Highlights

9.1 **Customer Expectations**

9.2 **Customer Communication**

All businesses have someone whom they serve. Those who are served may be called clients, customers, patrons, or patients, depending on the type of business. For example, if you are working in a doctor's office, the people you serve are called patients. If you work in retail, those you serve are usually called customers. If you work for an arts foundation, your customers are usually called patrons. Regardless of how you refer to those you serve, remember that they want to be understood, listened to, cared for, and treated fairly and individually. Those whom you serve expect you to treat them as "special."

In order to treat a customer as "special," you must make the customer perceive that he or she is valuable. To the customer, you are the company. Customers expect you to make the organization work for them. They expect you to understand the big picture and be able to answer their questions, solve their problems, give them product use ideas, and refer them to just the right people for just the right things.

As part of your study on this topic, review Chapters 7 and 8. Many of the guidelines for getting along with coworkers and supervisors also hold true for relating well to your customers. Getting along with customers is a skill that may be challenging at times, but it does not need to be difficult. Treating each customer as you would like to be treated, trying to learn his or her needs, making every effort to satisfy those needs, and making the person feel valued will be good steps toward relating well to clients and customers.

Customers will keep coming back if you supply them with quality products and services that are delivered in a timely manner with a sense of empathy and a focus on reliability.

"Do what is right. Do the best you can. Treat others as you would like to be treated."

—Lou Holtz

QUALITY PRODUCTS AND SERVICES

Every customer expects quality products or services. If the customer does not receive this quality, the customer is gone. No business of any size will stay in business long if its products or services do not meet the expectations of the consumer. Customers generally expect merchandise that is long-lasting, reasonably priced, of high quality, clean, and safe. If you work for a company that you feel is not selling quality products that meet the expectations of its customers, you may want to consider changing positions.

Some businesses do not sell products or tangible items. These businesses deal in services that you cannot actually keep in your possession as you would, for example, a shirt, a pair of shoes, a bottle of cologne, or a DVD.

Businesses such as beauty salons, plumbing services, insurance companies, and hospitals sell **intangibles**, things that you cannot actually touch or possess.

Companies that sell intangible services must offer the same level of service as those selling products. The customer who buys an auto insurance policy expects that the policy will take care of covered damage to his or her car. The customer who uses the services of a beauty salon for a permanent expects his or her hair to be curly when he or she leaves the shop. Customers want a desired service to be performed dependably, accurately, and consistently.

RELIABILITY

Any business that wishes to stay in business must be reliable. **Reliability** is the ability to supply what was promised, dependably and accurately. If you tell a customer, "This custom-crafted chair is solid wood. No veneer was used in its construction. I'll see that the chair is delivered to you tomorrow," you must deliver a chair tomorrow that is solid wood. A promise not kept could cost you a customer.

Contact the customer immediately if you cannot make good on a promise. Do not blame the computer, the delivery service, the weather, or use any other common excuse. Tell the customer what happened and why your promise has been broken. For example, you might say to the customer when you determine that the chair is not solid wood, "this is Jim at the Merchandise Mart. I sold you the solid wood chair yesterday. As it was being loaded on the truck today, I realized this is not a solid wood chair. The seat is veneer. This was my error. I want to apologize for the misinformation, and I regret any inconvenience this may cause. Do you still want me to send the chair over to you today?" Your reliability and honesty will be remembered the next time this customer is in the market for your products.

Customers usually respond well when they understand the reason you are unable to make good on a promise or fulfill a request. Provide them with reasons, not excuses. Also, never make a promise or commitment about a product just to get a sale. Service begins with the sale. Making promises you can keep is what reliability is all about.

EMPATHY AND UNDERSTANDING

Customers want to be treated as individuals. Each customer has wants, needs, desires, expectations, and emotions. Recognize your customer's expectations so that you can better serve him or her. Each customer is different. Consider the different needs of Matthew and Melissa. Matthew is purchasing a sweater as a gift for his wife. He may be nervous about being in a woman's

Customers expect quality service from those who sell intangibles.

on the job

Jessica works in an exclusive boutique that sells shoes. A frequent customer comes in and buys several pairs of sandals. The customer then wanders over and takes a look at the dress shoes. She picks out a very expensive pair of shoes and asks Jessica if they are available in her size. Jessica checks the storeroom and finds that the store is out of her size. She tells the customer that she is sure that she can get her a pair from the manufacturer in three to five days. Jessica is pleased with the big sale to this customer. After the customer leaves, Jessica calls the manufacturer and requests that the shoes be shipped. The manufacturer tells her that it is late in the season, and they don't have the size shoe needed. They have one a half-size smaller. Jessica says, "Oh, send them. She'll never notice the difference." The manufacturer also tells Jessica they should arrive in seven to ten days at the home of the customer.

What should Jessica do next? What should she say to this good customer? What may happen if a follow-up call is not made?

department, and he may be unsure of exactly what type of sweater he wants to purchase; in general, he is looking to you for guidance. You could help Matthew by asking him questions to determine what would be a most suitable gift. "What color do you have in mind? Does your wife like bright or pastel colors? Are you looking for a sweater for work wear, evening wear, or casual wear?" You could show him a variety of sweater styles.

On the other hand, Melissa is shopping for a sweater for herself and is comfortable in the department; she knows her size; she knows exactly what she is looking for; and she really does not want to be bothered with your help. Melissa would require a different approach. You would direct her to where the sweaters are stocked and offer to answer any questions, step back, and be available to respond to her questions or requests. In other words, you would be empathetic to the feelings of your customers based on their wants and needs.

Empathy is participating in another's feelings or ideas. You need to acknowledge and affirm the emotional state and wishes of the customer. Customers want to know that you appreciate them and their business. If customers have problems with your products or services, make an effort to assure them that you understand and plan to take action. For example, if a customer brings back a small appliance that does not work, he or she is probably going to be angry or, at the very least, unhappy. Understand these feelings. Use a phrase such as, "I can understand why this makes you unhappy. Let's get this situation corrected to your satisfaction." Imagine yourself in the customer's position.

Wayne works in the appliance center of a major department store. A customer storms into the department and says, "What's wrong with this company? It used to be that I could depend on all of your appliances. I can't count on you or anyone else these days. I bought this iron from you last week. Its temperature gauge is defective. I burned a hole in a very expensive shirt." Wayne replies, "I can understand your anger about the shirt and the iron. Let's check out another iron and be sure it works correctly. We would also like to make an adjustment on the price of the iron to cover the damage to the shirt."

In short, people want company representatives to listen. They want to be noticed. And if things go wrong for them, they want things to be made right.

TIMELINESS

Customers insist on timeliness. It seems that members of society are always in a hurry and demand immediate satisfaction. You may use a mail service that promises overnight delivery, you may drop your clothing at a dry cleaner that promises one-hour service, or you may order from a menu that promises ten-minute service or you eat free. Companies that cater to time-conscious customers are everywhere you look. And their success affects your customers' expectations of your willingness and ability to do the same. Small wonder that your customers may be demanding tighter deadlines and faster service than ever before. When they do, they expect you to be responsive. Customers are often unhappy with anything less than "immediately." Your customers are busy people—their time is a valuable resource. Other organizations are aware of the time-consciousness of their customers. If you cannot serve them in a timely fashion, someone else will keep your customers happy.

Smart Tip ▼ ▼ ▼

Here are some techniques that show your customers that you respect their desire for immediate and timely attention.

- If you are working in retail, be sure that *all* customers are acknowledged when they arrive.

- Establish eye contact with customers, so that they know you are interested in serving them. If you are helping someone else, they at least know that you are aware that they are waiting for help.

- Look each customer in the eyes as you talk about the assets of your product. Don't allow your eyes to dart around the room as this will indicate your full attention is not on the customer.

- If you are working in an organization that does a lot of business via the telephone, answer the phone quickly.

- If you must step away from a phone call, let your customer know why and how long you will be gone. If the customer prefers, call him or her back.

- Never offer deadlines you cannot meet.

▲ ▲ ▲ ▲ ▲ ▲ ▲ ▲ ▲

RECOGNITION AND ACKNOWLEDGMENT

Recognize your customers, and whenever possible, call them by name. Everyone likes to hear the sound of his or her name, to be acknowledged and recognized. People also like to have you indicate the reason that you remember them—something they bought, a mutual friend, a hobby, or something about one of their children. Customers like to hear comments about themselves, such as "Hi, Ms. Applebee. Glad to see you back in the store. How is your new dryer working?" or "Thanks for shopping with us, Angie. I'll look forward to helping you again soon" or "Hello, Mr. McClurg, how is that new grandbaby?"

You can pick up name clues from customers' checks, business cards, credit cards, desk signs, or office doors. Remembering names requires work. Try to associate a person's name with some unique characteristic he or she may have. This can help you recall names later. A genuine effort to remember names will serve you well.

Use *I* instead of *we* or *they*. To a customer, the company begins and ends with you. Using *I* shows that you understand and accept this responsibility. Saying "the policy is . . . ." or "*they* won't allow . . . ." tells the customer that you consider yourself "just a clerk" and not a part of the company organization. If that's the way you feel, you won't ever be able to help them. You become an interchangeable part, rather than an individual, and you are viewed as part of the problem. Feeling and acting like "just a clerk" can also affect your self-image—and may keep you from getting ahead.

Of course, there are times you really can't do anything. But even if all you can say is, "Let me talk to the manager and see what I can do," it makes you look more helpful, more like you're part of the solution.

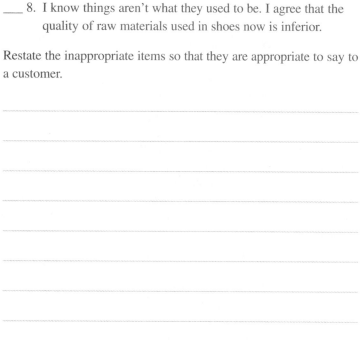

SELF CHECK

The following are statements that may be appropriate or inappropriate to say to customers. Place a check before the appropriate statements. Be prepared to justify your answers.

_____ 1. Hi, Mrs. Jordan. How did your kids like your new dress?

_____ 2. Your hairstyle is not becoming. Let's give you something new!

_____ 3. I need to put you on hold. I have another phone ringing.

_____ 4. We'll have that order out to you in 24 hours. (you hope)

_____ 5. Come back in when you know what you want.

_____ 6. Maxine, welcome to the store. I have something I think you will like.

_____ 7. Mr. Adams, your house has not been well maintained. It does not have good marketability.

_____ 8. I know things aren't what they used to be. I agree that the quality of raw materials used in shoes now is inferior.

Restate the inappropriate items so that they are appropriate to say to a customer.

Technology
at Work

Check these sites for additional opinions and thoughts on customer expectations.

**www.imtc3.com/
   expectations.html
www.williecrawford.com/
   loyalty.html
www.nkarten.com/mce.html**

chec*k*point

1. **Every customer expects**
   a. good products and services.
   b. a special "deal."
   c. to make small talk with you.
   d. to return merchandise.

2. **What does reliability mean in the context of this chapter?**

   _____

   _____

   _____

   _____

3. **Empathy means**
   a. offering the customer a cup of coffee.
   b. ignoring the customer because he or she is angry or upset.
   c. acknowledging and affirming the emotional state and wishes of the customer.
   d. serving the customer with a smile.

4. **What are some examples of intangibles?**

   _____

   _____

   _____

   _____

5. **When you cannot deliver on a promise to a customer, provide him or her with**
   a. reasons, not excuses.
   b. another promise.
   c. a free piece of merchandise.
   d. nothing.

applications

1. Explain what you think is meant by the old adage "Each customer is like a tree that branches out everywhere—you never lose just one customer."

2. What can happen as a result of having a customer not served?

3. Who benefits when you relate well with clients or customers? Why?

4. Why is timeliness important to serving your customers?

_____

_____

_____

_____

5. Rewrite the following remarks so that the same information is transmitted but in a more empathetic, and more helpful, way.

"We don't carry those jeans in your size."

_____

"Your flight has been canceled."

_____

"The table you ordered is out of stock."

_____

"We don't deliver packages weighing less than 20 pounds."

_____

6. This text presents a few ways for you to recognize your customers and remember their names. What techniques or tips can you add? How do you remember names?

_____

_____

_____

_____

You are now aware that customers have many expectations. You must try to live up to these expectations in order to retain customers. Research shows that there are some messages that customers do not like to receive, such as "I can't be bothered" or "I don't know."

Remember, if you say one thing, but your body language sends the opposite message, the customers will only receive the body language message.

Many customer satisfaction surveys indicate that customers stop buying from companies because of the indifferent way they are treated. There's more: Disgruntled customers usually tell other people why they stopped buying from a particular company. Whether your communication with customers is in person, through e-mail, or over the telephone, be sure the messages you send are focused on meeting your customers' needs.

"There are no unimportant people."

—MALCOLM FORBES

BE ATTENTIVE

You would probably never say it aloud to a customer, but your comments or body language may communicate the message, *"I can't be bothered."* If you commit all of your attention to one customer and fail to acknowledge a new customer walking into your area, you have delivered this message. If you are in a conversation with a coworker and do not give your immediate attention to a customer, you have communicated the negative message. Here is an example of what can happen.

"Don't find a fault. Find a remedy."

—HENRY FORD

Sally walked into a gift shop on her lunch hour. She knew what she wanted and she was in a hurry. She picked up her item, a gift bag, and a card and hurried up to the cashier station. She didn't see anyone to help her. She looked around and saw an employee restocking shelves. She called to the employee and said, "I am ready to check out." The employee finished the shelf she was working on and then got up to assist Sally. The employee didn't apologize for the delay. She rang up the sale and handed the purchases to Sally. Sally was livid. She vowed not to shop in the store again, and she related this experience to her coworkers.

DON'T BE A "KNOW-IT-ALL"

When you try to have every answer, even for a customer's objections or explanations of why something isn't needed, you may be sending the message, "I know everything." Customers do not like this. They like you to be informed about your product or service, but they do not appreciate power selling or trying to force them into a decision that they are not yet ready to make. Don't assume that you know everything about how your customer is going to use the product or service. For example, let's assume you are selling a love seat. Comments like "It will look beautiful in your home" or "It will accent your room" are inappropriate unless you have been in the home. It is important that you know your merchandise, but do not beat your customer over the head with your knowledge, and do not make statements about things you do not or cannot know.

BE KNOWLEDGEABLE

Customers arrive at your place of business because they expect you to be able to serve them. They have a right to expect that salespeople are knowledgeable about their products. Replace the words, *"I don't know,"* with *"I'll find out." "The book isn't in stock,"* with *"Let me find out how soon we can get you a copy."*

Customers are demanding. And they have every right to be. Today's customers have more options than ever before. They are also more knowledgeable than ever before due to the huge amount of product and services information available on the Internet. If your organization (you) does not offer what they want or need, if you don't interact with them in a manner that meets or exceeds their expectations, they will take their business elsewhere.

TREAT CUSTOMERS WITH RESPECT

Be sure that you treat all customers with the same quality service. Would you serve a young teenager wearing cutoff jeans and an oversized T-shirt the same way you would serve a person in a business suit? You should.

Every customer is an individual and deserves your attention. The teenager you may have avoided because you think he or she cannot afford the product and is only looking may well turn out to be a great customer today and in the future. All customers are individuals who deserve your attention. You must forget any biases you may have about certain customers because of the way they dress or their ages, races, or sizes. You are in business to serve all customers. The following example illustrates how you can lose a sale by letting your biases interfere.

Sam went into the showroom of an automobile dealer. He was dressed very casually, as he liked to be. The dealer sold very expensive sports cars. Mel, the representative on duty, sized Sam up and decided (1) he was just a looker, (2) he couldn't afford a sports car, and (3) he just wanted

on the job

Ann was in a large discount lawn and garden store. She was searching for an extension for a drainpipe to be used at her home to carry water away from the basement. She asked the first floor clerk she spotted, "Where would I find a drainpipe extender?" Glen, the clerk, wasn't sure, but he said, "Try over in the lawn supply area." The lawn supply area was on the opposite side of the building. She arrived in the lawn supply area and eventually met a new clerk, Edna. She asked Edna for a drainpipe extender. Edna looked confused and said, "I don't think we have any. Is there anything else I can help you with?" Ann was a bit disheartened and said, "No." She began to conduct her own search of the area. She found the aisle with the extenders. The pieces were very long and she felt she only needed a three-foot piece to get the water to flow away from her house. A sign at the end of the aisle stated, "Cut to fit your needs." Again, in search of a clerk, she found Rudy. She asked Rudy, "Is it possible to have this extender cut to about three feet?" Rudy said, "Lady, it's only about five feet long. I am sure it will work just fine for you." Ann handed Rudy the extender and said, "I think I might have better luck in another establishment."

Will Ann likely return to this establishment? How many people will she tell about her experience? What problems have these salespeople created for their company? How could they improve their customer communication?

to buzz around the block a few times in one of the beautiful sports models and get it dirty. Sam looked at several models, picked up some brochures, sat in a couple of the models, stood around like he wanted some questions answered, and eventually left.

The next day, Mel was en route to work when he noticed a beautiful new sports car, bearing temporary tags, in the lane next to him. Mel looked at the driver. You guessed it; it was Sam. Sam had purchased a very expensive sports car from Mel's competition. The competition was more than happy to answer Sam's questions and give him the attention all customers deserve.

BE HELPFUL

Whenever a customer comes to you for help, you must provide that help by being sensitive to his or her needs. Never put down a confused customer or demean the customer in any way for misinformation that he or she may share with you. Customers sometimes need to be educated. Recognize the customer has misinformation and give him or her the correct information without talking down to the customer. If you do not handle the situation with care, the next time the customer is in need of products or services, he or she will not seek them at your place of business.

You don't know everything, but keep in mind that today's customers expect to be reassured by the people they deal with. In large part, this is facilitated by a mastery of a few simple "people skills." In addition, a combination of both style and product knowledge wins accolades and brings customers back again and again.

Eva entered a huge retail establishment that specialized in products for the home. She was not familiar with this type of store and was overwhelmed by its size. She was shopping for a new kitchen sink. After following the store signs, she found her way to the kitchen sink display. Gary Jurgens, a clerk in the kitchen supply area, arrived and asked how he could be of help. She said, "I need a kitchen sink. And, I don't even know what questions I should ask." Gary asked Eva several questions about the sink that she currently had in her home. He asked her if she wanted a cast-iron, stainless steel, or one of the new synthetic material models? Eva didn't know. He carefully explained the advantages and disadvantages of each.

Gary explained the differences in the prices and the range of price for each model. Eva was concerned about whether or not the sink would fit. Gary explained that the standard for kitchen sinks is 33" × 22" and that each of the sinks he had shown her fit the standard. Gary explained that Eva would, in addition to the sink, probably need faucets, strainers, and perhaps connections to the water lines,.

Gary provided Eva with all the information she needed to make a wise decision. Will Eva be a repeat customer?

DON'T TAKE IT PERSONALLY

As you relate to clients and customers, remember that this is business/work. Do not take the remarks of the customer personally. There may be some situations where the customer may be verbally abusive. The customer may threaten, accuse, or make critical statements about you and the business.

If this happens, understand that the customer is upset about some phase of the business, not you personally, even though some remarks may have been directed at you. Focus your attention on determining and satisfying the customer's needs. Most often you will need to make some type of adjustment to satisfy the customer.

Never argue with the customer. This will only make the problem worse. Do not try to defend yourself with comments, such as "It's not my fault," "I didn't manufacture this product," or "I wasn't your salesperson." These remarks will only further annoy the customer. Allow the customer to vent his or her frustration rather than trying to shut it off with an argumentative statement. Stay calm and professional and try saying, "I understand your anger. Let's find a solution to the situation." Usually, once the customer feels that you understand the problem and plan to make an adjustment, he or she will calm down and deal with the solution

on ethics

Arnie is an employee in a small engine shop that specializes in the sale of lawn mowers. One afternoon, Arnie spends a long time with an exacting customer named Martin, selling him a self-propelled lawn mower.

Martin shows up a few days later with the mower in the back of his pickup truck. Martin storms into the salesroom and begins yelling. "This worthless piece of junk you sold me is a poor excuse for a lawn mower. I don't know how you get away with selling this type of trash!"

After Martin shouts and carries on for a bit, Arnie asks him some questions about why and how the mower has disappointed him. Arnie spots the problem with the mower and realizes that it's simple to fix. Arnie says, "How can we make you a happy customer?" Martin replies, "I want a new, different model mower." Arnie walks over to the display and says, "This one will serve you well. I'll have it lifted into your truck." Martin says, "Well, all right—but this one had better give me better service than the other piece of junk."

Martin drives away. Arnie chuckles to himself, "Dummy, you just got a mower with less power than the one you originally purchased. It's a much cheaper mower. That will teach you to rant and rave at me. I'll clean this one up and sell it again."

How do you feel about how Arnie handled this situation? Who are the losers in this situation? What would you have done in this situation?

in a reasonable manner. (Of course, if a customer becomes physically abusive, do not hesitate to call for assistance. However, with a little diplomacy, it is unlikely that you will see a situation escalate to this level.)

IS THE CUSTOMER ALWAYS RIGHT?

The popular phrase, "The customer is always right," is tossed around a great deal in business. You know that it is not possible for anyone to be right all of the time. Customers may not always be right; however, they are always customers. If the customer is not right, your job is to manage the experience so the customer eventually is right and remains your customer. Do not let the customer feel that he or she was wrong in having elected to do business with your organization.

Just because what the customer says sounds wrong to you, don't assume that it is. It may be that they don't express themselves very well or that the instructions they should have received were vague or missing. Look for teaching opportunities. What information could your customers have used before the misunderstanding occurred? Make sure they get it now.

Some customers do try to take advantage of you and your company. First, it is important to recognize that truly dishonest customers are pretty rare. But they do exist. Eventually, you will have to be firm with these customers and tactfully demonstrate that in this situation you cannot give credibility to their claim. Of course, company policy may help you in dealing with these customers. Be patient and work with the customer until he or she is satisfied with the outcome.

> *"Your most unhappy customers are your greatest source of learning."*
>
> —BILL GATES

Adam (customer): Hey, I purchased this blower/vacuum from you last Thursday and it doesn't work. It must be defective or broken.

Val (clerk): What is the trouble? Are all the parts in the box? How can I help?

Adam: I can't get it to blow leaves. I want my money back.

Val: Let's take a look. Putting these together can sometimes be quite a trick. (Val opens the box and immediately sees the problem. Adam hasn't put the blower/vacuum together correctly. She pulls the product out and quickly assembles the blower correctly.)

Adam: I tried that and it just wouldn't work.

Val: Let's see if I can get it to work. (She plugs in the blower/vacuum, sprinkles some packing pieces on the floor, and flips the on switch.) There we go. It is working.

Adam: Well, I'll be. Let me see what you did again.

Val: (demonstrates) Any questions?

Adam: No. I think I can accept the blower now. Thanks.

Val: I'm sorry that you had to take the time to bring this back to the store. The directions in the box could probably be improved.

Adam: Thanks.

Val handled this customer's concern without telling him he was wrong. She listened to his concern. She asked him some questions in search of the problem. Val let him know that she wanted to help. She sent Adam on his way with a working blower/vacuum that wasn't broken and was ready to be used.

LISTEN TO AND BELIEVE YOUR CUSTOMERS

Sometimes you may think a customer is totally wrong about a complaint. However, after all the information is heard, the customer turns out to be right. Listen to the customer's entire story before you respond. Always give your customers the benefit of the doubt. If you have harshly treated their request or complaint, you're going to find yourself embarrassed. You can save yourself some embarrassment by getting all the details before responding. Observe what can happen in the above situation.

EDUCATE YOUR CUSTOMERS

Many times, customers will experience a problem because they do not follow or find the directions carried with the merchandise. If a customer mistakenly washes and shrinks a new blouse, you can tactfully show the customer the label sewn in the collar that says the garment should be

> *"A few words of regret is a way of saying you care, a show of sensitivity to the ragged edges of another's emotion."*
>
> —ROBERT CONKLIN

A friendly attitude and product knowledge are necessary when working with customers.

PHOTO: © DIGITAL VISION

dry-cleaned only. This educates the customer about the importance of reading clothing direction labels. Better yet, if you know the blouse will shrink, point out the care instructions at the time of purchase. The customer will be grateful for being spared ruining the garment. It is always better to point out important information beforehand.

Here's another example: A customer returns a motion-sensor light. The light will go on when any motion occurs within 30 feet of the light. The customer returns the light, saying it does not work. You say, "I'm sorry. Let's see if we can figure out what went wrong." You open the box and pull out the directions. Step-by-step you go through the directions and check with your customer to see what step may have been omitted. It is likely that this process will lead to the problem. If not, you can do an exchange or a refund, and not offend the customer.

Of course, educating the customer begins with educating yourself. Read the material about the product(s) you are selling that is provided by the manufacturer. Check the Internet for additional product information. Spend some time thinking about the products you are selling and how they will be used by the customer. Listen to the customers buying your products for ideas to pass on to other customers. Customers expect you to know the features, advantages, and benefits of whatever it is your company makes, does, or delivers. No one expects you to know everything, but the salesperson who has to read a product manual or label in front of the customer just to figure out how to turn on the item doesn't create a good impression.

on the job

Jake is a clerk in a dry cleaner. An annoyed customer came in and said, "I specifically pointed out the grease spots on this suit when I brought it in, and when it was delivered to me, the spots were still there. Doesn't this dry cleaner know how to remove an identified grease spot?" Jake was very annoyed with the attitude of the customer. He replied, "If you indeed did point out the grease spots, they would have been noted and removed. We can take care of grease spots on this type of fabric without any problem." The customer replied, "I did note them." He then pulled out his claim check and showed Jake that the accepting clerk had written down that there were grease spots on the left lapel of the suit. The customer then picked up the suit and said, "I'll take this suit and my dry cleaning business elsewhere. I don't appreciate being called a liar. I want the money I paid to have this suit cleaned returned." Jake said nothing; he went to the cash register and returned the cost of the dry cleaning to the customer.

What did Jake do wrong? How could Jake have better handled the situation? Could this customer's business have been kept?

ATTITUDE

The idea that the customer is always right is clearly not a true statement. However, the *attitude* to be demonstrated to the customer is a good and positive feeling. The attitude expressed is that the customer is right. You should never argue or dispute the word of a customer, but make a genuine attempt to see the customer's point of view.

check**point**

1. How can you send the "I can't be bothered" message to a customer without saying a word?

   _____

   _____

   _____

   _____

2. When dealing with a customer who is complaining about a product, give your customer
   a. good advice.
   b. the benefit of the doubt.
   c. good deals.
   d. service when he or she deserves it.

3. How can you avoid making an unhappy customer angrier?

   _____

   _____

   _____

   _____

4. The correct attitude to express toward customers is that they are
   a. to come in again.
   b. sometimes right.
   c. never right.
   d. always right.

5. If you work in a retail store and you have a little time when customers are not in your work area, what might you do with this free time to strengthen your selling skills?

   _____

   _____

   _____

   _____

applications

1. Rate yourself on your customer service skills. (If you are not in a position to serve customers, rate how you think you would react.) Give yourself a 1 if you **never** use the skill, a 2 if you **rarely** use the skill, a 3 if you **sometimes** use the skill, or a 4 if you **often** use the skill.

a. _____ I know my products and services.

b. _____ I work to meet customer expectations.

c. _____ I listen when customers complain.

d. _____ I don't take customers' remarks personally.

e. _____ I use positive body language when communicating with customers.

f. _____ I demonstrate empathy toward my customers.

g. _____ I acknowledge customers immediately.

Total _____

If your total score is 25 or more, you are doing a good job in relating to clients and customers. If your score is 20 or more, you are doing a fair job in relating to clients and customers. If your score is 18 or below, you need to work harder to relate to clients and customers.

2. Josie walked into a shoe store and wandered around looking for a dressy shoe style. She asked the salesperson, "Are these shoes on sale?" The salesperson said, "I don't know." Josie walked a bit farther and picked up a shoe she liked and asked, "Do you carry these in black?" The salesperson replied, "I don't know." Josie looked at the sale rack, selected a shoe, and asked if it was available in a size 8. The salesperson said, "If they aren't on the rack, we don't have them."

a. What do you think about the salesperson's responses? Why?

_____

_____

_____

_____

b. What hints and suggestions would you have for the salesperson?

_____

_____

_____

_____

c. Do you think Josie will be back to shop at this store in the future? Why or why not? What would you do if you were Josie?

_____

_____

_____

_____

3. Think of a time when you believe you were improperly treated by a salesperson in a retail store or automobile service department. Explain what happened and why you think you were mistreated. What would you have done differently if you were the salesperson?

_____

_____

_____

_____

_____

9 Points to Remember

chapter

Review the following points to determine what you remember from the chapter.

- Clients and customers are your business, and they expect good service. Customers expect quality products and services, reliability, empathy, timeliness, and recognition.

- When communicating with customers, always be attentive, knowledgeable, respectful, and helpful. Never communicate the following messages verbally or through your body language: I can't be bothered. I know everything. I don't know. I don't want your business. You don't know anything.

- Do not take negative remarks made by a customer personally. Do not argue with the customer, because this will only disturb him or her further. Listen to your customer, and communicate that you want to satisfy his or her needs as soon as possible. Your body language may send a negative message while you are communicating in words that are positive.

- Customers are not always right. However, you want to communicate through your words, actions, and attitude that you believe that the customer is always right. Be sure that you listen to your customers, give them the benefit of the doubt, and educate them about your products or services whenever possible.

How did you do? Did you remember the main points you studied in the chapter?

key terms

Place the letter of the item in the definition column that matches the key word.

Key Word	Definition
___1. Intangibles	a. Ability to supply what was promised
___2. Reliability	b. Participating in another's feelings or ideas
___3. Empathy	c. Things that you cannot actually touch or possess

activities and projects

1. Fill in the blanks with an appropriate word or phrase.

a. Any business that wishes to stay in business must be _____.

b. Establish eye contact with every customer to _____.

c. "I can't be bothered" and "I don't know" are phrases _____.

d. To make a customer feel special, try to _____.

2. What are some positive phrases you could say to a customer as he or she is leaving after making a purchase of several small gardening tools? Remember that your livelihood depends on customers.

_____

_____

_____

3. Complete this statement: "I'm responsible for providing my customers with . . ."

_____

_____

_____

4. Henry Ford said, "Don't find fault, find a remedy." What do you think he meant? Relate this quote to getting along with a customer.

_____

_____

_____

5. In the space provided, list everything that Hernando did *correctly* in the following telephone scenario with William.

William: Do you have idiots working in your shipping department? I ordered a new television model called Majestic and received a model called Vivid. I want the model I requested delivered to my home immediately.

Hernando: Let me find the record of your order. May I have your name and address please?

William: My name is William Ankenman. Why do you need my address?

Hernando: Your address will assure that I am pulling up the correct record. Oh, no need. I have an order for a William Ankenman at 334 Lyncrest Drive. Is that correct?

William: Yeah.

Hernando: Okay. I'm pulling up your file on the television purchase. It should be on my monitor in just a moment. Ah. There it is. Mr. Ankenman, we have an order here for a Vivid placed on June 4.

William: Well, you must have keyed in the wrong model.

Hernando: That could happen. Let me find the original paperwork. I'm going to put you on hold for a couple of minutes. Is that okay with you?

William: Yes, just hurry up.

Hernando: Sorry to keep you on hold, Mr. Ankenman. I do have the original purchase order here, signed by you, and you did specify the Vivid model. If you like, I can fax or send you the original document.

William: No, don't bother. It looks like I made the mistake.

Hernando: The Vivid model is a quality product. I would encourage you to watch it for a couple of days before you make a decision to return it. Many of our customers report that they are especially pleased with the audio from this model. Would that be something you would like to consider?

William: Well, I don't know. It's just that I ordered the Majestic. My neighbor has one and likes it.

Hernando: Tell you what, you try it for a week and I'll call you to see how you like the Vivid. There is no difference in price. In the meantime, I'll place an order for a Majestic. It should be here within a week and then you can make a decision. How does that sound to you?

What did Hernando do correctly?

_____

_____

_____

_____

_____

case studies for critical thinking

DVD DILEMMA

Paul is a clerk in a video store. He helps customers find selections and operates the checkout register. A regular customer, Troy Obermier, comes barging into the store and slams down a DVD of the movie *The Perfect Storm*. He says in a very loud voice, "I checked this DVD out an hour ago for some houseguests who wanted to watch it, but it doesn't work. The DVD appears to be blank. There's something wrong with this copy. Why don't you check these movies before they leave the store? I had to drive all the way across town because of your inefficiency. This DVD better not have messed up my equipment. I want a good copy of this film." Paul replies to Troy, "This is Saturday night. Do you expect a popular movie like *The Perfect Storm* to be on the shelves? Look for something else."

1. What did Troy want, need, and/or expect?

2. Did Paul handle the situation correctly? Why or why not?

3. Write down a suitable reply from Paul. Keep in mind that there are no copies of the desired movie available.

TOUGH EXCHANGE

Mia works in the small appliances section of a department store. Cedric brings in a hand mixer and tells Mia that he wants to return it for cash. Mia asks for the receipt. Cedric tells her that the mixer was a gift. He doesn't want it as he already has a mixer. Mia says, "Our store policy is no cash returns without a receipt." Cedric replies, "I don't care whose policy it is. I don't need two mixers. What do you expect me to do with two mixers? I want to see the store manager." Mia says, "I don't care what you do with two mixers. I'm just telling you that without a receipt you are not going to return this mixer for cash. The manager will just tell you the same thing."

1. Did Mia do the right thing in explaining the company policy to Cedric?

_____

_____

2. Did Mia do anything to irritate the customer or increase the problem?

_____

_____

3. Was Cedric's desire to return the mixer for cash reasonable?

_____

_____

4. What will likely be the result of this conversation?

_____

_____

5. How would you have handled Cedric's request if you were in Mia's place? Keep in mind that you should follow store policy.

_____

_____

Case 9.3

IS THE CUSTOMER ALWAYS RIGHT?

Harvey sells an intangible product—homeowners' insurance. Harvey is a hardworking salesperson and strives to meet the needs of his customers. Elaine and Broderick Shaeffer have had a homeowners' insurance policy with Harvey's company for several months. Elaine calls Harvey one evening and reports that their roof suffered wind damage during a storm last week. Harvey acknowledges her call and tells her that he will be out soon to assess the damage. Harvey and one of the company adjusters go to Elaine and Broderick's home and find that several shingles are missing on the north side of the house. The damage is unusual. With permission from Elaine and Broderick, Harvey talks with the Shaeffers' neighbors and finds that they have incurred no damage. Three shingles are lying on top of the Shaeffers' trash.

Harvey takes a look at them and based on what he sees, he believes they have been pulled out of place by hand. The adjuster agrees. The Shaeffers have an old roof that will soon need to be replaced. Harvey suspects that the damage was not caused by the wind.

1. Should Harvey tell Elaine and Broderick that they have lied about the damage?

_____

_____

_____

2. Should he tell them that these shingles were pulled out to try to get the insurance company to replace an aging roof? Why or why not?

_____

_____

_____

3. Should Harvey file a report with his company and report that the roof will need to be paid for by the company since the Shaeffers' policy covers wind damage? Why or why not?

_____

_____

_____

| Case 9.4 | TOO MANY STUDENTS IN THE STORE |

The Brown Company has a sign on the door that only two students are allowed in the store at one time after 3 p.m. The store is near the junior and senior high schools and many students stop by after school to get soft drinks from the vending machines.

1. Is the store acting properly in excluding students in groups from the store?

_____

_____

_____

2. If you were a student, how would you feel about this practice?

_____

_____

_____

Self-Motivation

| think about it: | Oscar was a student in an internship program. The telephone rang in the office of his instructor-coordinator, Ms. Cardona. |

"This is Georgette Wilson, Oscar's training sponsor. Can we talk about a problem we're having with him?" "Of course," Ms. Cardona said, "what's going on?" "Well, as you know, in this kind of business, we can't always hover over our people and tell them every little thing to do. But when Oscar comes to a slack period or when he completes an assigned job, he disappears. Usually I find him in the coffee room, reading a novel at his desk or talking on his cell phone." "I understand," Ms. Cardona said, "we'll have a talk."

Later, in discussing the matter with his instructor, Oscar said, "But, Ms. Cardona, I always do what I'm told, and they tell me I do good work. What do they expect?"

Is Oscar's way of using his free time acceptable? What should his employer expect him to do when he comes to a slack period?

© BRAND X PICTURES

chapter focus

After completing this chapter, you should be able to:

1. Explain what causes a person to be motivated.

2. Explain the importance of being a willing worker.

3. Overcome the tendency to avoid or delay unpleasant tasks.

4. Show the initiative to do and learn more than is expected or required.

5. Display an open and eager attitude.

6. Be conscientious and dependable.

7. Understand the importance of using good judgment.

8. Admit mistakes and errors in judgment.

Chapter Highlights

10.1 Show Initiative

10.2 Be Responsible

Part of the ability required to do your job well is the result of your education, technical training, and experience in doing the work you are hired to do. However, to be successful, you must apply what you know and use your skills effectively, and this takes motivation.

Your first job may call for following orders implicitly, doing what you are told to do without question. There may not be many opportunities for acting on your own—for showing **initiative**. In time, however, you will grow through experience and practice and will be given greater responsibilities. You may be called upon for more independent thinking and action.

SOURCES OF MOTIVATION

Self-motivation is a drive within you to get things done. How can you acquire this drive if you do not possess it now? As your needs change, the spark that motivates you will change also.

Right now you may be working for grades—a passing grade or a high one. Or you may be interested in the approval of someone whose opinion is important to you. The term that many psychologists use for this is **external motivation**. This means that the drive to achieve comes from outside yourself.

In time, external motivation may be partly replaced by **internal motivation**. Internal motivation is the kind that comes from within, such as the satisfaction that comes from doing a good job.

BE WILLING TO WORK

When a person is hired to do a job, the employer expects the employee to be willing to work. However, many workers appear to spend their time in other ways. Being self-motivated means that you have overcome the desire to just relax and avoid hard work.

Smart Tip ▼ ▼ ▼

Here are four clues that tell your supervisor or employer how willing a worker you are:

- **You willingly perform the tasks that are assigned to you.**
- **You arrange your duties so that the work is completed on time after the assignments have been made.**
- **You take great pains to be accurate because mistakes can be costly.**
- **You take pride in your work.**

▲ ▲ ▲ ▲ ▲ ▲ ▲ ▲ ▲

TAKE ON UNPLEASANT TASKS

Any job contains a certain amount of drudgery. This is especially true in entry-level jobs that require little training and experience. These jobs consist mainly of routine work that may not be challenging or interesting.

If you are faced with a non-challenging job that is messy, dull, or physically exhausting, the natural reaction is to find some excuse to avoid or delay getting down to work. You may get a drink of water or adjust the ventilation. You welcome distractions and interruptions and find it hard to return to where you left off.

The way to overcome this natural tendency and to develop self-motivation is to take control of your desire to slack off. Simply *force yourself to face the task at hand.* Save that drink of water as a reward at the end of your first completed task. Adjust the ventilation after completing another task. If you use this technique the first few times, you will form the habit of concentrated effort. With this habit, you will find yourself becoming a much more productive worker.

ACT ON YOUR OWN

As a newcomer to the world of work, you may find it hard to know just how far you should go in showing initiative. Sometimes the rules of the organization make it necessary to follow a set pattern in everything that is done.

In most cases, however, the follow-the-rules-without-exceptions phase lasts only a short time. (Here, "rules" refers, of course, to the structure of the job, not the behavior requirements established by law or by the company.)

When you are not expecting it, you may be faced with a crisis. For example, the manager who is to sign all orders may be in the hospital or out of town. When something like this happens, the only thing you can do is weigh the matter carefully. Ask yourself, What will happen if I simply follow the rules? Could I lose an order?

If the consequences of following the rules could be worse than acting on your own, you must have enough initiative to take action. The only requirement is that you think through the situation carefully and make your decision on the basis of the best information you can get.

Occasionally you will have the opportunity to show initiative when you cannot be sure that your actions will be appreciated. You may face possible disapproval whether you act or not. However, failure to act in a crisis when there are no rules to guide you may be the worst thing you can do.

The following list contains suggestions for evaluating your self-motivation. If you find traits in this list that you would like to acquire, begin now to try to make them a part of your personality.

Most of the time, do you . . .

Accept the challenge to work at a task that does not appear to offer immediate interest or pleasure?

Yes_____ No_____.

Choose to postpone pleasure rather than postpone work?

Yes_____ No_____

Avoid procrastination, not waiting until the last minute to start a task?

Yes_____ No_____

Concentrate by learning to work in the presence of distracting influences, such as noise, physical discomfort, or interruptions?

Yes_____ No_____

Persist in finishing a task even when you are weary, and work late when the occasion demands it?

Yes_____ No_____

LEARN ON YOUR OWN

Another way to show initiative is by learning all you can about the business and your place in it. You also show initiative by:

- taking courses to prepare yourself for a promotion.
- learning how to do work that must be done even though it has not been definitely assigned to you.
- learning how to think and act swiftly in emergencies.
- learning how to handle new and unusual situations that arise.
- volunteering, on your own time, to assist more experienced coworkers with tasks you may someday be assigned to do.

"Perhaps the most valuable result of all education is the ability to make yourself do the thing you have to do when it has to be done whether you like it or not."

—THOMAS H. HUXLEY

on the job

Anna is a receptionist at a busy production plant. The plant manager has given strict orders that his home phone number not be given to anyone under any circumstances. One day, when the plant manager is at home with the flu, a production supervisor calls in a panic. "I need him to make a decision," the supervisor tells Anna. "I can't take responsibility for it and I need that decision now! Otherwise the whole production run could be ruined."

What are Anna's options? Which one do you think would be best in this situation?

better prepared to attempt new things and to be creative.

In the long run, your employer and your coworkers will benefit from your increased capacity for doing your job and helping them with theirs.

BE OPEN AND EAGER TO LEARN

Learn to view new and unfamiliar situations as stepping-stones to learning. Be enthusiastic about putting new ideas into effect, and be open to new experiences and learning opportunities. A beginner does have a lot to learn. People know that, but they do not expect the learning process to go on forever.

You can learn by listening and paying attention to suggestions from coworkers.

Another valuable benefit of learning on your own is that you may be able to fill in for a coworker who is absent. Being able to apply what you learn in one situation to a different set of circumstances is a valuable skill. You can plan and carry out new duties with minimal help from others. You are

© GETTY IMAGES/PHOTODISC

Technology at Work

Technology can be both something you need to learn for your job and a valuable source for learning on your own. There is a wide variety of computer tutorials, as well as popular consumer publications, that can help you learn about software that you may need to use. But don't overlook the Internet as a valuable source of information on a wide range of topics.

Online universities make courses available electronically. Searches for business and organizations related to your work can help you learn more about the field you're in. Powerful search engines, such as www.metacrawler.com, or human-guided search resources, such as www.about.com or www.looksmart.com, can help you find information on almost any topic, field, or industry.

The beginner who needs to be told something only once is considered unusually bright. The one who learns new routines with minimal instruction is rare indeed. Everyone makes mistakes, but the beginner with a good work attitude works to not make the same mistake twice.

Cultivate an "I can do it" attitude. You can be proactive, looking for answers. You should not need to have work laid out or be told repeatedly how to perform a task. Listen carefully the first time, and pay close attention to demonstrations of tasks. If possible, always take notes so that you can perform the task the next time with little or no assistance.

DO MORE AND BETTER THAN EXPECTED

A valuable key to success is to do more than your employer expects of you. Another is to set higher standards, so the quality of your work is *better* than expected. When the work that you do is outstanding, you look good to your employer and you are recognized as an outstanding performer. This also makes your supervisor and your working team look good.

Like the rewards for many other positive qualities, the reward for going beyond what is expected may be delayed. If you see no immediate benefit for your extra effort, your own satisfaction will be reward enough. You will probably learn more.

However, it is very likely that your employer will recognize and appreciate what you have done. He or she will think of you as a person who is a self-starter and as someone who can be depended upon to get the job done without much supervision. In the long run, you may have an advantage as you compete for a raise, a promotion, or a better position. Eventually others will notice that when there is a need for someone to "go the extra mile," you can be depended upon.

Smart Tip ▾ ▾ ▾

Here are some examples of going beyond what is expected:
- **Performing difficult, tedious, or unpleasant tasks when you might be expected to leave it for someone else.**
- **Performing your work with poise, dignity, and patience although conditions at work or in your private life may be distressing.**
- **Setting high standards and working hard to reach them.**
- **Paying attention to details.**
- **Displaying a high level of concentration.**
- **Working late to complete a job.**
- **Making an extra effort to please a dissatisfied customer.**

▲ ▲ ▲ ▲ ▲ ▲ ▲ ▲ ▲

focus on ethics

You may have heard people speak, usually admiringly, of someone who they described as having a "good work ethic."

What do you think it means to have a good work ethic? In addition to possible financial or career rewards, what internal, personal benefits does someone gain from having a good work ethic?

check*point*

1. Explain the difference between external motivation and internal motivation.

    _____

    _____

    _____

2. Under which type of motivation is the most work likely to be accomplished? Explain your answer.

    _____

    _____

    _____

3. What can you do to avoid time-consuming delays and distractions that prevent you from working hard at unpleasant, boring tasks?

    _____

    _____

    _____

4. If the consequences of following the rules are worse than acting on your own, before you take action you should make your decision based upon _____ and _____.

5. What should Shannon do? She works as a receptionist. A customer calls during the lunch hour asking for the new price on a rechargeable battery pack for his power drill. He says that the catalog price is wrong and wants an up-to-date price quotation. Should Shannon
    a. leave her desk and go into her supervisor's office to look for the new price on his computer?
    b. tell the customer to call back after lunch?
    c. promise that the supervisor will call back after lunch?
    Choose the response that you think is best and explain why you feel it is Shannon's best option.

    _____

    _____

    _____

applications

1. Ask a coworker or another student to share his or her ideas about handling unpleasant work assignments. Choose someone whom you know to be conscientious about doing something that is obviously unpleasant. Ask what motivates him or her, and record the responses below.

_____

_____

_____

_____

_____

2. Consider the following situations. What, if anything, *could* you do and/or what, if anything, *should* you do if you were confronted with each situation?

a. The coffeemaker and the area where the staff drinks coffee are dirty and cluttered.

_____

_____

_____

b. A coworker who delivers the mail, although conscientious about delivering first-class mail, is throwing away some of the third-class mail without delivering it. He says, "No one wants it anyway."

_____

_____

_____

c. You regularly attend a meeting of your work group. Time is wasted because two or three people talk about sporting events and social activities that have nothing to do with the intended purpose of the meeting.

_____

_____

_____

d. You are an administrative assistant to a construction estimator who travels a lot. You notice that he spends a half hour or more each day arranging for airline tickets and car rentals.

_____

_____

_____

e. The forklift in the warehouse is used by about a dozen people. You notice that it is not getting routine maintenance. Doing the maintenance is not part of your job description. After asking around, you learn that no one is specifically assigned to do it.

_____

_____

_____

3. A coworker who is in a position you would like to move into is scheduled to retire next year. How might you prepare to secure the job for yourself?

_____

_____

_____

_____

_____

4. Your company is updating all of the equipment for the production department to make copies and send faxes, as well as the software for each computer in the department. How could you learn the equipment and new software if no training is to be provided?

_____

_____

_____

_____

Be Responsible

To be **responsible** means to be answerable or accountable for something within one's power to control. The definition includes being dependable and reliable.

Employers expect responsible behavior. They try their best to hire responsible individuals as employees. Employers look for evidence of responsible behavior in reports of education and work experience. Also, they expect to see this trait mentioned in letters of recommendation from former employers and other references.

Part of being responsible includes:

- working hard.
- paying attention to details.
- concentrating on your work, even when it is unpleasant.
- showing effort and perseverance toward goal attainment.

BE DEPENDABLE

If someone describes you as **dependable**, consider it a great compliment. In most cases, it means that you do what you say you will do. It sounds simple, and yet workers with the best of intentions are often labeled as undependable. They postpone work until it is too late or fail to appear when they are needed. It is important to understand that, if someone accepts a job, he or she is, in fact, "saying" that he or she will do the work as specified, so "do what you say you will do" is not limited to actual conversations.

Sometimes, people feel that they will disappoint someone if they say no, so they say they will get a report out by five o'clock even though they know they will not be able to do it. Truly dependable people, however, do not say "yes" unless they are certain they can carry out their promises.

In effect, when you say you will do something, you create a contract. A written contract might seem more important to you, but a spoken promise is just as important. If you are a dependable worker, you will do your work well and not make excuses. Being dependable also means that you will be at work at the time you are expected to be there. Consider what happens when you are late for work. Everything you do becomes shaded by the fact that you were late. You are behind with your work, so you hurry to catch up; because you hurry, you make mistakes; making mistakes causes you to become flustered, so you hurry more. This circle of hurry and errors goes on all day. However, even if you succeed in doing your work well despite being late, remember that an employer may still view you as being undependable if you are chronically tardy.

On the other hand, if you come to work on time or early, you are relaxed when you start your first task. Relaxation helps you work rapidly and accurately. Working in this way brings you a feeling of satisfaction, and this feeling helps you with the next task at hand. The result is a circle of excellence that works for you all day.

Punctuality is easily controlled. First, examine your situation and identify the possible causes of tardiness. Is it difficult for you to wake up? Do you allow too little time for all that you have to do before you leave for work? Do you have transportation problems, such as unexpected traffic congestion or unreliable bus service? After

"Nothing will work unless you do."

—MAYA ANGELOU

"Forget yourself in your work. . . . Throw yourself, body and spirit into whatever you are doing. The truth is that, in every organization, someone is taking notice of any employee who shows special ability."

—HARRY B. THAYER

determining the potential causes of tardiness, take action to eliminate or avoid them. For example, you might set the alarm clock for an earlier time or place it across the room so you will have to get out of bed to shut it off. Plan your early morning activities the night before to ensure that you will have plenty of time—with some to spare. Some things, such as setting your clothes out, mixing your orange juice, and preparing your pet's food, can be done before you retire.

Attendance and punctuality form an important block in building your success. However, sometimes emergencies arise— but there is still a right way to handle things. If you know you can't avoid being late, call in. And always call if you can't get to work. Of course, if you know ahead of time that you must be late or absent (doctor's appointment or jury duty, for example), inform your employer as soon as possible.

BE CONSCIENTIOUS

Being **conscientious** suggests following the dictates of one's conscience. In a work situation, it suggests one who is **meticulous**, someone who is concerned and careful about details. It also suggests that the worker stays with a job until it is done well. The conscientious worker would not deliberately waste time or avoid work. His or her conscience would not allow the employer's time, resources, or money to be wasted.

Sometimes you might see respected workers doing things that you do not feel are productive or done in a meticulous way. In some cases, it may appear to be normal and acceptable. But be careful. First, not everyone's job is the same, so a behavior that would be unacceptable for one employee may be what is required of another. However, even if others are wasting time,

on the job

Meng worked as a dishwasher in a restaurant about five miles from his home. On the way to work on his bicycle, Meng had a flat tire, which took nearly an hour to repair. While he was at the service station fixing the tire, he could have telephoned to let his supervisor know he would be late. But he was somewhat shy, and the prospect of explaining his problem over the phone made him feel uncomfortable. So Meng was nearly an hour late as he approached his place of employment. Now the anxiety he felt about facing his employer was even greater. Not having the courage to go to work late, Meng did not show up at all. To make things worse, he did not call to explain his absence.

How do you think the supervisor responded when Meng returned to work the next day?

their behavior does not give you permission to follow their negative example.

A variety of behaviors are described in the Self-Check that follows. As you review the results of this self-test, ask yourself how motives might affect your response to some of the items. If you learned that all of the actions described were intentional ways of slowing down or avoiding work, would it change your response to any item(s)?

Ask yourself (here and in work situations) why you are doing something. Are the motives behind the action something that you are proud of? Was there a good reason to do it? Or were you putting off work? You may justify the action by saying it is okay; everybody does it. There's no rule against it. Any given behavior may not be against the rules, but does it violate the norms of the workplace?

"Opportunity is missed by most people because it is dressed in overalls and looks like work."

—THOMAS EDISON

Following are examples of employee behavior that might not be considered conscientious. Which of these behaviors would cause you to have a twinge of conscience? In the space provided, write yes or no. Insert a question mark (?) if you are uncertain about whether or not the behavior violates your conscience.

_____ 1. Waiting ten minutes for someone to help you proofread ten pages.

_____ 2. Delivering a package that could be mailed instead.

_____ 3. Going to someone's office for a conversation instead of using the telephone.

_____ 4. Beginning coffee breaks and lunch periods early or finishing late.

_____ 5. Carrying on social conversations (on the phone or in person) during working hours.

_____ 6. Doing your personal work (without anyone else knowing about it) during working hours.

_____ 7. Working slowly to make the work fill up the time available for it.

_____ 8. Daydreaming when you should be concentrating.

_____ 9. Performing a task yourself when it could (and should) be done more efficiently by someone else.

_____ 10. Wasting time talking about doing a job instead of getting to work and doing it.

_____ 11. Refusing to do something that you could do because "It's not my job."

_____ 12. Pretending not to notice customers waiting to be served.

_____ 13. Sending a coworker a joke through the company e-mail.

In the business world, time is money. In addition to conserving and using time well, the conscientious worker is not content with mediocrity. Doing a good job without wasting time is what your employers will expect and what you should expect of yourself.

EXERCISE GOOD JUDGMENT

Showing initiative without exercising good judgment can be dangerous, if not disastrous. As you try to decide what action to take, it can help to put yourself in your employer's place. Ask yourself how you would expect an employee to proceed. For instance, if you see a lot of clutter around your work area, it is likely that taking the initiative to clean it up would be appreciated.

However, if you have an idea for a more efficient way to perform a routine task, doing the task a different way without first checking to see if it is all right may be viewed by some supervisors as showing a lack of concern or poor judgment. A good strategy is to explain your idea to someone in charge and be sure you have approval to proceed.

There are times when you cannot avoid a difficult decision, when you must use your best judgment and take action right then and there. For instance, suppose a customer is upset because he received the wrong merchandise. As a salesperson, you should certainly show your concern. You should give assurance that something will be done about the situation, whether you have been previously instructed to do so or not. There is the possibility that what you promise may not be what your supervisor would want, but it would be worse to lead the customer to believe that you do not care or that the store does not guarantee its merchandise.

It takes courage to show initiative. It also takes courage to admit your mistakes when you have used your initiative with poor judgment. It is usually best in the long run to face the consequences of your mistake, and be open and honest about it. If you cover up your mistakes, you will spend much time making excuses, blaming others, or trying to find an alibi.

When you admit an error in judgment, you may feel ashamed, or you may even be punished, but eventually you will be respected for your honest admission. And a reputation for integrity is a valuable trait.

© BRAND X PICTURES

Good judgment is required in dealing with distressed customers, clients, or patients.

Smart Tip ▾ ▾ ▾

There are times when you face a situation that calls for good judgment, and you feel at a loss because you do not have confidence in your ability to make the best decision. Here is what you should do:

- **Take a brief time out to think.**
- **Review what you know that is relevant to the situation.**
- **Consider the reasonable options (what different actions might be taken).**
- **For each option, review the positive and negative consequences that might occur.**
- **Weigh the alternatives, choose the best, and make a decision.**

▲ ▲ ▲ ▲ ▲ ▲ ▲ ▲ ▲

focus on ethics

Your supervisor was late for work this morning. You knew that a production deadline would not be met unless you were to take the initiative to make copies of an order for materials and fax it to the supplier. You sent the fax, but now realize that you copied the wrong order. There are several others who might have copied the order and sent the fax. At this time, no one knows that you were the one who did it.

What are your choices?
What should you do?

check*point*

1. What are the most important elements of being responsible?

   _____

   _____

   _____

   _____

   _____

2. Being conscientious suggests that one is being guided by one's

   _____

   _____

   _____

   _____

   _____

3. What does it mean to be a dependable worker?

   _____

   _____

   _____

   _____

   _____

4. What are the benefits of admitting your mistakes?

   _____

   _____

   _____

   _____

   _____

applications

1. You ride the bus to work. The schedule allows you to arrive either twenty-five minutes early or three minutes late. What would you do? Explain your decision.

2. Assume you have been promoted to supervisor. One of the people with whom you formerly worked is now working in your unit. She is habitually late for work but is doing a good job otherwise. It is your duty to talk to her about her tardiness. In a short essay, explain the main points you would make in talking to her about this problem. If it is convenient, share your ideas with others in your class. Draft the main points you would include below.

3. In a small group, discuss the value to both a company and an individual of being dependable and conscientious. Identify some steps individuals might take to improve their dependability. Then suggest ways in which you could encourage others to be dependable.

4. List two or three situations in which you think you could take the initiative without checking with a supervisor, and one or two situations in which you think good judgment would dictate getting approval.

_____

_____

_____

_____

_____

5. Think of a time when you exercised dependability. What was the situation and how did you decide to act the way you did? Did it require you to use good judgment? If so, how?

_____

_____

_____

_____

_____

10 Points to Remember

chapter

Review the following points to determine what you remember from the chapter.

- Motivation can come from outside yourself—external motivation—or you can be motivated from within—internal motivation.

- When a person is hired, the employer expects the employee to be willing to work. Your self-motivation is reflected in your willingness to work hard.

- You should be able to be productive and effective in performing tasks that may not be pleasant. To do that, sometimes you have to force yourself to face the task at hand.

- Your employer and coworkers expect you to show initiative. You will be expected to be open and eager to learn. The learning process should not go on forever; you should eventually be able to perform on your own. A key to success is to do more than is expected of you. However, good judgment is essential if you are to avoid mistakes.

- You should project an eager attitude. Showing initiative includes taking advantage of every opportunity to learn on your own, make decisions, and act independently without always being told what to do.

- A sense of responsibility that includes being dependable and conscientious leads to habits that make you more productive.

- Showing initiative without exercising good judgment can be dangerous, if not disastrous. Put yourself in your employer's place; ask yourself how he or she would proceed. Consider the reasonable options and what consequences, both positive and negative, could occur if you choose that option.

- It takes courage to admit your mistakes, but it is usually best in the long run to do that. A reputation for integrity is a valuable trait.

How did you do? Did you remember the main points you studied in the chapter?

key terms

Define each term in the space provided.

Initiative

Self-motivation

External motivation

Internal motivation

Responsible

Dependable

Conscientious

Meticulous

activities and projects

1. Take an inventory of the tasks you regularly perform on your present job. Use scratch paper to make a list of the tasks. Then give each task a rating: 1 = very pleasant, 2 = neither pleasant nor unpleasant, 3 = very unpleasant.

a. Calculate the percentage of 1, 2, and 3 ratings to get an idea of how much of what you do in your typical working day is unpleasant for you.
I spend _____ percent of my typical working day on unpleasant tasks.

b. Consider your motivation. Do you approach the unpleasant tasks with the same level of enthusiasm as the more pleasant ones?
My motivation for unpleasant tasks is the same, _____ somewhat less, _____ much less_____ compared with my motivation for pleasant tasks.

c. Write an assessment of your motivation and describe your needs (if any) for improvement. Also (if needed), outline your plan for self-improvement in this area.

2. Wherever you work you are likely to be involved with others as a member of a working team. This means that you interact with coworkers: What they do affects you and what you do affects them. If someone is not dependable or is irresponsible, it can hamper the team effort. Following are three examples. For each, explain how the incident might have influenced the productivity of the team.

a. At a fast-food restaurant that opens for business at 9 a.m., the person responsible for turning on the french-fry cooker arrived at 8:45 a.m. In the rush to get ready for customers to arrive, she forgot to switch it on. It takes twenty minutes to heat up.

b. A salesperson working in the women's shoe department finds several pairs of shoes in the stockroom and takes them out on the sales floor for a customer to try on. Instead of returning the unsold shoes to their proper location, he leaves them on a convenient top shelf. He plans to put them where they belong after the "rush hour."

_____

_____

_____

_____

c. One of the two people in an automotive service shop who is assigned to install and balance new tires fails to show up for work because he could not get his car started on a cold, snowy morning.

_____

_____

_____

_____

3. This activity is designed to help you take an inventory of your external and internal motivation. First, in the spaces provided below, write six things you do that you consider challenging and difficult—things you have a hard time getting done. Some examples are cleaning and organizing a storage room, being on time for appointments, or balancing a checking account. Then, for each item, decide _why_ you do it. What motivates you? After you have listed the various motives, ask yourself, "Does this motivation come from within, or am I being motivated by something outside myself? Am I responding to internal motivation or external motivation?"

I find it challenging and difficult to_____

_____.

My motive for doing it is _____

_____.

The motivation comes _____ from within _____from outside myself.

I find it challenging and difficult to_____

_____.

My motive for doing it is _____

_____.

The motivation comes _____ from within _____from outside myself.

I find it challenging and difficult to_____

_____.

My motive for doing it is _____

_____.

The motivation comes _____ from within _____from outside myself.

I find it challenging and difficult to_____

_____.

My motive for doing it is _____

_____.

The motivation comes _____ from within _____from outside myself.

I find it challenging and difficult to_____

_____.

My motive for doing it is _____

_____.

The motivation comes _____from within _____from outside myself.

I find it challenging and difficult to_____

_____.

My motive for doing it is _____

_____

_____.

The motivation comes _____ from within _____from outside myself.

4. You work in a situation where coworkers are expected to fill in for each other when someone is absent from work. In what ways might you prepare for the time when you will be assigned to fill in for someone else?

_____

_____

_____

_____

_____

_____

5. You are scheduled to attend a one-week seminar that is being offered by your company to upgrade employees' skills in working as a team. You are not sure that you should attend because you already work on a team. What do you think you should do?

_____

_____

_____

_____

_____

case studies for critical thinking

NEGLECTING THE UNPLEASANT TASK

You are the supervisor of a Humane Society shelter for stray and unwanted pets. One of the five paid employees is a nineteen-year-old woman, Alice. She appears to love the animals and is very good at all her assigned tasks except one: keeping the cages clean and odor-free. You were perfectly clear in your instructions and there is no doubt that she is the one—the only one—responsible. She was told to monitor the situation and do the work when it is needed. You are disappointed in Alice's performance because it appears that her idea of what is "clean and odor-free" is simply unacceptable to you.

1. Should you prepare a schedule for cleaning and deodorizing and post it for Alice? Why or why not?

2. As a friend and mentor, what suggestions might you offer to help Alice develop more initiative in working at unpleasant tasks?

PROBLEM OR OPPORTUNITY?

Frederick is a trainee in a bank. One of his jobs is to check the computer overdraft report and call the customers to notify them that they are overdrawn. Usually he is instructed to transfer funds from a savings account, but in this case a customer asks Frederick to transfer funds from another bank electronically. Frederick hesitates. Then he asks, "Can you withdraw the funds and bring a cashier's check to be deposited in your account?" The customer responds, "You mean you want me to make a trip to the other bank and then to yours when it would be so much easier to just let the computer and the telephone do it?"

1. What could Frederick say to the customer at this point?

_____

_____

_____

2. When he ends the call, what should Frederick do?

_____

_____

_____

3. What are some possible outcomes?

_____

_____

_____

Case 10.3

JOB OR CAREER?

Laura is a salesperson in a clothing department of a department store. The sales staff in the store is paid a weekly salary. No commission is paid for the amount of merchandise sold. Laura is very industrious and is usually the first to greet a customer. After serving her customers, Laura returns the clothing to the racks. She then keeps busy arranging merchandise or studying new items that have been recently put in stock. She is always pleasant and courteous. Dale, who works with her, tells Laura she is foolish to work so hard when she receives no extra pay. Laura knows that Dale's attitude is characteristic of the feeling of many of the members of the salespeople.

1. What potential benefits do Laura's attitude and actions offer her as an employee, and what benefits do they offer her as an individual?

_____

_____

_____

2. If Laura's excellent work results in a promotion, can you think of any advantages that her attitude will give her in a position of greater responsibility?

3. Why do you think the other salespeople feel as they do about their work?

4. If you were in charge of Laura's department, how would you handle this situation of attitude on the part of some of the sales personnel?

Case 10.4

How Much is Too Much?

Sonia supervises the shipping and receiving department of a university library. She has several part-time student helpers. Usually they are able to keep up with the flow of incoming mail. However, after weekends or holidays the books and magazines pile up, and it may take several days for Sonia and her crew to get caught up. Most Mondays and days after holidays, Sonia works from one to three hours overtime to catch up.

1. Because Sonia works on a salary, she gets no overtime pay. Should she continue working overtime? If not, how should she handle the situation? What problems might occur—both for her and the library—if she refuses to work overtime?

2. Sonia catches the flu and misses three days of work. When she returns, she finds the backlog of undelivered mail so great that she has to work eleven hours per day for a week. Her supervisor does not seem to know about Sonia's overtime work. What should Sonia do? How can she let her employer know about her work? Nearly all salaried workers are expected to put in unpaid overtime; however, is there a point at which you think Sonia should refuse overtime work?

Self-Management

| think about it: | Greg, Carlos, and Ramona were talking after a staff meeting. They had been advised that productivity was slipping in some sections and that top |

management was expecting supervisors to encourage workers to be more efficient and productive.

Carlos said, "Some of my associates are unproductive simply because they don't know how to schedule their time. Others are disorganized, and a few just fall apart when the pressure is on."

"How do you keep your section running so well, Ramona?" Greg asked.

Ramona smiled. "Well, I do training when there's time, but my best asset is Jean, who handles customer service. She concentrates on the job at hand and isn't distracted. She's very task-oriented, but flexible; when something new comes up, she adapts to it. She's organized and schedules her time effectively. She manages herself and her resources well. And, most important, she manages to stay cool when everything gets crazy."

Greg smiled. "I wish I could entice her to come to work in my section. Any chance of that?" Ramona laughed and said, "No way! She sets a great example for the rest of my crew. I would not trade Jean for anyone else in the company."

What habits has Jean developed that make her so efficient on the job?

© GETTY IMAGES/PHOTODISC

chapter focus

After completing this chapter, you should be able to:

1. Explain the importance of orderliness in the workplace.
2. Develop a realistic, workable schedule for efficient time management.
3. Explain the importance of efficient management of material resources.
4. Describe underlying causes and effects of stress.
5. Explain how stress can be managed and reduced.
6. Develop a plan of action to manage and reduce stress in your personal life and at work.
7. Improve your ability to work while under pressure.
8. Exhibit self-control and maintain professional composure.
9. Keep your ambition and motivation at a reasonable level.
10. Maintain control of your health with diet and regular exercise and, if possible, participate in a wellness program.
11. Avoid and manage stress by taking time to play or doing something that you enjoy.

Chapter Highlights

11.1   Efficient Work Habits

11.2   Stress Management

Efficient Work Habits

As you have learned, two critical aspects of your preparation for success in the workplace are (1) education and training, so that you will have the required knowledge and skills, and (2) a high level of self-motivation, including initiative and responsibility. A third aspect of your career preparation has to do with how you manage yourself—being efficient in your work habits and being able to cope with the stress that can hamper your productivity. This chapter can help you with this self-management.

If you have good self-management skills, your life and work are well **organized**. This means that your behavior is methodical, logical, and directed toward goals or outcomes that you have clearly in mind. You have both the motivation and the ability to be orderly, efficient, and systematic in your personal life and in your employment. This includes organizing the things around you at home and at work. It also includes organizing your time.

ORDERLINESS

It seems natural for some people to be comfortable with disorder in their surroundings. At home you will find their clutter everywhere—in the kitchen, the bedroom, the garage, the closet. Others are very orderly and cannot tolerate clutter. Being extremely sloppy and disorganized leads to serious problems at home, at school, and especially at work. On the other hand, being driven to extreme orderliness in every aspect of living can create problems, too. Perhaps you have had the experience of living or working with an excessively orderly person and with someone who is totally

disorganized. If so, you will understand that for a person to fit in and get along, it is essential to strike a balance between the two extremes.

While disorderly habits may be tolerated in one's private life, it is unusual to find a workplace where they are considered acceptable. Some employers think it is intolerable. Would you like to work in a situation where everything is in total disarray? Probably you would not. Lack of organization is the cause of a tremendous waste of time in the workplace. It can cause frustration and chaos for customers, employees, and managers.[1]

On the other hand, there are many benefits that come from having an orderly work environment. It encourages efficiency and helps to eliminate mistakes and inaccuracy. Orderliness also helps to prevent wasting time, materials, and other resources. The ultimate benefit is productivity and profit for your employer. This in turn benefits your customers and you.

In addition to material and financial benefits, being orderly and well organized on the job has psychological benefits. A major source of frustration is eliminated and praise, rewards, and promotions are more likely. Finally, there is the reward of self-satisfaction. Being orderly just makes you feel better about yourself.

TIME MANAGEMENT

Efficiency is appreciated and rewarded in the world of work. Part of the meaning of efficiency has to do with how well a task is performed. However, if you were to ask supervisors and managers to identify the most important efficiency factor, most would probably choose **time management**—a program in which all

> *"Being busy does not always mean real work. The object of all work is production or accomplishment and to either of these ends there must be forethought, system, planning, intelligence, and honest purpose as well as perspiration. Seeming to do is not doing."*
>
> —THOMAS EDISON

resources, including time, are efficiently used to achieve something important. Samuel H. Klarreich recommends (and outlines a procedure for) efficient time management as a solution to the problem of stress in the workplace.[2] Inefficient time management, more than anything else, paves the way for wasting time and, therefore, reducing productivity and profit.

What does one do to manage time? Some good suggestions are offered by Ken and Marjorie Blanchard in *The One Minute Manager Balances Work and Life.*[3] The process is similar to money management. With money management, you have income that makes money available, and you use the money by spending it. The written plan for allocating money to various uses is a budget. With time management, you look at time as the resource to be used. A calendar and a clock tell you how much of this resource is available, and a schedule is used to show how it will be used. Following is a step-by-step procedure for efficient time management.

1. Identify tasks to be completed.

When job analysts study an employment position, they start by conducting a **job and task analysis**. This is a process by which a job or position is carefully studied to produce a list of all the specific activities required to get the job done. The position under study is subjected to a **job breakdown**, which results in a specific list of tasks to be performed. The analyst will continue the process by considering each task, one at a time, to determine what the worker needs to know, what personal qualities or traits are required, and what training or skills are needed. All the tasks within this analysis make up a **job description,** which gives the content and essential requirements of a specific job or position.[4] The job description for your position can be very helpful in identifying the tasks to be completed.

on the job

You take your car in to have the electrical system checked. The sign over the door to the work area reads, "Customers not allowed in the shop." The door is ajar, and out of curiosity you look in. You see grease, dirt, trash, and clutter everywhere. There is a puddle of oil under the lubrication area. Dirty rags are lying around, and a rack for wrenches and hand tools is nearly empty. The tools on the workbench are in disarray or on the floor. There is a large stack of old tires in one corner and piles of boxes with used parts in another. A mechanic wearing a grimy baseball cap backwards walks across the shop and kicks several empty cardboard cartons out of his way. He calls out, "Larry, where's my 17 millimeter socket?"

- Are you going to leave your car in this shop?
- Are the mechanics going to be careful and conscientious as they check your car?
- Will they be efficient? Will they waste any time (at customer expense) because of their disorderly shop?
- As you think about the places where you do business, how often do you see this kind of disorganized work environment? Is this situation typical of the efficient, productive, successful workplace?

If you are employed now and do not have a job description available, here is what you can do to identify the tasks to be completed. Review what you have been assigned to do. If possible, ask your instructor or work supervisor to help by going over your various assignments to determine exactly what you are expected to do—not what you are supposed to know, what skills you need, or how the job is to be done. Simply list the tasks in no particular order. Keep in mind that tasks consume time. If there is something on the list that is not time-consuming, cross it off.

"Employ your time well . . . you may delay but time will not."

—Benjamin Franklin

Smart Tip ▾ ▾ ▾

To make it easier to use the information, prepare a 3" x 5" file card for each task. Write a brief description of the task at the top of the card. You will use space on the front and back of the card to record information produced later.

▲ ▲ ▲ ▲ ▲ ▲ ▲ ▲ ▲

2. Rank the tasks in order of importance.

Now that you have an inventory of the tasks that you are expected to accomplish, review them to evaluate their importance. With all the tasks in view, ask, "Which is the most important?" If there are some that appear to be equal in importance, ask, "Which should be done first?" If that question does not help you identify one that is clearly most important, choose one at random and label it number one. Then follow this procedure until all the tasks have been assigned a number. Finally, sort your cards so that they are arranged in order.

3. Determine time requirements.

To determine the time requirements for each assigned task, you must carefully consider the following questions:

- How much time is required to accomplish the task?
- How much time is available for it?
- What is the deadline? If there is not a specific deadline, what would be a reasonable, acceptable time for completion?

Now write the results of your analysis on the card for each task. (If you are new to a job, you may wish to discuss this with an instructor or supervisor to get his or her input on reasonable amounts of time for various tasks.)

C. Northcote Parkinson, after analyzing the efficiency (or inefficiency) of the British Royal Navy, concluded that in an office organization, "*Work expands to fill the time available for its completion.*" This conclusion became known as **Parkinson's law**.[5]

Here is an example of how Parkinson's law might affect you. You are expected to mow the lawn. If you have just an hour before you are to meet some friends to go play soccer, you get the job done within that time frame. But if you have three hours on a lazy afternoon, the job somehow takes that long (including time out for lemonade and two telephone conversations).

4. Develop a workable schedule.

You now have a stack of cards. Each card has information about a task: its importance, the time it will take to complete it (assuming Parkinson's law has no affect on it), the time available for completion, and task deadlines. With this information, you can develop a schedule showing what you will do and specifically when you plan to do it.

There are many different ways to go about scheduling. One way is to prepare a daily list of "Things to Do Today." You may also make such a list on a weekly or monthly basis. Tasks can be moved from one list or schedule to another one if needed.

An example of a weekly work schedule is shown in Figure 11.1 on page 303. More elaborate and detailed systems for scheduling are available in most bookstores.

Whatever system you choose, it is important to use accurate estimates of time requirements and to be conscientious and realistic about including important deadlines. You should think of a deadline written in your schedule as a commitment—a promise to do something according to your schedule.

Your schedule should be flexible, however. You can pencil in new items, as needed. Adjustments are made occasionally based on an accurate evaluation of your progress. Along with maintaining your schedule, you may also revise and update the card file as an ongoing record of progress and accomplishments.

Using a schedule to plan and monitor your activities can help you be efficient and make the best use of your time. But you should not become a slave to the schedule. Occasionally (and for some jobs, often) you may be overwhelmed with work. Unexpected and unplanned demands will be made on your time. The time you planned to use for a specific task may have to be used for something else; you will have to "make time" for the task, squeezing it into the schedule sometime in the future. The best that you can do under such circumstances is to use the information that appears in the schedule and revise it using your best judgment.

Make compromises, adjustments, revisions, and continue monitoring and making new plans. (And always add the new tasks to your "to do" list, so you can see where your time went and be reminded of how much you accomplished.) Be sure to cross off tasks when they are completed or moved to another list. There is a great psychological benefit and feeling of accomplishment to marking off the completed tasks.

RESOURCE MANAGEMENT

The most important—and probably the most expensive—resource your employer has is you. You, your coworkers, supervisors, and management personnel are the human resources of the enterprise. Everything in this chapter up to this point has been concerned with the efficient management of human resources. This brief section is concerned with efficient management of material and facility resources.

In any position of employment, you will have responsibility for resources that

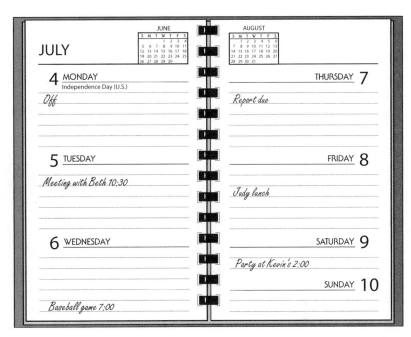

FIGURE 11-1 *A weekly work schedule.*

can be expensive. If you have a job, think about what you see all around you in your workplace. Imagine a workplace that might be in your future. Is there a building that is heated, air-conditioned, and well-lighted with facilities such as restrooms, a cafeteria, and more? Are there cars, trucks, computers, filing cabinets, product displays, and machines or equipment for production? Do you see supplies and materials that are to be used in getting the job done?

All these resources are available to help you do your job well. They are provided to help you keep your productivity and the quality of your work within accepted standards. You will be expected to conserve these resources and make good use of them.

Remember, from your employer's point of view, "Time is money." The material and facility resources for which you are responsible represent money as well. Waste and misuse have negative effects on productivity and profits.

on ethics

Workers in a copper mine are allowed to take materials and supplies as needed from the supply room. During camping season, the purchasing agent notices that the supply of flashlight batteries is used at three times the normal rate. When the purchasing agent presents this information in a staff meeting, one of the supervisors comments, "It's no big deal. Why make an issue of it?"

Is this an important issue? What should be done?

Technology at Work

Your computer or personal digital assistant (PDA) can be used to organize your life and work. Several easy-to-use software programs are available. A palm-sized PDA can store and retrieve phone numbers, calendar entries, to-do lists, and short notes, as well as access your e-mail and Internet sites. Several Internet sites offer free Web-based calendars for recording personal schedules, which can interface with your PDA.

check*point*

1. Clutter in your workplace helps to show your employer that you are busy.
    True_____ False_____
2. Waste and misuse of material resources can have negative effects on
    _____ and _____.
3. Label the following activities according to the order in which they should occur—1st, 2nd, etc.
    _____ develop a schedule
    _____ determine time requirements
    _____ identify tasks to be completed
    _____ rank tasks by importance
4. Two good ways to design and develop your time-management system are

    _____

    and_____

5. Two important benefits of orderliness are

    _____

    and_____

applications

1. Think about some personal examples of Parkinson's law based on your experiences.

a. List three occasions when the amount of time it took to perform a task was influenced by the amount of time available.

_____

_____

_____

b. What are some of the underlying causes of your behavior in the examples described above?

_____

_____

_____

c. What are some ideas for preventing or avoiding the effects of Parkinson's law?

_____

_____

_____

2. Jasper Matsura has a basket on his desk marked for incoming work. He has asked his supervisor several times to place any work for his attention in this basket, since his desk tends to get cluttered because of interruptions throughout the day. Nevertheless, his supervisor repeatedly comes in asking for work that Jasper has never seen. When he looks through the piles of paper on his desk, Jasper finds the requested items. Do you think Jasper has handled the problem correctly? Why or why not?

_____

_____

_____

3. It is important to know how you use one of your most valuable commodities—your time. In this activity, you are to keep track of the time you use in a one-week period. Use a chart, such as the one below, for each day. Record the actual time for each activity during the day. For example: "7:30 a.m. to 8:15 a.m. Exercise." It is important at least once per day to review how you spent your time and record it on your chart.

TIME   **ACTIVITY**

_____   _____

_____   _____

_____   _____

_____   _____

_____   _____

_____   _____

_____   _____

_____   _____

4. Using the chart above as an example of how you usually use your time, list some ways that you can become more efficient and use your time more wisely. If you feel you are efficient, write briefly why you think you have become so efficient in time management.

_____

_____

_____

_____

_____

Dictionary definitions do not quite capture the meaning of **stress** as it is seen and experienced in the world of work. You may hear stress described as an "emotional factor that causes bodily or mental tension."

A practical way of defining stress is the feeling one gets from prolonged, pent-up emotions. If the emotions you experience are pleasant and desirable—joy, elation, ecstasy, delight—you usually feel free to let them show. They are not suppressed. Therefore, positive emotions do not usually cause stress. Negative emotions, on the other hand, are more often held inside. They are hidden. You suffer quietly and you experience stress.

However, stress is not necessarily bad for you. Dr. Peter Hanson, in *The Joy of Stress,* points out that "you can make stress your best ally in achieving personal and professional excellence."[6]

CAUSES AND EFFECTS OF STRESS

Just as there is great variety in the range of emotions you might experience, there are many possible manifestations of stress—in your private life and in your working life. An interesting source of information on this topic is *The Complete Guide to Stress Management* by Dr. Chandra Patel.[7] Here are some words used to describe the emotions associated (as cause and effect) with stress.

- Anxiety
- Pressure
- Misery
- Strain
- Desperation
- Tension
- Anger
- Panic
- Dejection

on the job

Roberto recently started working as a supermarket checkout clerk. He has set for himself a goal of being an assistant manager within a period of three years. He works extremely hard at his job and strives to learn everything he can by observing others and asking questions about the grocery business. After one year, Roberto is promoted to assistant produce manager. He is thrilled. In his eagerness to continue to climb toward his goal, he puts in voluntary overtime, helps everyone in his department, and provides special services for preferred customers.

Roberto ignores the fact that he has not taken any vacation time. Some nights he is unable to sleep because he is thinking about some phase of his new position. He is losing weight and frequently feels tense. His stomach is often upset, and he experiences a burning sensation. After checking with his physician, Roberto learns that he is developing a gastric ulcer.

What might be other causes and effects of the stress buildup for Roberto?

Prolonged stress can be devastating; burnout, breakdown, and depression are some of the potential results of long-term, unmanaged stress.[8] By wearing a mask, you may expect to hide stress caused by problems in your personal life and not let them influence your performance on the job. This will probably not work. The more you try to hold your emotions in, the greater the pressure buildup will be.

Stress in Your Private Life Influences Your Work and Vice Versa

There is simply no way to survive the experience of long-term stress without damage to your private and work life. It is almost impossible to insulate one from the other. If you are under stress because of something that is going on in your work situation, it will be very difficult to maintain your positive attitudes and productive work habits. The most tranquil and satisfying personal life will be upset by the effects of stress that may occur in one's working environment. Similarly, being under emotional strain and having stress in one's personal life is bound to have a negative effect at work.

Think about someone in your life who has shown evidence of being under stress. How did you recognize that there were problems? What are some physical signs and effects that were apparent? What are some attitudes and behavioral evidence that you noticed? Remember that eventually the signs of stress show.

Sometimes Stress can Have Desirable Effects

You may have heard someone say, "I like to work under stress. If I have a deadline to meet, I work harder." Physical stress builds muscle. For some people, "test anxiety" improves performance; for others it hampers their performance. The problem is to be able to avoid crossing the line between improved performance and harmful stress.

Stress Affects the Body

It is clear from medical research that stress can influence heart function, cause high blood pressure, and raise levels of blood cholesterol. Dr. Peter O. Kwiterovich, director of the Lipid Research Clinic at Johns Hopkins School of Medicine, in his book *Beyond Cholesterol,*[9] points out that "current studies now suggest that people who anger easily or have a low tolerance for frustration may be more likely to develop coronary heart disease. Those who . . . have a greater change in their heart rate and blood pressure may also be more likely to develop coronary

heart disease, especially if they are exposed to situations where this occurs frequently. What we do not know is how to alter these reactions to stress. . . . However, it seems a matter of common sense to keep your stress levels low."

For most people, the body seems to adjust to stress. At least it does so in the short run. But sustained and increased stress may cause harmful physical and psychological problems including depression, anxiety, insomnia, irritability, heartburn, stomach disorders, headaches, heart disease, and more.[10]

Everyday Frustrations Cause Stress Buildup

From the time you wake up until you go to sleep, you may be confronted with a succession of stressful situations. Managing to get yourself (and possibly a spouse and children) out of bed and ready to face the day can be a challenge to your patience and ingenuity. Driving to school or work can be harrowing, especially if you're running late. You may experience frustration in arranging to get the car repaired. You may face conflicts in school or at work, such as coping with unrealistic deadlines, equipment failures, or unexpected bad weather. If part of your job is selling, you may experience feelings of rejection when most of your customers say "no."

A series of stressful and frustrating experiences throughout the day can cause you to lie awake at night in an emotional turmoil—unable to get needed rest. You face the next day with less emotional and physical stamina. After another stressful day and another night without rest, you may have even less emotional strength and stability. Therefore, stress buildup, if not resolved, continues day after day.

Problems in Our Personal Life can be Devastating

Surviving the normal, everyday stress described above can be difficult. But far

"Depression, gloom, pessimism . . . these slay ten human beings for every one murdered by disease . . . Be cheerful."

—FRANK CRANE

more serious and painful circumstances can create long-term stress.

More serious stressful circumstances may include separation from loved ones, personal illness or illness of a loved one, death of someone you care about, or conflict with a spouse or close friend. Other major causes of stress are problems with drug and alcohol abuse, domestic violence, care of children and elderly relatives, accepting a new job, chronic mental illness, injury, physical handicaps, even moving to a new home if you've lived in the same place for more than ten years. The list goes on and on.

Managing your personal finances can be another stressful experience. This can be a problem no matter what your income level, but it is especially difficult if you must support a family and do not earn enough to live comfortably. Unpaid bills, unwise use of credit, and budget limitations can make life difficult.

A Common Cause of Stress is Dealing with Life's Transitions

This is especially true when a person must cope with too many transitions all at once. For example, Sue Ellen has just completed a program in fashion merchandising. She is eager to get started on her new job. Her mother is ill and requires care. Her father died a few months ago. Sue Ellen's new job requires that she relocate to a town one hundred miles from home. The move, a new career, and a change in family relationships may cause excessive stress for her. Too many changes have arrived at the same time.

In Some Jobs, the Work Itself May Cause Stress or Tension

One factor that causes stress is **monotony**, or doing a task repeatedly. Another is being expected to do more work than your skills and the allotted time will allow. In contrast, sometimes not having enough to do can create stress.

A change in jobs or new job responsibilities, such as a promotion or a different assignment, can cause stress. There may be too many kinds of tasks for which you are not well prepared. You may be subjected to stressful working conditions—noise, interruptions, temperature extremes, poor lighting, or unsafe situations.

Some jobs are unavoidably stressful because of the nature of the work itself. Some examples are law enforcement, health occupations, fire fighting, air traffic control, news reporting, crisis intervention, or emergency services. Even though most hazardous jobs have many safeguards to protect workers, work that is dangerous is stressful. However, no matter where you work, some stress is sure to occur.

STRESS SIGNALS

If you are experiencing long-term stress, you may or may not be aware of it. Even if you are, you may choose to avoid facing up to your problems. When the solutions are not obvious and easy, it may feel better to hide the problem—even from your inner self. Following are some signs and symptoms of stress that you should be concerned about.

You May be Depressed and Not Realize It

Depression is an emotional disorder that is marked by unexplained sadness, inactivity, and a feeling of emptiness. According to Benson and Stuart, "Depression encompasses a number of feelings and behaviors including feelings of loss, defeat, discouragement, and hopelessness. It can range from 'feeling blue' to feeling that life is meaningless. The future is viewed with 'doom and gloom' pessimism. Depression also involves a loss of self-esteem and feelings of inadequacy."[11]

If you are experiencing depression, you may lose interest in your

"Stress is an ignorant state. It believes that everything is an emergency."

—NATALIE GOLDBERG

work and withdraw from family, friends, and everything that enriches your life. If you experience persistent, deep depression, you should seek professional help.

Physical Symptoms can be Warning Signals

In *The Wellness Book: The Comprehensive Guide to Maintaining Health and Treating Stress-Related Illness*, Benson and Stuart suggest that the physical warning signs of harmful stress may include these:

- pounding of the heart
- dryness of the throat or mouth
- insomnia
- feeling constantly tired
- inability to concentrate
- chronic pain
- change in appetite
- nightmares
- difficulty breathing
- overpowering urge to cry
- an urge to escape
- trembling
- panic attacks

Often stress signs are ignored, as they seem to come and go. If these symptoms are totally disregarded, more serious conditions may develop.[12]

Stress can Cause Mood Swings

If you are under a great deal of stress, your behavior may become unpredictable. You may do things that are not typical of your behavior. If you lose your temper or express extreme disgust with others or yourself for no apparent reason, you may be experiencing too much stress. If you are uncomfortable with a new position or additional responsibilities, you may experience personality changes brought on by too much stress.

Unfortunately, you may be unaware of the changes in your mood or behavior. The changes may have to be pointed out to you

by others. It is normal to experience a few of these symptoms at times, but enduring any of them often over a long period of time indicates unhealthy stress. C. W. Metcalf and Roma Felible in *Lighten Up: Survival Skills for People Under Pressure*, offer a variety of suggestions for controlling your mood swings.[13]

KEEP STRESS UNDER CONTROL

There are many effective ways to handle stress. One of the several excellent books on keeping stress under control is *Coping with Job Stress* by Herbert M. Greenberg.[14] Other references on stress management may be found in the Supplemental Enrichment Resources for Chapters 10 through 12.

Of course, you can't avoid stress; in fact, you wouldn't want to avoid all stress—because you'd never grow. However, you can manage your life so that you survive the emotional down times without allowing stress to engulf you. Also, you can work to eliminate controllable stress factors, such as running late or not getting enough sleep. But when stress is constant or too great, your wisest option is to find ways to reduce or control it. You need not, and should not, live your life in emotional stress and discomfort. Stress can be successfully managed. Here are some suggestions that may help.

Understand the Causes of Stress

Understanding why you are under stress is important. This may seem obvious, but it requires a deliberate, conscious effort to pause and simply ponder your situation. By now, you are familiar with what is called the **stress response**, the emotional or physical symptoms of uncontrolled stress. Now you need to try to discover the **stressors**, the factors that create the stress in your life.

Prepare a Written Assessment of Your Stress Factors so You can Visualize and Understand Them

This written self-analysis can help prepare you to gain control of the stress in your life. For example, you may write: "I feel tired most of the time. My lower back seems to ache all through the day and night. I miss deadlines and run behind schedule." After your analysis of stress responses and consequences is written, consider each item and ask why. "Why am I feeling tired? Why does my back ache? Why do I run behind schedule?" Careful consideration of the answers to the "why" questions will reveal stressors, such as deadlines, anxieties, trying to do too much, managing time or money poorly, or poor health habits.

It may help to talk things over with someone with whom you feel comfortable and secure. A good friend or a professional counselor can help you explore possibilities and clarify your thinking about what is causing stress in your life. These talks will release pressure, make you feel better, and help you see a new side of a problem. If you find yourself preoccupied with a difficulty, turn to a good listener and discuss what is troubling you. In the process of describing your problem, you may find a solution.

Deal With the Stressors

Develop techniques to deal with the causes of stress. The longer you avoid dealing with the stress factors, the more stress will build up. If tension comes because you have put off an unfinished task, restructure your priorities so you can get the task you have been avoiding out of the way and off your mind. Take the tasks that you have been neglecting, write them down, and check them off as you take care of them. Make it a point to talk with any person causing

The following checklist can help you with a self-assessment of the symptoms of stress in your life. Check those that you experience sometimes or often.

_____ persistent low energy

_____ persistent headaches

_____ chronic skin problems

_____ frequent stomach upset

_____ compulsive eating

_____ chronic insomnia

_____ temper outbursts

_____ moodiness

_____ inability to concentrate

stress in your life and resolve your differences.

You may find yourself ignoring the causes of stress by simply saying, "I'm not feeling well," "I'm just tired," or by taking your frustration and stress out on others with unkind thoughts, words, or actions. This kind of behavior only increases stress.

Develop your Ability to Work Under Pressure or Unusual Conditions

When you can't reduce the stressors, you need to manage your stress response. Almost everyone, at least at some point, has to meet deadlines, keep several tasks going at once, resolve problems that come up, and do extra work when necessary. However, when the pressure mounts, you can relieve it. Relaxation is the key, but most people must train themselves to relax when the pressure is on.

on the job

Bill was a first-line supervisor in a plastics molding department. After arriving at work thirty minutes late, he found that Joe, a new employee, had set up a production run incorrectly. Joe did not start the run, but if he had it would have taken several hours to correct the mistake. Bill lost control of his temper, used abusive language in reprimanding Joe, and threatened to have him fired. Later, Bill discussed the problem with the plant manager, a trusted and caring friend. "I blew up at Joe because it was the last straw," he said. "I had just come to work after a series of terribly frustrating experiences. My neighbor had a loud party last night, and I couldn't get to sleep. So I phoned and asked him to tone it down. When I finally did get to sleep, I overslept and was late for work. On my way to the garage, I noticed that about three feet of my new hedge had been torn out.

When I confronted my neighbor about it, he denied everything and accused my wife of ruining the hedge when she went to work earlier. When I finally got to work worrying about the deadline, I saw that Joe had the setup wrong. I just lost it."

Why did Bill lose his temper when he reprimanded Joe? How should he have handled the situation?

DEVELOP SELF-CONTROL

Sometimes, because of work pressures and frustrations, a person can "blow up" and lose emotional control. Here is an example.

Self-control is the ability to direct the course of your behavior; it is the capacity to manage your own thoughts, feelings, and actions. In the *On The Job* example, Bill allowed his personal problems and frustration to affect his behavior on the job. Employers expect and appreciate employees who are able to leave their personal problems at home. This can be difficult. Self-control is evident when you are in control of your emotions and actions. It requires men-

Smart Tip ▼ ▼ ▼

Here are some tips on how to relax when the pressure is on:

- **Stop for a moment (especially when you feel your muscles tightening up) and take a few deep breaths. You may even want to post a sign that says "breathe" in large letters.**
- **Do a relaxing exercise. Swing your hands at your sides and stretch.**
- **If your work situation allows it, take a "power nap." Lie down and totally relax for a few minutes.**
- **Find time outside your work to do some things that you enjoy.**
- **Learn meditation techniques or yoga.**
- **Leave your workplace briefly for a brisk walk or other vigorous exercise.**
- **Find a quiet place to read a magazine or novel during a break or at lunch.**
- **If possible, have pictures of serene, peaceful scenery (forests, meadows, mountains) visible or accessible. This "mini-vacation" for your eyes is a powerful inducer of the relaxation response.**
- **Look up.**
- **Keep something humorous on hand, such as a book of jokes. Laughter is great medicine to help us relax.**

▲ ▲ ▲ ▲ ▲ ▲ ▲ ▲ ▲

tal discipline and personal willpower, but it is vital if you are to do your best on the job.

Concentrating on your work, which is a key element of becoming efficient and productive, requires self-control. Most people want to be efficient and productive, but doing the job well often requires personal discipline. When a supervisor oversees the work, external motivation helps you settle down to work. However, if you have a job that you must do without direct supervision from others, you must have the self-control to do the job to the best of your ability.

CONTROL YOUR ACHIEVEMENT MOTIVATION

It is only natural to want to achieve. For some people, this desire can be almost an obsession. Psychologists refer to these hard-driving people as having **Type A personalities**. More easygoing, relaxed people are described as having **Type B personalities**. In *Beyond Cholesterol*, Dr. Peter O. Kwiterovich points out that "Type A people are competitive, impatient, always pressed for time, doing many things at the same time, and motivated by achievement. Type B people are more relaxed and tend to take things in stride."[15]

If you face the challenge of reining in your Type A behavior as you struggle to achieve, you may need to slow your pace. One of the reasons you are under stress is that you put yourself in high gear for long periods of time. These periods of highly motivated behavior may prove to be too much for your emotional and physical health.

Stop and reflect on your life. As you are working toward a goal, you will reach points where it is appropriate to stop and reward yourself for a job well done. This reward period will allow you to relax and get away from the pressure.

Take it Easy on Yourself
It is impossible to pay attention to all areas of your life simultaneously. Take care of things as you can. Do not expect perfection in yourself or others. Realize that there are some things you cannot control. Learn to

accept what you cannot change or alter. Ask yourself if you are aiming at the unreasonable or the impossible. If you are trying to live up to someone else's expectations, or expecting others to live up to your standards, you may be setting yourself up for failure. Remember, you are only human; imperfections are acceptable—and inevitable.

Manage Your Time Better
Time management can reduce stress, especially if you are a Type A overachiever. You may simply be trying to do too much. When you plan and schedule your work and your personal life, it will be easier to be realistic about your achievement motivation. Strive to work as efficiently as you can and continually seek ways of streamlining your work. Work to complete tasks on time and in an expedient manner.

Attempt to break down big jobs into reasonable blocks of work. This is a good way to tackle what seems like an overwhelming task and to feel rewarded as you complete each step. Delegate and share work with others when appropriate and acceptable. Avoid attempting to do everything yourself. Keep your workload under control.

MAINTAIN GOOD HEALTH
What you need to do to maintain good health depends on the kinds of problems that cause stress in your life. Following are some suggestions for alleviating stress and improving your physical health. They are recommended by Richard Carlson in *Don't Sweat the Small Stuff at Work: Simple Ways to Minimize Stress and Conflict While Bringing Out the Best in Yourself and Others.*[16]

"Take a rest; a field that has rested gives a bountiful crop."

—OVID

Get Regular Exercise
Exercise can help to relieve stress.[17] An effective exercise program can "burn up" the tension that builds in your body during a long period of stress. Activity, such as

Keep stress under control and be more productive.

© GETTY IMAGES/PHOTODISC

ommended by Martha Davis in *The Relaxation and Stress Reduction Workbook.*[19] Dr. Barry Sears, in *The Zone*, suggests that cutting down on fatty meats, dairy products, eggs, sweets, and salt will help maintain good physical and mental health.[20] It is also recommended that eating more fruits, vegetables, poultry, fish, and whole grains can be beneficial. And since poor health is a source of stress, you are reducing the risk of an additional stressor in your life.

BE GOOD TO YOURSELF

If you experience stress as a result of working too hard for too long without a break, you should try to "get away from it all."

Smart Tip ▾ ▾ ▾

Ask your doctor if vitamin supplements are right for you. A daily dose of the following vitamins can help to reduce your risk of heart disease.
- **A high-quality multiple vitamin**
- **Vitamin E**
- **Vitamin C**
- **Vitamin B complex**
- **Beta carotene**
- **Folic acid**
- **Aspirin**
- **Omega 3 fish oil**
- **Niacin**
- **CoQ-10**

Note that the B complex and C vitamins are especially helpful in high-stress periods. It is common for professional athletes, for example, to take extra B and C vitamins before important events.[21]

▲ ▲ ▲ ▲ ▲ ▲ ▲ ▲ ▲

moderate walking, can relieve tension and relax your body. Other activities that provide physical release from stress are playing tennis, running, dancing, bicycling, yoga, and other forms of exercise you enjoy. If you have had a stressful morning, skip the coffee break and try a walk break.

Get Involved in a Wellness Program
Employers across the country are realizing that their employees may need help, support, and encouragement to cope with mental and physical health problems. As a result, many companies have started **wellness programs**—programs designed to help employees maintain or improve their health—or have joined a local health agency's program. Participation in a wellness program can help you counteract the effects of too much stress before it becomes harmful to you.[18]

A healthful diet is an important component of a good wellness program, as rec-

Redirect your thoughts to something pleasant and relaxing for awhile to "recharge your batteries."

Go and have some fun. An exotic vacation can certainly help in coping with stress. If you can, do it. Fortunately those of us with less time and money can "get away" simply by changing our pace or taking a break from our routine. Weekends, holidays, and hours after work can relieve stress if you spend some of the time doing things you enjoy. Do you like to meet friends after work? Do you have a hobby such as sewing, reading, woodworking, gardening, hiking, square dancing, or working on restoring your classic car? Plan time to do the things that help you relax and give you pleasure. Reward yourself for all of your hard work. Take some time to enjoy yourself.

Look on the bright side. Attempt to develop a positive outlook on life. Always strive to concentrate on what is positive. Look beyond yourself, and avoid spending too much time thinking about failure. Whenever the opportunity arises, try to turn negative statements made by others into positive ones. If a coworker says, "We'll never get this report done," respond, "If we work together, I think we can do it!" A positive thought will introduce a new spirit and get everyone working hard to achieve. A positive spirit will indeed help reduce stress.

chec**k**point

1. **What are some common physical and behavioral symptoms of stress?**

   _____

   _____

   _____

   _____

   _____

   _____

   _____

   _____

   _____

   _____

2. **Write "A" or "B" in the appropriate spaces. People with Type ____ personalities are hard-driving. People with Type ____ personalities are easygoing.**

3. **Holding in and hiding your negative emotions can make it possible for you to conquer stress. True____ False____**

applications

1. Think about your own responses to stress to answer the following questions.

a. Does your body send out any warning signals when you are under stress? What are the signals?

_____

_____

_____

b. Do you have any special tactics you use to control your emotions when you find yourself in a stressful situation? Explain.

_____

_____

_____

2. Schedule an interview with a health-care professional. Prepare a series of questions for that individual about the impact stress can have on the physical and emotional health and well-being of a person. Write a short essay about what you learned in the interview. Write a few questions you would like to ask here before you go to the interview.

_____

_____

_____

3. Describe four stressful situations that you experience from time to time. Opposite each situation you describe, write an idea that might help you to manage it.

SITUATION	HOW TO MANAGE IT
(1.) _____	_____
_____	_____
_____	_____

SITUATION	HOW TO MANAGE IT
(2.) _____	_____
_____	_____
_____	_____
_____	_____
(3.) _____	_____
_____	_____
_____	_____
_____	_____
(4.) _____	_____
_____	_____
_____	_____
_____	_____

4. Think of a situation in which someone at school or work caused you to experience stress. What happened in the situation? What do you think caused the person to react the way he or she did? How could you have avoided the situation? What steps did you take to overcome the stress?

_____

_____

_____

_____

_____

11 Points to Remember

chapter

Review the following points to determine what you remember from the chapter.

- Employers value order. Being orderly in your work can lead to better job performance, rewards on the job, and self-satisfaction.

- Efficient time management includes an analysis of the tasks that consume your time. To manage your time efficiently, rank the tasks in order of importance. Consider the time available, how much time the task requires, and deadlines for completion of the work. Use this information to develop a realistic, workable schedule.

- A competent worker is expected to manage facility and material resources efficiently. Waste and misuse can have negative effects on productivity and profits. When time and material resources are wasted, the impact on your employer is the same as if money were taken. A conscientious worker would not deliberately avoid work or use any tactic that leads to inefficiency and less productivity.

- Sustained and increasing stress can affect your physical health. Everyday activities can also be stressful, and problems in your personal life can cause extreme stress. Stress is one of the causes of various ailments that affect our body and our ability to act in situations that we cannot control. Research has shown that stress is a factor in many diseases.

- There are many effective ways to handle stress. The first step is to identify the causes of your stress and carefully consider the possible reasons for allowing them to develop. Deal with the stressors and develop your ability to work under pressure.

- Talking with a friend or counselor can help you understand the underlying reasons for stress in your work and personal life and help you plan for better stress management. Some strategies that have proven to be effective in managing stress are being less demanding on yourself and managing your time better.

- You should expect your work environment and the demands of your job to create pressure. To be successful you must learn to cope with the pressure of the work environment and not let it reduce your productivity.

- Self-control is important in the workplace. It requires self-discipline and willpower. You should make an effort to be sure that problems and frustrations in your private life are not allowed to affect your performance on the job.

- Ambition and motivation to achieve should be kept to a reasonable level, so that they do not create extreme stress in your life.

- You should maintain control of your health with diet and regular exercise and, if possible, by participating in a wellness program. Many companies provide fitness centers and professionals to help with activities for exercise and wellness. Take advantage of these when offered.

- You can get away from the personal and work situations that create stress by taking time to play or doing something that you enjoy. Vacations or simply working on a hobby or project that you enjoy can help reduce stress.

How did you do? Did you remember the main points you studied in the chapter?

key terms

Define each term in the space provided.

Organized

Efficiency

Time management

Job and task analysis

Job breakdown

Job description

Parkinson's law

Stress

Monotony

Depression

Stress response

Stressors

Self-control

Type A personality

Type B personality

Wellness programs

activities and projects

1. Marilyn was graduated from high school, obtained a job in a nearby city, and moved in as housemate with Tony and Chad. After a month Tony and Chad were nearly ready to ask Marilyn to move out because she had failed to do her share of cleaning and seemed content to let the kitchen become an eyesore. When Marilyn left the door to her room ajar, and Tony and Chad saw the cluttered mess inside, they decided to take action. They first cleaned and organized the kitchen. Then they went into Marilyn's room and did a thorough "tidying up." They left a note on the bed: "This sets the standard. If you want to continue living with us, please turn over a new leaf and keep our home as neat and clean as you see it now."

a. Assuming that Marilyn needs to develop new habits compatible with those of her housemates, imagine the habits Tony and Chad have that Marilyn should develop. List them below.

b. Marilyn responds with a note on the kitchen table that reads: "Thanks for cleaning my room. But I left home, and don't need a parent to take care of me. I think you two are too meticulous and it's not reasonable to expect me to keep my room the way you keep yours." In a friendly conversation, what might Tony and Chad say to Marilyn?

2. Develop an efficient time management plan for one week. If you are attending school, if you are employed full-time or part-time, or whatever your routine might be, include all your important, time-consuming activities. Follow the procedure as explained in this chapter to develop a schedule, showing how you will use your time over the seven-day period.

_____

_____

_____

_____

_____

_____

_____

_____

3. Has there been a time in your life when you went through a difficult period involving a lot of change? The changes might have been the result of moving to a different community, the ending or beginning of a romantic relationship, attempting to lose weight or quit smoking, attending a new school, having a new housemate, experiencing the death of someone you cared about, going through losing one job and having to find another, or having a serious illness or injury.

a. Describe the situation. What happened and how did it make you feel?

_____

_____

_____

_____

_____

_____

_____

b. What did you do to help yourself cope and adjust to the changes? How well did your coping and adjusting techniques work? What might you do differently if another difficult situation arose?

_____

_____

_____

_____

_____

_____

_____

_____

4. Regular exercise, control of your diet, and other wellness activities can help you manage stress in your life. Analyze your situation. What are you doing about exercise and physical recreation? What are you doing and what should you be doing to improve and maintain good health? Prepare a plan and schedule.

_____

_____

_____

_____

_____

_____

_____

case studies for critical thinking

OVERWHELMED

Wolfgang learned to repair stringed instruments as a teenaged apprentice in his father's violin-making business. His father was dedicated to and immersed in his craft and specialized in making replicas of famous instruments for professional musicians. He set his own working schedule and enjoyed the luxury of having no deadlines or interruptions. The violin workshop was, to others, disorganized and cluttered, and often Wolfgang's father would spend his time "puttering" with some artistic detail, such as the purfling—the ornamental inlaid border on the top of a violin. He was never in a hurry and was seldom concerned about anything but the task at hand.

In his early twenties Wolfgang went into business for himself. He obtained a small-business loan at a local bank, rented a shop in a suburban mall, advertised his stringed-instrument repair business in the Yellow Pages, and his business blossomed. He found himself busy with instrument repairs, and word-of-mouth publicity brought more business than Wolfgang had expected. However, Wolfgang found that he simply could not operate this business the way his father had. His customers were not like those of his father. They were not willing to pay a high price for artistic details. They expected to pay a reasonable price for the work; they expected to have the work done in a reasonable time and on time; and they expected to be able to drop in or phone and get Wolfgang's immediate attention.

After a few months in business Wolfgang took stock of his situation. He was hearing his customers complain; he was feeling stress and distress because of frequent interruptions; he was embarrassed at the disorganization and clutter of his shop; his cash flow was not sufficient to pay for hiring someone to share his workload. It was apparent that Wolfgang would have to make some changes or go out of business.

1. What are Wolfgang's most serious self-management problems?

_____

_____

_____

2. Analyze the situation and identify the most critical examples of wasted time and resources.

_____

_____

_____

3. Outline a plan of action for Wolfgang that might result in improvements in his efficiency and productivity.

_____

_____

_____

Case 11.2

Up the Ladder

Helen and Marilyn were seated together on an airplane trip to a travel agency managers' convention. Helen started the conversation. "How's business, Marilyn?" "Best ever, Helen. But I'm a bit worried about how it's going to be after next week. My best agent has been hired away by your agency." Helen smiled, "I know. And I expect my business to improve. We're lucky to get Mei-ling. In your letter of recommendation, you shouldn't have been so candid about her ability." "I wish we could have offered her a management position," Marilyn responded. "Mei-ling is the most efficient agent we have. Not the most intelligent. Not the best educated. Not the most experienced. But the most efficient!"

1. What do you think are some of the work habits that might have helped Mei-ling succeed?

_____

_____

_____

2. As Marilyn interviews candidates for the vacant position, what are some questions she might ask? Make a list of four questions and, for each, tell what useful information she might obtain.

Question
1: _____

_____

Information _____

_____

_____

Question
2: _____

_____

Information _____

_____

Question
3: _____

_____

Information _____

_____

Question
4: _____

_____

Information _____

_____

Case 11.3

WORKING UNDER PRESSURE

A coworker and close friend works as an administrative assistant for five real estate agents. She also answers the phone and greets potential clients when they drop in at the agency office. She shares her feelings as follows: "It seems like I'm in a swamp with a bunch of alligators. The agents are constantly bringing in work that they want done immediately. They always seem to expect me to drop everything to do their work. When the workload slacks off, I feel so disorganized; it seems impossible to get caught up. I can't concentrate on anything for very long because clients keep coming in and interrupting me. Then there's the telephone—the worst interruption of all. I think I'm going to scream!"

1. As a trusted colleague, what advice would you give?

_____

_____

_____

2. If your advice is followed, what might happen to improve the situation?

_____

_____

_____

Case 11.4

OVERWORKED

Lisa has been in the position of assistant manager for a fast-food operation for two months. She supervises fifteen full-time employees and ten part-time workers. She does all the food and beverage ordering, takes care of promotional items and advertising, and opens and closes the restaurant every day. The cleaning service is often late or does not show up at all, and Lisa ends up cleaning the floor, the equipment, and the rest rooms.

Lisa finds herself snapping at dependable employees and faithful customers. She often feels tense and has an upset stomach and annoying headaches. Lisa sees her family physician and is told that perhaps she is working too hard and too many hours. Lisa does not see any alternatives. She continues to work as she has in the past.

1. What could possibly be the result of Lisa's situation?

_____

_____

_____

2. Why do some people work themselves into situations similar to this?

_____

_____

_____

3. What additional information would you like to know about Lisa that might help you advise her?

_____

_____

_____

_____

_____

_____

_____

_____

4. Would you recommend that Lisa give up the position? If not, what would you recommend that she do about her workload?

_____

_____

_____

_____

_____

_____

_____

_____

Thinking Skills

think about it: The human resources manager of a large department store is talking to a marketing instructor. The purpose of the teacher's visit is to find potential training stations for marketing students. The manager is saying, "We need good people for sales positions. We do *not* need salesclerks. We do *not* need management trainees. Under our new management philosophy, everyone has to be a manager. We expect those we hire to be able to do what we used to expect only of supervisory personnel. In fact, we don't think of our merchandising managers as supervisors anymore. And the people they used to supervise are no longer called salesclerks. They're now called sales associates. They are paid better now than they were when we expected them to work in the shadow of a supervisor. But more is expected of them. When a problem comes up or when a decision has to be made, they handle it. Now we expect them to do the work and to manage themselves as well. They no longer have someone they can go to for direction. They have to do their own thinking. Are you training your students to think?"

Are you prepared to be your own supervisor, with the problem-solving and decision-making skills this employer expects? Are these expectations realistic? What suggestions would you offer to the marketing instructor and her students?

© RUBBERBALL PRODUCTIONS

chapter focus

After completing this chapter, you should be able to:

1. Explain the importance and value of being able to think analytically and creatively.

2. Describe analytical and creative thinking abilities and skills.

3. Explain when and how to use analytical thinking and creative thinking strategies.

4. Plan and work toward improving your thinking abilities and problem-solving skills.

Employers Want People Who Can Think

Leaders in education and business agree that the skills required for decision making and problem solving are easy to recognize in the workplace. However, they are not so easy to teach as the how-to-do-it skills that are the main focus of most career and technical education programs. Therefore, there is a tendency for teachers to emphasize the technical knowledge and skills required by employers and to avoid or neglect the more difficult challenge of teaching students to think. As a consequence, many graduates arrive at the workplace unprepared for an important part of the work they will be assigned to do.

A typical employer's complaint was expressed by Sharon, the manager of a Colorado Holiday Inn Express. "The first thing I have to work on when I train a new employee is to teach her [or him] to think. If she [or he] works at the reservation desk or answers the phone, it's just one problem after another and I can't be there to coach her [or him] and answer all of her [or his] questions. She [or he] has to learn to analyze the situation at hand and come up with a solution." Sharon employs fourteen people, and she takes pride in being able to keep job turnover (and the time she spends training new employees) at a minimum.

"The new emphasis in education for the workplace of the future is on the three Rs . . . READING, WRITING AND REASONING."

—FORMER U.S. LABOR SECRETARY ELIZABETH DOLE

CRITICAL THINKING

A popular term for the one kind of thinking that is highly prized and appreciated in the workplace is critical thinking. Another term for **critical thinking** is *reasoning*. It includes the ability to use logic and to analyze information to solve problems and make decisions. Specifically, what does one do when reasoning or thinking critically?

A person with critical thinking ability is able to:

- **Distinguish between verifiable facts and value claims.**

  Example: An advertisement reads: "This herbal remedy reduces arthritic pain by 50 percent." This is not a verifiable fact because "pain" cannot be measured precisely using mathematical calculations.

- **Determine the credibility of a source of facts or value claims.**

  Example: If research on the effectiveness of an herbal remedy is not mentioned in the advertisement or if there is reference to "numerous testimonial letters from users," one would judge the credibility to be less than if there is reference to experimental research in a recognized medical journal.

- **Distinguish between warranted or unwarranted reasons or conclusions.**

  Example: An auto mechanic is "troubleshooting" to determine the cause of a "misfire" when your car engine is idling. If he puts his ear to the exhaust pipe and says, "It sounds like a sticking valve lifter," you would have less confidence in his conclusion than you would if he had connected a computer analyzer to your car's computer and said, "This code tells us that a spark plug is probably fouled."

- **Distinguish between relevant or irrelevant facts, claims, or reasons.**

  Example: Relevant: "This person should be selected for employment as a travel agent because he has traveled extensively in foreign countries." Irrelevant: "This person should be selected for employment as a travel agent because he has excellent grades in accounting classes."

- **Detect bias.**

  Example: Recognizing that when a person who is an expert golfer says, "It is my unbiased opinion that golf should be included in our high school physical education program," that person is actually presenting a biased opinion.

- **Identify unstated assumptions.**
Example: A very attractive man is selected as a salesperson in the appliance department. The female manager says, "We hired him because we want a guy who, if necessary, can do heavy lifting." What the manager does *not* say is that he was also hired because she and the female customers will enjoy having an attractive man in the store.

CREATIVE THINKING

Alex F. Osborn, in *Applied Imagination,* defined creativity as "the ability to visualize, to foresee, and to generate ideas."[1] (**Visualization** is the ability to "see with the mind's eye.") E. Paul Torrance, in *Guiding Creative Talent,* suggested that creativity is "the process of sensing problems or gaps in information, forming ideas or hypotheses, testing and modifying these hypotheses, and communicating the results."[2]

The creativity tests developed by Torrance measure the following specific creative thinking abilities:

- **Fluency: the ability to produce many ideas quickly**
Example: In the plumbing department of a large home builder's supply store, several fifty-gallon barrels of pieces of pipes and fittings have accumulated. Several of the department employees are taking a refreshment break and the department manager says, "What can we do with all this? It's a waste to just put it in the dumpster. What are some ideas for using short pieces of pipe and fittings?" If the group produces a large number—possibly twenty or thirty ideas (some good, some not so good, some ridiculous)—they will be demonstrating "ideational fluency."

on the job

Gregory is someone who appears to be very smart. He has scored in the top 5 percent in almost every test he's ever taken. He had a 4.0 grade point average in high school, including some college courses he was allowed to take during his senior year. Gregory had everything that smart college students are supposed to have, and he was invited to enroll at a top college. In a conversation with the school counselor, Gregory's college advisor said, "There's no doubt that he was smart. He could memorize anything. At the beginning, he performed just the way the tests predicted. He did extremely well on multiple-choice tests and was great in class, easily answering questions about assignments. But it did not stay that way. In upper grades, there was a lot more essay writing, rather than multiple-choice testing. Students were expected to not only process information, but also to come up with their own ideas. Gregory wasn't even in the top half by the time he finished."

What does this story tell you about the limitations of relying mainly on developing knowledge by memorization and rarely being challenged to develop thinking skills?

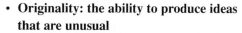

- **Originality: the ability to produce ideas that are unusual**
Example: Some of the ideas for using the pieces of pipe are quite obvious. But ideas that it seems no one else would think of—very clever ideas—are original. Making wind chimes, boat anchors, and using them for reinforcing poured concrete may be original ideas.

- **Flexibility: the ability to produce a variety of ideas.**
Example: Often, one idea will trigger another, then another, until a list of similar ideas is produced. One idea might be an anchor for a rowboat, another for a sailboat,

"Many highly intelligent people are poor thinkers. Many people of average intelligence are skilled thinkers. The power of the car is separate from the way it is driven."

—EDWARD DEBONO

etc. Or someone might suggest welding pipe sections together to produce an artistic piece—a dinosaur. This triggers the idea for making a gorilla, then a moose, etc. This tendency to get in a "mental rut" shows a lack of ideational flexibility. When many different categories of ideas are produced, flexibility is being demonstrated.

- **Elaboration: the ability to add interesting detail to ideas**

    Example: David decided to make a Father's Day card for his dad who is an avid windsurfer. He used paper in a variety of colors, scissors, a razor blade, and Elmer's glue. The sailboard, the windsurfer, the sail, and cutout letters appeared in an attractive design. A tiny purple comma was used for punctuation. A bright yellow cloud was shown with "wind" (tiny paper strips) and a "face" (eyes, eyebrows, pursed lips).

- **Curiosity: the ability to ask revealing questions**

    Example: Carmen is a realtor. She has a lunch meeting with Diane who says she is looking for a condo. Carmen asks many questions: "Where do you live now? What did you do before you retired? Will you plan to rent your condo part-time or live in it full-time? How do you plan to finance your purchase? Will you want a garage, a boat slip, a view, access to a golf course, a pool?" After many revealing questions and answers, Carmen will be able to help Diane find a condo that is "just perfect."

- **Imagination: the ability to make wild guesses**

    Example: Sometimes, as you work at solving a challenging problem or making a difficult decision, you need to know *why*. Cases in point might be the mechanic "troubleshooting" your car's misfire, the computer technician considering

"Imagination is more important than knowledge."

—ALBERT EINSTEIN

Technology at Work

There is a considerable amount of technology available for improving thinking skills, from video- and audiotapes to computer software. Instruction ranges from games for improving basic skills to software that simulates complex business situations.

The Internet also offers a wealth of opportunities for practicing and improving thinking skills. Consider searching for *Mind Games* or *Thinking Skills* to find sites that offer online instruction and thinking games for free or serious thinking courses (software, videos, or books) for sale.

what caused the computer to crash, or pondering the aftermath of a friend's "tantrum" that seems to have no reasonable cause. Imagination, as applied to creative problem solving, helps one to think of interesting possible answers to puzzling "why" questions—questions about possible causes and consequences.

In addition to the abilities listed above, the highly creative person has an attitude of self-confidence. One way to identify the creative people in a group is to simply ask, "Are you creative?" Those who say "yes" probably are.

Highly creative people are strongly motivated to use their creative potential. They are typically open-minded to the ideas of others. They show unusual curiosity, sensitivity to problems, and an attitude of "constructive discontent" with things as they are. They are challenged and interested when they see opportunities to help change things for the better.[3]

Critical Thinking and Creativity are Equally Important

One might expect highly intelligent people more likely to be highly creative. This is not necessarily true. There have been many careful research investigations over the past forty years concerning the relationships between intelligence and creativity. The evidence shows that creativity and IQ test scores are unrelated. Therefore, you should realize that few people are both highly intelligent and highly creative. And few are neither. There are many who score high on IQ tests but earn average scores on creativity tests. Also, there are many who score high in creativity but average on measures of intelligence.[4]

check✓point

1. **Creativity is closely associated with which trait?**
   a. dependability
   b. imagination
   c. orderliness
   d. patience

2. **Critical thinking involves**
   a. imaginative thinking
   b. memorization
   c. logic
   d. incubation

3. **A thinking ability closely associated with critical thinking is**
   a. flexibility
   b. elaboration
   c. memory
   d. detecting bias

4. **A thinking ability associated with creativity is**
   a. curiosity
   b. analysis
   c. synthesis
   d. logical thinking

5. **Being able to add interesting details to ideas is part of _____.**

6. **Detecting bias is something a person might do when involved in**
   a. rhetoric
   b. creative thinking
   c. elaboration
   d. critical thinking

applications

1. John Mansfield said, "Man's body is faulty, his mind is untrustworthy, but his imagination has made him remarkable." To what extent do you believe this to be true? Discuss.

2. Think about your past experiences at work and in school. Write a brief explanation of three instances when creativity on your part either improved or actually saved a situation.

3. Working alone or in a small group, think of as many reasons as you can why employers value critical thinking skills or creative thinking skills. Also discuss and record the different types of jobs where one skill might be more important than the other.

4. With a team of your classmates, review a few local newspapers and view several newscasts (television news programs) to determine if any bias exists. If you find biased reporting, explain it and why you think the information is biased.

Despite the fact that there is no clear, systematic explanation of exactly what happens when a person is engaged in thinking, these abilities can be recognized and improved. Something very worthwhile can be accomplished by following systematic problem-solving procedures. Following is a closer look at two procedures or strategies for solving problems, one using analysis of important information or critical thinking, the other using what is commonly referred to as creative thinking to produce valuable information.

PROBLEM SOLVING

A problem-solving procedure can be visualized as a funnel, as shown in Figure 12-1. At the top is an assortment of information that is logically processed, then narrowed down to a conclusion or solution to the problem. In other words, the information is used to reach the conclusion by using logical analysis. Therefore, this strategy for solving problems is referred to as **analytical problem solving**. Creative thinking ability gives one the power to do **creative problem solving**.

The step-by-step procedure shown in Figure 12-1 can be modified for different situations and, with slight variations, it can be used for both analytical problem solving and creative problem solving.

Following are the specific steps for both analytical and creative problem solving. Study and compare the two outlines. You will see that the distinction between creative problem solving and analytical problem solving is in what happens at the point where possible solutions to the problem are needed.

Analytical Method
Step 1. Identify and clarify the problem.
Step 2. Gather pertinent information.

OUTLINE OF A PROBLEM-SOLVING STRATEGY
1. Recognize that a problem exists and that there is a discrepancy between what is and what should or could be.
2. Identify possible reasons for the problem or discrepancy.
3. Devise and implement a plan of action to resolve the problem.
4. Evaluate and monitor the results of implementing the plan, and revise the plan as indicated by the findings.

FIGURE 12-1 *Outline of a problem-solving strategy.*

Step 3. Use logical analysis to determine possible solutions.
Step 4. Evaluate the alternative solutions.
Step 5. Choose the best solution.

Creative Method
Step 1. Identify and clarify the problem.
Step 2. Gather pertinent information.
Step 3a. Use brainstorming to produce possible solutions.
Step 3b. Develop and refine the ideas for solution.
Step 4. Evaluate the alternative solutions.
Step 5. Choose the best solution.

You will notice that in one method analytical problem solving is used to come up with ideas for decision making. Here, conclusions are reached by studying and thinking carefully about the facts or evidence. When this happens, critical thinking and logic are used. For example, if a

"A man is not idle because he is absorbed in thought. There is a visible labor and there is an invisible labor."

—VICTOR HUGO

Employers appreciate the worker who can solve problems.

© DIGITAL VISION

"In the space age the most important space is between the ears."

—Thomas J. Barlow

"Some men see things as they are and ask why. Others dream things that never were and ask why not."

—George Bernard Shaw

person shows up for work moving slowly, with a "glassy stare" and slurred speech, one might assume that he or she is under the influence of drugs or alcohol. Other logical assumptions might be that the person had been in an accident or did not get enough sleep.

However, if you ask the question, "What are the possible causes for someone exhibiting this type of appearance and behavior?" you would be using a **creative thinking** approach. A popular term for this problem-solving strategy is **brainstorming**. The purpose of brainstorming is to create as many ideas as possible. During the brainstorming session, critical judgment is avoided because if a person thinks his or her idea might not be a good one, it might not be shared with the group. The results of the brainstorming session are reviewed and the value of the ideas is judged at a later stage in the process.

To help you visualize how problem solving works in employment situations, study the

following examples that take you through the steps of problem solving. One shows how a travel agent might use this strategy in resolving a problem with a dissatisfied customer. The other is an example of a construction supervisor using the same problem-solving strategy when timber piles break.

As you study these examples, keep in mind that analytical skills come into play at various steps in the process and that creative skills are needed for others. Be alert to whether the approach being used is analytical or creative.

The Travel Agent's Problem

1. Recognize that a problem exists and that there is a discrepancy between what is and what should or could be.
A customer comes into the travel agency with a complaint. She is obviously dissatisfied with her travel experience.

2. Identify possible reasons for the problem or discrepancy.
The travel agent talks with the customer to determine the nature of the problem. She asks questions and looks for clues in the answers. She reviews the customer's file. At the conclusion of her investigation, the travel agent decides what should be done to satisfy the customer.

3. Devise and implement a plan of action to resolve the problem.
The travel agent contacts a representative from the company at fault to notify them of the customer's complaint. She negotiates compensation for the customer with a company representative and notifies the customer of the compensation offer.

4. Evaluate and monitor the results of implementing the plan, and revise the plan as indicated by the findings.
The travel agent makes a follow-up contact with the customer to learn the results of the interaction between the company and the customer. When the customer and the company express satisfaction, the case is closed.

on the job

A pottery manufacturer uses old newspapers to wrap dinnerware for shipment. Production has been slowing down. The supervisor notices that the workers are spending time reading the newspapers and that they talk about what they read while they are working. Slowest of all are the more experienced workers and those who are the most outgoing and sociable.

What are some of the possible underlying causes of the work slowdown? What are some clever, interesting, and unusual ideas for improving productivity in the preparation of dinnerware for shipment?

Determining a customer's wants and needs requires creative thinking.

© DIGITAL VISION

The Construction Supervisor's Problem

1. Recognize that a problem exists and that there is a discrepancy between what is and what should or could be.

The construction supervisor discovers that timber piles are breaking before they reach the specified level of load bearing.

2. Identify possible reasons for the problem or discrepancy.

The construction supervisor analyzes how and why the timber pilings break during the piling operation. He reassesses the strength of the materials, the equipment specifications, and the skills of the workers under his supervision.

3. Devise and implement a plan of action to resolve the problem.

The construction supervisor evaluates and selects the appropriate equipment to accomplish the project. He chooses the right kind of timber pilings based on the strength, diameter, and cost to meet project specifications.

4. Evaluate and monitor the results of implementing the plan, and revise the plan as indicated by the findings.

As the new equipment setup and timber pilings are used, the construction supervisor carefully observes the work being done. He inspects the completed work and is satisfied that the new pilings will not break under the load they are required to bear.

focus on ethics

A business is having quite a few problems. Some of these problems revolve around dealings with suppliers and employees. Other problems relate to money. The manager of the business knows that things aren't working well, but he hopes that if he ignores everything, things will work out somehow. Or maybe he'll just look for another job and leave the company in the situation it is in.

What outcomes will likely result from the manager's choices? Who, besides the manager, would be affected? What advice would you give the manager?

DEVELOP YOUR THINKING SKILLS

Having the *ability* to think is of no value unless you learn how to use it. You also need thinking *skills*. Developing these skills can give you the power to *use* your thinking abilities, to apply them practically.

The dictionary defines skills as "technical expertness" and "proficiency." It includes "using one's knowledge effectively" and "a learned power of doing a thing competently—a developed aptitude or ability."

The distinction between abilities and skills is that abilities are like the tools you use for thinking. Skill is what you need to develop if you are to make good use of the tools. For example, a camera is a tool for a photographer. To take good pictures, the photographer must have a good camera. But that is not enough. He or she must also have picture-taking skills, including the desire to photograph something of interest. You must develop your thinking skills if you are to take advantage of your thinking abilities.

It is important for you to understand that whatever thinking abilities you have, those abilities can be improved. And more importantly, the skills required to use those abilities can be learned. Knowledge is acquired by reading, listening, etc. Attitudes develop under the influence of emotional experiences. Physical (or psychomotor) skills are developed through coaching and practice. It is the same for intellectual skills, such as reasoning and creative problem solving. Knowing what to do and having the benefit of coaching and repeated practice—these are the keys to learning to think.

"Like most behavior, creative ability probably represents, to some extent, many learned skills. There may be limitations on these skills by heredity; but I am convinced that through learning one can extend the skills within those limitations."

—J. P. GUILFORD

on the job

Celia's former high school counselor was talking with one of her college professors. The professor said, "Her grades, letters of recommendation, IQ, ACT, and SAT scores were good but not great. Her first year here, she did average work, although she did improve. Surprisingly, however, she turned out to be the easiest student to place in a good job. And this surprised me. She did not appear to have very high analytical ability or creativity, yet she could do a job while others were having trouble. Celia, it turns out, had learned how to play the game. She made sure she did the kind of work that was valued by her employer. She had savvy—a kind of practical grasp of things. And that doesn't show up on IQ or creativity tests."

Why do you suppose Celia was able to develop the "savvy" that allowed her to excel in the workplace?

A competent worker:

- *Uses imagination*
- *Combines ideas in new ways*
- *Makes connections between unrelated ideas*
- *Reshapes goals to reveal new possibilities*
- *Organizes and processes symbols, graphs, pictures (as in visualizing a building from reading a blueprint)*
- *Solves problems by logical analysis*

A worker uses Thinking Skills to

Learn

Reason

Think creatively

Solve problems

Make decisions

—SCANS COMMISSION[5]

Smart Tip ▼ ▼ ▼

When you are in the spotlight of judgment or evaluation, remember to:

- **Be aware of what is expected of you and by what standards your decisions will be judged.**

- **Pay attention and learn from the feedback you get. Use it for self-improvement.**

- **Accept criticism gracefully; do not pretend the person who is giving the criticism is at fault.**

▲ ▲ ▲ ▲ ▲ ▲ ▲ ▲ ▲

Do you prefer numbers, facts, evidence, and order? _____

If yes, your strength may lie in critical, analytical thinking.

Are you good at visualizing? Do ideas just pop into your head? _____

If yes, your strength may lie in creative thinking.

Which problem-solving strategy seems to make the most sense to you, analytical or creative?

How could you use problem-solving strategies in everyday life?

Critical and creative thinking can be improved with practice. Take fifteen minutes and list as many ideas as you can think of for practicing these skills without having to wait for real problems to occur.

Which of your ideas do you think are the best?

check*point*

1. **The first steps in analytical and creative problem solving are**
   a. the same.
   b. different only in the underlying assumptions.
   c. different in strategy.
   d. different in the approach that is used.
2. **Creative thinking ability**
   a. may be improved with highly emotional experiences.
   b. may be improved with practice and coaching.
   c. can improve only with psychotherapy.
   d. never changes.
3. **If you are using the creative method to solve a problem, you will likely**
   a. use logic.
   b. use brainstorming.
   c. exercise critical judgment.
   d. use convergent thinking.
4. **If you are using the analytical method to solve a problem, you are likely going to**
   a. use logical analysis.
   b. use divergent thinking.
   c. visualize possible solutions.
   d. brainstorm for solutions.

applications

1. Take a walk through a busy shopping area and find two similar business places that are close to each other, where one obviously has more customers than the other. Working alone or with one or two classmates, work through the problem-solving process.

a. What problems exist where there is a discrepancy between what is and what should or could be?

_____

_____

_____

b. What are some possible causes or reasons for the discrepancies?

_____

_____

_____

c. What specific actions should the management of the less-patronized business take? Devise a plan that will help to resolve the problems.

_____

_____

_____

2. Most people do not fully use their creative potential because their motivation to be creative is squelched or suppressed (by others or by themselves). Some reasons are fearing risk and failure, conforming to the expectations of others, being lazy, and wanting to be sure an idea is a good one before communicating it. Think about what has happened, what is happening now, and what might happen in your future. List ten things that might suppress your creativity. Then think of strategies you could use to overcome those things.

a. _____

_____

_____

b. _____

_____

_____

c. _____

_____

_____

d. _____

_____

_____

e. _____

_____

_____

f. _____

_____

_____

g. _____

_____

_____

h. _____

_____

_____

i. _____

_____

_____

j. _____

_____

_____

3. Your employer has a problem with the errors that are being made in handling customer relations problems. He has asked you to devise a plan to correct the problem. What method of problem solving would you use? Why?

_____

_____

_____

_____

_____

_____

12 Points to Remember

chapter

Review the following points to determine what you remember from the chapter.

- More than ever before, employers look for and appreciate employees who are able to think on their own. They seek out and reward workers who can make decisions, solve problems, and handle critical and creative thinking activities that were traditionally in the domain of supervisors and managers. Critical thinking and creative thinking are intellectual skills that are needed, increasingly appreciated, and used at all levels in the modern workplace.

- Critical thinking skills allow a person to do analytical problem solving and to make logically sound judgments and decisions. Creativity helps a person to visualize, to foresee, and to generate ideas. Fluency in producing ideas, originality, flexibility, elaboration, curiosity, and imagination are factors in creative thinking. Both creative and critical thinking are important. A person can be highly gifted in one kind of thinking and only average in the other.

- The problem-solving procedure is essentially the same for analytical problem solving and creative problem solving. The distinction is that creative problem solving requires brainstorming techniques to produce a variety of good alternative solutions while analytical problem solving requires logical analysis to recognize or arrive at potential solutions.

- Improving your thinking abilities and skills is worth the effort. It takes some coaching and repeated practice, but it can enhance your value as a worker and make you more effective and productive.

How did you do? Did you remember the main points you studied in the chapter?

key terms

Define each term in the space provided.

Critical thinking

Visualization

Fluency

Originality

Flexibility

Elaboration

Curiosity

Imagination

Analytical problem solving

Creative problem solving

Creative thinking

Brainstorming

activities and projects

1. While working on a spreadsheet, your computer shuts down. The screen goes off, the blinking lights go dark. You need to find the problem, fix it, and get back to work. Use your analytical thinking skills and creativity as you ask yourself the following questions and consider the answers:

- Have any other lights or power failed?
- Do I smell smoke or see evidence of anything burning?
- Are all electrical cords still plugged in?
- Is there a fuse between the power source and the computer?
- What is the weather like outside?
- Is the computer on the same circuit as the microwave and toaster in the lounge?
- Was the computer operating perfectly at the time of the shutdown?

a. In the following space, list five additional questions that might be logically relevant to the computer failure.

b. Assume that you find your computer to be on the same circuit as the appliances in the lounge and that someone used the toaster at the same time as someone else was using the microwave. What might you conclude?

c. From the list above, and from the list you produced in response to *a*, choose three questions. For each, specify an answer to the question and, therefore, a plausible conclusion about the cause of the computer shutdown.

Question

Answer

Conclusion

Question _____

Answer _____

Conclusion _____

Question _____

Answer _____

Conclusion _____

d. In which part of this activity was creativity used? In which part was analytical thinking used? Explain your answers.

_____

_____

_____

2. Test your creative thinking abilities. Working either alone or in a small group, have a brainstorming session for exactly ten minutes. In that time, write down as many clever, interesting, and unusual ideas as you can think of for using empty plastic beverage containers. Now evaluate the results of your session.

a. Obtain a *fluency* score by counting the number of ideas, regardless of quality. Over 50 is excellent, 30 to 50 is good, and less than 30 suggests you need to suspend judgment, try harder, and be more creative.

Fluency Score_____

b. Obtain an *originality* score by considering how many of the ideas are really unusual. If at least 10 percent of the ideas appear to be so unusual that probably no one else would think of them, your originality score is excellent. Five percent is good. Less than that shows a lack of originality.

Originality Score_____

c. Obtain a *flexibility* score by counting the number of times you changed categories in responding. When this happens you somewhat "shift gears" mentally. For example, in 15 responses you list five as containers, seven as decorations, and three as floating objects. Your flexibility score would be 3. A flexibility score of 12 or more is excellent, 7 to 12 is good, and less than that suggests that you have a tendency to get in a "mental rut" and stay there.

Flexibility Score_____

3. Try out your problem-solving skills, either alone or in a small group.

a. Look around your school, workplace, or community. Find a problem that is important enough to motivate you to work on it. Write a paragraph to describe the discrepancy between what is and what should or could be.

_____

_____

_____

_____

_____

b. Identify the possible reasons for the problem or discrepancy. Use logical analysis to sort out the situation, the way you would if you were trying to unravel a mystery.

_____

_____

_____

_____

_____

c. Use creative thinking. Have a brainstorming session to produce a variety of interesting ideas about possible solutions of the problem or discrepancy. Make a list of your ideas and arrange them with the best ideas at the top of the list.

_____

_____

_____

_____

_____

d. Devise a plan of action to resolve the problem or remove the discrepancy. Again, use logical analysis and creative thinking as you did in *b* and *c* above. Write the plan in terms of (1) objectives or goals to be accomplished, (2) strategies and implementation plans, (3) ideas on how the achievement of objectives or goals will be evaluated, (4) a time schedule, and (5) an estimated budget.

case studies for critical thinking

UNEXPLAINED BEHAVIOR CHANGES

You are an agent in a large real estate firm. Your coworker and close friend, Carmen, is usually cheerful, energetic, skilled in communicating with potential buyers and other realtors, efficient and accurate in managing the paperwork and details of her job. Several days ago a change came over Carmen. Occasionally you find her sitting at her desk, simply staring out the window. She never smiles and often seems to ignore the people around her. She has made several careless mistakes with credit reports and loan applications, and when these errors were called to her attention she was defensive and blamed the clerical staff. You speculate about the possible reasons for this change in Carmen's behavior and come up with four plausible explanations: depression, stress, a personal crisis, or job burnout.

1. In a private, heart-to-heart conversation, with the objective of determining what is going on to cause these behavior changes, what questions might you ask?

2. With the answers to the questions you have asked in #1, outline a step-by step procedure using analytical problem solving that might help you to help Carmen get her life back to normal.

CAREER TRANSITION

Mercy has been enjoying a professional career in interior design. Her husband Paul is doing well as a truck driver hauling freight for a food wholesaler. Their first baby is on the way, and Mercy faces the possibility of leaving an interesting job that she has been devoted to for several years. Their second-story apartment is small, their parents live out of town, and most of their friends work all day. The prospect of Mercy having to interrupt her career is discouraging because of her strong creative urge and enjoyment of dealing with people. However, the possibility of being a full-time parent is appealing.

1. Specifically, what are the problems Mercy and Paul need to solve?

_____

_____

_____

2. Identify three possible solutions, including evidence to support your conclusions, and outline the advantages and disadvantages of each.

_____

_____

_____

Case 12.3

TIRED OUT

Merlin's Tire Shop has been in business for seventeen years. Tire sales have been steady, and Merlin has been collecting about twenty worn-out tires per day, hauling them to a vacant lot in the suburbs. A new city ordinance classifies the pile of tires as a fire hazard, and the city manager orders that they be removed. The community trash disposal site has a policy of charging one dollar per tire, and Merlin calculates that his cost for using the trash disposal site would put him out of business.

1. Specifically, what are the problems Merlin needs to solve?

_____

_____

_____

2. Make a list of clever, interesting, and unusual ideas for using old tires to make something useful.

_____

_____

_____

3. Outline a plan that might allow Merlin to dispose of his used tires without going out of business.

_____

_____

Standards of Conduct   13

think about it: Nancy and Marshall, supervisors in a soft-drink distribution center, were sharing a table in the lunchroom. Nancy looked around for a moment and said, "Where's Yvonne? Doesn't she work here anymore?" "Well, I doubt that she ever actually worked for this company," Marshall said. "She's gone now, and the manager told me it's because she was working for Yvonne." "I think I know what you mean," Nancy said. "I hear they were very upset when they found out that she gave a copy of our mailing list to her friend in Houston. And I know she was doing homework for her accounting class during her afternoon break—a very long break." "Really?" Marshall responded. "I didn't know about that, but I did see her here when I came in to do some catch-up work Saturday morning. She was working at the office manager's computer, and I saw the printer turning out copies of her yard sale advertising. I wouldn't trust Yvonne to work for me!"

If you were an employer or supervisor, would you trust Yvonne to work for you? What did Marshall mean when he said that Yvonne was working for Yvonne? What did Yvonne do that demonstrated unethical behavior and a lack of integrity?

© IMAGE SOURCE

chapter focus

After completing this chapter, you should be able to:

1. Explain the meaning of personal integrity and ethical behavior.

2. Describe what you may reasonably expect as an employee and what employers typically expect in return.

3. Discuss the importance of loyalty to your employer.

4. Explain the importance of avoiding drug and alcohol abuse.

5. Explain the meaning of petty theft and identify a variety of typical examples.

6. Describe various forms of expense account abuse.

7. Describe various forms of abuse of fringe benefits and privileges.

Chapter Highlights

13.1 Integrity and Ethics

13.2 Honesty

The purpose of this chapter is to help you develop the beliefs and values that you need to be a good citizen in your community and in your workplace. It will help you understand what your employers and the citizens of your community expect—that you will conduct yourself with integrity according to the values and ethics that prevail in the world of work and in our society. You are encouraged to develop positive values and beliefs—integrity and ethics—which will guide your behavior as a worker and as a citizen.

Integrity is adherence to a code of moral values. It means that you do what is right—even under pressure, you do not compromise. A person's integrity is a reflection of his or her **ethics**. An ethical person recognizes a moral duty and obligation to conform to accepted professional standards of conduct—the rules of right and wrong.

It is possible to behave ethically, not because it feels right, but because you know that unethical behavior may have undesirable consequences. The issue of personal integrity comes into focus when you do what is right simply because it is right, and not because of negative external motivation. When you do something that does *not* feel right, you have violated your integrity. An excellent source of information about *How Good People Make Tough Choices* to maintain their personal integrity is the book by Rushworth M. Kidder.[1]

UNDERSTAND EMPLOYER EXPECTATIONS

The values and ethics that set standards for your conduct should be consistent with the expectations of society and the expectations of your employer. When you accept a job and an employer accepts you as a worker, a contract is made. You agree to work. The employer agrees to pay you for your work. But there is more to the contract.

- You expect to be allowed to learn and progress on the job.
- You expect good supervision and training.
- You expect the employer to be honest with you—and fair.
- You expect a reasonably safe, pleasant place to work.
- You expect to have occasional rest periods, time for lunch, extra pay for overtime work (unless you're an **exempt employee**), and other fringe benefits. An exempt employee is not usually paid overtime and is usually classified as an administrative or professional employee.[2]

This is a very substantial list of expectations. But you are not entitled to any of them without meeting an equally substantial list of employer expectations. Many of those expectations are highlighted throughout this book:

- A positive attitude
- Productive work habits
- Initiative and motivation
- Knowledge and skills

You can read about the opinions and ideas of a variety of respected business-people in a collection of articles about *The Essentials of Business Ethics,* edited by Peter Madsen and Jay M. Shafritz.[3]

KEEP YOUR STANDARDS HIGH

If you have several years of work experience, you realize that some people will have an "anything goes" standard of conduct while others will be strict in their views of what should and should not be done. It is up to you to set moral and ethical standards for yourself. Therefore, you should judge carefully as you develop "rules and regulations" for your personal behavior.

Your personal morality will be defined by how well you conform to the standards of what you personally believe to be right. However, your integrity in society and in the workplace will be judged on how well you conform to recognized standards of behavior, such as being honest and considerate and having a good work ethic.

You must also recognize that your standards may not match those of your employers and coworkers. What they believe to be right will also be an important consideration as you make the day-to-day decisions regarding your conduct. Obviously, if you violate the standards and expectations of your employers and coworkers, you face the possibility of negative consequences. Keep your own standards high, and maintain your integrity by using those standards as guidelines for your behavior.

A competent worker

- *chooses an ethical course of action.*
- *establishes credibility through competence and integrity.*
- *can be trusted.*
- *recognizes when making a decision or doing something that may break with commonly held personal or social values and understands the impact of violating these beliefs and codes on the organization, self, and others; chooses an ethical course of action.*

—SCANS REPORT[4]

"*It takes less time to do a thing right, than it does to explain why you did it wrong.*"

—HENRY WADSWORTH LONGFELLOW

"*Better keep yourself clean and bright; you are the window through which you must see the world.*"

—GEORGE BERNARD SHAW

on ethics

Arturo, a server-trainee in a restaurant, noticed that some of the waiters and waitresses were receiving consistently larger tips than he was. Finally, he discovered the reason for it. Sandy, the person assigned to help train Arturo, explained it this way. "What it amounts to is giving free drinks and salads," she said. "You refill soft-drink glasses but forget to add the extra drinks to the check. You serve salads that weren't ordered and tell the customers that they're on the house. Sometimes you just sort of forget to put drinks or salads on the check. Most often what the customers should have paid for the salads and drinks shows up in your tip."

What should Arturo do if he is to maintain his own personal integrity and ethics? How would you feel if you were Arturo's employer? What would you deserve and expect?

LOYALTY

Among the most important employer expectations is loyalty. Many employers complain that the young people of today do not understand the importance of loyalty in the workplace. In fact, some employers actually prefer to hire and promote older workers who have demonstrated their loyalty. Of course, age and physical maturity do not automatically mean that the worker will be more mature in job performance and attitudes. But as a young worker, you will have to prove yourself with respect to loyalty. Most employers are very intolerant of what they consider to be disloyal behavior.

Arturo in the Focus on Ethics finds himself in a **dilemma**—a situation where one way or the other he was bound to create a problem for himself. He must choose between loyalty to his employer on one hand, and what his coworkers might consider betrayal on the other.

To help you understand what loyalty means to an employer, try to put yourself in the employer's place. Ask yourself, "How would I feel about this situation if I were the owner or manager of this business?" How would you feel if you were Arturo's employer? What would you deserve and expect in that situation? You would probably expect him to tell you what is going on, respecting his obligation of loyalty. As it turned out, Arturo chose loyalty to the employer over loyalty to his coworkers. When Arturo left his job to return to college, the manager expressed appreciation for his loyalty. Also, Arturo was promised a job in the future and a good recommendation to any other prospective employer.

A loyal employee puts the employer's interests first.

"Drunkenness is nothing but voluntary madness."

—SENECA

Maintaining an ethical workplace is a difficult challenge for many employers. Wayne Dosick offers some practical suggestions in *The Business Bible: Ten New Commandments for Creating an Ethical Workplace.*[5]

AVOID DRUG AND ALCOHOL ABUSE

You may be the type of individual who never drinks alcohol or abuses drugs. If so, these standards of conduct will probably be an asset as you seek employment and advancement in the world of work. As with the other personality traits discussed in this chapter, employers have a variety of expectations. Basically, you will find employers having one of three points of view.

At one extreme is the employer who cares only about one thing—production. In this situation, no one will be overly concerned about what you do when you are not on the job. Your private life is your own business, as far as your employer is concerned. Whatever you do privately, your employer will only be concerned with how well you do the job you were hired to do. You will be expected to keep your personal life and affairs in control so they have no effect on your work.

At the opposite extreme are employers who assume that anyone associated with the company must live by certain moral and personal behavior standards. People employed by a church, local government, or a school or community organization have a public image to protect.

Between the two extremes described above are the employers who expect that personal problems, drugs, and alcohol abuse will not influence job performance. But in addition, they may want to maintain a favorable company image. For example, a bank, a retail store, or a real estate agency might feel that their business would be hurt if customers think the company's salespeople are not of the highest moral character. This point of view is especially common in small communities where company employees are recognized by everyone and where stories of improper behavior get around quickly.

The employment community recognizes that drug and alcohol abuse threaten the work environment in several ways. The Department of Labor estimates that the combined cost of drug and alcohol abuse is $276 billion annually.[6] These abuses can affect safety standards, productivity, loyalty, and morale. In addition, there are legal issues that address the rights of individuals. As a result, some companies and organizations have instituted initial drug testing in their hiring process. Most employers, especially in larger companies, now have company-sponsored employee assistance programs to help workers deal with drug and alcohol abuse, as well as other problems. These programs generally provide such services as counselors and doctors who can help with substance abuse, stress, and family problems. Most communities also offer programs through their social services agencies, including the sponsorship of a variety of support groups.

che**ck**point

1. Your personal morality will be defined by how well you conform to
   a. what your employer and coworkers believe to be right.
   b. what your parents and society taught you.
   c. what you personally believe to be right.
   d. company policies.

2. Your success in the world of work depends on your employer's views of your
   a. standards of behavior.
   b. opinions of morality.
   c. off-work personal habits.
   d. goals and aspirations.

3. Among the most important of employer expectations is
   a. perfection.
   b. social skills.
   c. loyalty.
   d. conformity.

4. Integrity is a (an)
   a. employer expectation.
   b. benefit.
   c. perquisite.
   d. social skill.

5. It is important to realize that if you violate the standards expected by your employer, you face the possibility of negative consequences.
   True_____ False_____

6. No company or organization should be concerned about your standards of conduct in private life.
   True_____ False_____

applications

1. A coworker asks you to let him use your Microsoft Office XP disk to install in his home computer. The disk belongs to your employer. Should you let him borrow it? If it belonged to you, would the answer be different?

_____

_____

_____

_____

2. A friend offers you a free pecan roll that she has shoplifted. Would you accept it? Why or why not?

_____

_____

_____

_____

3. A friend wants to borrow your homework because he did not have time to finish his because of an emergency. Would you lend it to him? Why or why not?

_____

_____

_____

_____

4. You promise to keep a secret, but to keep the promise you have to lie. Would you keep this promise? Explain your answer.

_____

_____

_____

_____

5. After you leave a restaurant, you realize you received 90 cents too much in change. Would you keep it? Why or why not?

_____

_____

_____

_____

6. You are in a grocery store and you see a sign over the bins of candy that says "No Snacking," but you really want some chocolate. Do you help yourself anyway? Explain your answer.

_____

_____

_____

_____

_____

7. You are a dishwasher in a restaurant. The manager offers to let you eat dinner before you end your shift. Would you order the most expensive item on the menu? Explain your answer.

_____

_____

_____

_____

8. You work in a clinic where one of the doctors is being sued for malpractice. You are in a position to see some of the correspondence between the doctor and the lawyers who are working on the case. Should you share this information with your spouse or a close personal friend who asks about it? Why or why not?

_____

_____

_____

_____

9. The speed limit is 30 mph in a residential area with many children. You don't see any other cars, and you don't see any police. You don't see any children. Do you exceed the speed limit? Explain your answer.

_____

_____

_____

_____

_____

When a supervisor writes a letter of recommendation saying, "Lou is an honest person," the message is that Lou can be trusted. Honesty is straightforwardness of conduct, adherence to the facts, honor, and a refusal to lie, steal, or deceive. The person with integrity and high standards of conduct resists pressure and temptation and remains honest. Your challenge is to set standards of honesty for yourself that will cause your employers and coworkers to admire and respect you.

Rather than reading a list of rules for honesty in employment, you will study some situations that might challenge your own honesty. As the possible alternatives to the situation are discussed, you will begin to understand what typical employers might expect of employees with reputations for being honest. Then you should be able to measure your own personal standards against those of your future employers. Hopefully, you will want to set high standards of honesty for yourself. In the long run, your honesty will be rewarded.

PETTY THEFT

When you take something from someone else with no intention of returning it to its owner, you are guilty of larceny. **Larceny** is theft and a **larcenist** is a thief. But any judge will tell you that many convicted larcenists do not think of themselves as thieves. For example, you may know someone who has taken merchandise from a store without paying for it. Do you think of these people who are guilty of shoplifting as criminals? You should, since shoplifting is a criminal offense.

There are many kinds of larceny in the workplace. **Grand larceny** is the legal term for stealing something of great value. **Petty larceny** describes the theft of something of

on the job

Pat and Jan were sharing a hero sandwich at the deli where they often met for lunch. "I'm amazed at what some people get away with today in business," said Jan. "If you want to, you can get away with anything." "It's the same at our bank. But you could find yourself unemployed—maybe in jail," Pat responded. "I'm not talking about crime," Jan said. "I mean things like sending personal e-mail on company time, using the postage meter for personal mail, taking extra time at breaks, using paper for personal use, taking supplies home for family members' use, showing favoritism to customers who bribe you with gifts, not reporting cash transactions to avoid income tax. I could go on and on—and they get away with it!" There was a pause. Then Pat said, "Do they really?"

What do you think? Do they get away with it? And do you think Jan is right when she says that she's "not talking about crime"?

© GETTY IMAGES/PHOTODISC

Petty theft from your employer is dishonest.

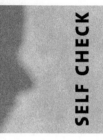

Knowing what is acceptable behavior and what is not, as your employer sees it, is not always easy. Asking first is always wise, but sometimes you just have to use your judgment.

Following are some examples of behavior that may take place in the workplace. What do you think about each item? Indicate your judgment as follows:

Honest and ethical 2
Honest but unethical 1
Dishonest and unethical 0

_____ Taking home small quantities of inexpensive office supplies, such as pencils, file folders, and transparent tape.

_____ Writing personal letters on company stationery, using company postage, and using company long-distance telephone lines for personal calls.

_____ Taking materials or supplies that the company produces or uses.

_____ Taking things that the employer has no use for and wants to dispose of, such as day-old bakery goods, used packing boxes, surplus or waste building materials, scrap paper, and free samples of merchandise or supplies.

_____ Using company computers, Internet access, and time for your own personal entertainment when you should be working.

SCORING: If your score is above 4, your standards are probably lower than your employer's. A score of 3 or less suggests that your standards of honesty are high.

learn about what is expected by simply asking, "Terry, do you mind if I take a truckload of sand to fill the sandbox I made for my cousin?" Or you might be less direct: "Dan, may I use the company long-distance line to call my parents in Minneapolis, or should I have the call billed to my home phone?" You may also learn what is acceptable and what is not by observing and talking with your coworkers. But be careful. You may find yourself, along with others, violating your employer's rules.

EXPENSE ACCOUNT ABUSES

Many business occupations involve travel, meals, and lodging at company expense. Selling "on the road," traveling to deliver merchandise or to service customers' equipment, and participating in business conferences are examples of business-related travel.

Some companies have liberal expense accounting policies. They trust the employee to keep personal records and simply report what was spent. Other employers enforce elaborate rules and regulations and require receipts. These detailed rules and record-keeping procedures are designed to protect the employer from employees who might use the expense accounting system to obtain extra income.

Some of the practices noted in the Self Check are clearly dishonest and unacceptable. Some appear to be questionable. Others may seem, to most people, to be perfectly acceptable. Your challenge, as always, is to learn what your employer expects of you in a given situation. Then you must avoid abuses that can damage your reputation for honesty.

As an inexperienced worker, you will need to make a special effort to learn your company's rules and policies. Be aware that you may encounter individuals who set a bad example—"bending the rules" or

"If you don't want anyone to know it, don't do it."

—CHINESE PROVERB

a lesser value or importance. The legal penalties are greater for grand larceny, but petty larceny is probably a greater problem for employers. Shoplifting by the employees in a retail business is only one form of the problem. Employee theft of supplies, equipment, and materials is another form of petty theft that causes employers great concern.

To protect your reputation for honesty, find out what your employer's expectations are and be sure your standards of conduct conform to those expectations. You can

Smart Tip ▼ ▼ ▼

Use expense accounts in a way that projects to your employer an image of concern about conserving and economizing the use of company resources—that is, in a way that strengthens your reputation for honesty.

▲ ▲ ▲ ▲ ▲ ▲ ▲ ▲ ▲

cheating whenever and however they can. Most of the time, however, you will find individuals who live by high ethical standards.

Here is an example of highly ethical and honest behavior. A sales representative was found to be reporting unusually low travel expenses. When the expense account auditor investigated, it was found that the representative owned a small car that used very little gasoline. The representative made sure the reimbursement covered only actual expenses, which were considerably less than other representatives driving larger cars or those reporting "inflated" mileage.

Here are some examples you might follow:

- Stay with friends or relatives, or stay at clean but safe less expensive hotels and pass the savings in hotel bills along to the employer.
- Take advantage of the lowest possible airfare and travel at an inconvenient time, if necessary, to get a lower-priced ticket.
- Eat inexpensive meals and find ways to conserve on food expenses.

However, if you are entertaining clients or customers, be sure that what you serve does not appear to be cheap. That does not mean that you would take the clients to the most expensive restaurants in town, however, as a general rule. Be sure you know the company

Here are some examples of questionable uses of expense accounts. Indicate your judgment as follows:

Honest and ethical 2
Honest but unethical 1
Dishonest and unethical 0

_____ Reporting more expensive meals than actually eaten.

_____ Asking reimbursement for meals not paid for (such as those received on an airplane).

_____ Including liquor (reported as food) on expense accounts.

_____ Reporting greater automobile mileage than actually driven.

_____ Riding the bus or subway but reporting taxi fares.

_____ Asking for full reimbursement when two people share a ride.

_____ Staying in exclusive hotels, traveling first-class, or eating at the most expensive restaurants.

_____ Asking reimbursement for expenses for vacation time (taking an extra day for recreation at the end of a business trip).

_____ Including personal long-distance telephone calls or in-room movies on a hotel bill.

SCORING: If your score is above 5, your standards are probably lower than your employer's. A score of 4 or less suggests that your standards of honesty are high.

policies for entertainment of clients or customers.

You should realize that, in the long run, both you and your employer benefit when you economize and help the company make a profit. Just as there are people who use the expense account to steal from their employers, there are people who use it to conserve and reduce expenses for their employers. You will probably find most of

"Live in such a way that you would not be ashamed to sell your parrot to the town gossip."

—WILL ROGERS

"There are few, if any, jobs in which ability alone is sufficient. Needed, also, are loyalty, sincerity, enthusiasm and team play."

—WILLIAM B. GIVEN

your coworkers' actions to be somewhere between the extremes. The majority of people are honest in reporting their actual expenses. You should not threaten your reputation as an honest person. When your employer discovers cheating, it could mean your job.

Consider this: When employees' personal standards of honesty are high, a relaxed, trusting relationship grows. Employers seldom question or even review the expense accounts reported by trusted employees. When necessary, the employees can report unusually high expenses without hesitation. Working in such an atmosphere is a pleasure. But it is far from pleasant working in an atmosphere of insecurity that results when employers see expense accounts being used as tools for petty larceny.

ABUSES OF FRINGE BENEFITS

Almost any job you can think of has certain fringe benefits and privileges. And almost every one offers some opportunity for exploitation—or dishonesty. Consider the following situations:

- Many retail stores offer employee discounts on merchandise.
- Employees of a small meatpacking plant are allowed to buy tenderloin at one-third of the market price.
- Employees of a large automotive service station are allowed to take any parts that may be discarded when repairs are made.
- Some automobile and motorcycle dealers allow their employees to drive used vehicles that are in stock.
- A television dealer allows service department employees to work on their own sets during evenings and weekends, with parts provided at the dealer's cost.

focus on ethics

Adrian works at a restaurant. He gets an hourly wage plus tips. He also gets free meals for himself and a 50 percent discount on food for anyone else in his family. Adrian decides to have a party. He uses his food discount privilege to buy $50 worth of fried chicken for $25. Also, he is in the habit of ordering the most expensive steak sandwich at closing time and taking most of it home, supposedly for his dog. Sometimes he just leaves it on his plate, and it gets thrown out.

How would you react to Adrian's habit if you were the owner of the restaurant?

Technology at Work

The Better Business Bureau: **The extensive Web site for this organization, which aims to promote "the highest ethical relationship between business and the public," includes consumer alerts about business scams, reports on charitable groups, and a database of businesses. You can file a complaint on-line, as well, if you have encountered dishonest business practices.**

http://www.bbb.org

These are only a few examples of the kinds of fringe benefits and privileges that employees might be offered. You probably can think of many more. Also, you can probably imagine many different ways that these benefits could be abused. Abuse of these privileges hurts the employer and can result in the privileges being revoked for everyone—so everyone suffers. These are the kinds of situations where your good judgment, your sense of fair play, and your basic honesty will guide you.

You may find it difficult at times to maintain higher standards of conduct. But to the extent that you are successful in doing so, your chances for success and personal satisfaction will be increased. Remember that the higher your standards, the more options you have. Prospective employers will be more interested in hiring you. You will be welcome in a greater variety of employment situations. Your chances for success and personal satisfaction will be increased in the long run, and you will take pride in yourself. You will be the winner.

chec**K**point

1. It is important to make sure your standards of conduct match those of your employer. True_____ False_____

2. Fringe benefit abuses almost never occur among management personnel. True_____ False_____

3. Almost every fringe benefit privilege offers some opportunity for
   a. promotion.
   b. exploitation.
   c. increased profit.
   d. management proliferation.

4. A larcenist is a person who
   a. is hired to find dishonesty in a company.
   b. does something legal and ethical.
   c. does something offensive and distasteful.
   d. is a thief.

applications

1. How might you, as a beginning worker, learn about the unwritten code of behavior that prevails in your workplace?

2. While honesty is good, there are times when kindness or good sense would dictate silence rather than being "totally honest" and blunt. In what situations might you need to use tact or silence? What guidelines can you use to help you handle these situations without compromising your integrity?

3. Research one or more incidents of bribery, kickbacks, or other dishonesty in business (including government business) that have been exposed in the news. What were the results of the investigations? What happened to the business and to the people involved?

4. You are attending a meeting at a city in a state located near one of your friends' home. You could easily rent a car and travel there after the meeting is over. You are authorized to rent a car and charge it to your expense account. Would renting a car to visit your friend be an acceptable charge to your expense account? Give reasons for your answer.

Points to Remember

chapter

Review the following points to determine what you remember from the chapter.

- The issue of personal integrity comes into focus when you let what you know is right guide your behavior. An ethical person who has integrity will sense a moral obligation to conform to accepted standards of conduct. Your integrity will be judged by how your behavior conforms to the recognized standards in your workplace. If you violate the standards and expectations of employers and coworkers, you face the possibility of negative consequences. You should be aware of accepted professional standards and use them as guidelines for your own behavior in the workplace.

- In addition to the compensation and the benefits provided by your employer, you may expect to be treated fairly and supervised and trained in a safe, pleasant work environment. In return, your employer will expect you to be motivated, to use the knowledge and skills required to be productive, and to have a positive attitude.

- Among the most important of the typical employer's expectations is loyalty. Young workers, especially, may have to demonstrate this quality to gain an employer's respect and trust. Honesty is another important expectation of an employer.

- Employers expect your standards of conduct to include avoiding drug and alcohol abuse. While some employers may be unconcerned about what you do in your private life, others may consider your personal behavior as a reflection on them and expect conformity to their standards. Most important, alcohol or drug abuse must not influence your productivity or behavior on the job.

- Taking something that does not belong to you without intending to return it is theft, plain and simple. The theft of something of great value is grand larceny, and the legal term for stealing something of lesser value is petty larceny. You should avoid taking anything without your employer's approval, and doing so is both illegal and unethical.

- Sometimes employees cheat their employers by using their expense accounts to obtain extra income that they do not deserve. Expense account abuse is a problem that concerns employers, and you should avoid it. A loyal, ethical employee will be conscientious in finding ways to conserve the employer's resources by keeping reimbursed expenses down.

- There are many fringe benefits and privileges that challenge a person's integrity and have implications for his or her moral standards. You should use good judgment and be honest and fair as you take advantage of what your employer provides.

How did you do? Did you remember the main points you studied in the chapter?

key terms

Define each term in the space provided.

Integrity

Ethics

Exempt employee

Dilemma

Larceny

Larcenist

Grand larceny

Petty larceny

activities and projects

1. Your company is involved in a sanitation issue in its meat division that has supposedly caused severe illness in several consumers who ate the meat. A reporter meets you at the gate after you get off and offers you a large sum of money to give him the details of the incident. What should you do? Should you accept the money?

2. Interview several employers to determine their policies for controlling or eliminating problems with employees whose standards of conduct do not meet their expectations. If possible, work with other students. In the interviews, you might ask the following questions. Prepare a report summarizing the answers.

a. To what extent is employee theft a problem in your business?

b. What action do you take when you discover a case of employee theft?

c. How effective is the action in preventing future theft?

d. What problems do you have with employees abusing special privileges or benefits?

_____

_____

_____

e. What actions do you take to prevent or control the abuses?

_____

_____

_____

f. What are some examples of employee misconduct with respect to ethical or moral behavior in your business?

_____

_____

_____

g. What policies do you have in place that remind and guide employees toward acceptable standards?

_____

_____

_____

3. Assume you have discovered that some of the employees in the supermarket where you work are stealing empty soft-drink containers and selling them to youngsters in the neighborhood at half their value. You see some of these children returning the same bottles for cash at the check-stand of your store.

a. What are your responsibilities to your employer? to your coworkers?

_____

_____

_____

b. What should the store manager do upon discovering the details of this situation?

_____

_____

_____

4. Review the issue of abusing fringe benefits and privileges in the workplace. Find, collect, and summarize three articles from newspapers, magazines, or television dealing with this issue in today's business world. Use the summary sheets below.

Resource: _____

Title of the article _____

Describe the privilege or benefit _____

_____

_____

_____

What was the abuse and why did it occur? Was it legal? Was it ethical? Explain your answers.

_____

_____

_____

_____

Resource: _____

Title of the article _____

Describe the privilege or benefit _____

_____

_____

_____

What was the abuse and why did it occur? Was it legal? Was it ethical? Explain your answers.

_____

_____

_____

Resource: _____

Title of the article _____

Describe the privilege or benefit _____

_____

_____

_____

What was the abuse and why did it occur? Was it legal? Was it ethical? Explain your answers.

_____

_____

_____

_____

_____

_____

_____

_____

case studies for critical thinking

To Draw or Not to Draw

Tim is working part-time in the drafting department of a small manufacturing firm. Since he has access to graphic supplies, materials, and equipment, he decides to use his coffee breaks and lunch periods to design and produce detailed sketches of a family room remodeling project for his home.

1. Should Tim ask permission, or should he feel free to go ahead with the project since he intends to do it on his own time?

_____

_____

_____

2. How do you think his supervisor should respond if Tim asks permission?

_____

_____

_____

3. What reasons might be given to justify refusing Tim's request?

_____

_____

_____

The Encounter

Hal worked the night shift as an admitting clerk in a hospital. About 3 a.m. he heard a noise in the pharmacy. He opened the door and saw Mrs. Swann, the hospital administrator, with a beaker of clear liquid in her hand. Mrs. Swann said nothing when she saw Hal. She simply set the beaker on the counter, then walked past Hal and out the door. Hal checked the beaker and found it to contain alcohol. Thinking it was none of his business and fearing that he might be fired if he said anything about it, Hal said nothing to anyone about the incident. Two months later Mrs. Swann was replaced as administrator with no explanation. But everyone on the hospital staff figured out the reason when Hal admitted Mrs. Swann to the hospital later as an emergency case with alcohol poisoning.

1. Did Hal make the right choice in keeping quiet about the incident? If not, what should Hal have done?

_____

_____

_____

2. If Mrs. Swann had caught Hal in the pharmacy with a beaker of alcohol, would she have overlooked the incident? If not, should she have overlooked it?

_____

_____

_____

Case 13.3

NO PERSONAL CALLS

Ruth McDonald is busy with her work when she receives a personal telephone call from her friend, Harry, who wants to find out about a weekend trip that is being planned. Harry is working at his first job. Ruth knows Harry does not realize that the office is no place for personal calls. Ruth does not want to hurt Harry's feelings, so she tries to be tactful. Finally, she says, "Harry, I must go now. Mrs. Maxwell is buzzing me. See you Friday."

1. Do you think Harry was made aware that he should not call Ruth during office hours?

Yes_____ No_____

_____

_____

_____

_____

2. Should Ruth have been more honest with Harry so he would understand how to behave in the future? Explain your answer.

_____

_____

_____

3. Can you think of a tactful way that Ruth could have informed Harry of the general rule regarding personal telephone calls during business hours? What would you say?

_____

_____

_____

Case 13.4

BUSINESS WITHIN A BUSINESS

Bertha works as an assembler in a sash and door factory. Scrap wood accumulates as the window and door frames are produced, and the owner of the business allows the employees to take the discarded wood for use in their fireplaces at home. Bertha's neighbor, Mr. Larson, offers to pay Bertha for fireplace wood and makes it clear that he will not mention the fact that he is paying Bertha for the wood. Bertha reasons that this is okay. She thinks, "The boss doesn't need to know. Anyway, I'm underpaid on this job, and I can use the extra cash."

1. Do you agree with Bertha's reasoning? Explain your answer.

_____

_____

_____

2. Under what circumstances, if any, would you expect Bertha's employer to approve of this arrangement?

_____

_____

_____

Case 13.5

THE FAXED CONFIDENTIAL INFORMATION

You walk by the fax regularly and sometimes see a fax when it is being received. Most faxes that come into this machine are for the vice president of sales. You note that many of the faxes are confidential and contain price quotes and other confidential sales data. You are tempted to mention one of the bits of information you noted recently at lunch one day, but something told you to keep quiet.

1. Should you read a fax that is marked confidential? What should you do if you are in charge of distributing the faxes to the persons to whom they are addressed? Do you have any responsibility if you are not in charge to keep the faxes confidential?

2. Is this an ethical situation in which you should disregard the ethics in favor of discussing information that no one else would have privilege to know? Your friends may be interested in some of the information that you learn during the day. What should you do?

Valuing Diversity

14

think about it: Olga grew up in Montana—big sky country. Her grandparents were immigrants from Norway, and she remembers that in her community there was occasionally a little good-natured teasing about her blonde complexion. She also remembers hearing her relatives tell ethnic jokes. Norwegian farmers were stereotyped as stubborn and not particularly intellectual. But underneath it all was a kind of pride and appreciation of Scandinavian culture.

After completing a two-year degree in accounting, Olga went to work in a Minneapolis bank and moved quickly into a management position. Yesterday she was told that the corporation was offering her an exciting challenge if she wanted it. They were sending her to El Paso, Texas, to set up the accounting system in a new branch bank. In addition, Olga would be assigned to train the Hispanic personnel. While she was well qualified for the assignment, she was a little nervous about this career opportunity. In discussing it with George, a trusted friend and coworker, she said, "I have never worked in a place where the culture is so different from mine. What do I know about the El Paso area—the people and their customs? Will they accept me?"

How will Olga adjust and feel at home in a culture that is so different from her own?

© GETTY IMAGES/PHOTODISC

chapter focus

After completing this chapter, you should be able to:

1. Explain how employers are coping with diversity and how they expect workers to adapt and react to it in the workplace.

2. Describe the ethnic and minority composition of the workforce.

3. Demonstrate tolerance and understanding for coworkers who might be subjected to discrimination, prejudice, and stereotyping, and how cultural conflict and misunderstanding can be avoided or resolved.

4. Explain how employers are required to recognize and avoid unfair or illegal discrimination and prejudice in the workplace.

5. Explain how employers are expected to respond to the federal statutes prohibiting employment discrimination in the workplace.

6. Explain what sexual harassment is and how it should be dealt with in the workplace.

7. Demonstrate understanding of how you might deal with personal experiences involving prejudice and discrimination.

If you are to develop your appreciation of anything—classical music, western dancing, soccer, or Japanese food—you must get involved and expose yourself to it. If you are to fit in and get along in a diverse working environment, you need to develop your appreciation for **diversity**, the increasingly varied social and cultural makeup of the workforce. That means exposure to and involvement with a wide range of people and traditions. Self-appreciation is a good place to start.

TAKE PRIDE IN WHO YOU ARE

If you are a member of a group that has been subjected to unfair treatment in the world of work, you realize the need for appreciating diversity. You also probably realize that, although you may be different, you certainly have no cause to feel inferior.

- As a female worker in a predominantly male workplace, you should see yourself as equal and deserving of fair treatment.
- As a person with a disability, you need not accept second-class status.
- Your ethnic and cultural heritage may be different, but it is not inferior.
- If you are an older worker, you need not accept the stereotypes associated with age discrimination.
- If your religious beliefs and practices place you in a minority in your community, you should not have to endure discrimination.

If you are African-American, Hispanic, Asian, or Native American, you are probably aware of efforts in your community to foster pride and appreciation of your cultural heritage. In the past, cultural heritage didn't seem as important. Sometimes people of different cultures were encouraged to abandon their traditional ways—to adopt a new identity. Others rushed to abandon traditions in their desire to be progressive or modern. Now we are seeing more of an effort to preserve traditional cultures and encourage appreciation of heritage—while still, of course, retaining pride in being part of the larger, unifying tradition of American citizenship.[2]

Notions of the superiority of one culture over another are being rejected. No matter what your background or status in society, the fact that your ethnic and cultural background set you apart should translate into an appreciation of yourself. Take pride in who you are.

WIDEN YOUR PERSPECTIVE

Having suggested that you take pride in who you are, the next step is to learn to appreciate other cultures. There are some popular buzzwords for our tendency to let self-pride dampen our appreciation of others. One of these terms is **egocentric myopia**. It simply means that we see and appreciate only what is close (our immediate environment), which gives us a distorted impression of being more important than we really are. Another term is **ethnocentrism**, coined by William Graham Sumner.[3] This term proclaims the assumption that one's own worldview is the only view.[4]

It is important for you to realize that an ethnocentric view of the world can influence how you feel about people from other cultures. The people around you can misunderstand you as well because they may have

A competent worker

- *respects the rights of others.*
- *bases impressions on performance, not on stereotypes.*
- *works well with men and women, people of different ethnic or social backgrounds.*
- *takes pride in his or her own culture.*
- *respects and appreciates other cultures.*

—SCANS[1]

a distorted image of you and your cultural heritage. You should take pride in who you are without feeling that yours is the only way to view the world or that your view of the world is necessarily *better* than the view of someone else. As you expose yourself to the diversity of perspectives among your coworkers, your own perspective will widen.

PAST INTOLERANCE OF DIVERSITY

It is natural for any society to take pride in itself—in its families, its communities, and its culture. The down side of this is that, often, this pride can lead to looking down on others who are different. In this country, we have cause for regret in the practice of human slavery, in the exploitation and oppression of Native Americans, and in the reluctance of men to allow women the right to vote. Of course, we should also take pride in the fact that we have outlawed all these things in the United States, while there are still many countries that practice slavery, exploitation, oppression, and even genocide.[5]

The founders of our nation realized that, when people are justifiably proud, they can also have unjustified feelings of superiority—feelings that can lead to oppression of those who are different. That is why the focus of the Declaration of Independence is on the fact that all people are created equal and that they should be accorded equally the rights of life, liberty, and the pursuit of happiness.

However, people often fear that which is different and will also often try to protect themselves from change, because change is frightening, too. As society has changed and larger numbers of Asian, Hispanic, and eastern European immigrants have flooded into the workplace, fear often created intolerance. A predominantly male workforce is

Smart Tip ▾ ▾ ▾

The more you learn about different minority groups and cultures, the more you will come to appreciate them. Here are some suggestions.

- **Attend cultural events, festivals, parades, and other activities sponsored by specific ethnic or minority groups.**
- **Patronize neighborhood restaurants or shop in ethnic grocery stores.**
- **Take the initiative to socialize with people of different cultures.**
- **Participate in diversity workshops or other training activities sponsored by your employer or your school.**
- **Volunteer to help with fundraising events involving persons with disabilities.**
- **Pay attention to political and social representatives as they write or speak in the media.**

▲　▲　▲　▲　▲　▲　▲　▲　▲

less than cordial in welcoming women. The culture of youth makes it harder for older workers. Persons with disabilities, Native Americans, and African-Americans all can have difficulty in the workplace.

Typically, these groups have less access to the better jobs. They have fewer opportunities for promotion, and they are paid less when they do the same work. However, people inside the traditional workforce and outside of it are beginning to realize that things must change. Laws have been passed, and this intolerance for diversity has begun to erode. While human nature is the same and some people will always feel threatened by differences, people on the whole are making an effort to learn about

"The resource of bigotry and intolerance when convicted of error, is always the same; silenced by argument, it tries to silence by persecution—in old times by fire and sword, in modern days by tongue."

—G. SIMONS

and accept other people's cultures and backgrounds.

Of course, it is important to remember that intolerance is not something that only "they" do. We are all capable of being intolerant, because we are all capable of feeling uncomfortable with differences. Remember, however, that tolerance doesn't mean agreeing with everyone. Our belief systems, political ideologies, and religions don't disappear. It simply means that you recognize and respect the rights of others, try to understand their cultures, accept the differences, and appreciate them as individuals.

THE WORKFORCE OF TODAY

The *Statistical Abstract of the United States: 2003* shows that there are several significant changes occurring in the composition of the labor force.[6]

- **The percentage of white males is changing in the workforce.** While the workforce in this country forty years ago was made up mainly of native-born white males, only one in six workers today are in that category.
- **The workforce is larger and growing.** In 1990 it consisted of 126 million workers. In 2020 the Department of Commerce predicts that it will include 158 million.
- **Increasing numbers of women continue to enter the labor market.** In 1990, 51 percent of white women, 58 percent of black women, and 53 percent of Hispanic women were employed. In 2010, it is expected that 62 percent of white women, 66 percent of black women, and 59 percent of Hispanic women will have

full-time jobs. In 1990, about 70 to 80 percent of the male population was reported to be employed. The predictions for 2010 are the same, with not much change over the 20 years.

- **More married women are employed.** In 1970, only 41 percent of married women had jobs. In 1990, that figure was 58 percent and in 2002 it was 61 percent. In 1970, 57 percent of single women were employed, and in 1990 and 2002, the figure was 67 percent.
- **The workforce is becoming better educated.** In 1992, 13 percent of workers had less than a high school education, 36 percent were high school graduates, and 26 percent were college graduates. In 2002, only 10 percent will have less than a high school education, 31 percent will be high school graduates, and 31 percent will have college degrees.

In 1990, Congress passed a law that increased legal immigration levels. Now ethnic minorities and immigrants are about one-third of the workforce. Hiring highly skilled immigrants is encouraged, and stiffer penalties are imposed on employers who are reluctant to do so.[7]

Now, as employers compete in the labor market for skilled workers, they are more accepting of diversity. But diversity in the workplace sets the stage for problems, such as prejudice, stereotyping, sexual harassment, and subtle discrimination. To help avoid and overcome these problems, many employers are voluntarily using affirmative action programs. They are working to accommodate persons with disabilities. They are working to avoid and eliminate sexual harassment. They are making changes that will help workers who are somehow different to fit in, get along, and feel accepted and appreciated.[8]

check**point**

1. As you expose yourself to the diversity of perspectives in your workplace, you can expect your own perspectives to _____.

2. The percentage of white males in the workforce is _____ increasing _____ decreasing.

3. Immigrants and minorities are about what percentage of the workforce? _____

4. Name two emotions that can lead to intolerance. _____ _____

5. A term for seeing one's own view of the world as the only view is _____

6. Employers try to hire workers of the same or similar cultures. True_____ False_____

applications

1. This is an activity designed to help you understand what your cultural values are and to recognize some differences among different cultures.

a. Develop a list of sayings or proverbs that are part of your culture, and the meaning or value they represent. For example, the axiom "Time is money" means that if you waste time, it is costly to you and your employer.

AXIOM	VALUE

b. Review the axioms and values with several people whose culture is different from your own. Identify examples where the axiom does not apply in their culture because their values are different. Make a list of examples you have found that indicate different cultural values.

2. Assume you are going to work (or are already at work) in a situation where you are different from most of your coworkers. Or use the workplace scenario about Olga at the beginning of this chapter. What are some of the problems or barriers that might make it difficult for you to fit in, get along, and reach out to provide support for others?

3. Select a large business enterprise in your community—a bank, hospital, government agency, car dealership or factory, for example. Telephone or make a personal visit and ask the manager or a company executive for permission to interview employees who have had successful careers in that enterprise. Specifically, choose to interview a woman and a male member of an ethnic minority group. In the interviews, ask them to share their views about problems and issues that might have been barriers to their success in the changing workplace. Take notes, and summarize what you learned in the space below.

Conflict that occurs because of cultural differences is called **cultural conflict**. Egocentric myopia and ethnocentrism reinforce it. Nevertheless, cultural conflict can be avoided if you are alert and sensitive and if you make an effort to learn about other cultures.[9]

on the job

Yoko and Alan were at lunch together. Alan had just returned from a meeting with two Japanese purchasing agents who were negotiating to purchase a large quantity of lumber. Alan looked at his tray of food and shook his head slowly. Yoko said, "Alan, are you okay? How are you doing in negotiating the lumber deal?" Alan looked up and said, "Yoko, you should be doing this. I just can't figure out how to relate to these guys. I have no idea why, but several times they acted embarrassed or insulted. The situation was tense. We just couldn't communicate!" "Well, to be honest, Alan, I'm not too surprised," Yoko said. "Let me tell you how to communicate with Asian executives."

What do you imagine Alan might have said or done to create the cultural conflict with the Japanese business-people? What actions could Alan have taken before the negotiations started to avoid this conflict?

BE RESPECTFUL OF OTHER CULTURES

Here is the rest of the conversation between Alan and Yoko. Alan had underestimated the cultural differences between nationalities and, therefore, had learned nothing about them. Yoko explained how he could have appeared more respectful of his business associates and been more effective in working with them.

Yoko continued, "Japanese usually prefer to spend more time on small talk that has nothing to do with the task at hand. Americans think a short time is sufficient. Japanese might spend more time in polite social conversation before getting down to business. Don't misinterpret this as not being serious about the meeting.

"Eye contact is another communication conflict. I was watching you. You would try to make eye contact, and they would try to avoid it. They would lower their eyes, and you would look right at them. When you looked down at your notes, they would look up.

"You noticed that they had a tendency to remain silent during the negotiations. You thought this meant that they were dissatisfied. They were just being polite and courteous. Facial expressions also enter into it. If things are not going well, Americans expect to see frowns. A respectful, tolerant smile may be misread as approval or agreement.

"Finally," Yoko said, "the word that got you into the most trouble is *you*. One should not address a Japanese businessperson directly, as in "What do you think?" It's more appropriate to ask, "What does the company think?"

BE SENSITIVE AND RESPECTFUL OF DIFFERENCES

Most cultural conflicts occur because people simply don't know what another culture values. An individual may assume that everyone else will somehow know what their motives are or what is important to them. But this is not the case. Here is an example of a cultural conflict and how it might have been avoided.

Sherman met Rose at a local hospital where they both volunteered their time. Rose grew up in a town in Mexico and had recently moved to the United States. After several weeks of working together at the hospital, Sherman invited Rose to dinner with him and his mother.

Sherman was very clear and specific in his invitation to Rose. Appetizers were to be served at 5:30 p.m., and dinner would be at 6 p.m. At 6:15 on the appointed day when Rose had not yet arrived, Sherman's mother felt very insulted.

Rose arrived at 6:30. She cheerfully greeted Sherman with a hug, and when introductions were made, she put her arm around his mother and greeted her warmly. Sherman's mother looked away, brushed Rose's arm off her shoulder, and walked briskly away without saying a word.

Your own background will influence how you react to the individuals in this story, but it should be evident how the conflict arose and how it might have been avoided. Rose would have created a better impression if she had understood that Sherman's mother might interpret her late arrival as an insult and that a physical gesture of friendliness might be considered disrespectful. Likewise, Sherman and his mother might have reacted better if they had recognized and understood that in Rose's culture, qualities such as punctuality are usually judged to be superficial when compared with the value of a good relationship.

All this information can provide clues that will help you be sensitive and respectful in your relationships with people of other cultural backgrounds.

MANAGE LANGUAGE BARRIERS

Perhaps the most obvious source of cultural barriers is language. What can you do when you find yourself unable to understand or make yourself understood? First, and most important, you can *avoid making incorrect assumptions.*

You should develop sensitivity to the values, dress, eating habits, and leisure-time activities that may reflect other people's cultures. For example:

How do you react when you see someone eating with chopsticks instead of a knife and fork?

_____

_____

_____

What relevance does "dress for success" have in a job interview for Muslim women who "cover"?

_____

_____

_____

Do you know the cultural values that are behind the attitudes toward treating illness in different cultures?

_____

_____

_____

How do you respond when you hear coworkers talking together in their native language?

_____

_____

_____

How do you interpret facial expressions or silence when speaking with a coworker from a different culture?

_____

_____

_____

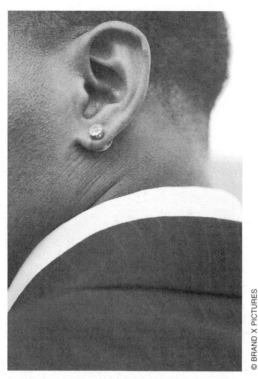

You must look beyond what appears on the surface to get to know the real person.

Smart Tip ▼ ▼ ▼

Following are some suggestions about how to be sensitive and show respect for cultural differences.

- **Study other cultures. Books, magazines, newspaper articles, television programs, and movies can help you learn about other cultures.**
- **Make friends with people from different cultural backgrounds. Ask them to explain some of their customs, beliefs, and practices.**
- **Observe people from other cultures in their natural interactions with one another. Notice gestures, facial expressions, and posture while they are conversing. Notice how they relate to children and to older people.**
- **Notice the customs and actions of people from other cultures while they are eating and drinking. Watch what they do while shopping, working, and playing.**

▲ ▲ ▲ ▲ ▲ ▲ ▲ ▲ ▲

Assuming that a person is poor or illiterate because he or she speaks broken English is unfair and unrealistic. In fact, that limited English-speaking ability may be greater than your ability to speak their language. Would you want to have someone judge your intellect by your ability to speak another language? You can generally assume, however, that they would like to speak English better, if that is not their first language, and you can offer them assistance by speaking clearly and explaining terms that are unfamiliar.

Second, you can *make an effort to learn another language.* While it is true that you can't learn every language that appears in today's workplace, you can learn one other language or, at least, learn how to be polite (please, thank you, hello, goodbye) in languages with which you come in contact.

Some suggestions on how to manage language barriers are:

- **Study the language.** You can take courses in high school, in college, and through adult and community education programs. Also, most bookstores and libraries offer audiotapes and books.
- **Use an interpreter.** This includes language interpretation—literally translating so you can talk freely with someone whose native language is different. It also means thinking carefully about what you see and hear. Ask, "What does this expression or behavior mean? What message is this person sending?"

- **Sharpen your foreign language skills** by speaking the language instead of English when you are talking with friends or coworkers who are fluent in the language. Ask them to correct your mistakes and coach you in pronouncing and speaking correctly.

HELP OTHERS MAKE CULTURAL ADJUSTMENTS

As part of your effort to adapt and feel comfortable in a workplace where there is so much diversity, you should take advantage of opportunities to help others make cultural adjustments. Some ways of doing this are to:

- read credible newspapers and magazines so that you will be well informed.

- become aware of the problems and issues that create misunderstanding and cause division rather than unity.

- explain your own culture to those of another culture. Compare the two cultures by finding similarities as well as differences.

- offer guidance if you see someone having a difficult time adjusting, but do so with sensitivity and respect. Explain aspects of local culture that they may not understand. Help them feel welcome, and help them understand and fit in.

- Take a stand on issues that promote respect for and appreciation of diversity.

Do not be afraid to reach out to your coworkers. Form supportive interpersonal relationships with those whose culture and traditions are different from your own. The same applies to other minorities who may find themselves isolated or subjected to discrimination—older workers, younger inexperienced workers, men or women who may be a minority in your workplace, persons with disabilities, members of minority religious groups, and those whose educational and social backgrounds are different.

Technology at Work

The Internet offers a tremendous amount of help in finding information about other cultures, countries, and traditions. Do a search using the name of the particular country or culture in which you are interested to find out more about it.

Many search engines also have links to their counterparts in other countries; you can check overseas newspapers or discover what sports, foods, or items of interest are current.

There are also sites, such as http://travlang.com, where you can learn useful phrases in a wide range of languages, see the words spelled correctly, and hear samples of pronunciation.

chec*k*point

1. Conflict that occurs because of cultural differences may be avoided if you are
_____ and _____ to what is going on.

2. Possibly the most obvious sources of cultural conflict in the workplace are
_____ barriers.

3. List four ways you can help others make cultural adjustments in the workplace.
Explain how you could implement your suggestions in the workplace or in a
school situation.

_____

_____

_____

_____

_____

_____

_____

_____

_____

_____

_____

_____

_____

_____

_____

_____

_____

_____

applications

1. Select a culture or minority group with which you would like to become better acquainted. Interview several members of that group. Use the workplace scenario about Japanese executives as an example of the kind of material you should include. Report on the following:

a. What are some interesting and unusual customs and behaviors that are part of the culture?

_____

_____

_____

_____

b. What are some beliefs and values that are characteristic of the culture?

_____

_____

_____

_____

2. Make a list of some things people say that indicate cultural stereotypes. Two examples are listed to get you started.

    French men are romantic.   German men drive fast.

_____   _____

_____   _____

_____   _____

_____   _____

3. Sometimes, without intending to, we show disrespect and insensitivity for people who are different. The use of nicknames is an example. Ask several friends, coworkers, and possibly relatives (especially those who are over fifty years old) to recall nicknames of people they have known. List the names below with your opinion about whether or not using the nickname shows disrespect.

	Disrespect?	
Nickname	Yes	No

Everyone has an inner sense of fairness, and when it is violated, a person may feel uncomfortable or angry. **Discrimination**, according to the dictionary, simply means to recognize differences. However, it has taken on a negative meaning as a word used to describe unfair treatment of a particular person or group due to race, gender, religious affiliation, or physical disability. The treatment is unfair because it is not based on what is real, but on stereotypes and prejudice.[10]

PREJUDICE AND STEREOTYPING

Discrimination is a behavior that is often based on an attitude. If you, as an individual, think that a particular race of people tend to be lazy, you display a discriminatory attitude. If you were an employer and refused to hire people of that race, you would be guilty of discrimination.

Prejudice is a term that is often used in connection with discrimination. It means to prejudge or form an opinion without taking the time or effort to judge in a fair manner.[11] Prejudice leads to treating a person unfairly. If you have decided that people belonging to a particular group are inferior, you will likely prejudge all people you meet belonging to that group. This does not just apply to people from other countries. Anytime you prejudge a person based solely on their being a member of some group, rather than on what he or she is like as an individual, you are being prejudiced.

Stereotyping occurs whenever you think of all members of a group as having the same characteristics, rather than viewing the members of the group as unique individuals.[12] If you stereotype an individual, you assign to that person a set of characteristics that may be unfair and undeserved.

on the job

Arlene has been working as a designer for a clothing manufacturer. Her record as an employee is excellent, but she has a tendency to worry about her job. During dinner with a friend, Arlene said, "I think I'm in for real trouble." "What's the problem?" her friend asked. Arlene replied, "They've added another designer in my division—a young Korean woman. The boss probably wanted someone who will work twenty-four hours a day and all weekend. You know how those foreigners are. She'll probably work for next to nothing." Her friend responded, "I don't know why you're so concerned. You're very talented and constantly complimented on your work." Arlene continued, "And she has an accent. You'd think that if she were going to live here, she could learn to speak the language. I don't know why they couldn't have hired one of the hundreds of local designers who are dying to get into the business."

Is Arlene's attitude toward her new coworker reasonable? Are her employer and coworkers likely to agree with her?

Stereotyping can also work in reverse. You may give people an unfair advantage by assigning them very positive traits because of stereotyping. For example, you may choose Edna as a friend because she wears expensive clothing, looks like a fashion model, and lives with her parents in a luxurious home. If you take a look at Edna as an individual, you may find a discrepancy between Edna's real personality and the image you have because of the stereotype. Stereotyping is not only unfair, it is likely to be inaccurate.

"To keep the Golden Rule we must put ourselves in other people's places. If we had the imagination to do that . . . fewer bitter judgments would pass our lips, fewer racial, national, and class prejudices would stain our lives."

—HARRY EMERSON FOSDICK

Learn to avoid prejudice and stereotyping. Discrimination, prejudice, and stereotyping can become so much a part of your life that you hardly notice them. All too often, prejudices feel comfortable. You do not think about them. You may even endure the discomforts of prejudice in order to keep a job. Today, however, there is an effort to make people conscious of their prejudices and the damage that can be done by those feelings.

When prejudice becomes a part of your personality as a worker or when you learn to accept unfair treatment based on prejudice, a type of decay sets in. Work becomes less satisfying. Conflict becomes a part of each day's work. Often your productivity will decrease. In order to be a better worker, you should remove these barriers to productivity and job satisfaction. You need to learn to recognize and not accept discrimination in the workplace. You must be sensitive to what is going on around you and recognize your personal prejudices in order to change them.

To deal with unfair discrimination in employment situations, one must first become aware of it. As you become aware of and sensitive to discrimination (including your own), opportunities to take positive action will appear. Here are some suggestions about how to take advantage of those opportunities:

- *Speak up and challenge those who make negative comments based on prejudice or stereotypes. Usually this can be done tactfully.* For example, "I understand your point of view on this issue, but it really isn't fair to judge an individual because she is a Native American."
- *Express your disapproval or walk away when someone tells a joke or story that makes fun of someone on the basis of prejudice or negative stereotypes.* For example, "I know you don't intend to be unkind, but if I were Polish, I'd be offended by jokes that make Polish people look stupid."
- *Bring up the subject of discrimination. When you see the opportunity in casual conversation at work, share what you are learning about prejudice and stereotyping. You may influence others to be more aware of and sensitive to these problems.* For example, "Isn't it great that more women are being promoted to management positions in the banking industry? Now I realize what Ellen was trying to say when she complained about having to train the young man who was to become her supervisor."
- *Avoid using a person's minority group label to identify him or her.* For example, say "Deliver the package to the receptionist" instead of "Deliver the package to the Asian woman at the front desk."
- *Learn and use the preferred terms for identifying minority group members.* For example, use "persons with disabilities" instead of "handicapped." Be very careful not to use unacceptable nicknames for nationalities and ethnic groups.
- *Resist and expose prejudice when you discover it.* In almost every working group, you will find someone who presents an image of being tolerant and fair-minded when actually he or she is motivated by intolerance and prejudice. It may be difficult or impossible to change the attitudes of such a person, but you can refuse to support or agree with acts of discrimination. Also, you may be able to express your disapproval and call attention to the discrimination in an effort to stop it.
- *Examine your own attitudes.* Are others being unfair or have you prejudged them? Is your own attitude creating problems? Do you need to unlearn some of your own prejudices?

WHAT THE LAW PROVIDES

The U.S. Equal Employment Opportunity
Commission (EEOC) was established in
1964 to enforce the following principal federal statutes prohibiting employment discrimination.[13]

- The Equal Pay Act of 1963
- Title VII of the Civil Rights Act of 1964
- The Civil Rights Act of 1991
- The Age Discrimination in Employment
  Act of 1967
- The Pregnancy Discrimination Act of
  1978
- Title I of the Americans with Disabilities
  Act of 1990
- The Sexual Harassment Law of 1991
- The Family and Medical Leave Act of
  1993

The EEOC receives complaints and
evaluates them, then either tries to work out
the problem or refers the complaint to the
courts. It develops guidelines to help organizations create and put legal hiring programs
into practice. This agency is supported and
used by state and local government entities.
For example, cities and counties may have
Community Action Boards, Human
Relations Commissions, Human Rights
Officers, and Citizen's Review Boards concerned with discrimination by employers
and government agencies.

According to Title VII of the Civil
Rights Act of 1964 and the Civil Rights Act
of 1991, employers are not allowed to discriminate in any area of employment based
on race, color, religion, sex, or national
origin.[14] Employers cannot discriminate in
recruiting, hiring, promoting, discharging,
classifying, or training employees. The
1991 act provides for monetary damages in
cases of intentional discrimination.

The Equal Pay Act of 1963, passed
before the Civil Rights Act, prohibits
discrimination on the basis of sex in
the payment of wages or benefits, as

Think for a moment about your attitudes toward
those who are different. Can you find evidence in
your past behavior suggesting that you might have
participated in some form of stereotyping or prejudice? If you feel comfortable about sharing this
information, make notes about a few examples in
the space below.

_____

_____

_____

_____

_____

well as working conditions and work
responsibilities.[15]

Affirmative action is a hiring policy
that many private and public employers use
to correct the effect of past discrimination
against minorities and women. Under affirmative action plans, employers list the discriminatory barriers in their organization
that are limiting to minority applicants and
current employees. Then plans are set up to
eliminate those barriers. In the past, some
employers were legally required to develop
and follow affirmative action plans. Now
affirmative action is encouraged on a voluntary basis. A good reference on this topic
is *Affirmative Action,* edited by Brian J.
Grapes.[16]

As employers changed their policies
for recruiting, selecting, and hiring, a problem with reverse discrimination emerged.
The most common objective of affirmative
action is to create a workforce with fair
representation of women and minorities.
The obvious strategy for achieving this goal
is to give preference in hiring and promoting to workers who would have been subjected to discrimination in the past. When

"People are pretty much alike. It's only that our differences are more susceptible to definition than our similarities."

—LINDA ELLERBEE

this preference is used, it can result in **reverse discrimination**, barring qualified individuals from being hired simply because they are not from a minority group. While affirmative action may seem to be fair and reasonable as a solution to problems created by past discrimination, reverse discrimination is still discrimination and is unfair.[17]

As noted *In the Employment Law Guide—Laws, Regulations & Technical Assistance Services,* revised April 2003, the Department of Labor's regulations prohibit discrimination in such employment practices as recruitment, rates of pay, upgrading, layoff, promotion, and selection for training. Employers may not make distinctions based on race, color, religion, sex or national origin in recruitment or advertising efforts, employment opportunities, wages, hours, job classifications, seniority, retirement ages, or job fringe benefits such as employer contributions to company pension or insurance plans.[18]

The Department of Labor's regulations, cited above, make it very clear that your race, color, or ethnic background should not be determining factors in whether or not you will be hired. In the process of recruiting, selecting, and hiring workers, employers are prohibited by law from asking certain questions concerning race, color, or national origin.[19] Any employer may ask whether the applicant is a citizen of the United States. Questions regarding an individual's ability to speak or read a foreign language are also permitted. However, questions regarding ancestry or native language are not allowed. Asking "What language did you speak at home as a child?" is illegal.

Religious discrimination is not fair and obviously not legal, if the Department of Labor's regulations are followed. Over the past few decades, much of the discrimination against certain religions has diminished, although it has not completely disappeared.

As a job applicant, you should be advised concerning normal hours or days of work required by the employer. An employer may ask if you are willing to work the required schedule. An employer may not, however, quiz you about your religious denomination, practices, affiliations, or holidays.

The language of Title VII of the Civil Rights Act of 1964 indicates that you cannot be discriminated against because of your gender. This type of discrimination has been and continues to be a major issue in our society. As the traditional role of women has changed, more and more women are entering the workforce. Men, too, have taken a look at the roles assigned to them and are discovering that they have additional options. These redefined roles have caused some concern on the part of employers. Employers are concerned about the following:

- How much time will family obligations take?
- How often will the employee be absent for family commitments?
- How much time will be required away from the workplace if a new baby becomes a part of the family?
- Who is responsible for child care in the home?

An employer may not ask your marital status or family status, and you do not need to provide information about whether you are single, engaged, married, divorced, or separated. Employers may not ask questions about a spouse's income or questions regarding the number and ages of children or plans for pregnancy. As an applicant, you may be asked if it will be possible for you to meet specific work schedules or if there are any activities, commitments, or responsibilities that may hinder you from doing your job.

Other questions that may allow the employer to learn about your family status (without asking directly) can relate to your expected duration on the job or anticipated absences. These questions may only be asked if they are asked of all applicants and weighed equally in evaluations for both sexes.

Age discrimination is not legal according to the Age Discrimination in Employment Act of 1967.[20] Discrimination because of a person's age is referred to as **ageism**, a term coined by Dr. Robert Butler, president of the International Longevity Center-USA in 1969.[21] Younger workers are often hired because they are less expensive and are stereotyped as more flexible and willing to learn. Younger workers can also be placed at a disadvantage because they have little experience. Older workers may be hired because of their experience, knowledge, and maturity. However, they may be discriminated against because their understanding of methods and technology is considered dated. By law, it is illegal to discriminate against hiring a person based solely on age. While employers may require a work permit (issued by school authorities) providing proof of age for younger workers, an employer may not require a birth certificate as proof of age before hiring.

Traditionally there has been discrimination and prejudice in the workplace against those whose character does not meet with the general standards of society. Criminals, members of subversive organizations, those who are poor credit risks, and others who are considered to be "undesirable" are often not hired to work even though they have the abilities to perform in a given occupation. In many cases, however, the law requires that such individuals should have equal opportunity in employment with people of "acceptable" character.

An important regulation helps prevent discrimination against people who may have been arrested for, but not convicted of, a crime. It prohibits inquiry as to whether a job applicant has ever been arrested. Questions concerning an applicant's conviction (and if so, when, where, and the disposition of the case) are allowed. No questions may be raised regarding your credit rating, charge accounts, or other financial matters. You may be asked about the type of education and experience you obtained in military service as it relates to a particular job, but you may not be asked about what type of discharge you received from the service.

The Pregnancy Discrimination Act of 1978 under Title VII of the Civil Rights Act of 1964 prohibits an employer from refusing to hire a woman because of a pregnancy-related condition as long as she can perform the major functions of her job. Women affected by pregnancy or any related condition must be treated the same as other applicants or employees with similar abilities or limitations.[22]

The law protects the rights of persons with disabilities.[23] Discrimination in the workplace against people with disabilities was, for a long time, a common occurrence. However, in July of 1990, the Americans with Disabilities Act (ADA) was passed to make such discrimination and prejudice unlawful. Title I of the act deals with employment.

The ADA prohibits discrimination in hiring by not allowing the employer to specifically ask if the job applicant is disabled. The person may be asked if he or she is able to perform the essential tasks and functions of the job. However, that is a fair question and should be asked of everyone. The employer is not required to hire a person who is not competent to do the job.

Another important provision of the ADA is that employers are not allowed to give special treatment or make special requirements of disabled persons. For example, a physical examination may not be required unless all job applicants are required to have one.

After the disabled person is hired, the employer must make reasonable accommodations so that the employee will be able to stay on the job and perform effectively. Some examples are these:

- The job may have to be restructured, or reassignments may have to be made.
- Special equipment may have to be acquired, or modifications may have to be made to existing equipment or devices.
- The entire workplace and its facilities must be accessible. For example, if the door to the lunchroom is too narrow to accommodate a wheelchair, it may have to be widened.

It is possible for the employer to avoid making some of the accommodations if it can be shown that being expected to make them is unreasonable. The employer must show that the accommodations would entail "undue hardship, difficulty, or expense."

Employers are required to make reasonable workplace accommodations for the disabled worker.

Due to the provisions of the Sexual Harassment Law of 1991, you have a legal right to be free from sexual harassment.[24] **Sexual harassment** is coerced, unethical, and unwanted intimacy. It is not only an issue of sex; it is also an issue of power.

Sexual harassment can occur at any level of an organization. Supervisors can be harassed by subordinates, as well as vice versa. Men can harass women, and women can harass men.

The Supreme Court has ruled that remarks, gestures, and even graffiti can be considered forms of sexual harassment. Rude sounds, whistling suggestively, jokes about sex, derogatory rumors, notes or signs posted in a person's work space, brushing up against bodies, and unwelcome touching are forms of sexual harassment.

Sometimes the perpetrator is not aware that his or her behavior is considered harassment. What may be intended as friendly teasing can come across to the victim as bullying. Flirting may come across as sexual harassment. The key to recognizing the difference is how the victim feels about it. Most acts of sexual harassment are power plays that are degrading in nature. Nobody has the right to harass another person.

Sexual harassment may make the victim feel that there is no way out of the situation, and it can lead to a good deal of personal sacrifice. A victim may feel obligated to quit a job due to the harassment or may expect to be fired from the job for resistance.

If resisting and reporting the harassment fail to resolve the problem, you have several options for taking legal action.[25] The equal opportunity laws and civil rights agencies can provide help for those who feel they are being sexually harassed. Some forms of harassment (such as physical assault) are crimes. Do not hesitate, in that case, to go to your local police department. If the form of harassment you encounter is

© GETTY IMAGES/PHOTODISC

not specifically a crime, there are other remedies. Unions and human resources departments can provide internal contacts. You may also file complaints on a federal level with the EEOC and on a local level with human rights agencies.

If you are being sexually harassed, you should speak up. Ignoring or tolerating the situation can often lead to a cycle of ongoing harassment and victimization. You need to be assertive and establish strong personal boundaries. You should tell coworkers to stop when their behavior is offensive and inappropriate. Bystanders, too, must speak out against harassment when it occurs, or they can appear to condone it. If you feel you are being harassed on the job, remember that you have the right to be free from pressure or abuse. You have the right—and you owe it to yourself—to resist!

Subtle discrimination is discrimination that is not obvious and is seldom brought out in the open. It is based on appearance, values, or some other personal characteristic. In this category one finds discrimination against overweight people, short people, tall people, single people, lesbians and gay men, divorced people, and recovering alcoholics, to name a few. You may be a victim of this type of discrimination, or you may be guilty of subtle discrimination against others.

Subtle discrimination should be recognized and addressed. This form of discrimination may not be entirely covered by law, but it can be just as harmful as the types of discrimination previously discussed in this chapter.

AVOIDING, RESISTING, OR FIGHTING DISCRIMINATION OR PREJUDICE

To this point, we have considered the many different aspects of discrimination and prejudice in the work world. You have been encouraged to be alert and sensitive to these problems. This section is concerned with what you might actually do if you are faced with discrimination or prejudice.

Keep in mind that the effects of prejudice and discrimination are destructive. Prejudice can be eliminated by developing acceptance and understanding of other individuals. Tolerant people are those who are secure and can separate the important from the unimportant. For instance, does it really make a difference to you if Phyllis eats bean sprouts at break time? Should her eating habits really make a difference in how you feel about her?

A willingness to accept and try to understand others as they are will go a long way in helping you preserve good working relationships.

There are several options available to you if you feel you are a victim of discrimination. Consider the following steps on pages 396–397.

> *"Aggressive fighting for the right is the greatest sport in the world."*
>
> —THEODORE ROOSEVELT

Smart Tip ▾ ▾ ▾

If you feel that you are the victim of sexual harassment, you should resist. First, and most importantly, you should:

- **Confront the person who is harassing you. Tell him or her how you feel about what is happening and make it very clear that you want the unwanted behavior to stop.**
- **If the harassment continues, explain the situation to your supervisor. If the perpetrator is your supervisor, then go to his or her supervisor or to the human resources department.**

▲ ▲ ▲ ▲ ▲ ▲ ▲ ▲ ▲

focus on ethics

Six years ago Elizabeth was a very successful receptionist in a utility company. She had enjoyed her work and now was ready to return to the job market after taking time off to care for her elderly parents. She refreshed her professional skills by taking a computer class at a local community college. She prepared a résumé, updated her references, and began the interviewing process. But things seemed different now. It appeared people were talking down to her—treating her with less respect. When she finally obtained a position, she found herself in the back office of the company doing data entry work where she had little contact with the public. After several weeks on the job, she explained to her boss that she would like to be moved to a position where she could meet the public. He mumbled something about "We like to give the public an image of being a young, forward-looking company." Her coworkers did not seem to enjoy the "goodies" she brought to break time. They made comments about the importance of being trim and fit. Elizabeth was aware that she had put on quite a few pounds over the past few years, but could hardly believe that it would create a problem.

Did Elizabeth's employer do anything illegal? Was his behavior ethical? Were Elizabeth's coworkers guilty of subtle discrimination?

You Can Turn and Walk Away

There may be situations when you think the costs of confronting discrimination are too high. You may feel that the least painful choice is to walk away from the pressure. It may seem best to resign your position or ask for a transfer to free yourself from a situation. You may even refuse a job offer, feeling that the pressure of prejudice from your coworkers will be too great.

Simply turning and walking away may, at times, seem like the least painful option, but that leaves you with little hope or satisfaction. In the long run, what you do can affect others who may be in your position. Discrimination will not be brought to light. Unfair practices will continue. By leaving, you will be helping to maintain that discrimination.

You May be Able to Overcome Discrimination with Positive Resistance Over Time, and with Patience

The very nature of discrimination—generally based on stereotypes—is not specific or well thought out. Demonstrating that you do not fit the image of the stereotype by doing your best can do much to reduce or eliminate the issue. For example, when Anna, a woman in her late fifties, reorganized the entire filing system, eliminating the problem of misplaced files, her coworkers began to seek her advice. They no longer allowed the difference in age to keep them from including her. They no longer avoided contact with her.

Positive resistance does not mean that you should ignore or endure the discrimination. **Positive resistance** means clearly recognizing and confronting the discrimination. It means letting your coworkers know that you are aware of the discrimination and are uncomfortable with it. Unfortunately, not all discrimination can be eliminated with positive resistance. The next section deals with the strongest means of dealing with discrimination.

Fighting for Your Rights May be Your Best Option

A good resource on this topic is *Job Discrimination—How to Fight—How to Win!* by Jeffrey M. Bernbach.[26] If you feel your rights are being violated, you have remedies under the law for dealing with this discrimination. Guidelines about where and how to file a formal complaint are available in the Appendix of *Coping with Discrimination* by Gabriel I. Edwards.[27] However, if you are a victim, your first impulse may be to get even with the offender. This alternative always does more harm than good. Often it simply increases the prejudice and, as a result, the discrimination.

Revenge can take many forms—from vandalizing to physical assault. These actions are illegal and carry serious consequences that are far more damaging than any pleasure you may receive from getting even.

The appropriate way to fight is to follow these steps.

1. Your first action should be to attempt to correct the situation from an on-the-job perspective. Contact a member of your human resources department or union if this option is available to you. An investigation will be conducted. If just cause is found, grievance procedures can be initiated. This may be as far as you need to go to correct the discrimination.

2. If you receive no satisfaction from these sources, your next step will be to contact either an attorney or a governmental agency dealing with discrimination. On a local level, you may contact a human rights agency, such as a state equal employment opportunity commission. On the federal level, you should contact the Equal Employment Opportunity Commission (EEOC).

Be aware that if you have a legal case against your employer for discrimination, you must be prepared to face a not-always-sympathetic public that may include your coworkers. If you decide to proceed with court remedies, do not make it a halfhearted attempt. Backing away after you have taken the initiative can be worse than losing. Always keep in mind your right to be judged for yourself—free of stereotypes and prejudices. *You have the right to fight discrimination and prejudices!*

> *"Don't be in a hurry to condemn because he [sic] doesn't do what you do or think as you do or as fast. There was a time when you didn't know what you know today."*
>
> —MALCOLM X

chec**k**point

1. A hiring policy that attempts to restore fairness in hiring is _____.

2. A form of discrimination that can apply to older or younger workers is _____.

3. Sexual harassment may include
   a. looks.
   b. remarks.
   c. touching.
   d. all of the above.

4. The agency that enforces laws pertaining to discrimination is
   a. ADAC
   b. ACRAA
   c. OOA
   d. EEOC

5. Prejudice has to do with
   a. judgment.
   b. illogical thinking.
   c. illusion.
   d. equity.

6. Reasonable accommodations for a person with a disability does not include
   a. wheelchair ramps at the main entrance.
   b. restructuring job assignments.
   c. offering additional training to compensate for the disability.
   d. making expensive modifications to a piece of equipment.

7. Check the questions that are not legal in employment interviews and applications.
   a. ___ Which language did you speak at home as a child?
   b. ___ Are you a citizen of the United States?
   c. ___ What is your ethnic background?
   d. ___ What is your religious affiliation?
   e. ___ Are you able to lift at least forty pounds?
   f. ___ Are you married, single, or divorced?
   g. ___ May we have a copy of your birth certificate?

applications

1. Finish the following sentences with your first thoughts. Share your ideas with a classmate if you feel comfortable doing that. As you review the answers, examine them for prejudicial content.

a. Overweight people _____

b. Bosses _____

c. Alcoholics _____

d. Foreigners _____

e. Farmers _____

f. Old people _____

g. Blondes _____

h. Cats _____

i. Welfare recipients _____

2. Create a list of questions that you feel would be discriminatory in an employment interview. Check with a human resources manager or attorney to find out which of your questions would be illegal and which would not.

_____

_____

_____

3. Discuss in a small group how you might respond to an employer who asked questions during an employment interview that you knew were discriminatory and illegal. Role play an interview. Remember that some interviewers may be inexperienced and may not know that a question is illegal, so practice answering in a way that takes this into account, as well as creating responses

for when it is obvious that the person knows that he or she is asking an inappropriate question. Draft a few ideas in the space below.

_____

_____

_____

4. Can you think of an example of subtle discrimination against you or someone close to you? If you can, in the space below, describe the situation. If you cannot, interview someone who has experienced subtle discrimination and is willing to share what happened.

a. What was the discriminatory action or behavior?

_____

_____

_____

b. Specifically, what do you suppose was the reason or underlying motive for the discrimination?

_____

_____

_____

c. How did the victim of the subtle discrimination react or respond?

_____

_____

_____

d. What was done, or what might have been done, to prevent future occurrences of this kind?

_____

_____

_____

chapter

Points to Remember

Review the following points to determine what you remember from the chapter.

- Diversity in the world of work can create problems of prejudice and cultural conflict, but employers are working to avoid these problems. They expect workers to be able to fit in and get along and to help others to do so. This includes taking pride in who you are, learning to understand the values and views of others who are different, and making an effort to learn about other cultures and traditions. Being sensitive to differences, making an effort to overcome the language barrier, taking a stand on diversity, and making an effort to attend diversity seminars and workshops all help to overcome barriers to understanding. Employers are making an effort to accommodate differences in cultures and in physical requirements of workers. Employers are more aware of laws and regulations and are enforcing the regulations and laws so that workers feel safe and work in more pleasant environments.

- The workforce of today is steadily becoming more diverse. There are more women, more individuals with disabilities, more older workers, and more ethnic minorities and immigrants. Native-born white males are no longer a majority in the workforce—in fact, they have become a minority, with only one in six workers falling into this category.

- Cultural conflict can be avoided when workers are sensitive and respectful of differences among cultures. Helping others to adjust and fit in can be rewarding. Getting and giving help with language

barriers is an important step. Taking a stand on important issues of promoting acceptance of others and suggesting improvements when things are not right can lead to unity and overcome divisiveness. Most important, you can reach out to your coworkers and form supportive interpersonal relationships with those who are different from you.

- Discrimination is unfair treatment due to attitudes about race, gender, religion, and a variety of other personal characteristics. Prejudice and stereotyping are underlying causes of discrimination in the workplace. The Equal Employment Opportunity Commission (EEOC) is a government agency that helps with implementation and enforcement of Title VII of the 1972 amendment to the Civil Rights Act of 1964. It also helps private and public agencies and business enterprises develop and implement affirmative action programs. Affirmative action plans are designed to correct the effects of discrimination. Employers are not allowed to use discriminatory practices in hiring, promoting, or firing. Some of the unlawful practices include asking questions or using selection criteria that would permit the employer to give preference to or reject job applicants because of race, color, national origin, religious affiliations or practices, gender and family status, age, and personal character that do not meet society's standards.

- Employers must abide by a number of federal statutes prohibiting discrimination in the workplace. The Americans with

Disabilities Act (ADA) was passed in 1990. It includes a number of regulations that ensure fair access by persons with disabilities to many jobs that were formerly unavailable to them. Employers are required to disregard the disability and make selections on the basis of job performance capability. They are also required to make reasonable accommodations so the worker will be able to work effectively. In addition employers must abide by the Civil Rights Act and its amendments, the Sexual Harassment Law, the Age Discrimination in Employment Act and others as they pertain to discrimination in the workplace.

- Sexual harassment is unacceptable behavior in the workplace. The most important step in eliminating sexual harassment is to confront the perpetrator. Next, if

necessary, make the situation known to those with greater authority. If the harassment is a criminal act, help should be obtained from law enforcement agencies. Human resource departments, human rights officers, and the EEOC may also provide assistance. Hiring an attorney to represent you in a lawsuit would be a final step to protect your rights.

- Prejudice and discrimination, including subtle discrimination, may be offset when you develop tolerance and understanding of the problems experienced by those with whom you live and work. When that fails, it may be appropriate for you to avoid, resist, or fight discrimination and prejudice in the workplace and in your personal life.

How did you do? Did you remember the main points you studied in the chapter?

key terms

Define each term in the space provided.

Diversity

Egocentric myopia

Ethnocentrism

Cultural conflict

Discrimination

Prejudice

Stereotyping

Affirmative action

Reverse discrimination

Ageism

Sexual harassment

Subtle discrimination

Positive resistance

activities and projects

1. During our childhood and teenage years, we learn our attitudes and values from people whom we admire and respect. This may be the source of some of our prejudices. Prejudice may also develop if a person has had a bad experience with a member of another race or ethnic group. The bad experience is then generalized to the whole group.

a. Do you have prejudices? If so, what are they?

_____

_____

_____

b. Do members of your family or close friends have prejudices? If so, what are they?

_____

_____

_____

2. The circle made with your thumb and forefinger is a familiar gesture that may have totally different meanings in different cultures. For example, it can mean A-OK (USA, UK, Europe), "he's a zero or a failure" (France), an obscene accusation (some Mediterranean countries), or "give me change in coins" (Japan). Was there a time when another person's gesture or body movement confused you or someone else? Describe what happened in the space below.

_____

_____

_____

3. Assume that you are an employer looking for a top-notch computer technician. A person in a wheelchair with one obviously disabled hand is applying for the position. List five questions that might be used to evaluate this disabled person as a job applicant. You are to avoid questions prohibited by law.

_____

_____

_____

4. Norico is an artist in an advertising agency. Most of her coworkers are male. Consider each of the following events and decide whether or not it is a case of sexual harassment. Explain why or why not. You may also wish to discuss how Norico should react, and what she might do to prevent further problems.

a. A single coworker asks her for a date.

b. A much older supervisor asks her for a date.

c. A coworker gives her a hug in greeting.

d. A male coworker tells her she has "cute legs."

e. A male coworker tells her a joke with sexual implications.

f. She hears the same joke, but is one of a group. She is the only female.

g. She wears a low-cut blouse and is told, "If you've got it, flaunt it!"

h. Several times a male coworker touches the back of her neck as he passes by.

case studies for critical thinking

Case 14.1

LANGUAGE BARRIER

Greg, an assistant manager in an auto parts store, was moved from his Ogden, Utah position to one in Brownsville, Texas. The transition was difficult for Greg partly because he found himself in a very different cultural environment. He became angry when several of his coworkers would chatter among themselves in their native language. He suspected they were talking or laughing about him, or just wasting time. He found himself being irritable with them. He complained about them to the store manager.

1. If you were the store manager, what advice would you give to Greg to help him manage his cultural discomfort?

Case 14.2

FROM ANOTHER WORLD

A week had passed in Accounting 101. The thirty students had become acquainted with one another. Study groups were emerging. Small groups were having lunch together. But two students, Laura and Jim, sat in the back of the room and were not included in anything. During the introductions on the first day of class, Laura and Jim said that they were from the Four Corners area—the Native American reservation. They did not say much to each other, and they said absolutely nothing when called upon to answer questions in class. Usually they were a little late arriving, and they were always the first ones out the door. No one, it seemed, took an interest in getting them to join in and become active members of the class.

1. Assume you have decided to help Laura and Jim fit in and get along with other students in the class and survive the rigorous demands of the course. What are your suggestions to Laura and Jim for specific goals and a plan for accomplishing them?

2. What might you learn from Laura and Jim? In what ways might you and other class members benefit from reaching out to these two who seem to be from another world?

Case 14.3

REASONABLE ACCOMMODATION?

Charles had a difficult time finding a job, but finally he was hired to work in the equipment room of a health and fitness club. When he was nine years old, Charles was stricken with an illness that left him with damage to his central nervous system. He is unable to walk and has difficulty with eye and hand coordination. In addition, his speech is slightly impaired. His coworkers are friendly and helpful, and Charles likes the work. But he is a bit slow because of the extra effort required to move around the facility in his wheelchair. There is a step at the doorway of the weight room. Charles is assigned to work behind a counter that he can barely see over. But the most difficult problem is communicating with coworkers and customers. Charles has to speak very slowly to be understood. Often he is misunderstood. On one occasion, after asking him to repeat something a second time, a coworker said, "Oh, just forget it!" and walked away.

1. Assume you are the manager of the health and fitness club and part of your job is hiring and supervision. You are having second thoughts about whether or not Charles will fit in and get along in his new job. What are you going to do? Explain how and why.

---

2. Assume you are a coworker assigned to work with Charles doing the same work. You are concerned that he is apparently not able to do the job as well as you, and you find yourself doing some of his work. You like Charles. He seems to get along with people and has a pleasant personality. But it is sometimes frustrating for you because he is so slow—both in his actions and his speech. What are you going to do? Explain how and why.

Case 14.4

WRONG RELIGION?

Leon applied for a job as a retail clerk with a local department store. Based on the area of town where he lived, the human resources director, Gladys, asked if Leon was a Seventh-Day Adventist. When Leon said that he was an active member, Gladys gave him no further consideration because the store was open on Saturday. Gladys knew that Adventists observed Saturday as their day of worship.

1. Was Leon subjected to unfair discrimination because of his religion? Explain.

_____

_____

_____

2. What question might have been asked, legally, to obtain the information Gladys wanted?

_____

_____

_____

Case 14.5

AGE DISCRIMINATION

After receiving an outstanding application from Charles Nelson for the position of teller at Security First Bank, the human resources director decided to call him in for an interview. Charles is 57 years old. He is an accountant who was required by his former employer to "retire early" because of a management reorganization. When the human resources director entered the outer office and saw Charles waiting, he asked, "May I help you? I am Tom Parks, director of human resources." Charles replied, "I'm here for an interview for the teller position." The director looked at Charles's job application, then at the floor. After a short pause he said, "Quite truthfully, we have a problem. For this position we are looking for someone less than 35 years of age."

1. What would be the ethically and legally correct actions for the human resources director to take in this situation?

_____

_____

_____

2. What actions might Charles take to ensure that he is not subjected to discrimination because of his age?

_____

_____

_____

_____

_____

_____

_____

3. What could be the problem with the application?

_____

_____

_____

_____

_____

_____

_____

Getting the Job

think about it: Clete Hansen completed high school and plans to go to college someday. His financial situation will not permit him to further his education immediately, so he begins looking for work. He scans the daily newspaper and circles a position for a management trainee job at a fast-food restaurant. He checked the state employment agency Web site and found an interesting service position at the local telephone company. He followed up on both leads and was granted interviews. At the interview for the fast-food restaurant, he found that he would need to take a six-month training course in management at the headquarters of the fast-food chain and possibly relocate. He wanted to continue to live with his family and put some money away for college so relocation was out of the question. His second interview was for a representative position at the phone company. His job would be to demonstrate to new customers how to use their cell phones. The workplace impressed Clete, the human resources staff was pleasant, and he thought it looked like a nice place to work. His training would be primarily on-the-job. He was offered the position. Within a few weeks, Clete realized this was not the job for him. He had trouble communicating with customers. He was impatient with customers who didn't listen during his demonstration and then came back the next day with what he considered "dumb" questions. He was not an outgoing, people person. Clete was very uncomfortable with serving the constant stream of customers. He dreaded going to work every day. Clete soon realized that he needed to think about his future and get into a position where the work suited his aptitude and personality.

© DIGITAL VISION

What questions should Clete have asked during the interview? What advice would you give to Clete as he prepares to think about another position?

chapter focus

After completing this chapter, you should be able to:

1. Plan a successful job campaign and check out all possible sources.

2. Prepare a quality resume.

3. Complete a job application form.

4. Write a professional letter of application.

5. Conduct yourself in a positive manner during a job interview.

6. Prepare a thank-you letter as a follow-up to the job interview.

There is more to finding a satisfying job than just picking up a paper or responding to a "hiring" sign in a window. Circumstances or timing may make these your only options for the short term, but long term you want a job that matches your skills, training, and talents and suits your personality in an environment that you enjoy. You will probably also want a position that offers potential for growth.

In order to accomplish this, you need to do some thinking and preparation.

To choose the job that is best for you, you can use the formula $Q + I = JP$. Here, Q is qualifications, I is interest, and JP is job possibilities as shown in Figure 15-1.

Once you identify your qualifications and interests, you will be ready to look for job possibilities that fit your qualifications and interests. This formula can be a valuable tool in finding a satisfying job.

MAKING YOUR INVENTORY LIST

The first step in preparing for the job campaign is to take a good look at yourself. Make a list of everything you can think of that might have a bearing on your success—that is, your qualifications. At this point, do not try to organize or prioritize the information. Just get it down on paper.

Sample Listing of Personal Qualifications

Attended Tory High School
Experience as babysitter
Science Club member
Photography Club member
Business Club member
Community volunteer for Red Cross
Experience as a grocery clerk
Participated in walk-a-thon to raise money for diabetes research
Experience with word processing and database programs
Participated in Save-the-Wetlands project
Directed community theater production
Excellent written and oral communication skills
Graduated with honors

The second step in preparing your campaign is to list your interests and likes. Again, do not try to organize or prioritize at this time.

> *"A job search that doesn't have a definite plan is likely to become only a search with no job."*
>
> —UNKNOWN

QUALIFICATIONS	+	INTERESTS	=	JOB POSSIBILITIES
Education		Hobbies		
Personal Traits		Clubs		
Special Training		Sports		
Unique Skills		Favorite Subjects		
Special Certifications or Licenses		Projects		
		Other		

FIGURE 15-1 *Job-seeking formula.*

Sample Listing of Personal Interests

Golfing	Photography
Science/Medicine	Waterskiing
Reading	Watching football
Being outdoors	games
Fishing	Music
Working with people	Windsurfing
Walking	

ORGANIZING YOUR INVENTORY LIST

When you have written down all the items you can think of, you should organize them into separate classifications. Some of the headings you might consider will include the following:

- Education
- Work Experience
- Special Talents or Abilities
- Organizational Memberships
- Hobbies and Interests

As you organize this list, select items from your qualifications and interests lists. Drop those items that are perhaps not as important to you. Take a large sheet of paper and turn it the long way. Enter your headings across the top of the sheet. Below the headings, list the items from your inventories that belong in each category. (See the example in Figure 15-2.) Check your inventory to see if the items match some of the requirements for jobs you are considering.

CHECKING YOUR APTITUDE

An **aptitude** is a natural talent, ability, or capacity to learn. Having an aptitude for something makes learning things related to your aptitude much easier. For example, if you have an aptitude for math, working with figures, percentages, and other types of math comes more easily for you. Consider occupations that suit your aptitude. The occupations for a person with a good math aptitude might include work in the areas of accounting, computer programming, or positions in a financial institution.

You may already know a lot about your own aptitudes. One way you learn about your aptitudes is by listening to others. Your friends or neighbors may say, "You'd be a great accountant, because you are so good at math," or "A job with the public would be good for you, because you're so likable." In these comments, your friends or acquaintances are talking about what they perceive to be your aptitudes.

You probably will discover that you are interested in doing the things for which you show an aptitude. If you have an aptitude for writing, there is a good chance you will enjoy a job in which you will have the

		ME		
Education	**Work Experience**	**Abilities**	**Memberships**	**Interests**
High School Diploma	Grocery Clerk	Computer Word	Theater Club	Science/ Medicine
Tory HS	Babysitter	Processing	Red Cross	Reading
Honor Student	Directed Theater Production	Communication Database	Science Club	Working with People
			Photography Club	Fishing
			Business Club	

FIGURE 15-2 *Inventory of information.*

opportunity to write. However, you may not always enjoy doing the things you do well. Just because you can do a good job putting a database together does not mean that the activity brings you great satisfaction.

Aptitude tests measure your ability to learn something. Aptitude tests help people discover which occupations match the skills they can develop easily. These tests may be given by career or school counselors or employers to determine your aptitudes.

The assumption behind these tests is that people differ in their special abilities and that these differences are related in a predictable manner to their later achievements. The aptitude test measures a broad spectrum of abilities (for example, verbal, comprehension, number operations, and mechanical knowledge). The aptitude test yields a profile of scores rather than a single intelligence quotient. Aptitude tests have been developed to measure professional potential and capabilities (law, medicine) and special abilities (clerical, mechanical).

One well-known aptitude test is called the General Aptitude Test Battery (GATB).

on the job

Jose applied for a position as a ticket agent for a major airline. He saw an ad in the paper and thought the job sounded like something he would like, so he called for an interview. During the interview, Jose was asked, "Do you meet the qualifications for this position?" "Oops," Jose thought to himself, "I didn't read what they were." Jose said, "Yes, I guess so." He was also asked, "Are you interested in the airline industry?" Jose said, "Well, I like to fly whenever I have the opportunity." Next question, "Tell me about your experience with computers." Jose replied, "I haven't worked much with computers. My previous jobs have been in sales." The next question was, "Can you lift 80 pounds?" Jose replied, "I cannot because I have lower back problems." The interviewer cut the discussion short and said, "We'll get back to you. I don't think you have the qualifications we are seeking. I would encourage you to think more about your abilities, interests, and capabilities before you apply for another position."

Was Jose prepared for this interview? Had Jose thought about his interests and abilities? What do you think about the advice given by the interviewer?

Technology
at Work

These days job openings can be anywhere in the world. You can take a number of approaches to find an open position. Networking, the Internet, newspaper want ads, hot lines, private employment agencies, public employment agencies, temporary agencies, job fairs, and internships are all ways to find jobs.

When considering those that are a distance from where you now live, take into consideration the cost-of-living differences, moving costs, and the characteristics of a new city. Using the Internet is one way to find such information. Several job sites provide formulas to calculate the salary you would need if relocating to a different area of the country.

As an example, visit this Web site. Locate a city you would like to live in. What do you find attractive about this city? What is the difference in the cost of living between your current location and the new city?

http://www.homefair.com

See http://assess.nelson.com/group/gp-gatb.html for an insight into the provisions of this battery of tests. It is used by many state employment agencies. You may want to try to arrange to take this or another aptitude test. These tests measure your ability to work with numbers and words, to work with your hands, to distinguish between shapes and forms and see relationships between objects, and to perform mechanical and clerical tasks.

After you have considered your qualifications, interests, and aptitudes, list some jobs you think you would like to try. Each job you consider must match your qualifications, should match your aptitudes, and, ideally, should relate to some of your interests or preferences. A good resource to use as you are putting your qualifications and interests together is the *Occupational Outlook Handbook (OOH)*. This document is a nationally recognized source of career information developed to provide assistance to individuals making decisions about their futures and their lives. The handbook is available online (http://www.bls.gov/

The *Occupational Outlook Handbook is available online and is a valuable resource in a job search.*

oco/home.htm) or at any public library. It describes what workers do on the job, working conditions, the training and education needed, earnings, and anticipated job prospects in a wide range of occupations. The OOH is updated every two years so you will be looking at current information.

chec**✓**point

1. What are the elements of the job-seeking formula?

_____

_____

_____

_____

_____

2. What is an aptitude?

_____

_____

_____

_____

_____

3. Why might you want to consider your aptitudes when looking for a job?

_____

_____

_____

_____

_____

4. Where would you go to find a copy of the _Occupational Outlook Handbook_ ? What information will you find in the _Handbook_ ?

_____

_____

_____

_____

applications

1. Prepare an inventory list of your qualifications and interests. Put them in a format similar to the one shown in Figure 15-2. Do this activity with care, as you will be utilizing the information in a future assignment (Application #1, Section 15.3).

2. Do you think your qualifications or your interests are more important to an employer? Why? How might this affect the planning of your job campaign?

3. Review the On the Job activity in this section.

a. List the reasons why you think Jose may have applied for the ticket agent position. Were these reasons good enough to actually seek an interview?

b. What qualifications would you assume a ticket agent needs?

c. If Jose would have prepared a qualifications and interests survey, what do you suspect he would have found?

_____

_____

_____

4. List four positions that are of interest to you and that fit some of your natural talents and interests. Look up each of these positions and list the qualifications in the space provided. Ask your instructor or a friend to review the positions with you and determine which job best fits your aptitude, personality, and skills.

(1) _____

_____

_____

(2) _____

_____

_____

(3) _____

_____

_____

_____

(4) _____

_____

_____

_____

Once you have determined your qualifications, interests, and aptitudes, you are ready to begin looking at job resources and job leads. A **job lead** is information about a possible job opening.

PEOPLE

People you know can be of special help to you because they care about you and your future. Let everyone know that you are interested in employment. Tell everyone you meet that you are in the job market. The more people you talk to about your job search, the more leads and information you will discover. Also, encourage others to tell you about their job experiences—the high points and the low points. You can consider this information when it is time to make a decision.

This process of sharing and exchanging job information is **networking**. You may become active in service organizations in your community in order to expand your networking opportunities. Check your local newspaper to see if it lists networking opportunities. The public library can also be a source of information on networking, as well as offering other valuable references and tools (books, videos, Internet access) for your job search. For additional information on networking, here is a Web site you may want to check out: http://www.enetsc.com/JobSearchTips14.htm.

Do not be too proud to ask those who know you for personal assistance in getting a job. The old saying, "It's not what you know, but who you know" holds some truth. There is nothing wrong with having a friend or family member assist in your search to get a job for which you are qualified. Some of your friends, family members, or acquaintances may work for

businesses that pay a referral bonus when an employee recruits a successful job candidate.

Encourage those who know you to help you decide what kind of employment is best suited to you. You may not always hear what you expect to hear.

NEWSPAPER HELP-WANTED ADVERTISEMENTS

Take advantage of the help-wanted advertisements (ads) in your daily newspaper(s). These are not only a source of job openings, but also show trends in the type of openings that are most common. Do not just skim these ads. Read each ad carefully before you respond to it. The help-wanted ads are written and paid for by employers. If an advertised job is not exactly what you are looking for but is related, you may want to follow up on the ad if you think it has potential. Do not waste the employer's time and yours by calling or writing about jobs for which you positively do not qualify.

Be sure to follow up on an advertised job opening immediately. A delay may lose the job for you. Be sure to check the Sunday edition of the newspaper. Sunday news editions usually have the largest job ad section. In fact, some employers only advertise jobs in the Sunday newspaper.

EMPLOYMENT AGENCIES

An **employment agency** is a business that brings together a potential worker and an employer to fill a job opening. You may find help through state-supported or private agencies.

> *"A man who qualifies himself well for his calling, never fails of employment."*
>
> —THOMAS JEFFERSON

on the job

Jolene is very interested in getting a position in one of the hospitals or medical facilities in her new community. She has the credentials and experience to work in respiratory therapy. She has just moved to this community. She spots an ad in the Sunday edition of the local newspaper. The ad has a section describing positions available at Bryan Hospital. The ad does not specifically indicate that there is an opening for a respiratory therapist. Jolene calls the human resources manager listed in the ad and talks with her about her qualifications. Jolene indicates she is new in the community; she has credentials and experience in respiratory therapy work. She acknowledges that the ad didn't specifically say that Bryan had such a position. She says, "I would like to know if you anticipate any expansion or openings in the respiratory therapy area." The resources manager says, "No, I think we are well staffed in that area. However, I suggest that you call St. Thomas Medical Center. I have a friend on their staff who just mentioned to me that they are looking for a respiratory therapist." Jolene thanks her and makes a call to St. Thomas.

What two job resources did Jolene use in this example? What did Jolene do correctly in this scenario? Will you consider Jolene's technique the next time you are job searching?

State Employment Agencies

Every state has a job service agency that helps people find employment. The name of the agency varies from state to state. Look for the agency in the local telephone directory, call the general state government office number, or search the Internet for your state government offices. Your state agency will have many job listings in a wide variety of occupations. The staffs in these agencies have knowledge of the business, industry, and government jobs available within the state.

Most states also have a Web site that you can check for available jobs. In many states, you may submit your resume on a Web site so employers know you are looking for work. Employers take advantage of these Web sites, also. If you cannot locate a Web site for your state, call the State Department of Labor to see if one is available to you. If you are mobile and considering positions in other areas of the country, most state Web sites have links across the nation.

There is no fee charged for the services of the state employment agency. The goal of the agency is to make as many placements as possible so that few people are unemployed and the economy of the state is healthy. State agency employment services may include career counseling, career and technical assessment, resume preparation, interviewing skills, and job-search workshops. Use the services available in your state.

Private Employment Agencies

Private employment agencies can also be useful in helping you find a job. If you contact a private agency, remember that this agency is in business to make a profit. When you complete the private agency application form, you will be asked to sign a contract. *Read the contract before you sign it.* Many private agencies charge fees to employers to find competent, qualified workers, but some private agencies charge the applicant for this service. The fee may be an up-front dollar amount or a percentage of the wages you will earn in the job placement. Also ask what services the agency offers and what period of time the contract covers. Often, private agencies will prepare resumes and letters, give aptitude tests, or offer other services that may be included in the fee or may cost extra.

If you decide to use a private agency, make sure you understand who will be paying the fee for the match between you and the employer. In addition, ask and verify what the procedure is if the job does not work out and you are dismissed for whatever reason within the first year of employment. Will the agency find you another position? Will there be an additional fee? You may also want to check with others who have used the services of private employment agencies to see if they were satisfied with the service provided.

CIVIL SERVICE POSITIONS

In a civil service position, your employer is the U.S. government. The U.S. government is the largest employer in the country. The government hires thousands of new employees each year for many different jobs in all parts of the nation. The pay and working conditions for government jobs are usually very good. Find out where the federal government offices are that accept applications for civil service positions to obtain information about these jobs. You will find the phone number for U.S. Government Offices in the telephone book. Or you may want to check the U.S. Office of Personnel Management Web site (www.opm.gov).

OTHER JOB RESOURCES

Do not overlook the school placement services that are often available in high schools, community colleges, and other postsecondary institutions. Employers often check with school placement services to obtain the names of individuals with qualifications they are seeking.

Consult the Web site www.dol.gov. This Web site is provided by the U.S. Department of Labor and it has a link to every state and territory. The state job links provide wage information, employment standards, and a section called Career Voyages that provides you with a list of "hot" occupations in every state.

If there are large companies and organizations in the area where you choose to work, you may want to do some **cold canvassing**. This means stopping by the human resources offices of these large businesses and completing an application. Let them know you are looking for a job and what skills you have to offer.

Make it a point to read bulletin boards with job postings. These are often found in supermarkets, discount stores, drug stores, government buildings, and community

Technology at Work

The Internet is becoming an increasingly important way to look for job openings. When you find an employer that interests you, check the company Web site to learn more about the company and any open positions. The following sites can get you started. And don't forget to check the Web site of your local newspapers.

America's Job Bank:
http://www.ajb.org

Monster Board:
http://www.monster.com

Career Builder:
http://www.careerbuilder.com

Nation Job Network:
http://www.nationjob.com

America's Employers:
http://www.americasemployers.com

Getting the Job

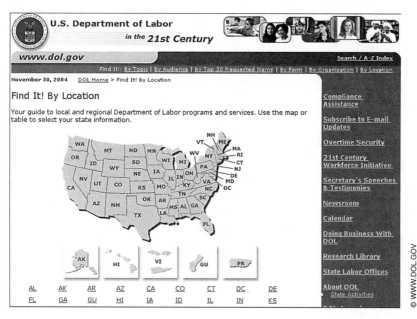

The U.S. Department of Labor Web site can help you find job information in every state.

centers. Watch for help-wanted signs in local businesses where you would like to work.

You should also look into the services of temporary work agencies. Trying out a variety of jobs on a temporary basis is a common first step for entry-level workers in many areas. In fact, temp-to-hire programs are becoming more common, even at levels higher than entry-level.

The more resources you use, the greater are your chances of finding a job that meets your needs. As you hunt, keep in mind that you are looking for a job that matches your qualifications and aptitudes, while trying to match up, if possible, at least some of your interests and preferences.

© WWW.DOL.GOV

chec**k**point

1. What is a job lead?

   _____

   _____

   _____

2. What is networking?

   _____

   _____

   _____

3. What are the two types of employment agencies?

   _____

   _____

   _____

4. What are civil service jobs?

   _____

   _____

   _____

5. What others sources can you go to for job information?

   _____

   _____

   _____

6. Why is the U.S. Department of Labor such a valuable resource?

   _____

   _____

   _____

applications

1. Check out the Sunday edition of your local newspaper or a newspaper from a community in your area. Refer to the jobs/want-ad section. Circle with a red pen the jobs for which you feel qualified. Circle the jobs you would be interested in applying for in black. Circle the jobs in which you are interested and for which you are qualified in blue. As you read, you may notice qualifications (such as *motivated* or *organized*) that you didn't include on your original qualifications list. Add these to your list as you discover them.

2. Make a list of the networking opportunities you have at the present time. Include contacts with family, community, church, organizations, etc. List organizations you could join or activities you could participate in to expand your networking circle.

3. Contact your state government service by phone, letter, or e-mail. Find out what services are available to you (such as job search assistance, seminars, workshops, resume assistance). Write a summary of your findings.

4. Schedule an interview with a private employment agency to find out what services and advantages they offer. Ask to see their policy on who pays for their services and a fee schedule. Prepare a list of questions to ask before you call or visit the agency. Alternatively, you could contact a temporary agency to see if they have a temp-to-hire option. Summarize your findings below for a class discussion. Use additional paper if you need more space.

_____

_____

_____

_____

_____

_____

_____

_____

_____

_____

5. For the experience of using the U.S. Department of Labor Web site, go to the link for the state of South Carolina and identify the median annual income for a veterinary technologist and the anticipated growth rate for this job.

Median Annual Income for Veterinary Technologist _____

Anticipated Growth Rate _____

Search for the same information in the *Occupational Outlook Handbook*.

Medium Annual Income _____

Anticipated Growth Rate _____

Job Search Documents

As you work on your job campaign, you will need to prepare a resume. A **resume** (also often spelled résumé) is a written summary of your education, work experience, and other qualifications for a job. You will also need to know how to put together a letter of application, sometimes called a cover letter. In these documents, you will want to "look good," as the letter and the resume may be your first introduction to a prospective employer. "Looking good" means having prepared attractive, readable, and accurate documents.

RESUME

The resume is sometimes referred to as a *personal data sheet* or a *curriculum vitae* (Latin for "course of one's life," often shortened to *c.v.*). As you begin to prepare the resume, use the sheet that you prepared earlier that lists your qualifications and interests. Think of the resume as an advertisement for you. This resume should sell you and your skills. The resume can be left with employers, attached to your application form, sent with your letter of application, and shared with those with whom you are networking. Share your resume with everyone interested in helping you find a job.

There are many acceptable formats for resumes. One will be presented in this chapter. You may want to experiment with other formats. Libraries, bookstores, textbooks, and Web sites will offer numerous resources that discuss the merits of various formats for various purposes and stages in your career. However, other than the basics, the most important aspects of the resume are its content and appearance.

The resume must always be keyed. Errors on a resume are totally unacceptable.

Also, the resume should be clean, without stray marks or smudges. In addition, because employers may scan your resume for electronic storage, it is wise to avoid fancy type-faces, italics, or underlining. Use space, bold-faced type, capitalization, or type size to separate or highlight information. The resume should be one or two pages and produced on quality paper. Remember that this resume is a "snapshot" of you and should be designed to sell you.

Resumes are typically divided into the following information categories: Personal Information (presented as a heading), Career Objective, Education, Work Experience, and Special Certifications or Licensing. If your personal interests relate directly to the job for which you are applying, refer to that information in your application letter or you may list them on your resume. References should be provided on a separate sheet of paper. They are not usually included on a professional resume today.

Personal Information

This section of the resume should include your full name (nicknames are not appropriate), your complete address, your telephone number (include your area code), and e-mail address (if you have one). It is not appropriate to list your height, weight, religion, marital status, or age. These have nothing to do with your ability to perform a job. You may choose to eliminate the word *RESUME* at the top of the page as that is the style preferred today. Figure 15-3 shows the heading of the resume.

Career Objective

State simply and briefly the type of work you want to do. The employer will want to match your interests with the company's

```
Dean Franklin Burkholder
8121 Imperial Circle
Lincoln, NE 68506-1836
(402) 555-4588
dfburkho@rko.net
```

FIGURE 15-3 *Resume heading.*

needs. Your objective may be general or specific. For example, a general objective might state: "Full-time position as a laborer in a large manufacturing company." A more specific objective might say: "Full-time position desired as a house framer for a home builder." In Figure 15-4 (on page 429) note how a career objective is positioned beneath the personal information. This part of the resume is optional. If you are applying for temporary work or wish to use the resume for several applications, you may eliminate the career objective. Keep in mind that using the same resume for several applications may be a disadvantage. You should customize your resume to fit each job and each application in order to give you the best chance for an interview.

Education

The education section of your resume should support your objective. An employer will look for schooling or training that will be essential for doing a job. List the highest level of education you have successfully completed. List the name of the school, the address, the dates you attended, and your area(s) of study. If you were graduated and earned a diploma or certificate, include these accomplishments. If you have earned a GED or are working on it, put that in this section. Employers will be impressed by your initiative.

Any special course, on-the-job training, or military service should be listed in this section. You can see how sample education information is listed on the resume for Dean Franklin Burkholder shown in Figure 15-4. Note that, as you begin your career, your education is probably your strongest asset, and that is why it appears below the objective. As you progress in your career, work experience will become more important and relevant, and Education will appear following Work Experience. The general exception would be if you were changing careers and had taken special courses related to your new objectives. The key is to have the qualifications most likely to "sell" you closest to the top of the resume.

"Genius without education is like silver in the mine."

—BENJAMIN FRANKLIN

Work Experience

Prospective employers like to see what work experiences you have had. This is a very important section of the resume. You should list your previous jobs in reverse chronological order. That is, list the present or most recent job first, then the next most recent, and so on, until you have all your jobs listed. Include the following information about your previous employment: name of your employer, employer's address, employment dates, job title, duties, and (if appropriate) accomplishments or specific skills used. Yes, you do list jobs from which you have been fired. There is no need to indicate that you were dismissed, but be prepared to explain the circumstances in the interview. It is not uncommon to have a less-than-perfect work history. In Figure 15-4 on page 429, you can see how work experience is listed.

Certifications or Special Licensing

In this section, you will want to list any special certifications or licensing that you have obtained that may apply to the position for which you are applying.

Personal Interests

This section is optional, but it gives the employer a chance to look at the total person. Keep your list of interests short and to the point. Be sure to list those interests that may support your qualifications for the position. You may include such information as your hobbies, sports you enjoy watching or participating in, any community service work, groups you belong to, or other things you enjoy. The interests should relate to the job you are seeking. Consult the inventory that you prepared as you were beginning the job search process. In Figure 15-4, you see that Dean works in a gift shop and he lists his skills in taking inventory, as they relate to the job he is seeking.

References

References are not usually included on most resumes today. You should prepare a separate page and include the names, titles, addresses, and phone numbers of three or four individuals who can recommend your work habits, skills, or character.[1] The people you use as references should be over the age of eighteen and should not be related to you. Be sure you get permission from your references before you use their names. Your references might include a coworker, a current or former teacher, a former employer, or possibly a career counselor. If

focus on ethics

Grace is applying for a position in a state government agency. She would like to serve as an administrative assistant for the director of the Health and Human Services Department. She puts together a resume that she thinks her prospective employer might want to see. Grace indicates that she has completed a two-year community college program in the area of office technology. Grace indicates that in high school she took business classes and was graduated in the upper 10 percent of her class. Also, she adds that she has worked in the Department of Revenue for two years. In the personal interest area, Grace indicates that she is an avid reader of biographies and science fiction.

Grace puts together an impressive resume. However, she is not truthful on the resume. She has attended a community college but she only completed two courses in the office technology program. She completed high school without taking any business courses and did not graduate in the upper 10 percent of her class. She worked as a temporary worker for the Department of Revenue during one tax season. She hasn't read a book since she left high school.

What risk(s) is Grace taking when she falsifies this information? What questions might trip Grace up during the interview? What assumption might an employer make about a potential employee who has falsified her resume?

you have been in the workforce, always list at least one former employer. Be sure you have the permission of that employer to list his or her name, just as you will for all of your references.

References may be listed on your resume, or you can simply use the phrase *References: Available upon request.*

Today, a separate reference sheet, as shown in Figure 15-5 on page 430, is preferred rather than listing references or the italicized phrase on your resume. When the number of job applicants has been narrowed to a few, the employer may ask for this list of references.

"You will find it a very good practice always to verify your references sir."

—MARTIN ROUTH

Dean Franklin Burkholder
8121 Imperial Circle
Lincoln, NE 68506-1836
(402) 555-4588
dfburkho@rko.net

Objective: To be employed by a large supermarket and work with inventory.

Education: Tory High School, Lincoln, Nebraska
College Preparatory Program
Was graduated, May 2004

Certificate: Hammell Community College Data Entry Training Program
Earned Certificate: September 2004

Work Experience: Sumner's Grocery Store
56th Street & Adams Avenue
Lincoln, NE 68506
June 1999-present
Checker

J. L. Lewis
1432 Apple Road
Adams, NE 68333
April - June 1999
General yard work and gardening.

Personal Interests: I volunteer 8 hours per week in the children's ward at the hospital. In this position, I often stock and count inventory of items in the gift shop.

FIGURE 15-4 *Resume.*

JOB APPLICATION

When you decide to apply for a position or visit the employment office of a business, go to the human resources office. Go alone. Do not take a friend or relative. The employer is interested only in you.

Before you leave home, be sure that you have the necessary tools to apply for a job. Have your social security number, two black pens and a pencil, and any information that you have put together about former jobs, your educational background, your list of references, and your military service (if any). If spelling is a problem for you, take a small pocket dictionary to help you, and use it.

Any job for which you apply will require that you complete a job **application form**. This form is used by employers to get

---

References for Dean Franklin Burkholder

Oliver Upton (Supervisor)
Sumner's Grocery Store
56th St. & Adams Ave.
Lincoln, NE 68506
(402) 555-4321

Rinji Mori (School Advisor)
Hammell Community College
2930 South 37
Lincoln, NE 68506
(402) 555-5678

Martha Overton (Hospital Gift Shop Manager)
2432 Winding Way
Lincoln, NE 68506
(402) 555-1234

FIGURE 15-5   *References.*

the basic information about people who apply for positions in their place of business. Figure 15-6 (pages 432–433) shows a typical application form. You may want to complete the application form in Figure 15-6 at home for practice and take it with you as a guide in completing the employer's application form. However, remember that each company has its own application form, and each form is a little different. Follow the instructions on the form you receive for completing the application form.

The completion of the form should be taken seriously, as it will show the employer

- basic information about you.
- how well you follow directions.
- what you have achieved in your education.
- how neat you are.
- a summary of your work experience.

If you do not understand a particular question on the form, ask the person who gave you the form for assistance. If there is a word on the form that you do not understand, check your pocket dictionary for help.

The Civil Rights Act of 1964 prohibits discrimination in employment because of race, color, religion, sex, or national origin. Title VII of the Civil Rights Act was amended in 1972 and includes virtually all forms of job discrimination. This amendment became known as the Equal Employment Opportunity Act. The agency created to oversee compliance is called the Equal Employment Opportunity Commission (EEOC).[2]

The Age Discrimination in Employment Act of 1967 prohibits discrimination because of age. The only question that may be asked legally about your age is, "Are you eighteen years old or older?" An employer's application form can ask only job-related questions. For example, the employer cannot legally ask if you are married, divorced, or single, because marital status does not affect your ability to do a job. Other laws have been passed that prohibit various types of

© GETTY IMAGES/PHOTODISC

Don't leave home for the interview without the necessary tools and information.

discrimination. You may want to become familiar with these laws as they may affect you as an applicant or later as an employee.

Tips for Completing the Application Form

The following tips will help you successfully complete job applications. Read through the entire application before you start writing anything!

- **Follow directions.** Read each question with care and put down only the information that is requested. If the form says please print, then *print*. If the form says circle your answer, *circle* it. If there is a space to write the position you desire, write in the position(s) in which you are interested. Never just put in *anything* or *anything available*. Be as specific as you can about the job you want.
- **Be neat.** Print or write clearly so that your answers can be read easily. Use a black ink pen unless instructed otherwise. A black pen is usually preferred because the employer may want to photocopy the application, and black ink will photocopy best. Scan the document quickly to determine if answers are written above or below the

APPLICATION FOR EMPLOYMENT

(PRE-EMPLOYMENT QUESTIONNAIRE) (AN EQUAL OPPORTUNITY EMPLOYER)

PERSONAL INFORMATION

DATE _____

SOCIAL SECURITY
NUMBER

NAME

| | LAST | FIRST | MIDDLE |

PRESENT ADDRESS

| | STREET | CITY | STATE | ZIP |

PERMANENT ADDRESS

| | STREET | CITY | STATE | ZIP |

PHONE NO.   ARE YOU 18 YEARS OR OLDER?   YES ☐   NO ☐

EMPLOYMENT DESIRED

POSITION

DATE YOU
CAN START

SALARY
DESIRED

ARE YOU EMPLOYED NOW?

IF SO, MAY WE INQUIRE
OF YOUR PRESENT EMPLOYER?

EVER APPLIED TO THIS COMPANY BEFORE?   WHERE?   WHEN?

EDUCATION	NAME AND LOCATION OF SCHOOL	NO. OF YEARS ATTENDED	DID YOU GRADUATE?	SUBJECTS STUDIED
COLLEGE				
HIGH SCHOOL				
GRAMMAR SCHOOL				
TRADE, BUSINESS, OR CORRESPONDENCE SCHOOL				

The Age Discrimination in Employment Act of 1967 prohibits discrimination on the basis of age with respect to individuals who are at least 40 years of age.

GENERAL

SUBJECTS OF SPECIAL STUDY OR RESEARCH WORK

U.S. MILITARY SERVICE
NAVAL SERVICE   RANK

PRESENT MEMBERSHIP IN
NATIONAL GUARD OR RESERVES

FORMER EMPLOYERS (LIST BELOW LAST FOUR EMPLOYERS, STARTING WITH LAST ONE FIRST).

DATE MONTH AND YEAR	NAME AND ADDRESS OF EMPLOYER	SALARY	POSITION	REASON FOR LEAVING
TO				
FROM				
TO				
FROM				
TO				
FROM				
TO				
FROM				

(CONTINUED ON OTHER SIDE)

FIGURE 15-6 *Job Application.*

REFERENCES: GIVE THE NAMES OF THREE PERSONS NOT RELATED TO YOU WHOM YOU HAVE KNOWN AT LEAST ONE YEAR.

	NAME	ADDRESS	BUSINESS	YEARS ACQUAINTED
1				
2				
3				

PHYSICAL RECORD: DO YOU HAVE ANY PHYSICAL LIMITATIONS THAT PRECLUDE YOU FROM PERFORMING ANY WORK FOR WHICH YOU ARE BEING CONSIDERED? ☐ YES ☐ NO

PLEASE DESCRIBE:

IN CASE OF
EMERGENCY NOTIFY

NAME	ADDRESS	PHONE NO.

I CERTIFY THAT THE FACTS CONTAINED IN THIS APPLICATION ARE TRUE AND COMPLETE TO THE BEST OF MY KNOWLEDGE AND UNDERSTAND THAT, IF EMPLOYED, FALSIFIED STATEMENTS ON THIS APPLICATION SHALL BE GROUNDS FOR DISMISSAL.

I AUTHORIZE INVESTIGATION OF ALL STATEMENTS CONTAINED HEREIN AND THE REFERENCES LISTED ABOVE TO GIVE YOU ANY AND ALL INFORMATION CONCERNING MY PREVIOUS EMPLOYMENT AND ANY PERTINENT INFORMATION THEY MAY HAVE, PERSONAL OR OTHERWISE, AND RELEASE ALL PARTIES FROM ALL LIABILITY FOR ANY DAMAGE THAT MAY RESULT FROM FURNISHING SAME TO YOU.

DATE   SIGNATURE

DO NOT WRITE BELOW THIS LINE

INTERVIEWED BY   DATE

HIRED:	YES	NO	POSITION	DEPT.

SALARY/WAGE   DATE REPORTING TO WORK

APPROVED   1.   2.   3.

EMPLOYMENT MANAGER   DEPT. HEAD   GENERAL MANAGER

FIGURE 15-6   *Job Application. (continued)*

questions. Avoid crossing out your answers, writing too large or too small, or making smudges on the paper. You will avoid these errors if you plan ahead. Think about your answer and the space you have for it before you write it down.

- **Be honest in all your answers.** Your signature means that you have answered each question truthfully and to the best of your ability. It is a legal document once it is signed, and being untruthful is usually considered grounds for refusing employment or, if discovered later, for dismissal. If a question does not apply to you, draw a straight line or write NA for not applicable. This lets the employer know that you *did* read the question.

If the application asks for a desired salary and you have little or no experience, write *starting wage.* If you are experienced and have extensive education, write *negotiable.* **Negotiable** means that you want to discuss salary.

on the job

Lorene saw a job in the newspaper that she thought sounded interesting. She quickly put together a resume and letter of application, and called the company for an application form. The company suggested she bring in her letter and resume and at that time she could fill out the form. She stopped on her way home from her present job to turn in her paperwork. Just as she got out of the car, she proofed her resume, spotted a couple of spelling errors, and corrected them with a red pen. She only had a red pen with her. She didn't have her social security number. She had to guess at the addresses of her last two employers. She forgot to sign her letter of application, and she didn't see the signature line on the application form.

Did Lorene give a good first impression? Do you think she has damaged her chances of getting an interview?

LETTER OF APPLICATION

If you apply for a job through the mail or if you need to visit the company to drop off the application package, it is appropriate to include a letter of introduction with your resume. This letter is called a **letter of application** or cover letter. If you apply for the position, and the employer asks for an application letter via e-mail, the letter would be called a cover message. This letter or message is an important document. The application letter or message will create the first impression of you for the employer. If you really want the position, invest the time to create a brief, but strong message.

The letter must

- be keyed and formatted so that it is easy to read.
- be organized logically.
- be clean and neat.
- be brief.
- be keyed accurately on $8\frac{1}{2} \times 11$ inch good quality paper that matches your resume paper.

Keep your application letter short (under 300 words). If your cover letter is longer than one page, you are perhaps trying to put in too much information. Employers are busy people and are looking for a brief introduction to you.

There are seven steps to writing a successful letter of application. Refer to Figure 15-7 to see how the letter is set up.

Step 1: Your Address.
Include your street address, name of city, state, and ZIP code.

Step 2: Date.
The month, day, and year of the writing of the letter.

Step 3: Inside Address and Salutation.
Include where the letter is going and to whom. A greeting to the person receiving the letter is called the **salutation**. If you do not know who will receive the letter, use a

8121 Imperial Circle   **(Step #1)**
Lincoln, NE 68506
July 17, 2005   **(Step #2)**

Personnel Office
Value Supermarket   **(Step #3)**
P.O. Box 832
Lincoln, NE 68506

Dear Personnel Director:

I am seeking the position you advertised for an inventory clerk in the grocery business in the Sunday edition of the *Lincoln Star*. Your need for someone who is interested in the grocery business is an excellent match to my experience and enthusiasm for the grocery business.   **(Step #4)**

My experience in the grocery store business has been interesting and rewarding. Presently I am working the customer service desk of Sumner's Grocery Store. My duties include cashing checks, selling postage stamps, helping customers find products, ordering special products for customers, and stocking shelves. I have had some formal training in computer work and inventory control. Enclosed is my resume for your review.   **(Step #5)**

I will welcome the opportunity to come in for an interview to discuss the position at your convenience. My telephone number is 555-4588. Please call me any day before 1 p.m.   **(Step #6)**

Sincerely, **(Step #7)**

(Sign your letter in this space.)

Dean Franklin Burkholder

Enclosure: Resume

FIGURE 15-7   *Letter of Application.*

general salutation, such as Dear Personnel Director or Dear Human Resources Manager. If you know the name of the director or manager, use it.

Step 4: First Paragraph of the Letter.
Explain why you are writing the letter. Keep your statements simple. You are writing the letter to apply for a job. Tell the reader where you learned of the job opening.

Step 5: Second Paragraph of the Letter.
Write two or three good sentences about yourself that you think will be important to the employer. Give only information about yourself that is related to the job for which you are applying. This is a very important paragraph because it talks about why you are ideal for the position. The advertisement to which you are responding should give

Technology at Work

The information in this chapter shows you just one sample of a resume and job application letter. Of course, there are many variations, and you may want to see how they look. Check these Web sites for additional information on creating resumes and writing letters of application. You will also pick up some additional job application tips and recommendations at these sites.

http://www.jobweb.com/
Resumes_Interviews/resume_guide/
sampleres.html

http://www.jobweb.com/search/sitemap
.html

Many large companies are using text-searching or artificial-intelligence software to track resumes. These systems use optical scanners to input resumes or accept resume files transmitted through e-mail or a Web site. They then search the resumes for the skills needed to match one of their job openings. Use the following guidelines for making your resume scannable and/or cyber-ready:

- Use specific words in your resume that you think companies will use to perform key searches.
- Study current job listings for popular key words appropriate to the field in which you are interested. Put these key words in your resume in a coherent and well-worded manner.
- Try to use these key words as nouns rather than as verbs in your resume.
- Use a typeface such as Helvetica or Courier at a size of 12 points or a little larger.
- Do not use underline, bold, italic, bullets, or graphics in your resume.
- Print the resume in letter quality, or transmit it as an ASCII or text-only file.
- If you are printing your resume, use white or off-white paper rather than colored paper.
- Avoid folding or creasing a printed resume.

you a good idea of what information should be included and which skills or aptitudes you should highlight. You should refer the reader to your enclosed resume in this section of the letter.

Step 6: Final Paragraph of the Letter.
Ask for an interview. Tell the reader where, when, and how to reach you. Invite the reader to contact you. It is also okay to say, "I'll follow up with you in a few days (or by the end of the week)." If you say you are going to follow up, do so.

Step 7: Closing.
Use a business closing to the letter. A good closing would be "Sincerely." Sign the letter. If you sign the letter, it shows your attention to detail and it is good business etiquette. Be sure to place "Enclosure" below your typed name.

Be sure to proofread your letter of application several times. Mistakes in a letter of application are totally unacceptable. Notice as you proofread and edit your letter how many sentences begin with "I." Rewrite a few of these to make the activities or the information the subject of the sentence.[3] Check to be sure that your letter uses strong words. For example, "Your need for someone who is interested in the grocery business is an excellent match with my experience in and enthusiasm for the grocery business." This would be a better statement than "Please consider me for the inventory clerk opening."

chec**k***point*

1. What step needs to be taken before you prepare your resume?

    _____

    _____

    _____

2. What supplies should you carry to a session where you will be completing an application form?

    _____

    _____

    _____

3. What do you mean if you write "negotiable" in reference to salary on an application form?

    _____

    _____

    _____

4. Why is the letter of application important?

    _____

    _____

    _____

5. Place a + (plus sign) by the item(s) that will assist you in being a successful applicant. Place a − (minus sign) by the item(s) that will not assist you in being a successful applicant.
    a. _____ Failing to follow up on your application.
    b. _____ Signing your application letter.
    c. _____ Preparing a neat, well-written cover letter.
    d. _____ Stretching the truth on your application form.
    e. _____ Keying a neat, well-prepared resume.
    f. _____ Skipping the preparation of a list of references.
    g. _____ Ignoring application questions that you don't think pertain to you.
    h. _____ Using as a closing the phrase "Your Friend."

applications

1. Prepare a well-organized resume for yourself. Before you begin, go back to the inventory list of your qualifications and interests that you completed in Application 1 on page 417. This list will help you get started on the resume. Include appropriate personal information, education information, previous job experiences, personal interests (only if applicable to the job), and references (on a separate page; see Application 2 below). The resume should be one that you could use in applying for any job. Be sure that the resume is keyed perfectly. Have a teacher or someone you know who employs people review and critique your resume.

2. Prepare a list of people you might use as references with any resume. (Think about employers, teachers, coaches, school counselors, ministers, scoutmasters, and others who would be able to comment on your work or character.) The list you used in Application 1 above is a good start. If you are likely to be searching for a job in the near future, contact these individuals to get their permission to be used as references, then gather the needed information (names, titles, addresses, telephone numbers) and prepare a references sheet that you could give a prospective employer.

3. Rewrite the following application letter in the space provided (or key the letter on a separate sheet of paper). Your letter should meet the guidelines established in this chapter. Use your home address as a return address. The letter should provide a good introduction for Elwood Kile.

Company's name and address:

Schwarz Paper Company
Carlsbad, CA 32630-2669
800 Pacific Street
Candace Imes, Personnel manager

I want to come to work at your paper company as a shipping clerk. I will call you for an interview next week. If you want to call me before next week, you can try to reach me on my cell phone (724)343-3433. One of my friends works for your company and she said that she wanted me to apply. My friend is Claudia Osberg. She thinks I would make a great shipping clerk. I graduated from high school two years ago and I've been looking for a good job since that time. I enjoyed my math and accounting classes. I have been working at the Burger Time Restaurant and I receive the supplies, wait on customers, and I have assisted with the franchise accounting. My resume is enclosed. After you review the letter, you will know I am the man for the job. Sincerely, Elwood Kile

---

---

4. Prepare a letter of application using the format presented in this section. Following the steps given, assume you are applying for a job at the Goodline Diary Company. You select a job that you think could be found at a diary company that would suit your experience, qualifications, and interests—factory work, quality control work in quality assurance, janitorial services, or office work. Alternatively, you might wish to select an ad from the local paper and write a letter using the ad as your guideline.

The Job Interview

This is your big chance. You have submitted your letter of application and a resume, and you have completed an application form. The employer is interested in you or he or she would not have taken the time to schedule an interview.

PREPARING FOR THE INTERVIEW

Learn all you can about the company before you go for the interview. If you have had any contact with the company or ever used one of its products, be prepared to say something positive about it. Be sure that you know what products or services are provided by the business.

FIGURE 15-8 *Turn off your cell phone or pager before entering the office of a future employer for an interview.*

Have everything you may need at the interview ready to take with you. These include your social security number, two black pens and a pencil, an extra copy of your resume, and a list of your references. Place your resume and references in a file folder or envelope to keep them fresh. By all means, turn off your cell phone or pager before you enter the office of the interviewer (see Figure 15-8). It would be considered very rude and distracting to get a call or page during the interview.

Consider your personal appearance as you prepare for the interview. The clothes you select should be based on the type of job for which you are applying. If you are applying for a construction job or factory work, you may want to wear neat, clean work clothes. If you are applying for an office or sales job, wear business attire. Men should wear a dress shirt, slacks, and a tie. Women should wear a businesslike dress, suit, or skirt and blouse. A well-tailored matching pantsuit is acceptable in most companies, but you may want to check out the attire before you go for the interview.

If you are in doubt as to what to wear, walk by the company to see what employees are wearing as they leave work or go to lunch. Dress as the employees dress and you cannot go wrong, although it may be a good idea to dress a little better than the employees if attire is casual. It isn't necessary to buy a new interview outfit, but make sure that whatever you wear is clean and in perfect repair. The interview requires a sharp appearance, because first impressions are so important. You will want to look your best.

Of course, be sure to attend to personal hygiene. Shower or bathe and brush your teeth, of course, and be certain to use deodorant, but avoid excessive use of perfume, cologne, or aftershave. You want the interviewer to remember you and your qualifications, not your smell.

INTERVIEW QUESTIONS

Be prepared to answer the standard interview questions. Please review and practice answering the standard questions in Figure 15-9. Your answers should be complete and honest and consistent with the information you have provided in your letter of application, resume, and application form. Remember that these questions may or may not be asked. Each employer has his or her own set of questions.

You may want to have a friend ask you the standard interview questions as practice for the real interview. Be sure you answer the questions honestly. Don't just give the answers that you think the employer wants to hear; give the answers that express your thoughts and feelings. There are two excellent Web sites that will be of further help to you as you think about possible interview questions and your responses. Check out http://www.sla.org/content/jobs/index.cfm and http://www.pohly.com/interview.html

THE INTERVIEW PROCESS

The interview is a chance for the interviewer to meet you. You have prepared yourself, and you will interview well. Be on time. You should arrive at least five minutes before your scheduled interview. If you are not familiar with the area, drive by the area the day before the interview. As you drive by, check out the availability of parking. Go to the interview *alone*!

Introducing Yourself

Introduce yourself to whoever is in the reception area of the hiring office. Speak loudly enough to be heard, and do not forget to *smile* ! Being courteous to the receptionist is especially important since this is the first person who will have met you at the office. Rude or unkind behavior may be reported later to the interviewer. The person in the reception area probably will take you to meet the interviewer or call him or her to come to get you in the reception area. Introduce yourself to the interviewer and speak confidently. Use the interviewer's name if possible. For example, say, "Good morning, Mr. Jones. I'm Dean Burkholder."

STANDARD INTERVIEW QUESTIONS

Are you looking for temporary or permanent work?

What do you want to be doing in five years?

Why do you want to work for this company?

How did you become interested in this company?

What jobs have you held?

Why did you leave those jobs?

Do you prefer working alone or with others?

What are your strengths? What are your weaknesses?

What do you like to do in your spare time?

What makes you think you can do this job?

Why should I hire you?

FIGURE 15-9 *Interview questions.*

Do not offer to shake hands unless the interviewer offers first. However, be ready to shake hands. When shaking hands, grasp the interviewer's hand firmly. Limp handshakes are not impressive. However, crushing handshakes are not acceptable at all.

Don't sit until you are offered a seat. When you sit, be relaxed but sit straight in the chair. No slouching allowed. Do not place any of your belongings on the employer's desk. Put your things beside you, in your lap, or on the floor.

Responding to Questions

As the interviewer begins asking questions, talk freely. The interviewer will likely ask you **open-ended** questions. These are questions that require more than just a yes or no answer or a one-word answer. For example, if you are asked what subject you enjoyed most in school, do not say, "English," and then stop. You might say, "I enjoyed English because it provided me the opportunity to learn more about literature. I also enjoyed the opportunity to put my thoughts on paper." It is never appropriate to try and be "cute" or funny by saying something like: "I enjoyed recess."

If you do not know an answer, say you do not know. Do not try to fake it. Be honest and sincere in answering all questions.

Also, do not be afraid of a moment's silence as you contemplate a question that has been asked. Indicate that you heard the question and are thinking about it, either by saying something like "let me think about that a moment" or simply "hmmm," so the interviewer will understand your silence. Don't let the silence last too long, but use it to collect your thoughts. Interviewers will understand that you cannot be prepared for every question, and they will appreciate your thinking about what they've asked. As time goes by, however, there will be fewer questions that surprise you.

It is illegal for an interviewer to ask questions about the following topics:
- Your age (unless they need proof in the form of a work permit)
- Place of birth (it would give national origin)
- Race or color
- Religion
- Marital status

If the interviewer asks you questions that you feel are inappropriate and have nothing to do with your ability to fill the position, you must decide quickly how to handle them. You could say, "I'll be happy to answer that question if you first tell me how you will use the information." Or, if you feel that the interviewer doesn't know the question is inappropriate, you may just want to answer it. If you are hired, you may want to share with the interviewer at a later time that he or she shouldn't ask questions that are illegal under the Fair Employment Practices Act.

During the questions, keep your eyes on the interviewer, and try to meet his or her eyes often. The following are absolutes in the interview setting.
- Keep your hands still.
- Never chew gum or smoke during an interview.
- Do not lean over the interviewer's desk.
- Never read or give the impression you are reading items on the interviewer's desk.
- Keep a pleasant smile.
- Keep eye contact with the interviewer.

Listening

Listening during the interview is an important key for success. Listen as the interviewer introduces himself or herself, so you are certain to get the name and title correct. Listen to the information anyone may give you about the job and the company; it may help you formulate your own questions or may answer questions you had. Listen so you understand each question. If you do not listen carefully and misinterpret a question, you may jump ahead and answer a question you have not heard. Listen to hints about how this job might or might not suit your needs or fit your qualifications or preferences.

Asking Questions

The interviewer will probably give you a chance to ask questions toward the end of the interview. Be prepared. If you are not, you will appear uninterested in the job. All of your questions should be related to the job. Some sample questions might include:

Why is this position open?
What are the work hours for this position?
What challenges might I anticipate in this position?
Is there an opportunity to work overtime?
What training does the company provide?
What are the expectations for the person who will fill this position?

If nothing has been said about salary, it is appropriate to ask what the salary is for the position. However, this should not be the first question you ask. You would want to ask about the compensation in a way to show that you are interested in all aspects of the position: "Could you review for me the compensation and benefits offered with this position?"

Be sure that the questions you ask have not been answered previously at another point in the interview.

Closing the Interview

Your cue to depart from the interview is when the interviewer stops asking questions and you have no more questions to ask. The interviewer will probably say something such as, "Well, if you have no more questions . . ." to let you know that he or she is finished. If you do not have any more questions, smile and rise in preparation for departure. If you have not been offered the job, ask when you will be notified of the interviewer's decision. Thank the interviewer for his or her time and leave. You may offer to shake hands. Again, be sure it is a firm handshake.

"Nobody ever listened himself out of a job."

—Calvin Coolidge

Follow Up

After the interview, there is one more opportunity for you to impress the interviewer. Write him or her a thank-you letter. The letter will bring your name to the mind of the interviewer again. The letter should be brief, neat, well written, and keyed or handwritten. Simply thank the interviewer for the time spent with you. Mention that you are interested in the position (if you are). If you forgot to say something in the interview about one of your qualifications, you can mention it in the thank-you letter. If you are not interested in the position, a thank-you letter is also in order.

The thank-you letter should be sent even if you do not want the position. You want to stay on good terms with all employers since you may be interested in another position in this organization at some time in the future. Provide a courteous and plausible reason for not pursuing the job opportunity. Perhaps you want to continue your education, you want to pursue another type of position, or some other reason that would keep the lines of communication open for the future. Send your letter immediately after the interview. Figure 15-10 on page 444 is an example of an acceptable thank-you letter.

8121 Imperial Circle
Lincoln, NE 68506-1836
July 19, 2005

Mr. Don Wilson
Personnel Department
Value Supermarket
P.O. Box 832
Lincoln, NE 68506

Dear Mr. Wilson:

Thank you for the time you spent with me yesterday discussing the inventory clerk position at Value Supermarket. I appreciate your making the extra effort to show me around the store. The store is beautiful and looks like a very pleasant place to work. I am very much interested in the position. I believe my inventory experiences that we discussed will be valuable in this position.

I look forward to hearing from you about the hiring decision soon.

Sincerely,

(Signature)

Dean Franklin Burkholder

FIGURE 15-10   *Sample thank-you letter.*

Smart Tip ▼ ▼ ▼

Job hunters often make the same mistakes. Avoid this list of common errors.

- **Poor eye contact. You may be nervous and a bit unsure of yourself. This situation may cause you to avert your eyes. Fight this.**
- **No goal. Don't say, "Any job will do" or "I'll take anything." Don't sound desperate.**
- **Poor appearance. Wear appropriate clothing. Look your best.**
- **No questions prepared. If you don't have questions, you will appear unprepared or uninterested.**
- **Little enthusiasm. Enthusiasm is what the interviewer is seeking.**
- **Asking about salary and benefits too soon. These are important points, but don't ask about them as your first questions.**
- **Not asking for the job. Tell the interviewer you are interested (if you are) and indicate that you think the job is a good match for you.**

▲ ▲ ▲ ▲ ▲ ▲ ▲ ▲ ▲

SELF CHECK

Are you ready for the job search? Use this checklist in preparing for the job search process. (You may want to make several copies of items 7 through 13 to use for each job for which you apply.)

1. __ Determined my qualifications and interests.
2. __ Discussed my aptitudes with others.
3. __ Networked with friends.
4. __ Prepared a resume.
5. __ Practiced interviewing.
6. __ Prepared my list of references.
7. __ Prepared a job application letter.
8. __ Proofread my application documents.
9. __ Reviewed the rules about preparing the job application.
10. __ Planned what to wear to the interview.
11. __ Studied the products and/or services of the business.
12. __ Prepared questions to ask the interviewer.
13. __ Sent thank-you follow-up letter.

chec**k**point

1. What should you plan *not* to take with you to the interview?

_____

_____

_____

_____

2. How should you dress for an interview?

_____

_____

_____

_____

3. What questions are illegal or inappropriate to ask of an applicant?

_____

_____

_____

_____

4. Why is it important to listen carefully during an interview?

_____

_____

_____

_____

5. How do you know when the interview is over?

_____

_____

_____

_____

6. What does sending a follow-up letter accomplish?

_____

_____

_____

_____

_____

_____

_____

_____

_____

_____

_____

_____

7. Place a + (plus sign) by the item(s) that will assist you in being a successful applicant. Place a − (minus sign) by the item(s) that will not assist you in being a successful applicant.

____ a. Taking a friend with you to the interview.

____ b. Wearing a clean and pressed pantsuit.

____ c. Keeping your cell phone on to impress the interviewer that you are in demand.

____ d. Keeping eye contact with the interviewer.

____ e. Saying that you will take any job available.

____ f. Chewing gum so that you appear relaxed.

____ g. Listening carefully to information provided by the interviewer.

____ h. Sending a follow-up letter thanking the interviewer for his or her time indicating you are interested or not interested in the position available.

applications

1. Write your answers to the following standard interview questions. What will you say if you are asked the following questions?

a. What do you want to be doing in five years?

_____

_____

_____

_____

b. What are your strengths? What are your weaknesses?

_____

_____

_____

_____

c. What do you like to do in your spare time?

_____

_____

_____

_____

2. Write a sample follow-up letter and key it as you would for a job interview situation. Assume you have just interviewed for a bank loan officer trainee program. You are very much interested in the position. You talked with Josie Harris, Personnel Director. Use the name and address of a bank in your community.

3. Assume you have just interviewed for a management trainee position at a finance company. You are not interested in the position because you would be required to enroll in an out-of-state training program. You talked with Monica Bushnell at the Liberty Finance, 820 Braddock Point, Columbia, SC 29201. Write a follow-up letter; then key it and proofread it.

15

chapter

Points to Remember

Review the following points to determine what you remember from the chapter.

- Finding an enjoyable and satisfying job is hard work. Prepare for the job campaign by listing your qualifications and interests. Focus your search based on these lists. Also, consider your aptitudes—your natural talents and abilities. You can examine your aptitudes by completing an aptitude test and listening to others tell you about your strengths. Once you have determined your qualifications, interests, and aptitudes, you need to begin looking at resources that will help you find employment. Let everyone know that you are looking for a job. People can be a valuable job resource. Read the help-wanted ads in the newspaper. Visit your state employment agency or a private employment agency. Keep in mind that a private agency is a for-profit business and fees may be charged. Check with government offices, school placement services, temporary work agencies, and bulletin boards that post job opportunities. Do not be afraid to walk into a business and ask for an application.

- Prepare a resume to advertise yourself to others. The resume should include the following: personal information, education, work experience, certifications or licensing, personal interests if applicable to the position, and references on a separate sheet of paper. You may also want to include an objective line, if you know fairly specifically what you want to do. The resume should be keyed on good quality paper and should be limited to one to two pages.

- Special care should be taken when you complete an application form for any position. Be sure that you are prepared (with pens and information) to complete the form, that you answer all questions truthfully, and that you take the special care to do neat work. The employer can tell a lot about you by how you complete the form. Read over the entire form before you begin to answer anything in it.

- A letter of application should be sent when you are applying for a position by mail or if you are taking the application letter with you for a preinterview. The letter must be keyed and well prepared. Use good quality paper that matches your resume. Be sure you proofread your application letter. Mistakes are not acceptable.

- The job interview is your chance to shine. Prepare for the interview by finding out all you can about the company, planning what you are going to wear and where the interview is going to take place, reviewing standard interview questions, preparing questions that you wish to ask, and being on time. Go alone to the interview.

- After the interview, follow up with a thank-you letter to the person or persons who interviewed you. Thank-you letters may be keyed or handwritten and should be sent immediately after the interview.

How did you do? Did you remember the main points you studied in the chapter?

key terms

Place the letter of the item in the definition column that matches the key word.

Key Word	Definition
____1. Aptitude	a. Source containing job descriptions, earnings, and anticipated job prospects.
____2. Aptitude tests	b. Indicates to the employer that you want to discuss salary.
____3. Job lead	c. Stopping by human resources and completing a resume even though a job is not posted.
____4. Networking	d. Greeting to the recipient of a letter.
____5. Employment agency	e. Measures your ability to learn something.
____6. Cold canvassing	f. Used by employers to get basic information.
____7. Resume	g. Sharing and exchanging job information.
____8. Application form	h. Information about a possible job opening.
____9. Negotiable	i. Letter of introduction.
___10. Letter of application	j. Written summary of your qualifications for a job.
___11. Salutation	k. Brings together a potential worker and employer to fill a position.
___12. *Occupational Outlook Handbook*	l. Natural talent or the ability or capacity to learn.
___13. Open-ended question	m. Requires more than a one-word answer.

activities and projects

1. Write (key) a letter of application to Mr. Douglas Crosier, 5442 South Cumberland, Columbia, SC 29210. Mr. Crosier is the human resources officer for the Abilene Paper Company. Assume you are qualified for the position he advertised in the *Times Register* for a front-office receptionist. The letter must be keyed. Attach the resume that you have prepared as a part of your work in studying this chapter.

2. Write (key) a follow-up letter to Mr. Crosier. You have had the interview, but you are not interested in working as a receptionist because the pay is low. However, you know they will be hiring factory crews in the fall. You would like to be considered for one of those positions. Draft a few notes below that you will consider using as your reasons for rejecting the position. Then write your letter and key it in appropriate format.

3. Prepare a quality letter of application for the following ad you read in the *Los Angeles Times*. Assume that the position meets your qualifications, aptitudes, and interests.

Well-groomed person desiring to work F/T as host in upscale restaurant. Exp nec. Perm with flexible hrs. No wkend work. Available immed. Write the mgr at Bon Appetite, 28 Longacre Road, Carlsbad, CA 92008.

4. Assume your letter of application got you an interview at the Bon Appetite (see Application 3). Prepare a list of questions you would ask at the interview at the Bon Appetite Restaurant.

5. Research two jobs listed in the *Occupational Outlook Handbook* in which you have an interest. You can locate the handbook at http://www.bls.gov/oco/home.htm or in any city or school library. Record the following information about each job: (1) What does the work of the job include? (2) What training and education is required? (3) What salary might you expect? Discuss your findings with your instructor. As a result of your research, are you going to pursue a position in either of the jobs you reviewed? Why? Why not?

case studies for critical thinking

IN THE WRONG PLACE

Hassam was graduated from high school and was eager to go to work. He took an aptitude test before leaving high school, and he completed an inventory of his qualifications and interests. After taking a good look at himself, Hassam decided that he would like to work in a health occupation. He applied for a position at a hospital. The only work available was a job in the diet kitchen. Hassam accepted the job without applying anywhere else. After two months on the job, he was miserable. The job required that he work a split shift 5 a.m. to 9 a.m. and 4 p.m. to 8 p.m. He had no contact with patients. He found little job satisfaction in filling trays and placing them on carts to be sent to patients.

1. What mistake(s) did Hassam make in selecting the job?

_____

_____

_____

2. Should Hassam stay with the job?

_____

_____

_____

3. Should Hassam try to find other work within the hospital?

_____

_____

_____

4. What additional information would you like to have available to you in order to further assist Hassam?

_____

_____

_____

Case 15.2

FINDING A FUTURE

Rosaria was graduated from high school and spent a year in a community college studying computer-assisted drafting, but she did not complete the program. She was a server at a restaurant for a few months but quit the job because she did not like the work. Rosaria was fired from a job at a recreation center for being frequently late to work. Now she is working for a temporary job service but not earning enough money to be on her own.

1. What suggestions would you make to Rosaria about her future in the work world?

_____

_____

_____

2. Do you think Rosaria's situation is unusual? Why or why not?

_____

_____

_____

3. Should Rosaria list the recreation center on her resume?

_____

_____

_____

Case 15.3

FIRST IMPRESSIONS

Audra applied for a position in an advertising firm. She read the ad in the local paper, and she met the qualifications. She called and received an interview time. She selected from her wardrobe a pair of hip-hugger jeans, a spaghetti-strap shirt, and sandals. She had received compliments on the outfit so she determined it looked good on her. She decided to forget about printing a resume. They could find out whatever they needed to know about her from the application form. Audra and her boyfriend arrived a few minutes late for the interview. Her boyfriend was kind enough to drive her to the interview so she asked him to come in with her rather than sit in the car. She was concerned about her breath so she decided to chew gum during the interview. She didn't prepare any questions for the interview. She thought about it, but decided the questions would come to her during the session. At the close of the interview, she was thanked for coming in for an interview and that she would be informed of her status as a candidate within a few days.

1. Do you think Audra got the job? Why or why not?

_____

_____

_____

2. What suggestions would you have for Audra for the next interview?

_____

_____

_____

3. What do you think about her decision to "forget about" the resume?

_____

_____

_____

4. What other information would you like to know about Audra in order to assist her in getting a job?

_____

_____

_____

Case 15.4

WHAT IS CARLA'S FUTURE?

Carla is a middle-aged woman who has two children in middle school. She is married to a self-employed insurance salesman. Carla has been out of the job market for many years. She is considering going back to work part-time to help out with household expenses and upcoming college expenses. Carla was graduated from high school, completed an office management program at a local community college, and worked as an office manager before her children were born. She applies for an office position at the Allegra Insurance Agency. The advertisement indicates that Allegra is looking for a full-time employee with a pleasing personality, good computer and office skills, access to a car, and willing to do some travel to neighboring communities. Carla gets an interview. As she has graduated from a community college in an office program, she assumes she meets all the qualifications. She tells the interviewer that she will work full-time; she figures that she will work through the school year and then tell them she wants to only work part-time when her children are out of school. The interviewer doesn't specifically ask if she has a car. So, she doesn't say anything about the car situation. They are a one-car family. The interviewer finds Carla a pleasant person. She indicates that she has good office skills. She is offered the position.

1. Should Carla accept the position? Why? Why not?

2. Was Carla truthful with the interviewer? If yes, explain. If no, explain.

3. Do you feel that Carla is qualified for the position? Why or why not?

4. If Carla was graduated from the community college program before her middle school children were born, do you think she has retained the skills learned? Do you anticipate any other problems with her skills?

5. What do you think about Carla's not mentioning that she doesn't have access to a car?

_____

_____

_____

_____

6. How do you think the management at Allegra will react when Carla tell them that she wants to work only part-time when school is out?

_____

_____

_____

_____

7. If she doesn't take the job at Allegra, what advice would you give Carla about her job search?

_____

_____

_____

_____

Workplace Success

| think about it: | Antoinette was overjoyed and eager to begin her new job. She had conducted a great job campaign, interviewed well for a good position |

at Riverside Hospital, and landed the job. When she arrived on her first day, her coworkers greeted her warmly and then went on with their busy days. Her supervisor gave her stacks of forms, procedures, and instructions. She answered countless e-mail and telephone messages, but had to promise to get back to patients because she could not locate the information she needed. She dropped a box of files and had to spend about thirty minutes re-alphabetizing them. By 5 p.m., she was near tears. It seemed as if there was so much to learn and everything was taking place so fast. She wondered how she would ever learn everything that was required. One of her coworkers, Simpson, walked out to the parking lot with her and said, "I'm sure this was a confusing day for you. I remember my first day. I thought I would never catch on to everything. However, each day got a little easier. See you tomorrow." Antoinette took a deep breath and said, "Thanks. I needed to hear those words." Antoinette recognized that her earlier concerns were normal for the first day on a new job. Things would get better and she would succeed on this new job.

© BRAND X PICTURES

Do you think Antoinette's feelings at the end of the first day were normal? Were Simpson's comments appropriate?

chapter focus

After completing this chapter, you should be able to:

1. Prepare for the first day on the job.

2. Identify the elements essential for keeping a job.

3. Establish goals and create a career path.

4. Conduct yourself professionally in a performance appraisal.

5. Determine if and when you should change jobs.

Chapter Highlights

16.1 **First Day on the Job**

16.2 **Keeping Your Job**

16.3 **Planning Your Career**

16.4 **Moving Ahead**

Your first day on the job is an important one. You only get one chance to make a good first impression, so make it a good one. You'll probably be a bit nervous and uneasy, but you will be eager to get started and show you have the knowledge and skills to do the job. You will probably spend a good part of your first day in the human resources department and with your immediate supervisor. You will fill out employment forms, get information about your workplace, and instructions from your supervisor and others.

EMPLOYMENT FORMS

One of your first orders of business at a new job will be to complete payroll and benefits forms. You should be prepared to show your driver's license and social security card for identification and payroll purposes. Every month a portion of your paycheck will be put into a federal social security account called FICA, an abbreviation for Federal Insurance Contributions Act. Your employer matches this sum by putting in an equal amount in your account. You will appreciate the contributions you and your employer have made when you reach retirement age and begin to draw on the benefits.

You will also complete a Form W-4 Employee's Withholding Allowance Certificate. This form authorizes the company to withhold money from your paycheck to pay your federal and state income taxes. The amount withheld from your check depends on your income level, your marital status, and the number of allowances (dependents) you claim. In addition, you must complete Form I-9 Employment Eligibility Verification required by the Department of Homeland Security, U.S. Department of Justice. The purpose of this form is to establish identity and employability. All employees, citizens and noncitizens, hired after November 6, 1986, must complete Section 1 at the time of hiring. The employer verifies and completes other portions and retains the form on file.

You will also complete insurance forms and learn about the benefits package provided by your company. Be sure that you fully understand the insurance and other benefits of the organization. Ask questions! If there are options, for example in your insurance program, you may want to take home the written information and review it before you sign options for disability, dental, eye care, and other insurance. Review all of the material carefully and decide which options are affordable and best meet your needs.

INTRODUCTIONS

You will meet your supervisor and some of your coworkers during the first day on the job. Make every effort to be polite and to appear competent and professional. Also, strive to remember the names of coworkers. It may help to repeat names of coworkers as they are introduced. "Alicia, I would like you to meet one of your coworkers. This is Jeff McNeely." Alicia might reply, "Pleasure to meet you." However, a better reply would be "Jeff McNeely, it is a pleasure to meet you" or "I am pleased to meet you, Jeff." However, by saying the full name, Alicia will be more likely to remember Jeff's name.

Suggestions for the first day include:
- Make sure your appearance is neat and clean. People notice your hair, teeth, complexion, eyes, and, most of all, your smile.
- Walk with confidence and purpose.
- Dress appropriately for your organization. When in doubt about what to wear, dress conservatively and professionally.

- Offer a firm handshake to supervisors and coworkers you meet.
- Do not hesitate to introduce yourself to others. Say something like, "Hi, I'm [name]. I just started working in the accounting department." Others will automatically introduce themselves. If you don't hear or understand the full name, ask for it. "I'm sorry. I didn't hear your full name."

JOB DESCRIPTION

You were probably given a job description during the job interview process, but it is a good idea to revisit it when you start the job. A **job description** is a written explanation of the tasks, duties, and responsibilities of a particular job.[1] Job descriptions are important for a number of reasons. Note the following about job descriptions:

- They clarify who is responsible for what within the organization. They also help define relationships between individuals, between departments, etc.
- They help the employee understand the responsibilities of the position. This not only enables the employee to assess the importance of everything he or she is accountable for, but also provides a sense of where the job fits into the company as a whole.
- They help job applicants, employees, supervisors, and human resources professionals at every stage in the employment relationship, from recruitment to retirement. They provide information about the training, knowledge, and skills needed for a job. They can prevent misunderstandings by telling employees what they need to know about their jobs.
- They help management analyze and improve the company's organizational structure. They reveal whether all responsibilities are adequately covered.

- They provide a basis for job evaluation, wage and salary surveys, and an equitable wage and salary structure.

As the job description is a very important document, read it, ask questions about it, and after you have been on the job for awhile, review it to be sure that it adequately represents what you are doing on the job. If not, visit with your supervisor about it.

RULES OF THE JOB

Rules for employees are a little different in every organization. A new employee learns these rules and makes every effort to comply

on the job

Olivia was anxious about her first day on the job. She was eager to get to work. When she arrived at her new workplace, she reported to the human resources office. She completed her Forms W-4 , I-9, and insurance forms and listened to the explanation of the benefits package of the company. She was then taken to her workstation and introduced to her supervisor, who walked her through the entire facility so she could get a picture of the full operation. The supervisor showed her where to clock in and the location of the restrooms and cafeteria. She talked about the company rules as she took Olivia around the facility. They then went to her office where Olivia was given a company handbook and a briefing on company rules, policies, and safety procedures. They went back to Olivia's workstation, and her supervisor introduced two of her coworkers. Olivia glanced at her watch and realized she had been on the job for nearly four hours and had not yet begun to work. She was eager to start her job.

Would you perceive that Olivia's experience would be a usual first day in some facilities? How would you compare Olivia's first day with Antoinette's first day as described on page 459 in the "Think About It" scenario.

with them. The rules of the workplace are most often found in an employee handbook. If you do not understand a rule, ask your supervisor for clarification. If you choose to work for a small company, such a handbook may not exist, but this does not mean there are no rules. You will need to ask about them.

The excuse "I didn't know about the rule" is never acceptable. Learn the rules of your workplace and follow them.

Some of the rule topics you will want to check into immediately are:

- Expected work hours
- Parking arrangements
- Breaks and meal arrangements
- Security and identification procedures
- Use of company equipment and services—computer, e-mail, Internet access, telephone, fax, and copier
- Vacation, sick, and personal leave policies
- Smoking policy on company property
- Whom to call if you are ill or unable, for a good reason, to come to work.

Some of these basic policies and rules may have been explained to you at the interview. If not, be sure you ask about the policies before the end of your first workday. You may want to keep a small notebook handy and jot down questions as they occur to you so that when the opportunity presents itself you can check on the concerns and/or questions that have come up during your first day.

For another example, if you are in any type of medical, pharmaceutical, human resources, or healthcare facility, you must be aware of the rights of patients and others and how the Health Insurance Portability and Accounting Act (HIPAA) affects records, conversations, privacy of information, and other communications.[2]

Safety Rules

In addition to the general rules, a company may also have safety rules that are published and posted for all employees. Safety rules are most important if you are employed in a manufacturing setting or an area where heavy equipment or hazardous materials are being used. You may be required to wear safety shoes, gloves, and glasses/goggles, a helmet, a mask, or clothing that protects you against hazardous conditions. Your company must enforce these rules to meet government and insurance standards.

Every employee has the right to safe working conditions. If you are unsure about how to operate a piece of equipment, ask for help. Don't ever begin using machinery or equipment until you have had instruction. Be sure to observe all safety rules and report any unsafe conditions immediately to your supervisor.

"Understood" Rules

Some rules are not written, but rather they are "understood." It is wise to learn these rules quickly and follow them. For example, a company may prefer that no one wear jeans or t-shirts with words on them to work. This may not be a written policy or rule. It is simply not done in the company. You will learn these unwritten rules by observing, listening, and questioning. Other rules you will instinctively know. For example, *be on time, go to work every day*, and *return from breaks and lunch on time*. If you are in a food service position, you would be expected to know that *hand washing, proper handling of dinnerware, and good health habits* would be essential. In all positions, it may not be written, but you are expected to be kind, courteous, and thoughtful of your customers and coworkers. Above all, you are expected to put in an honest day's work for an honest day's pay.

che**c**kpoint

1. What is the purpose of Form W-4?

   _____

   _____

   _____

2. How will you introduce yourself to a coworker?

   _____

   _____

   _____

3. What technique could you use to help remember the names of new coworkers?

   _____

   _____

   _____

4. What is a job description? Why is it something you will want to review and study with care?

   _____

   _____

   _____

5. What rules of the job should you make sure that you know by the end of your first day of employment?

   _____

   _____

   _____

6. Why are safety rules in the workplace necessary?

   _____

   _____

   _____

applications

1. Obtain a current copy of a Form W-4 and Form I-9 and review the contents of the form. The W-4 form can be obtained from the IRS Web site (www.irs.gov) under "Forms & Publications." Form I-9 can be obtained from the U.S. Department of Justice, Department of Homeland Security (http://uscis.gov/). Determine how you will complete the forms. Write below where you think you would get the information required to complete the W-4 and I-9 forms.

2. Visit an industrial organization in your area and ask to see copies of the safety rules of the company. Also, ask to see the safety warnings, safety lines, and precautions that are in place in the company. If the company is large, it will probably employ a safety engineer. Ask if you can interview the safety engineer and ask questions about safety precautions and equipment required in the organization. List some of the questions you would ask the engineer or another person tasked to do safety inspections and regulations.

3. It is your first day on the job in a large telemarketing firm. Write out three greetings that you might extend to your coworkers.

a.

b.

c.

4. List five unwritten rules of the job that you would anticipate if you were employed as a teller in a large bank.

a. _____

b. _____

c. _____

d. _____

e. _____

5. Research the requirements for privacy under the HIPAA regulations. Interview a pharmacist, a physician's assistant, or someone else in the medical field to learn how these regulations have changed the way they handle records and deal with patient privacy.

_____

_____

_____

_____

_____

_____

_____

_____

_____

_____

_____

_____

Keeping Your Job

In today's competitive workplace, you will need to begin thinking about "how do I keep this job?" Job insurance is up to you; at the minimum, you will need to care for your work area, develop good work habits, cooperate with coworkers, follow instructions, and pay attention to workplace politics.

WORK ENVIRONMENT

The work environment includes the physical aspects, such as your work area, as well as other aspects, such as your daily work habits.

Work Area

Your employer is required to provide a safe place for you to work. You are responsible for keeping your work area in a safe and good condition. Your work area should be kept neat and organized in order for you to perform most efficiently. A tidy work area will signal to others that you are a professional. If there is a problem with your area, you will need to tell the supervisor so that the problem can be corrected. If you share your work area with coworkers, you must respect their rights and feelings in order to help maintain a good, safe work environment for everyone.

Work Habits

Establish good work habits from the beginning of your new employment. This list of habits will start you off on the right foot with your employer.

- Do not waste supplies.
- Take orders and follow directions willingly.
- Follow the "understood rules."
- Ask questions and remember the answers.
- Dress appropriately for the type of work you are doing.
- Be pleasant and friendly.

EMPLOYMENT INSURANCE

There are several personal characteristics that you will want to exhibit on the job to ensure that you keep your position. These characteristics are detailed in the following paragraphs.

Do your best

Your employer and coworkers expect you to do the job you were hired to do. Doing your job to the best of your ability has another benefit. It allows you to feel good about yourself and build your self-esteem. Self-esteem is necessary for job success. The benefits of doing your best are shown in Figure 16-1.

Do not just do what you are told. Employees who truly do their best notice

Safety is of concern to employers and should be of great concern to you.

© DIGITAL VISION

DOING YOUR BEST

Approval by your coworkers.
Approval by your supervisor.
Continued employment.
Improved level of self-esteem.

FIGURE 16-1   *The benefits of doing your best.*

other jobs that need to be done. They do the little extras without being told. Put effort and energy into whatever you do on the job. The process of starting a task or project without being told to do so is called showing **initiative**. If you see a task that you would like to do but need additional knowledge or training, ask if training is available or seek experiences outside the workplace.

Be productive

The amount of work you produce in some positions is very important. In fact, in some positions you may be paid by the amount of work you produce—the number of bricks placed in a day, the number of lines of programming code written, the number of garments sewn, the number of patients seen, or the number of customer calls made. Your employer is always looking for quality work done in an efficient manner.

Look for ways to improve

After you are comfortable and feel competent doing your job, look for new knowledge or skills that you can master. (Review the ON THE JOB scenario. Danielle was seeking new knowledge as a way to improve.) Watch the experienced workers do their jobs. Ask them to show you how to do some advanced tasks. Do not be afraid to ask for new, challenging assignments and opportunities.

Let your supervisor know when you are willing to take on additional responsibilities. However, before you do this, be *sure*

on the job

Danielle was hired to be an administrative assistant in a large environmental agency. She had good computer skills and spent many hours at the computer each day. Her supervisor did many presentations to citizen groups, service clubs, and other agencies regarding environmental rules and regulations. On several occasions, Danielle had the opportunity to hear her supervisor, Harriet Tipton, speak. Harriet was a good speaker and held her audience well. Danielle, however, noticed the audience was having trouble seeing the charts, figures, and graphs Harriet was placing on an overhead projector. Danielle was aware of the advantages of using PowerPoint presentations and thought to herself, "I could strengthen her presentation if I knew how to use PowerPoint." She checked her equipment and found that the software for building PowerPoint presentations was available in her agency. Danielle called the local community college and asked what training might be available. She was told that a short course was available at a minimal cost.

What are the next steps for Danielle? Should she tell Ms. Tipton that her presentations need improvement? Should she enroll in the course and surprise her supervisor with her new skills?

you are doing an excellent job on your present duties. If opportunities for extra training are made available, sign up. The more you learn and do on the job, the more valuable you are to your employer. If you are not performing as well as you would like in a particular area, seek training or help.

Accept responsibility for your job

You will make mistakes because you are human. Do not be afraid to admit your mistakes, but be sure that you learn from your mistakes. Whatever

"Have confidence that if you have done a little thing well, you can do a bigger thing well, too."

—DAVID STOREY

> *"Great services are not canceled by one act or by one single error."*
>
> —BENJAMIN DISRAELI

> *"Those who duck responsibility will also duck success."*
>
> —UNKNOWN

you do, do not try to hide your mistakes or blame them on someone else or ignore them. Accept responsibility for your work and your errors. Keep upgrading your work habits and your work skills. The more confidence you have, the fewer errors you will make.

Have a great attitude

The "can do" attitude shows you believe in your own ability to succeed. This type of attitude will help you accomplish your assigned job tasks to the best of your ability.

It may sound a little trite, but why not display the words *can do* prominently somewhere in your immediate work area? Each time you see the "can do," you will be reminded that you do have the ability to succeed.

Employers can teach you the skills you need. You, on the other hand, must develop good attitudes. The following Smart Tip would be a good checklist to review every week that you are on the job.

Use this Smart Tip as a personal checklist each day to see how you are doing.

Smart Tip ▼ ▼ ▼

Show your good attitude by:
- **listening to suggestions.**
- **showing a desire to please.**
- **giving a day's work for a day's pay.**
- **not making excuses for errors.**
- **respecting the opinions of others.**
- **trying to see things from the points of view of others.**
- **being willing to change.**
- **complaining seldom, if ever.**
- **helping and praising others.**
- **smiling often.**

▲ ▲ ▲ ▲ ▲ ▲ ▲ ▲ ▲

focus on ethics

Mandy worked in a large company. One of her jobs was to check all incoming office supply invoices against the merchandise received at her company, Travert Computer Ware. She liked her work and had been complimented on the job she was doing. Mondays were always very busy days at Travert. One Monday, Mandy signed, in haste, for a huge order of office supplies from Supply Mart. Mandy did not take the time to check the items received against the invoice. She signed for the materials and set them aside. When things slowed down a bit, Mandy took a look at the invoice. She realized that four large items on the invoice were missing from the merchandise received. Work was going well for her and she didn't want to admit the error. She figured that no one in a company this large would ever know that the items were not in the shipment; therefore, she decided not to mention the shortage to her supervisor.

What may happen as a result of Mandy's decision? What recommendations would you have for Mandy?

Mix with others

Don't allow yourself to be an isolationist. You need to work with your peers, supervisors, and others and be a part of the team. You can learn from others.

Accept criticism positively

You must be prepared to accept suggestions and criticism on the job. Criticism is suggestive remarks about your job performance.

In an earlier chapter you read that criticism is a form of self-improvement. If no one points out what you are doing wrong, you cannot improve. Respond to criticism in a positive way. Do not overreact and assume that you are a failure. Tell yourself you can and will continue to improve. Do not think negatively about the word "criticism." Criticism can be your best friend in the workplace.

Keep a good sense of humor

You have read in earlier chapters about the importance of a sense of humor for fitting in and getting along in the workplace. Having a sense of humor includes being able to laugh at yourself. Know how and when to use humor in the workplace. Do not take yourself so seriously that you forget to laugh. Showing a sense of humor does not include telling jokes that hurt or degrade others or telling jokes that are crude. A person who tells these kinds of jokes is not held in high regard by coworkers or supervisors. Demonstrating a sense of humor does not mean continually telling jokes, acting foolish, pulling pranks and practical jokes, or attempting to be the "company clown." You could get a few laughs from coworkers, but they begin to see you only as a clown. Worse yet, your supervisors might see you as a goof-off.

Treat others with respect

Chapters 7, 8, 9, and 14 were devoted to fitting in and getting along with coworkers, supervisors, and customers. You may want to reread these chapters as you think about the topic of "keeping the job." Getting along with all types of people can be tough. It takes patience and understanding. Accept people and their differences. When you accept someone, you create a beginning point for building a good relationship with that person. For example, if you and a coworker belong to different races,

simply accept that as fact and value that difference. Valuing individual differences means accepting people who are not like you, taking a positive attitude toward differences, learning from others who are different, and recognizing that similarities are more important than differences. You will have coworkers unlike you in gender, race, mental ability, physical condition, age, religion, geographic origin, education, ethnic heritage, culture, and lifestyle.

"Criticism should be a plow that plows a furrow only to sow in it seeds that will grow."

—JEROME P. FLEISHMAN

on the job

Ole was just hired as a clerk for a large state government agency. He was starting to feel comfortable with his new duties and environment. He felt his work was going well. Janice, one of his superiors, had been particularly helpful to him as he learned the requirements of his work. She had coached him in many aspects of the new job. He felt that he owed part of his success to her mentoring. Today Janice tells him that the agency head should be fired—he is ineffective, incompetent, and unreasonable in his deadlines and expectations. She wants Ole to sign a petition to send to the governor's office requesting that the agency head be replaced. Janice tells him that many of his coworkers are signing the petition. She states further that the agency head does not treat women or minorities fairly. Ole has never met the agency head and has no reason to sign such a petition. Janice tells him that if he wants to fit into the organization he had better sign. Ole is troubled by her request and confused about how he should proceed. Ole knows that Janice has been with the agency for a long time and she has an interest in being agency head.

What suggestion(s) would you have for Ole? What do you think about Janice's tactics? How can Ole win in the situation?

Count on your mentor for help and guidance; this person can also lead you through workplace politics.

© GETTY IMAGES/PHOTODISC

FINDING A MENTOR

As you transition into a new position, you are going to need some help in the form of a mentor. A **mentor** is a trusted counselor or guide who is sometimes called a coach. This mentor can be a very valuable resource to you and can help you quickly learn the rules and some of the "understood rules" mentioned earlier in the chapter. Some organizations assign an experienced employee to new employees as a mentor to give them guidance, assistance, and support as they learn a new job. If this is not a policy of your new organization or company, seek out a mentor on your own. Select someone who is experienced and with whom you feel comfortable.

WORKPLACE POLITICS

You will need to keep on top of and understand workplace politics if you want to keep your position. **Workplace politics** is an undefined force in an organization that develops because people want to protect themselves or gain power. The "politicking" that goes on is usually done to benefit an individual rather than to benefit the organization. The best policy is to play fairly and openly with others and leave office politics to the politicians.

Think about an ordinary political campaign. What do the candidates usually talk about? They talk about their good characteristics or record. Candidates also talk about their opponents' bad characteristics. Workplace politics are very similar to what goes on in political campaigns. People talk about their good personal qualities and talk disrespectfully about their supervisors, coworkers, and company officials. You cannot ignore these aspects of your work environment.

Unfortunately people tend to get involved in workplace politics that are

It is important to value differences on the job because it creates a good work environment. It benefits the business and the employees because satisfied workers are productive and happy workers, and it is the law. You may want to review Chapter 14 and reflect on what diversity means to you and your career. In addition, you may find it valuable to research the employment laws and how they apply to employees in your company and/or in your state. Federal and/or state laws are likely to govern various endeavors or behaviors in the workplace.

Businesses are required by law to provide equal employment opportunities to all employees without regard to race, color, religion, gender, national origin, age, disability, or veteran status. In addition to such legal requirements, workplace values dictate that employees treat each other fairly and with respect.

"Every human being, of whatever origin, of whatever station, deserves respect. We must each respect others even as we respect ourselves."

—U THANT

unproductive and destructive to the work environment. Gossip is a part of workplace politics. You may want to refer to Chapter 4, page 80 and reread the section relating to gossip and the rumor mill.

The best way to handle workplace politics is to stay neutral. That means you do not take sides. Be courteous and concerned about all of your coworkers and supervisors and concentrate on doing your job well. Above all, keep confidences.

check✔point

1. **What will result if you "do your best" on the job?**

    _____

    _____

    _____

    _____

2. **When should you let your supervisor know that you are ready for additional duties and assignments?**

    _____

    _____

    _____

    _____

3. **What should you do if you make a mistake on the job? What should you not do?**

    _____

    _____

    _____

    _____

4. **What are the indicators of a good attitude?**

    _____

    _____

    _____

    _____

5. What kinds of jokes are not appropriate in the workplace?

_____

_____

_____

_____

6. What does it mean to be an employer who offers equal employment opportunities?

_____

_____

_____

_____

7. Why is it important to value differences in the workplace?

_____

_____

_____

_____

8. Why is getting involved in workplace politics unwise?

_____

_____

_____

_____

_____

_____

_____

_____

_____

applications

1. Describe a situation in a workplace or in your personal life where you have demonstrated initiative.

_____

_____

_____

_____

2. What could you do if you were satisfied with the work you were doing but wanted to learn some additional knowledge or skills to make your workplace more efficient and develop your own skill set?

_____

_____

_____

3. Determine whether the following statements are true or false. Explain your answers.

a. _____ Coworkers should take a positive attitude about their differences.

_____

_____

b. _____ Sharing your traditions and customs with coworkers means that both of you will better understand each other.

_____

_____

c. _____ To value differences in the workplace, coworkers need to accept people who are different.

_____

_____

d. _____ Coworkers' differences are more important than their similarities.

_____

_____

e. _____ Criticism is a form of self-improvement.

_____

_____

4. Think of a situation either at school, in a school organization, or on the job in which a coworker continued to act "silly" and say and do what he or she thought were humorous antics. How was this received in this situation? Did the person gain anything by acting in this manner? Was he or she considered immature?

_____

_____

_____

_____

_____

_____

_____

_____

Create a vision for what you want your career to look like. Think big; if you plan to reach your vision you will have a greater possibility of reaching it.

The vision will become a reality if you plan and prepare to be successful in your present position and in the various jobs that will become part of your career path. A **career path** is a plan that you can follow that will lead to a position with more responsibility, satisfaction, or income. Success in a career consists of discovering your potential and developing it. It includes making the most of what you have to offer an employer, of sharpening your skills and remaining abreast of what is new in your chosen career. Your on-the-job hours should be satisfying—adding to your self-fulfillment and contributing to your professional growth and personal happiness. If you are happy during your hours at work, your overall mental and emotional health will be enriched.

© COMSTOCK IMAGES

There are no shortcuts to career planning; visualize your career, establish your goals, and go to work.

VISUALIZE SUCCESS IN YOUR CAREER

There are no shortcuts to success. There are no substitutes for planning if you want a satisfying career. Having a plan does not guarantee success, but planning by setting goals greatly improves your chances. Visualize where you want to be in your career in ten years, in twenty years, or at retirement. One of your life goals should be moving ahead in your career to reach your full potential.

You read in an earlier chapter about the importance of goal setting. Goals are steps you must take to progress from where you are to where you want to be. Now it is time to visualize the success you want to enjoy and develop a strategy to reach success.

A **strategy** is a plan of action to reach your goals. Plan your strategy and work your plan.

CAREER GOAL

The most common reason that people do not reach their potential or goals is because goals are never set. Having your goals in mind is not enough. Your goals need to be in writing. If your goals are in writing you can refer to them, you can review them, and you can stay on track because of them. Put your goals in a place where you can see them every day. As these goals are developed, keep your key interests in mind. What makes you happy? What energizes you? What topics can engage you for hours? Think about your hobbies and those subjects you love to talk about with family and friends. Your interests and hobbies can often be translated to a career goal that will bring you satisfaction.

"Vision is always a long view into the future as well as a fresh insight into the facts of the present."

—UNKNOWN

on the job

Simon was graduated from high school with honors. He did not want to go on for advanced education right away. He was unsure of what he wanted in the future. He wanted to go to work and do some career exploration. Simon took a job as a flag person on a road crew. He did not like it and quit. He tried working at a retail outlet and did not like it. He worked in an office for a few weeks as a temporary employee and became very bored with the job. After a couple of years and many unsatisfying job experiences, Simon decided it was time to put some focus on his future. He worked with an employment counselor, identified his qualifications and established his goals, and through testing determined his aptitudes. Simon soon had developed a strategy to reach for his new career goal—a physical therapy assistant. Simon volunteered in a local clinic while he worked on the educational requirements for this position. He worked part-time as an aide in a physical therapy office. Simon felt good about himself as he was finally on a career path.

Would you consider the years that Simon floated from job to job as wasted? Why is it so difficult to get started on a career path?

Be specific

To be meaningful your career goals must be specific. For example, perhaps you think you would like a career driving a truck. The goal "I want to drive a truck" is not specific enough. The goal might be "I want a steady job driving a semitrailer truck across the country for a large, well-established trucking company." Having specific goals makes it easier for you to plan your strategy for success.

Be realistic

Your goals must be realistic. Not everyone can be a brain surgeon, a corporate lawyer, a professional athlete, or the president of a Fortune 500 company. If you are 5'2'' and weigh 120 pounds you will probably never be a fullback for the Dallas Cowboys. However, this doesn't mean you will not be able to find a meaningful career in some other phase of the football industry—sports information, game announcer, publicity director, or referee. You need to look closely at your interests, abilities, and aptitudes as you set realistic career goals. It is good to stretch your potential and aim high but be fair and reasonable in the expectations you have of yourself.

Be honest

Your goals should be what you really want to do. Do not put down on paper things you think you should do or list careers that others think you should consider. If you put down a goal just because you think it will impress or please others, you will have trouble meeting that goal. Be sure your career goal is one you want to meet. This is your life! You should also recognize that if your goal is not specific and realistic, you will want to change or alter it. If you are being honest with yourself, you will know if changes are necessary.

GOAL PLANNING

Your goal will be specific, realistic, and honestly stated. Recognize that this career goal will be a long-range goal. The career goal will not be attainable tomorrow, next week, or even next year. Think big; think long term! You are planning a lifetime career.

Short- and Medium-Range Goals

You will need to set and write down short- and medium-range goals as stepping-stones to meet your long-range goal(s). Setting short- and medium-range goals is the second step in your strategy to make your career plan happen. These goals keep you on target.

For example, if your long-term goal is to be a head nurse in a large community hospital in the pediatric ward, your short-term goal might be to arrange for some volunteer work with sick children in a local hospital. A medium-range goal might be to find a job paying good wages in the health field as you work toward acquiring the education you will need to be a nurse. The completion of short- and medium-range goals will also give you a great deal of satisfaction and encouragement.

Can goals change?

You may need to change your goals because of life circumstances. You may need to change a goal because of poor health, economic conditions, or a family situation. Changes in the workplace may also take place. Career fields can shift in this rapidly changing technological world. You may move far beyond your expectations and exceed your goal earlier than planned. If changes occur, you need to be flexible and set a new long-term career goal. You may want to develop a Plan A and a Plan B to be sure that you have well-established goals. Also, as you grow older, your priorities, interests, and hobbies may change. Yes, your goals may change.

Energize yourself

Once your goals are written, your job is not done. You have only just begun. As you plan for your future career, never neglect your present job. Your present job is important; you are building a reputation as a worker. You are gaining knowledge and skills, and you are making contacts that will be important as you move toward your goals.

Make others aware of your goals. Share your career goals with others. Share the goals with people who are supportive of

Keep your goal in a spot where you will see it everyday.

you and who will encourage, push, and help you along the way. Sharing your goals with others will also increase your sense of responsibility, and you will have someone to help motivate you and share in your successes.

Use positive self-talk to keep yourself on track toward accomplishing your career goals. You must believe in yourself. Believe you can accomplish your goals, and you will have a much greater chance of achieving your goals. If you prepared your goals realistically, specifically, and honestly, you know they are attainable. Look at yourself in the mirror as you check your progress toward your goals and say, "I can complete this short-range or medium-range goal, and I'll be a (state your long-range career goal)."

"Aim at your career as the archer aims at the target."

—UNKNOWN

"A job is only a job until it becomes a commitment, and a commitment is only possible when people see the meaning in what they do."

—UNKNOWN

Whenever you are talking to yourself or others, use positive phrases when communicating your goals. Use phrases and words like those in Figure 16-2.

Avoid negative words and phrases such as *I'll try, I can't, Someday . . . maybe, That's impossible, I should, I should have*, or *I have to*. Positive words help communicate to others how important your career goal is to you.

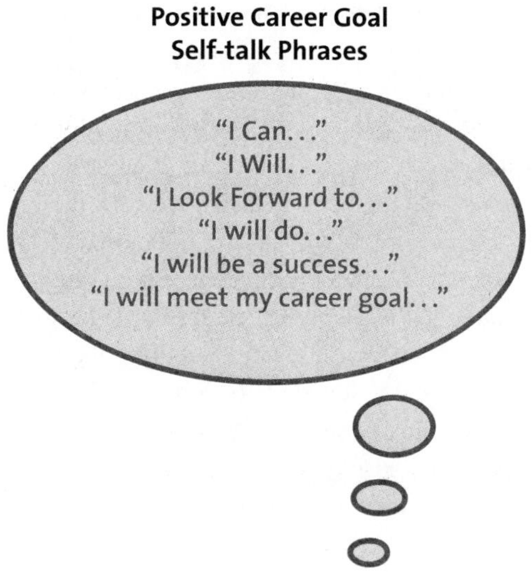

Positive Career Goal Self-talk Phrases

"I Can..."
"I Will..."
"I Look Forward to..."
"I will do..."
"I will be a success..."
"I will meet my career goal..."

Figure 16-2 *Phrases for positive career goal self-talk.*

478

chec*k*point

1. **What is a career path?**

   _____

   _____

   _____

   _____

2. **Why must goals be specific, realistic, and honest?**

   _____

   _____

   _____

   _____

3. **Where should your written goals be placed?**

   _____

   _____

   _____

   _____

4. **Why do you set short- and medium-range goals?**

   _____

   _____

   _____

   _____

5. **Why should you share your goals with others?**

   _____

   _____

   _____

   _____

applications

1. List three career goals that you have considered for yourself. Indicate how you might reach these goals.

_____

_____

_____

_____

2. Practice writing short-, medium-, and long-term goals by preparing goals for someone who wants to be an electrician, a computer technician, or an accountant. Be sure your goals are specific, realistic, and honest. (Use your imagination.)

_____

_____

_____

_____

_____

3. List some of the events that could cause a change in your career goal.

_____

_____

_____

_____

4. Write a specific, realistic, honest long-term goal for yourself.

5. Write short- and medium-term goals for the long-term goal written in Application 4.

6. You are helping a friend write his career goals. He is very interested in the field of medicine and wants to be a surgeon. His college grades have been average. His application to several medical schools has been denied. Write out the suggestions you might have for him.

Moving Ahead

As you progress toward your goals, you will need some measuring points. These can be found in your performance appraisals and the reward system within your workplace.

PERFORMANCE APPRAISALS

You will know how well you are doing on the job as a result of your performance appraisal. A **performance appraisal** is an official evaluation of your work. Your supervisor does the evaluation. He or she may use a special form geared for employees' performance evaluations.[3] An appraisal is a chance for your supervisor to tell you your strengths and weaknesses on the job.

Discussing your weaknesses is meant to help you become a better worker. It is not meant as a way to pick on you or to reduce your level of self-esteem.

Both you and your supervisor can learn from the performance appraisal conference. This conference gives your supervisor a formal opportunity to talk about your job, its responsibilities, and its potential for growth. Your supervisor can tell you how you fit in the company, if you need extra training, and if you are making the best use of your skills. The evaluation session also gives you a chance to speak openly about your view of the job. Your supervisor will probably encourage you to talk about any problems you see with your job, to ask questions, to share changes you would like to see made, and to offer suggestions for the betterment of the company.

When your evaluation session is over, both you and your supervisor will sign the appraisal form. The original copy will become part of your permanent personnel file. You will get a copy for your records. As the appraisal form goes into your permanent file, it is important for you to make a good impression during the appraisal conference. The appraisal conference may determine future promotional opportunities for you. Workers who make an effort to improve their work are often rewarded with raises and promotions.

RAISES AND PROMOTIONS

Your short- and medium-range goals will include efforts to secure raises and promotions.

Requesting a Raise

In most organizations your performance appraisal is directly related to any increase in pay you may receive. A good appraisal may result in a pay raise. If your company has no pattern set for salary increases, it may be appropriate for you to request a raise based upon a satisfactory performance evaluation. When you ask for a raise in pay, the request should be based on your work and accomplishments. Do not talk about your financial need or obligations. Before you ask for a raise, think about your accomplishments of the past year. Be prepared to tell your supervisor

- what new responsibilities you have accepted since you were hired.
- what new skills you have acquired and are now using on the job.
- how your work has made a special contribution to the company. In other words, you need to justify why you feel you are worthy of a salary increase.

Consideration for a Promotion

Part of getting ahead on the job is going up the career path in your company. You can move up the career path by getting a promotion from one level to the next. Promotion opportunities usually come from getting a positive rating on your performance appraisal. The positive or glowing appraisal says you have proven your ability to accept more responsibility and to do more challenging work. In addition to doing well on the performance appraisal, be the best at what you do, set goals, and get to know the company and the promotion policies.

Do you Really Want the Promotion?

In most situations a promotion means that you will need to accept more responsibility. You do not have to accept a promotion just because it is offered to you. Be sure that you weigh the advantages and disadvantages of accepting a promotion. The promotion should be one that is in line with your set career goals. If the promotion is not in your plan, you have a decision to make. You will need to change your career goals or turn down the promotion. A raise in salary and a new title are not always good reasons to accept a promotion.

Changing Jobs

There may come a time when you consider changing employers. This is part of the career path climb. Changing jobs can be difficult and stressful because of the relationships you have developed and the security you feel within the job. Changing jobs is an important decision. Be sure you change jobs for the right reasons.

Do not quit your present job until you find a new one. Prepare a written list of reasons to either stay or leave your present position. Avoid rushing into a job change without doing some planning. Look at all aspects of any new job you consider. Another job or company may look good on the surface. Be careful. If you do not do your research, you could end up working with a difficult supervisor, you could be given a heavy, unpleasant workload, or you could find yourself in a position with no growth potential. A job change should not be taken lightly. If the job change doesn't fall in line with your career path, extra thought must be given to it.

Smart Tip ▼ ▼ ▼

The right reasons for changing jobs are listed below. Consider them carefully as you look at promotions or job changes.
- **Your current employer can offer no advancement for you.**
- **Your current job does not further your career goal.**
- **The economy causes layoffs.**
- **Your department or job is eliminated.**
- **You do not agree with the policies and goals of the organization.**
- **You wish to move to a new geographic location.**
- **You have a changed career goal. This job does not fit into your plan.**

▲ ▲ ▲ ▲ ▲ ▲ ▲ ▲ ▲

Choose your Job Carefully

As you seek to build a satisfying career, do not sell yourself short just to obtain immediate employment. Your goal is to market your skills for the best possible measure of job stimulation and challenge, security, appreciation, and other rewards. The most important question to ask yourself before accepting a new job is, "Does this position move me toward reaching my long-term career goals?" Other questions to consider before taking a new job include:
- How stable is the company?
- What is the reputation of the company?
- What opportunities are there for advancement?
- What are the policies for promotion in the company?
- Will I need more education if I remain with this company?
- What security does the position offer?

- Will the work be interesting and challenging enough for me?
- Do I have the interests, qualifications, and aptitude for this position?
- Are there any negative characteristics about the job?

The best time to plan for advancement is before you take a job. One of the considerations to weigh is whether the job offers the possibility of promotion. For example, a well-established firm may offer more security than advancement. A new firm, on the other hand, may provide rapid advancement to those employees who are promotion material; yet the position may be less stable than with the established firm. You will need to examine your options.

Advantages of Changing Employers

While it is sometimes more comfortable to stay with your present employer, there may also be some advantages to making a change. Whenever you consider changing employers, review these advantages and make sure they are present.

- You may receive a better salary or fringe benefits package.
- You may increase your job interest by becoming involved with a new job challenge.
- You may gain knowledge, broaden your experience, and perhaps expand your career growth opportunities.

Upgrading your Skills

In the changing workplace environment, keeping up with the technical preparation in most jobs is a challenge. Your skills can become obsolete quickly. For example, you may have become proficient on a certain piece of equipment or software only to discover that your employer has installed an upgrade of the equipment or software you have been using. Or you may find that the methods, systems, and routines of a new position are entirely different from those you learned. What should you do?

First, keep a learning attitude. A learning attitude means that you pay extra attention and ask questions about new challenges and tasks. Ask for demonstrations of new systems or procedures. Pledge to yourself that you will remain flexible and accepting of change. You may want to make this pledge an ongoing part of your career goal.

Second, take advantage of training opportunities. On-the-job training may be offered to current employees needing to

on the job

Elaine has been employed by the Gothic Gallery for three years. She has enjoyed her work, and her schedule allows her to spend time with her two small children. Elaine is a single parent. She is offered a new position that will pay $750 per week. Her title will be Acquisitions Director. Elaine's new position will require her to supervise seven people who are currently her coworkers. Her new supervisory duties will include attending Gallery Board meetings two evenings per month, evaluating the seven people she supervises, and being responsible for the implementation of the goals set forth by the Gallery Board. The Gallery will expect Elaine to attend regional auctions to search for new works for the Gallery. Elaine is currently an hourly employee who is compensated for any overtime at time and a half. As a supervisor, she will not be eligible for overtime. Elaine now holds a forty-hour-per-week job and is paid $15 per hour. She gets time and a half for overtime and some weeks she works 44 to 48 hours when the Gallery has many visitors during the summer months. She carefully weighs the pros and cons of the promotion and thinks about her future and the future of her small family.

What advice would you have for Elaine? What topics should Elaine consider? Are there any questions you would advise her to ask the employer? What additional information do you need to help Elaine make this decision?

learn new skills, to new employees, or to employees who have been transferred into new positions. If such training is available, welcome the opportunity to learn something new. This will set you apart from the other employees. Learning something new is a guaranteed way of improving your vigor, effectiveness, and security.

As you consider job opportunities, select an organization that provides, promotes, and supports ongoing training as part of its policy.

Self-Training

You have a responsibility to your employer and to yourself to upgrade your skills and knowledge whenever possible.

Spend some time reading. Reading is an educational tool for thousands of self-made business leaders. If you have not developed the regular reading habit, decide to become knowledgeable in some area of interest that is job related. Get a book or some periodicals from the public library or do some online research. It will help if you set aside a special time for reading of this type. Reading will increase your vocabulary, horizons, and abilities.

Do not overlook professional magazines, periodicals, and Web sites devoted to hundreds of career topics; choose one that relates to your work, subscribe to it, and faithfully read it.

Educational Courses

Special course work related to your employment may be offered at a community college, a university, or your place of employment. College credit may be earned if it is desired. These courses provide an outstanding opportunity for the ambitious worker to improve and expand his or her knowledge and potential. Often local community colleges provide special classes. Many educational opportunities are available online as well.

Also look for online training and distance learning programs in technical and human relations skills. Many opportunities are provided through community colleges in partnership with local business and industry.

LEADERSHIP

If you want to advance in your career, you must develop leadership qualities. Supervisors are leaders. **Leadership** in this context is the ability to lead or direct others on a positive course. Effective leaders have traits that give them the ability to lead others. Do you have these traits? If part of your career plan is to someday lead others, now is the time to begin working on the development of leadership traits. Evaluate yourself using the Self Check on page 486.

HOW TO LEAVE A JOB

If you decide the best course of action is to leave your present job (or if you are asked to leave), do so professionally and courteously. Throughout your working life, references from past employers will be requested. For this reason you must leave your job calmly and on a pleasant and positive note. Do not leave angry or in a huff even if you were dissatisfied with the position. Give your employer at least two weeks' notice that you are resigning. Be sure to be on the job right up to your last working day. Resign properly from your current job. You want to maintain a reputation for fairness. Say good-bye to your coworkers and supervisors. If the job experience has been valuable, tell them so.

Before you walk out the door, you have several things to do that are in your best interest.

"Education is not the filling of a pail, but the lighting of a fire."

—W. B. YEATS

"A mind expanded never returns to its original boundaries."

—UNKNOWN

SELF CHECK

Evaluate your leadership qualities. If you feel that you have the quality, give yourself 5 points. If you have at least part of the quality, give yourself 3 points. If you need to work on the quality, give yourself 0 points.

_____ I respect and support the rights of others.

_____ I communicate in a clear and understandable manner.

_____ I am competent, confident, and honest.

_____ I am open-minded.

_____ I am positive about my group's work.

_____ I use good judgment and am comfortable making decisions.

_____ I am adaptable and comfortable making changes.

_____ I like to take risks and am not afraid of failure.

_____ I am willing to share knowledge and delegate tasks to others.

_____ I am good at influencing and motivating others.

_____ TOTAL

40–50 You are on your way to being a leader.

30–39 You have potential.

Technology at Work

If supervisory or leadership positions are listed in your career goals, you may want to check out Web sites devoted to leadership skills, supervisory techniques, and management skills. Try this to get you started:

http://www.etiquette42day.com/

If you want to check to see if your current salary is fair or what reasonable expectations would be in another job, check these Web sites.

http://www.salaryexpert.com

http://www.salary.com

http://www.jobstar.org

http://www.bls.gov/ncs/ocs/ **(This is a site provided by the Bureau of Labor Statistics. The data is usually a couple of years old but may give you some good base figures.)**

1. Check on whether or not you are entitled to **severance pay**, an allowance usually based on length of employment that is payable to a terminating employee. There is no law requiring severance pay; nevertheless, some employers offer this benefit especially if you are leaving a job because of a layoff or because the job has been downsized or eliminated.
2. Check to see how your final paycheck will be delivered to you and when it will be available.
3. Check to see if you are eligible to receive payment for unused vacation time or sick leave.
4. Check to see what happens to your health insurance benefits. The Consolidated Omnibus Budget Reconciliation Act (COBRA), passed in 1986, and other state laws provide continuation of health benefits for at least a period of time when an employee quits, is laid off, or is fired for any reason other than misconduct. Check the U.S. Department of Labor Web site, www.dol.gov, for the details on COBRA. The human resources department should help you with your insurance benefits paperwork.
5. Check into unemployment insurance in your state's Department of Labor; if you lose your job temporarily or permanently, you may be eligible for financial assistance. These benefits vary greatly from state to state.

chec**k**point

1. What should you be prepared to tell your supervisor when you request a raise?

_____

_____

_____

_____

_____

2. How do you decide whether or not to accept a promotion?

_____

_____

_____

_____

_____

3. What are the right reasons for changing jobs?

_____

_____

_____

_____

_____

4. How can you upgrade your skills?

_____

_____

_____

_____

_____

_____

_____

applications

1. Explain how you would prepare yourself to ask for a raise.

2. Check out one of the recommended Web sites that relate to salary. (See page 486.) If you are a welder in mid-America making $22 per hour, would you consider moving to San Francisco for a $30 per hour job? Why? Why not?

3. List the leadership characteristics that you currently possess. Give examples of how you have demonstrated these characteristics in school or on the job.

4. Explain to a friend the correct way to request a raise. Prepare an outline to follow as you make this presentation.

_____

_____

_____

_____

_____

5. Lucille has been a candy wrapping machine operator for five years. Lucille enjoys her work, likes her coworkers, and finds the salary and fringe benefits package offered by the company to be a fair one. She is happy doing repetitive work and likes the fact that when she leaves the company at night, she does not need to think about the job on her own time. Her performance appraisals are excellent. Mary Elton, her supervisor, calls her in and asks if she would like to be the supervisor of the fifteen wrapping machine operators. The promotion offers her an additional $200 per month; her work hours will remain the same. Lucille asks for time to think about the offer.

a. What questions should Lucille ask herself?

_____

_____

_____

b. What advantages and disadvantages does the role of a supervisor include?

_____

_____

_____

c. Based on what you know about Lucille, would you suggest that she accept the position? Why or why not?

_____

_____

_____

16 Points to Remember

chapter

Review the following points to determine what you remember from the chapter.

- Your first day on the job is an important one, as you will be making a first impression on your supervisor and coworkers. Work very hard to remember the names of those introduced to you on this busy first day. Also, the first day will be your opportunity to be introduced to the rules, including the understood rules and the safety rules of your company. Be sure that you understand the rules and clarify any questions you may have. Complete the required forms and consider carefully the benefits package options.

- To keep your position, you will need to establish good work habits and pay attention to keeping your work area orderly. You will need to do your best work, be productive, continually look for ways to improve, accept responsibility for your job and any errors that you make, be willing to work with others, keep a good sense of humor, and treat others with respect. Seek out a mentor to provide you with guidance and direction. Pay attention to workplace politics and take a neutral position.

- Your desire for success in a career takes work. Design a career path to lead you to success. It takes a plan and some goal setting. Having a plan does not guarantee success, but setting goals greatly improves your chances. Your goals must be specific, realistic, and honest. You need to have short- and medium-range goals to help keep you on target. Once your goals are established, you will need to make others aware of your goals, remind yourself of your goals each day, and energize yourself to work toward those goals. It is okay to change goals because life changes, also.

- As you move up the career path, you must do a good job in each position you hold. Your supervisor will evaluate your performance in performance appraisal sessions. These sessions provide your supervisor with a chance to report your strengths and weaknesses. They also provide you with an opportunity to ask questions and share your ideas and opinions. Raises and promotions generally result from outstanding performance appraisals. If you are offered a promotion, be sure that the promotion fits with your overall career goal. If it does not, turn it down or adjust your career plan.

- You may have opportunities to change employment. Be sure you change jobs for the right reasons. Carefully choose each job you accept and use your career path as your guide. Resign properly from your current job. Upon termination of a job, before leaving check out the possibility of severance, find out when and how you will receive your last check and whether or not you will be paid for unused sick leave or vacation pay, and check into the possibility of continuing your insurance benefits. If you have been dismissed because of a layoff or other negative situation, you will want to check out unemployment compensation benefits.

How did you do? Did you remember the main points you studied in the chapter?

key terms

Place the letter of the item in the definition column that matches the key word.

Key Word	Definition

___1. Job description

a. An allowance that may be payable to a terminating employee.

___2. Initiative

b. A plan that you can follow that will lead to a position with more responsibility, satisfaction, or income.

___3. Mentor

c. Ability to lead or direct others on a positive course.

___4. Workplace politics

d. An objective and impersonal written explanation of the tasks, duties, and responsibilities of a job.

___5. Performance appraisal

e. A trusted counselor or guide who is sometimes called a coach.

___6. Career path

f. An official evaluation of your work.

___7. Leadership

g. An undefined force in an organization that develops because people want to protect themselves or gain power.

___8. Severance pay

h. Starting a project without being told to do so.

___9. Strategy

i. A plan of action to reach your goals.

activities and projects

1. Think about being a supervisor. Your challenges as a supervisor will be many. Here is one scenario. Could you handle this situation?

One of your duties as the newly appointed assistant purchasing agent is the supervision of the stockroom. You spent five years working there for Rodney Simpson, who is in charge of the stockroom and has been with the company for 25 years. He devised and installed the manual inventory system currently being used. The system is now out of date and a new computerized system is needed.

A major concern is how to get Mr. Simpson's cooperation in making the change from the old system of records to one that is more efficient.

a. How will you initially approach Mr. Simpson? What will you say?

b. Assume that you gained his cooperation in the above item. What will you say to him when he makes the remark that this system has worked for 25 years and that it will probably serve the company well for another 25 years?

c. How will you tell him that a computerized system will be installed next month?

d. How will you prepare him for this installation?

_____

_____

_____

_____

2. Select a company in your area, and arrange to find out all you can about it. Talk with employees, clients and/or customers, and a person from management; read literature available about the company. (Be sure that you let the human resources department of the company know that you are doing this as a learning activity.) Your goal will be to determine, theoretically, if you would like to take a job with the company. You can keep the decision between you and your instructor. Answer the following questions in making your determination.

Company you selected _____

Position you would consider _____

a. How stable is the company? Will it be operating in five years?

_____

_____

_____

_____

b. What is the reputation of the company? What do others think about the company? Use some of the quotes you heard from others while doing your interviews.

_____

_____

_____

_____

_____

c. What opportunities for advancement exist within this company? Assume that you take an entry-level job. Where can you go from there?

_____

_____

_____

_____

d. What are the policies for promotion within the company? Are promotions based on seniority or on an employee's ability to do the job? Do internal candidates interview for promotions as positions become available or are promotions awarded for performance?

_____

_____

_____

_____

e. Will you need more education if you join this company? If so, how will you obtain it?

_____

_____

_____

_____

f. What kind of job security does this company offer? Have they had frequent layoffs?

_____

_____

_____

_____

g. Do you have the interests, qualifications, and aptitudes necessary to be an entry-level worker in the company? Explain.

_____

_____

_____

_____

h. What negative characteristics have you heard about this company? Will they have an impact on your decision?

_____

_____

_____

_____

Would you take a job with this company? _____
Why or why not?

_____

_____

_____

_____

3. Explain what is meant by the David Storey quotation, "Have confidence that if you have done a little thing well, you can do a bigger thing well, too."

_____

_____

_____

_____

4. Give some thought as to whom you would select as a mentor in a new position. Record your thoughts and answer the following questions.

a. How would you approach someone and ask if he or she would be interested in helping you by being your mentor?

_____

_____

_____

b. What qualities would you look for in a mentor?

_____

_____

_____

c. Are personal qualities more important than job qualities when you seek a mentor?

_____

_____

_____

d. Would you ask your supervisor to recommend a mentor? Why? Why not?

_____

_____

_____

e. How would you handle the situation if the person you selected as a mentor declined your offer? Your proposed mentor said, "I'm sorry, I don't have the time."

_____

_____

_____

case studies for critical thinking

FIRST DAY DILEMMA

Salvador arrives at this first day of work for Heritage Home Builders, Inc. He reports to the office of Heritage. The only person at the site is the office manager. She gives Salvador a Form W-4 and an I-9 Form and then asks him if he wants to sign up for the insurance program. Salvador completes the Form W-4 and the I-9 Form. However, because he does not understand the insurance program, he does not sign those forms. The office manager tells him that he is to report to a job site at 434 Lyncrest Avenue. Salvador drives to Lyncrest Avenue and finds one other employee who is roofing a house. Salvador introduces himself to the employee. The employee says, "Hello, I guess you're supposed to help me." Salvador had applied for the position of house framer, but with a little direction from his coworker, he begins roofing. Salvador's boss arrives at the site about 11:30 a.m. He introduces himself to Salvador and says, "Glad to have you with us!" and leaves the work site.

1. What information does Salvador not have at the end of his first day?

2. What questions would you have at the end of the day if you were Salvador?

3. How should Salvador go about finding the information he needs to know?

Case 16.2

IS A PROMOTION IN ORDER?

Marcus has been working at the Computer Superstore retail chain as a salesperson for several years. He knows the company's products and has proven himself to be a dependable worker. The position of buyer becomes available. Marcus wants the position because it involves travel and a pay increase and is a step toward his career goal to be a district manager of the chain of stores. The buyer would negotiate with major electronics suppliers across the country for the best prices. Marcus is very opinionated. He enjoys working with only a few of the other sales staff members. He feels that some of the sales staff are incompetent because they have not worked in computer programming, and he has. Marcus's performance appraisals have been satisfactory, but at each session the supervisor has reminded him that he needs to work on his "people skills."

1. Will Marcus get the promotion? Why or why not?

2. What leadership skills does Marcus possess? What leadership skills does he need to acquire?

3. Would you hire Marcus as a district manager?

4. As his present supervisor, what advice would you have for Marcus?

Case 16.3

IS IT TIME FOR A CHANGE?

J. B. has worked as a technician in a county government environmental planning office for three years. His appraisal reports have been excellent; he is well liked by his coworkers and superiors. He has one county official who doesn't like him, but J. B. overlooks this since the official doesn't hire or fire him. J. B. is a true environmentalist and his training and experience are in environmental planning. The government paperwork, general bureaucracy, outdated codes, rules, and regulations are a constant annoyance to J. B. His current work is to monitor housing developers as they design tracts to make sure that the "urban sprawl" does not interfere with the natural beauty of the mountains and other terrain that surrounds the county. His toughest task is to keep the developers within the rules and codes of development established by the elected county officials.

J. B. has been offered a position in environmental planning in another state where he will be doing similar work for a nongovernmental agency. The new position offers him a pay raise of $12,000. His work will assist land developers to design attractive developments that are aesthetically pleasing.

1. What should be considered by J. B. as he considers the offer to change positions?

2. Do you see any drawbacks of J. B. remaining in his current position?

3. What additional information would you need to help J. B. decide whether or not he should take the new position?

endnotes

Chapter 1

1. Marie Dalton, Dawn G. Hoyle, and Marie W. Watts, *Human Relations*, 2nd Edition, Thomson Learning, Cincinnati: South-Western Educational Publishing, 2000, p. 35.

Chapter 2

1. James O. Prochaska, John C. Norcross, and Carlo C. Diclemente, *Changing for Good: A Revolutionary Six-Stage Program for Overcoming Bad Habits and Moving Your Life Positively Forward*, New York: Avon Books, 1994.

Chapter 4

1. Mary Ellen Guffey, *Business Communication Process & Product*, Cincinnati: Thomson South-Western, 2003, p. 11.

2. As cited in Guffey, p. 70.

Chapter 7

1. Marie Dalton, Dawn G. Hoyle, and Marie W. Watts, *Human Relations*, 2nd Edition, Thomson Learning, Cincinnati: South-Western Educational Publishing, 2000, p. 144.

Chapter 8

1. Pattie Odgers, *Administrative Office Management*, 13th Edition, Cincinnati: Thomson South-Western, 2005, pp. 261–262.

Chapter 11

1. Don Aslett and John *Caldwell, The Office Clutter Cure: How to Get Out from Under It All*! Better Way Books, March 1, 1995.

2. Samuel H. Klarreich, *The Stress Solution*, Toronto, Canada: Key Porter Books, 1988.

3. Ken Blanchard and Marjorie Blanchard, *The One Minute Manager Balances Work and Life (One Minute Manager Library)* April 7, 1999.

4. *Pattie Odgers, Administrative Office Management*, Cincinnati: Thomson South-Western, 2005, p. 142.

5. C. Northcote Parkinson, *Parkinson, The Law*, Houghton Mifflin, 1980; B. Lewis Keeling and Norman F. Kallaus, *Administrative Office Management*, Cincinnati: South-Western Educational Publishing, 1996, pp. 33–34.

6. Peter G. Hanson, *The Joy of Stress*, Kansas City: Andrews, McMeel & Parker, 1986.

7. Chandra Patel, *The Complete Guide to Stress Management*, New York: Plenum Press, 1991.

8. Barbara Bailey Reinhold, *Toxic Work—How to Overcome Stress, Overload, and Burnout and Revitalize Your Career, New York:* Dutton, 1996.

9. Peter O. Kwiterovich, Jr., *Beyond Cholesterol*, Baltimore, Maryland: Johns Hopkins University Press, 1989.

10. Christopher Hobbs, *Stress and Natural Healing*, Interweave Press, 1997; Neal Pinckney, *Healthy Heart Handbook*, Health Communications, 1996; Judy Monroe, *Coping with Ulcers, Heartburn, and Stress-related Stomach Disorders.* New York: Rosen Publishing Group, 2000.

11. Herbert Benson and Eileen M. Stuart, *The Wellness Book: The Comprehensive Guide to Maintaining Health and Treating Stress-Related Illness*, October 1, 1993.

12. Ibid.

13. C. W. Metcalf and Roma Felible, *Lighten Up, Survival Skills for People under Pressure*, Reading, MA: Addison-Wesley, 1992.

14. Herbert M. Greenberg, *Coping With Job Stress: A Guide for Employers and Employees*, Upper Saddle River, NJ: Prentice Hall, 1980.

15. Ibid., Kwiterovich.

16. Richard Carlson, *Don't Sweat the Small Stuff at Work: Simple Ways to Minimize Stress and Conflict While Bringing Out the Best in Yourself and Others*, New York: Hyperion, 1998.

17. Valerie O'Hara, *The Fitness Option: Five Weeks to Healing Stress*, Berkeley, *CA:* University of California Press, 1990.

18. Ibid., Benson and Stuart.

19. Martha Davis, *The Relaxation and Stress Reduction Workbook*, Oakland, CA.: New Harbinger Publications, 2000.

20. Barry Sears, *The Zone*, New York: Harper Collins, l995.

21. Joseph C. Piscatella, *Take a Load Off Your Heart*, New York: Workman, 2003.

Chapter 12

1. Alex F. Osborn, *Applied Imagination*, Hadley, MA: Creative Education Foundation, 1993.

2. E. Paul Torrance, *Guiding Creative Talent*, Upper Saddle River, NJ: Prentice Hall, 1962

3. Ibid.

4. Ibid.

5. http://www.scans.jhu.edu/NS/HTML/ SkillsSimple.htm

Chapter 13

1. Rushworth M. Kidder, *How Good People Make Tough Choices*, New York: Morrow, 1995.

2. Pattie Odgers, *Administrative Office Management*, Cincinnati: Thomson South-Western, 2005, p. 184.

3. Peter Madsen and Jay M. Shafritz, *Essentials of Business Ethics*, Salinas, CA: Meridian, l990.

4. *Secretary's Commission on Achieving Necessary Skills (SCANS)*, http://www.scans.jhu.edu/NS/HTML/ SkillsSimple.htm.

5. Wayne Dosick, *The Business Bible: Ten New Commandments for Creating an Ethical Workplace*, New York: HarperBusiness, 1994.

6. Samuel Greengard, "Dealing with Addiction," *Workforce*, February 2003, p. 8, as cited in Odgers, *Administrative Office Management*, p. 210.

Chapter 14

1. SCANS 2000, Institute for Policy Studies, Baltimore, Maryland: Johns Hopkins University Press, 2001.

2. Renee Blank and Sandra Sipp, *Voices of Diversity*, New York: American Management Association, 1994.

3. http://en.wikipedia.org, August 2004.

4. John P. Fernandez, *The Diversity Advantage*, Lanham, MD: Lexington Books, 1993. See Chapter 2, "Racism, Sexism, Ethnocentrism, and Xenophobia."

5. Debbie Levy, *Bigotry*, San Diego, CA: Lucent Books, 2002.

6. U.S. Department of Commerce, *Statistical Abstract of the United States: 2003*. Issued December 2003.

7. U.S. Department of Labor, *Employment Law Guide—Laws, Regulations & Technical Assistance Services*. Revised April 2003.

8. Ibid., Fernandez.

9. Sandra Lee Smith, *Coping with Cross-cultural and Interracial Relationships*, New York: Rosen Publishing Group, l990.

10. Ibid., Levy.

11. *Merriam Webster's Collegiate Dictionary*, 10th Edition, 1996.

12. Ibid.

13. Margaret C. Jasper, *Employment Discrimination Law under Title VII*, Dobbs Ferry, NY: Oceana Publications, Inc., 1999; Ibid., U.S. Department of Labor.

14. Marie Dalton, Dawn Hoyle, and Marie W. Watts, *Human Relations*, 2nd Edition, Cincinnati: Thomson South-Western Publishing, 2000, p. 516.

15. Pattie Odgers, *Administrative Office Management*, Cincinnati: Thomson South-Western, 2005, p. 130.

16. Brian J.Grapes, San Diego, CA: Greenhaven Press, Inc., 2000.

17. Francis J. Beckwith and Todd E. Jones, *Affirmative Action—Social Justice or Reverse Discrimination*, Prometheus Books, 1997; Ibid., U.S. Department of Labor, p. 89.

18. Ibid., U.S. Department of Labor, p. 89.

19. Gabrielle I. Edwards, *Coping with Discrimination*, New York: Rosen Publishing Group, 1992.

20. Raymond F. Gregory, *Age Discrimination in the American Workplace*, Piscataway, NJ: Rutgers University Press, 2001.

21. David Carey, "Ageism a hot topic as boomers get older," *The Sun News*, Myrtle Beach, South Carolina, September 5, 2004, p. D1.

22. Ibid., Odgers, p. 131.

23. Brenda Stalcup, Ed., *The Disabled*, Greenhaven Press, 1997.

24. Margaret C. Jasper, *Harassment in the Workplace*, Dobbs Ferry, NY: Oceana Publications, Inc., 2002.

25. Steven Mitchell Sack, *The Working Woman's Legal Survival Guide*, Upper Saddle River: NJ: Prentice Hall, 1998.

26. Jeffrey M. Bernbach, *Job Discrimination*, Crown Publishing Group, 1996.

27. Ibid., Edwards.

Chapter 15

1. Mary Ellen Guffey, *Business Communication Process and Product*, Cincinnati: Thomson South-Western, 2003, pp. 535–537.

2. Pattie Odgers, *Administrative Office Management*, Cincinnati: Thomson South-Western, 2005, pp. 130–131.

3. Ibid., Guffey, p. 554.

Chapter 16

1. Pattie Odgers, *Administrative Office Management*, Cincinnati: Thomson South-Western, 2005, p. 142.

2. Neal McChristy and Scott Cullen, "Homing in on HIPPA," *Office Solutions*, January/February 2004, pp. 12–14, 16.

3. Ibid., Odgers, p. 175.

supplemental enrichment resources

This resource list has been developed to provide opportunities for additional in-depth study and review for students and instructors who use the 9th edition of *Personal Development for Life and Work*. These materials are likely to be available in your school, public library, local bookstore, or on the Internet.

Developing Your Success Identity (Chapters 1–3)

Eric Berne. *Games People Play*, Ballantine, 1996.

Nathaniel Branden. *The Psychology of Self-Esteem: A Revolutionary Approach to Self-Understanding*, Jossey-Bass, 2001.

Erin Brockovich. *Take It From Me: Life Is A Struggle But You Can Win*, McGraw-Hill, 2002.

Joyce Brothers. *Positive Plus: A Practical Plan for Liking Yourself Better*, Berkley Publishing Group, 1995.

Donald O. Clifton. *Soar With Your Strengths*, Dell Books, 1996.

Milton R. Cudney. *Self- Defeating Behaviors: Free Yourself From the Habits, Compulsions, Feelings, and Attitudes That Hold You Back*, Harper San Francisco, 1993.

Thomas A. Harris. *I'm OK—You're OK: A Practical Guide to Transactional Analysis*, Galahad Books, 1999.

Carole Hyatt. *When Smart People Fail*, Penguin, 1993.

Norman Vincent Peale. *The Power of Positive Thinking*, Prentice-Hall, 1952.

Lev Raphael. *Dynamics of Power: Fighting Shame and Building Self-Esteem*, Shenkman, 1991.

Martin E.P. Seligman. *Learned Optimism*, Pocket Books, 1998.

Martin E.P. Seligman. *What You Can Change and What You Can't: The Complete Guide to Self-Improvement*, Fawcett Books, 1995.

Judith Sills. *Excess Baggage: Getting Out of Your Own Way*, Penguin, 1994.

Charles L. Van House. *Teen Self-Esteem: A Common Sense Path to a Happy and Successful Life*, Life Lines Press, 1993.

Francine Ward. *Esteemable Acts: 10 Actions for Building Self-Esteem*, Broadway Books, 2003.

http://www.TestsTestsTests.com/growthtest.htm —Self Improvement Quotient Test and Quiz— Use this test as an open exploration. It will help you to see yourself more clearly and know where you can deepen your understanding. Sponsored by "The Sedona Method."

http://www.selfhelpsolutions.homestead.com/ BoostSEl.html—Techniques you can start to use now to build positive self-esteem in yourself. Presented by a licensed clinical psychologist.

http://www.leadersdirect.com/selfesteem.html— An overview of self-esteem and suggestions on celebrating yourself and receiving feedback from others. Includes a quiz to determine if you have low self-esteem.

http://www.self-esteem-nase.org/—National Association for Self-Esteem (NASE). An organization dedicated to fully integrating self-esteem into the fabric of American society so every individual experiences personal worth and happiness. Includes sections on parenting, educational programs, conferences and an offer to subscribe to *Self-Esteem Today Magazine*.

http://www.webheights.net/lovethyself/home. htm—Love Thyself: Resources for Improving Self-Esteem, Self-Confidence, and Self-Acceptance. Fear, anxiety, self-doubts, and insecurity haunt those crippled by low self-esteem. This comprehensive resource directs visitors to books, on-line articles, and programs to enhance the self-worth of adults and children.

Communication (Chapters 4–6)

Nowak Achim. *Power Speaking*, Allworth Press, 2004.

Lillian Brown. *Your Public Best, Second Edition*, New Market Press, 2002.

Jeff Davidson. *The Complete Guide to Public Speaking*, John Wiley & Sons, Inc., 2003.

Rosalie Maggio. *How to Say It*, Prentice Hall Press, 2001.

Laura Morice. "I Wish I Weren't So Shy," *Good Housekeeping*, August 2004, Vol. 239, Issue 2, pp. 98–100.

Michael F. Opitz and Matthew Zbaracki. *Listen Hear!* Heineman, 2004.

Jack Valenti. *Speak Up With Confidence*, Hyperion, 2002.

Lilyan Wilder. *Fearless Speaking*, John Wiley & Sons, Inc., 1999.

Richard Worth. *Communication Skills, Second Edition*, JG Ferguson Company, 2004.

http://www.communication-skills.net/index.htm

Working with Others, Supervisors, and Customers (Chapters 7–9)

Rhonda Abrams. *Wear Clean Underwear*, Villard Books, 1999.

Be Our Guest: Perfecting the Art of Customer Service. Disney Institute, Disney Editions, 2001.

Ken Blanchard, Thad Lacinak, Chuck Tompkins, and Jim Ballard. *Whale Done: The Power of Positive Relationships.* The Free Press, 2002.

Thomas Connellan. *Bringing Out the Best in Others*, Bard Press, 2003.

Jeffrey Gitomer. *Customer Satisfaction Is Worthless: Customer Loyalty is Priceless,* Bard Press, 1998.

Dandi Daley Mackall. *Team Work Skills*, JG Ferguson Company, 2004.

John C. Maxwell. *Attitude 101*, Thomas Nelson, Inc., 2003.

John C. Maxwell. *Learning the 27 Essential Qualities of a Team Player: Becoming the Kind of Person Every Team Wants*, INJOY, Inc., 2002.

John C. Maxwell. *Relationships 101*, Thomas Nelson, Inc., 2003.

Angus McLeod. *Me, Myself, and My Team*, Crown House Publishing, 2000.

Paul Meier and Robert Wise. *Crazymakers: Getting Along with Difficult People in Your Life*, Thomas Nelson, Inc., 2003.

Julie Morgenstern. *Making Work Work*, Simon & Schuster, 2004.

Bob Nelson. *1001 Ways to Take Initiative at Work*, Workman Publishing Company, Inc., 1999.

Tom Rath and Donald Clifton. *How Full is Your Bucket*, Gallup Press, 2004.

Thomas Stevenin. *Win-Win Solutions: Resolving Conflict on the Job*, Moody Press, 2000.

Harvey Thompson. *Who Stole My Customer*, Prentice Hall, 2004.

James Waldroop and Timothy Butler. *The 12 Bad Habits that Hold Good People Back.* Doubleday, 2000.

Ron Zemke. *Delivering Knock Your Socks Off Service, Third Edition.* Performance Research Associates, 2003.

http://www.psychological-hug.com/

Developing Your Productivity (Chapters 10–12)

Bob Adams. *The Everything Time Management Book: How to Get it All Done*, Adams Media, 2001.

Eve Adamson. *The Everything Stress Management Book*, Adams Media, 2002.

David Allen. *Getting Things Done: The Art of Stress-Free Productivity*, Viking, 2001.

Ingrid Bacci. *The Act of Effortless Living*, Vision Works, 2000.

Herbert Benson and Eileen Stuart. *The Wellness Book, The Comprehensive Guide to Maintaining Health and Treating Stress-Related Illness*, Simon and Schuster, 1993.

Robert Boostrom. *Developing Creative and Critical Thinking: An Integrated Approach*, National Textbook, 1992.

Francine Bouche. *Living Well with Stress*, Editions de Mortagne, 1989.

Richard Carlson. *Don't Sweat the Small Stuff at Work—Simple Ways to Minimize Stress and Conflict While Bringing Out the Best in Yourself and Others*, Hyperion, 1998.

Elizabeth L. Chelsa. *Practical Solutions to Everyday Work Problems*, Learning Express, 2000.

Marshall J. Cook. *Slow Down and Get More Done*, Better Way Books, 1993.

Edward De Bono. *Serious Creativity*, Harper Business, 1992.

Lynne Eisagurre. *The Power of a Good Fight: How to Embrace Conflict to Drive Productivity, Creativity, and Innovation*, Alpha, 2002.

Diane Fassel. *Working Ourselves to Death*, iUniverse.com, 2000.

Jack Foster. *Ideaship: How to Get Ideas Flowing in Your Workplace*, Barrett-Kohler Publishers, 2001.

Milo O. Frank. *How to Succeed in Business Without Working so Damn Hard*, Warner Books, 2002.

Herbert J. Freudenberger. *Burn Out: The High Cost of High Achievement*, Bantam Books, 1989.

Saul W. Gellerman. *Motivation in the Real World: The Art of Getting Extra Effort from Everyone Including Yourself*, Plume, 1993.

Peter G. Hanson. *The Joy of Stress*, Andrews, McMeel & Parker, 1986.

Marion E. Haynes. *Personal Time Management*, Crisp, 2000.

Christopher Hobbs. *Stress and Natural Healing*, Interweave Press, 1997.

Patricia J. Hutchings. *Managing Workplace Chaos: Solutions for Handling Information, Paper, Time, and Stress,* AMACOM, 2002.

Charles B. Inlander. *Stress, 63 Ways to Relieve Tension and Stay Healthy*, Walker and Company, 1996.

Samuel H. Klarreich. *The Stress Solution*, Key Porter Books, 1988.

Barry Lenson. *Good Stress, Bad Stress: Identifying and Managing Your Stress*, Marlowe & Co., 2002.

Harlan L. Lane. *Make Every Minute Count*, Marlowe & Co., 2000.

Michael MacCoby. *Why Work?: Motivating the New Workforce*, Miles River Press, 1995.

Charles C. Manz. *Business Without Bosses*, John Wiley & Sons, 1995.

Christina Maslach. *The Truth about Burnout*, Jossey-Bass, 1997.

Bruce S. McEwen. *The End of Stress as We Know It*, Joseph Henry Press, 2002.

C. W. Metcalf and Roma Felible. *Lighten Up, Survival Skills for People Under Pressure*, Addison-Wesley, 1992.

Annette Moser-Wellman. *The Five Faces of Genius: The Skills to Master Ideas at Work*, Viking, 2001.

Kevin O'Connor. *The Map of Innovation: Creating Something Out of Nothing*, Crown Business, 2003.

Alex F. Osborn. *Applied Imagination,*Creative Education Foundation, 1993.

Chandra Patel. *The Complete Guide to Stress Management*, Plenum Press, 1991.

Neal Pinckney. *Healthy Heart Handbook*, Health Communications, 1996.

Joseph C. Piscatella. *Take a Load Off Your Heart*, Workman, 2003.

Beverly A. Potter. *Preventing Job Burnout, Transforming Work Pressures into Productivity*, Crisp Publications, 1987.

J. Robin Powell. *The Working Women's Guide to Managing Stress*, Prentice-Hall, 1994.

Barbara Bailey Reinhold. *Toxic Work: How to Overcome Stress, Overload, and Burnout and Revitalize Your Career*, Dutton, 1996.

Jill Zimmerman Rutledge. *Dealing With the Stuff That Makes Life Tuff*, Contemporary Books, 2004.

James Scalla. *25 Natural Ways to Manage Stress and Prevent Burnout*, Keats Pub., 2000.

Laura Stack. *Leave the Office Earlier: How to Do More in Less Time*, Broadway Books, 2004.

Arthur B. Van Gundy. *Idea Power—Techniques and Resources to Unleash the Creativity in Your Organization,* Amacon, 1992.

RogerVon Oech. *Whack on the Side of the Head: How You Can Be More Creative*, Warner, 1998.

Janie Walters. *Blow a Bubble, Not a Gasket: 101 ways to Reduce Stress,* Quail Ridge Press, 2002.

Clare Warmke. *Guidelines and Prompts for Brainstorming*, How Design Books, 2003.

Zig Ziglar. *Success for Dummies*, IDG Books, 1998.

http://www.plainsense.com/Health/Stress/index.htm—Stress management resources from Plainsense.

http://www.mindtools.com—Under the category "Skills for High Performance Living," the Mind Tools site offers information on goal setting, time management, stress management, planning, and communication.

Developing Your Social Conscience (Chapters 13–14)

Terry H. Anderson., *The Pursuit of Fairness: A History of Affirmative Action*, Oxford University Press, 2002.

Francis J. Beckwith and Todd E. Jones. *Affirmative Action—Social Justice or Reverse Discrimination?* Prometheus Books, 1997.

Jeffrey M. Bernbach. *Job Discrimination II—How to Fight . . . How to Win!* Crown Publishing Group, 1996.

Renee Blank and Sandra Slipp. *Voices of Diversity*, American Management Association, 1994.

Ellen Bravo. *9 to 5 Guide to Combating Sexual Harassment*, John Wiley & Sons, 1992.

Christine Craft. *Too Old, Too Ugly, and Not Deferential to Men—an Anchorwoman's Courageous Battle Against Sex Discrimination*, Prima Publishing & Communications, 1988.

Amy DelPo. *Federal Employment Laws, a Desk Reference*, Nolo, 2002.

Gabrielle I. Edwards. *Coping with Discrimination*, Rosen Publishing Group, Inc, 1992.

John P. Fernandez. *The Diversity Advantage*, Lexington Books, 1993.

Lawrence H. Fuchs. *American Kaleidoscope: Race, Ethnicity, and Civic Culture*, Wesleyan University Press, 1991.

Bryan J. Grapes. *Affirmative Action*, Greenhaven Press, Inc., 2000.

Raymond F. Gregory. *Age Discrimination in the American Workplace—Old at a Young Age*, Rutgers University Press, 2001.

Sandra Grymes and Mary Stanton. *Coping with the Male Ego in the Workplace*, Longmeadow, 1993.

Lisa Gueren. *Workplace Investigation: A Step-By-Step Guide*, Nolo, 2004.

Edward T. Hall. *Hidden Differences: Doing Business with the Japanese*, Anchor, 1990.

Janet Hauter. *The Smart Women's Guide to Career Success*, Career Press, 1993.

Margaret C. Jasper. *Harassment in the Workplace*, Oceana Publications Inc., 2002.

Margaret C. Jasper. *Employment Discrimination Law under Title VII*, Oceana Publications, Inc. 1999.

Jill Karson. *Civil Rights*, Greenhaven Press, 2003.

Anne Levy. *Workplace Sexual Harassment*, Prentice-Hall, 2002.

Debbie Levy. *Bigotry*, Lucent Books, Inc., 2002.

Alfredo Mirande. *Gringo Justice*, University of Notre Dame, 1990.

Joan Nordquist. *Sexual Harassment: A Bibliography*, Reference and Research Series, 2002.

Tracy O'Shea and Jane LaLonde. *Sexual Harassment—A Practical Guide to the Law, Your Rights, and Your Options for Taking Action*, St. Martin's Griffin, 1998.

William Petrocelli. *Sexual Harassment on the Job: What it is and How to Stop it*, Nolo Press, 1998.

Barbara Kate Repa. *Your Rights in the Workplace*, Nolo, 2002.

Patricia Riley. *Growing Up Native American*, Avon Books, 1995.

Steven Mitchell Sack. *The Working Women's Legal Survival Guide*, Prentice Hall Press, 1998.

Jay M. Shafritz. *Essentials of Business Ethics*, Meridian, 1990.

George Simons. *Working Together—Succeeding in a Multicultural Organization*, Crisp Publications, Inc., 1994.

Sandra Lee Smith. *Coping with Cross-Cultural and Interracial Relationships*, Rosen Publishing Group, Inc., 1990.

Brenda Stalkup. *The Disabled*, Greenhaven Press, Inc., 1997.

Melvin I. Urofsky. *A Conflict of Rights—The Supreme Court and Affirmative Action*, Charles Schribner's Sons, 1991.

Mary E. Williams. *Racism*, Greenhaven Press, 2004.

CNN Looks at Diversity in the Workplace (video), South-Western, 2000.

http://www.eeoc. gov—Web site of the Equal Employment Opportunity Commission.

http://www.diversityinc.com—a Web magazine providing a wide range of information about workplace diversity.

http://www.ibe.org.uk—The Institute of Business Ethics

Getting the Job and Workplace Success (Chapters 15–16)

Bob Adams. *The Everything Job Interview Book*, Adams Media Corporation, 2001.

Jeffrey Allen. *The Complete Q & A Job Interview Book, Fourth Edition*, John Wiley, Inc., 2004.

Bill Breen. "New Rules for Landing a Job," *Reader's Digest*, Vol. 156, Issue 938, pp. 86–91.

Enelow and Louise M. Kiersmark. *Expert Resumes for People Returning to Work*, JIST Publishing, 2003.

Rick Frishman and Jill Lublin. *Networking Magic*, Adams Media, an F+W Publications Company, 2004.

Ron Fry. *Your First Interview, Fourth Edition*, Career Press, 2002.

Melissa Giovagnoli and Jocelyn Carter-Miller. *Networking: Building Relationships and Opportunities for Success*, Jossey-Bass, 2000.

Kim Johnson Gross and Jeff Stone. *Dress Smart Women: Wardrobes That Win in the Workplace*, Warner Books, 2002.

Christopher W. Hunt and Scott A. Scanlon. *Navigating Your Career*, John Wiley & Sons, Inc., 1999.

Stuart K. Levine. *The Six Fundamentals of Success*, Doubleday, 2004.

John C. Maxwell. *Your Road Map for Success*, Thomas Nelson Publishers, 2002.

Talane Miedaner. *Coach Yourself to Success*, Contemporary Publishing Group, Inc., 2000.

Diana Pace. *The Career Fix-It Book*, Sourcebooks, Inc., 2000.

Diane Stafford and Moritza Day. *Job Hunting Secrets*, Sourcebooks, Inc., 2004.

Paul D.Tieger and Barbara Barron-Tieger. *Do What You Are, Third Edition*, Little, Brown and Company, 2001.

Martin Yate. *Knock 'em Dead*, Adams Media, an F+W Publication Company, 2004.

http://jobsearchtech.about.com/library/weekly/aa041000.htm

http://www.rockportinstitute. com/resume_02.html

glossary

A

Active listening The process of interpreting the information being heard while still listening.

Affirmative action A hiring policy that many private and public employers use to correct the effect of past discrimination against minorities and women. Plans are set up to eliminate the barriers that are limiting to minority applicants and current employees.

Ageism Discrimination according to age which may affect the young or the older worker.

Aggression An emotional response to conflict.

Aggressive communication Communicating your feelings in a forceful manner without regard to the rights and feelings of others; opposite of passive communication.

Allegiance Demonstration of loyalty and commitment to a supervisor.

Analytical problem solving Information used to reach a conclusion or a solution to a problem by logical analysis.

Application form Form used by employers to get the basic information about people who apply for positions in their place of business.

Aptitude A natural talent, ability, or capacity to learn.

Aptitude tests Measurement of your ability to learn something.

Assertive communication Communicating by standing up for your rights but not impinging on the rights of others.

Attitude How a person feels about something, such as the attitude that the customer is always right.

Autocratic leader A leader who develops policies and procedures, defines and assigns tasks, and, in general, dictates how work is to be done; does not entrust activities to others.

B

Behavior modification An approach to self-improvement; theory behind it suggests that people act in ways that bring some kind of reward.

Brainstorming An approach in which as many ideas as possible are created. Critical judgment of any idea is avoided in the early stages of this approach.

C

Career path A plan that will lead to a position with more responsibility, satisfaction, or income.

Channel The mode or route that a message takes to get to the receiver.

Cold canvassing Stopping at the human resources offices of companies or organizations in the area where you wish to work, and completing an application to let them know that you are looking for a job.

Communication An act of transmitting information and meaning from one individual or group to another.

Conflict The difference of opinions caused by opposing attitudes, behaviors, ideas, needs, or goals.

Conscientious Following the dictates of one's conscience.

Cooperation The ability to work well with others while working toward a common goal.

Creative problem solving The power achieved to solve problems from using creative thinking ability.

Creative thinking An approach to solving problems by asking specific questions or brainstorming to find an answer.

Critical listening The process of separating the facts from the opinions while listening.

Critical thinking Another term for reasoning. It includes the ability to use logic and to analyze information to solve problems and make decisions.

Criticism Suggestions from others about the quality of your work; a form of self-improvement.

Cultural conflict Conflict that occurs because of cultural differences.

Curiosity The ability to ask revealing questions.

D

Delegate authority Entrusting an activity, decision, or responsibility to an employee.

Democratic leader A leader who seeks out employees' ideas, thoughts, and solutions, allowing the group to make the decisions; also called participatory management style leader; a leader who encourages participation in the workplace.

Dependable Doing what you say you will do.

Depression An emotional disorder that is marked by unexplained sadness, inactivity, and a feeling of emptiness.

Dilemma A situation where one way or the other a person is bound to create a problem for himself or herself.

Diligent worker A worker who does his or her work carefully and completely.

Discrimination A term that simply means to recognize differences; however, this term in the world today has taken on a negative meaning as a word used to describe unfair treatment of a particular person or group due to race, gender, religious affiliation, or physical disability.

Diversity The term applied to an increasingly varied social and cultural makeup of the workforce.

E

Efficiency A term that relates to how well a task is performed; a key factor of efficiency is time management.

Ego Feeling of self-worth

Ego conflict A conflict in which the individuals view "winning" or "losing" as a measure of their expertise and personal worth.

Egocentric myopia A term that means that we see and appreciate only what is close (our immediate environment) which gives a distorted impression of being more important than we really are.

Elaboration The ability to add interesting detail to ideas.

Emotion The critical factor in the development of attitudes.

Empathy The ability to participate in another person's feelings or ideas; to understand and feel another person's emotions.

Employment agency A business that brings together a potential worker and an employer to fill a job opening.

Enthusiasm To inject energy into your work.

Enunciation Pronouncing each part of each word clearly and correctly.

Envy The feeling of desiring something someone else has.

Ethics A reflection of a person's integrity.

Ethnocentrism A term which proclaims the assumption that one's own worldview is the only view.

Exempt employee An employee who is usually not paid overtime and is usually classified as an administrative or professional employee.

External motivation A term psychologists use that means that the drive to achieve comes from outside the person.

F

Facts Things that can be proven.

False conflict A situation in which a person thinks a conflict exists, but in reality it does not.

Feedback Information you can use to evaluate yourself, to judge how you are doing; the response to a message that allows the sender to know if the message was understood.

Flexibility The ability to produce a variety of ideas.

Fluency The ability to produce many ideas quickly.

Grand larceny A legal term for stealing something of great value.

Grapevine The informal circulation of information which is often inaccurate.

I

Imagination The ability to make wild guesses.

Imaging A technique in which you make a deliberate effort to imagine your renewed and improved personality.

Inflection The rising and falling of your voice.

Initiative The process of starting a task or project without being told to do so; the energy or aptitude displayed in the initiation of action.

Intangibles Things that you cannot actually touch or possess.

Integrity Adherence to a code of moral values. You do what is right, even under pressure.

Internal motivation A term psychologists use that means the drive to achieve comes from within, such as the satisfaction that comes from doing a good job.

Jargon The technical terminology or characteristic words and ideas that belong to a specific type of work or field of knowledge.

Jealousy The feeling of rivalry toward one who you believe has an advantage over you.

Job and task analysis A process by which a job or position is carefully studied to produce a list of all the specific activities required to get the job done.

Job breakdown A specific list of tasks to be performed on a job.

Job description A written explanation of the tasks, duties, and responsibilities performed on a specific job; the content and essential requirements of a specific job or position.

Job lead Information about a possible job opening.

L

Laissez-faire leader A leader who avoids giving specific directions to employees and permits them to work independently, giving only general guidance.

Larcenist A thief.

Larceny Theft.

Leadership The ability to lead or direct others on a positive course.

Leadership style Method used by the leader to get the work done.

Letter of application A letter of introduction sent with a resume; a cover letter.

Listening The process by which we make sense out of what we hear.

Long-term goals Goals for the future.

Loyalty Believing in your place of employment and being committed to it.

M

Mask To cover or hide one's true feelings.

Mentor A trusted counselor or guide who is sometimes called a coach. This person takes a personal interest in helping someone with training and development on the job.

Message A thought or idea that is transmitted.

Meticulous Concerned and careful about details.

Monotone Speaking with no change or inflection.

Monotony A factor that causes stress, such as doing a task repeatedly.

Negotiable On an application, a term used to mean you wish to discuss salary.

Networking The process of sharing and exchanging job information.

Nondirective approach A technique used by counselors that recommends that you reflect back what a person has said as you respond to him or her; this technique works particularly well with the complainer.

Nonverbal Without the use of words.

Nonverbal communication A message sent without the use of words.

O

Occupational Outlook Handbook Source containing job descriptions, earnings, and anticipated job prospects.

Open-ended question A question that requires more than a yes or no answer or a one-word answer; used in interview situations.

Opinions Thoughts or statements based on personal beliefs or feelings.

Organized Good self-management skills; a person's behavior is methodical, logical, and directed toward goals or outcomes that he or she has clearly in mind.

Originality The ability to produce ideas that are unusual.

P

Parkinson's law A term that C. Northcote Parkinson denoted which meant that "Work expands to fill the time available for its completion." He concluded this after his research of the efficiency (or inefficiency) of the British Navy.

Passive communication Communicating by giving in without expressing your feelings, thoughts, or rights.

Patience Capacity to bear pain calmly and without complaint.

Performance appraisal An official evaluation of your work.

Personal space Distance between you and your listener.

Persuasion The art of attempting to get others to adopt or agree with an idea.

Petty larceny A legal term that describes the theft of something of lesser value or importance.

Pitch The high or low sound of your voice.

Politeness Exhibiting courtesy and consideration to others.

Positive resistance Clearly recognizing and confronting discrimination.

Prejudice A term that is often used in connection with discrimination; means to prejudge or form an opinion without taking the time or effort to judge in a fair manner.

Problem-solving technique A conflict resolution technique that uses five questions to lead to a solution: 1) What is the conflict? 2) What are the facts? 3) What is the overall objective? 4) What are some possible solutions? and 5) What is the best solution?

Pronunciation Saying a word correctly.

R

Receiver The individual to whom a thought or idea is transmitted.

Reinforcement Reward for desirable behavior; a term used by psychologists to mean the reward which serves as reinforcement of the desirable behavior.

Reliability The ability to supply what was promised, dependably and accurately.

Resentment A feeling of displeasure over something believed to be a wrong, insult, slight, or injury.

Responsible A term which means to be answerable or accountable for something within one's power to control.

Resume or résumé A written summary of your education, work experience, and other qualifications for a job.

Reverse discrimination Barring qualified individuals from being hired because they are not from a minority group.

S

Salutation On a letter, the greeting to the receiver of the letter.

Selective communication Hearing or reading only what you want to hear or read.

Self-actualization A term for the process of growing to reach your greatest potential.

Self-control Ability to direct the course of your behavior; the capacity to manage your own thoughts, feelings, and actions.

Self-esteem Attitude about yourself is positive and constructive; you feel good about yourself.

Self-motivation Drive within you to get things done.

Self-pity Feeling sorry for yourself and your situation without looking at the good things in your life.

Sender The originator of a thought, information, or idea to be transmitted to another.

Severance pay An allowance that may be payable to a terminating employee.

Sexual harassment Coerced, unethical, and unwanted intimacy; not only an issue of sex but also an issue of power.

Shaping A technique used to help a group member work better within a group by reinforcing positive behavior and ignoring negative behavior.

Short-term objectives Stepping stones to the achievement of your goals.

Simple conflict Disagreement over a fact.

Stereotyping A situation that occurs whenever someone thinks of all members of a group as having the same characteristics, rather than viewing the members of the group as unique individuals.

Strategies or tactics Plans of action that will ensure the achievement of your objectives.

Strategy Plan of action to reach your goal.

Stress An emotional factor that causes bodily or mental tension; the feeling one gets from prolonged, pent-up emotions.

Stress response The emotional or physical symptoms of uncontrolled stress.

Stressors The factors that create the stress in a person's life.

Subtle discrimination Discrimination that is not obvious and is seldom brought out in the open; it is based on appearance, values, or some other personal characteristic.

Supervisor A person who is in charge of one or more workers.

Sympathy The ability to identify, or take on, another person's emotions.

Tact The ability to do or say the right thing when dealing with people or difficult situations; diplomacy.

Time management A program in which all resources, including time, are efficiently used to achieve something important.

Try-out experiences Something that helps you find and confirm your natural abilities and preparation for a career, such as enrolling in a course related to the field you want to explore.

Type A personality A term psychologists use to refer to hard-driving people. Type A people are competitive, impatient, always pressed for time, doing many things at the same time, and motivated by achievement.

Type B personality A term psychologists use to refer to more easygoing, relaxed people who tend to take things in stride.

Value-added qualities Personality traits that add value to your technical skills, knowledge, expertise, and work experience.

Values or beliefs conflict Conflict that arises when people differ in their thoughts about life in general or an aspect of life, and these differences are brought into focus on a particular issue.

Verbal Use of words.

Verbal communication Communication that is transmitted with the use of words.

Visualization The ability to "see with the mind's eye."

Volume The loudness or softness of your voice.

Wellness programs Programs designed to help employees maintain or improve their health.

Workplace politics An undefined force in an organization that develops because people want to protect themselves or gain power.

index